An Introduction to
Statistics in Psychol
Second Edition

D0120646

Pearson
Education

We work with leading authors to develop the strongest
educational materials in psychology, bringing cutting-edge
thinking and best learning practice to a global market.

Under a range of well-known imprints, including Prentice
Hall, we craft high quality print and electronic publications
which help readers to understand and apply their content,
whether studying or at work.

To find out about the complete range of our publishing
please visit us on the World Wide Web at:
www.pearsoneduc.com

An Introduction to Statistics in Psychology

A Complete Guide for Students

Second Edition

DENNIS HOWITT AND DUNCAN CRAMER

An imprint of **Pearson Education**

Harlow, England · London · New York · Reading, Massachusetts · San Francisco
Toronto · Don Mills, Ontario · Sydney · Tokyo · Singapore · Hong Kong · Seoul
Taipei · Cape Town · Madrid · Mexico City · Amsterdam · Munich · Paris · Milan

Pearson Education Limited
Edinburgh Gate
Harlow
Essex CM20 2JE
England

and Associated Companies around the world

Visit us on the World Wide Web at:
www.pearsoneduc.com

First published 1997
Second edition 2000

ISBN 0–130–17314–2

British Library Cataloguing in Publication Data

A catalogue record for this book can be obtained from
the British Library

Library of Congress Cataloging-in-Publication Data

Howitt, Dennis.
    An introduction to statistics in psychology : a complete guide for students/Dennis
Howitt and Duncan Cramer.— 2nd ed.
        p. cm.
    Includes bibliographical references and index.
    ISBN 0-13-017314-2 (pbk.)
    1. Psychometrics. I. Cramer, Duncan, 1948- II. Title.

    BF39 .H74 1999
    150'.1'5195—dc21

                                                                           99-045154

10 9 8 7 6 5 4 3 2 1
04 03 02 01 00

Typeset by 65
Printed and bound in Great Britain by Henry Ling Ltd., at the Dorset Press, Dorchester,
Dorset.

Contents

Introduction ix

Part 1 Descriptive statistics   1

  1 Why you need statistics: Types of data   3

  2 Describing variables: Tables and diagrams   9

  3 Describing variables numerically: Averages, variation
    and spread 20

  4 Shapes of distributions of scores 31

  5 Standard deviation: The standard unit of measurement
    in statistics 41

  6 Relationships between two or more variables:
    Diagrams and tables 53

  7 Correlation coefficients: Pearson correlation and
    Spearman's rho 62

  8 Regression: Prediction with precision 80

Part 2 Significance testing 91

  9 Samples and populations: Generalising and inferring . . . 93

 10 Statistical significance for the correlation coefficient: A
    practical introduction to statistical inference 99

 11 Standard error: The standard deviation of the
    means of samples 109

 12 The *t*-test: Comparing two samples of correlated/
    related scores 115

13 The *t*-test: Comparing two groups of unrelated/
    uncorrelated scores 127

14 Chi-square: Differences between samples of frequency
    data 142

15 Probability 161

16 Reporting significance levels succinctly 167

17 One-tailed versus two-tailed significance testing 172

18 Ranking tests: nonparametric statistics 176

Part 3 Introduction to analysis of variance 187

19 The variance ratio test: The *F*-ratio to compare two
    variances 189

20 Analysis of variance (ANOVA): Introduction to the one-
    way unrelated or uncorrelated ANOVA 195

21 Analysis of variance for correlated scores or repeated
    measures 214

22 Two-way analysis of variance for unrelated/
    uncorrelated scores: Two experiments for the price
    of one? 231

23 Multiple comparisons in ANOVA: Just where do the
    differences lie? 262

24 More analysis of variance designs: Mixed-design
    ANOVA and analysis of covariance (ANCOVA) 269

25 Statistics and the analysis of experiments 300

Part 4 More advanced correlational statistics 307

26 Partial correlation: Spurious correlation, third variables,
    suppressor variables 309

27 Factor analysis: simplifying complex data 319

28 Multiple regression and multiple correlation 334

29 Path analysis 346

30 The analysis of a questionnaire/survey project 360

Part 5 Assorted advanced techniques 369

31 Statistical power analysis: Do my findings matter? 371

32 Meta-analysis: Combining and exploring statistical findings from previous research 378

33 Reliability in scales and measurement: Consistency and agreement 396

34 Confidence intervals 407

35 The analysis of complex contingency tables: Log-linear methods 416

Appendix A Testing for excessively skewed distributions 442

Appendix B1 Large sample formulae for the nonparametric tests 445

Appendix B2 Nonparametric tests for three or more groups 446

Appendix C Extended table of significance for the Pearson correlation coefficient 450

Appendix D Table of significance for the Spearman correlation coefficient 453

Appendix E Extended table of significance for the *t*-test 456

Appendix F Table of significance for chi-square 459

Appendix G Extended table of significance for the sign test 460

Appendix H Table of significance for the Wilcoxon Matched Pairs Test 463

Appendix I Table of significance for the Mann-Whitney U-test 466

Appendix J Table of significant values for the *F*-distribution 468

Appendix K Table of significant values of *t* when making multiple *t*-tests 472

References 475

Index 477

A Companion Web Site accompanies *An Introduction to Statistics in Psychology* by Dennis Howitt and Duncan Cramer

Visit the *An Introduction to Statistics in Psychology* Companion Web Site at www.booksites.net/howitt to find valuable teaching and learning material including:

For Students:
- A password protected, interactive questions section
- Web links for key web sites

For Lecturers:
- A secure, password protected site with teaching material
- PowerPoint slides that you can download and alter
- SPSS updates to keep you informed of changes
- An electronic, downloadable version of the Instructor's Manual
- Access to interactive questions

Also: This regularly maintained and updated site will have a syllabus manager, search functions, and email results functions.

Introduction

This second edition of *An Introduction to Statistics for Psychology* aims to increase further its usefulness to students of modern psychology. Largely this involves extending the coverage of interpreting and reporting data, and adding chapters on techniques such as confidence intervals, meta-analysis, log-linear analysis and item and inter-rater reliabilities. The basic structure of the first edition has been retained though additions have been made at many points. In particular, the coverage of analysis of variance (ANOVA) has been consolidated by including conventional calculation procedures and describing the calculation of the analysis of covariance. Despite these changes, the basic concept remains the same – a modular statistics package that is accessible to a wide ability range of students throughout. We have attempted to achieve this while being as rigorous as possible where rigour is crucial.

Structure

This textbook is intended to cover most of the statistics that students need in a first-degree course in psychology.

- Part 1 covers basic descriptive statistics from tables and diagrams through to the correlation coefficient and simple regression.

- Part 2 covers basic inferential statistics – significance testing. So the significance of the correlation coefficient, the *t*-tests, and nonparametric testing are major features of Part 2.

- Part 3 covers the analysis of variance (ANOVA) up to the level at which the use of computers is recommended, not merely desirable. The most common and useful ANOVA designs are presented including one-way related and unrelated ANOVAs, two-way unrelated ANOVAs, mixed designs and the analysis of covariance. The computation of appropriate significance levels for multiple comparisons is given special attention.

- Part 4 covers more advanced correlational statistics such as partial correlation, multiple regression and factor analysis.

■ Part 5 is largely new to this edition and includes a miscellany of advanced techniques including meta-analysis, log-linear analysis, reliability and confidence intervals. Confidence intervals have been advocated increasingly in recent years as an alternative to conventional statistical significance testing. Log-linear analysis has been included for those working with complex crosstabulation frequency data.

Package

The textbook is part of a package of materials for the teaching and learning of statistics as applied in psychological research. The package consists of the following four parts:

■ This textbook, which provides an overview of the use of statistics in undergraduate laboratory work, practical work and final-year projects.

■ A computer book explaining how computations are easy to carry out using a standard computer package. The student may learn to use SPSS for Windows. This is commonly available at universities and colleges throughout the world. It is now user-friendly and solves many of the problems associated with the analysis of psychological data. Computer packages make it feasible to include more advanced statistical techniques than are normally included in statistics textbooks for psychology students.

■ An instructors' manual. This includes exercises, problems, multiple-choice assessment materials, calculation worksheets, and templates for producing overhead transparencies.

■ A Companion Web Site (see p.vii).

Level of difficulty

Throughout, the package is designed to remain at a relatively simple level even where complex statistics are being explained. The material is aimed at the vast majority of students who, although having some mathematical skills, nevertheless do not relish complex formulae and abstract explanations of obscure mathematical procedures.

Nevertheless, rigour is not sacrificed to this end. Students following our advice and recommendations carefully will be able to analyse virtually any data effectively and to a competent standard. To this end we have been scrupulous in ensuring that alternative statistical procedures are mentioned when the limits of applicability of a statistical techniques are breached. A good example of this is the inclusion of the Fisher Exact Probability Test when chi-square is not applicable because of small expected frequencies. Students' data sets are often fairly small and must be analysed as they are because the option of collecting more data is not available.

Flexibility

The textbook is designed as a menu of statistical techniques, not all of which need be sampled. Chapters 1 to 18 constitute a thorough but compact basic introduction to psychological statistics; they are suitable for use as a basic-level course as they cover descriptive statistics and common inferential statistics. Flexibility was another important feature planned for the package for the following reasons:

■ All instructors teach courses differently. The textbook covers most of the commonly taught techniques and many less common ones too. Instructors may omit some chapters without causing difficulties. The textbook contains pertinent basic and revision information within each chapter wherever possible. In other words, instructors will be able to select their favoured route through the material.

■ Some instructors prefer to teach statistics practically through the use of computers. This is made easy by this package which contains both a textbook and a computer manual.

■ Many students will have little difficulty in self-study of most chapters. Supervisors of student practical classes and projects may find this particularly appealing as they can direct students to appropriate parts of the textbook.

■ However, the flexibility is far greater than this. The package can serve as an introduction to statistics or as a textbook for an intermediate-level course. Not only is this simply better value for students; it means that the problems of transferring from one textbook to another are bypassed.

There is no right or wrong way of structuring modules in psychological statistics. What is appropriate depends on what the students know already, the aims and objectives of the module and, most importantly, the other modules that the students are taking especially those involving practical research experience. If statistics is taught as part of practical classes then it may be difficult to include formal lectures on the use of statistics. For these reasons and many others, this text is itself modular in construction. The physical order of the chapters in the text is merely one of several possible alternatives. Our choice is to give a thorough grounding in descriptive statistics before moving on to the basic principles of significance testing. This is partly because we feel that descriptive statistics are not always handled well by psychology students who too often regard statistical significance as equivalent to statistical analysis at the expense of understanding and describing their data.

Most lecturers will choose their own route through the material. For example, the chapters on correlation and regression may be omitted or deferred if the lecturer wishes to teach basic experimental design and analysis. For this reason, each chapter lists essential prerequisites in terms of the students' knowledge and also refers to later chapters if these are particularly relevant.

Professional relevance

It is increasingly obvious that the statistics taught to students and the statistics contained in journal articles and books are drawing apart. For that reason, the book contains introductions to techniques such as factor analysis, multiple regression and path analysis which are common in professional publications and generally easy to do using computer packages. Again, this section of the textbook may form part of an intermediate course.

Other features of the package

- Tables of statistical significance have been simplified extensively. Students find some books hard and confusing to use because the statistical tables are so obscurely or badly presented.
- Statistical formulae have been kept to a minimum. This is relatively easy since not too many formulae are necessary anyway.
- Every calculation is illustrated with a step-by-step example for students to follow. Where hand calculation is too difficult, the student is advised when it is essential to use a computer package.
- We have preferred to use methods and descriptions that communicate clearly and effectively to students even if they are at times not the most formally rigorous explanations. This introduces a degree of informality that might annoy the most statistically precise thinkers. We think it is for the greater good to avoid too abstract an approach.
- We have tried to provide insight into the ways in which psychologists use statistics.
- Practical advice on the learning and use of statistics in psychology is given at the end of every chapter of the textbook.
- The package is excellent value for the student as it meets all of their statistical needs for a first degree in psychology.

Acknowledgements

We are extremely grateful to Antoinette Hardy for help and advice from a student's perspective and for her careful checking of the manuscript. In addition, Rosemary Chapman's suggestions about student needs in statistics have been incorporated with our thanks.

Whilst every effort has been made to trace owners of copyright material, in a few cases this has proved impossible and we take this opportunity to offer our apologies to any copyright holders whose rights we may have unwittingly infringed.

Part 1

Descriptive statistics

Chapter 1

Why you need statistics

Types of data

1.1 Introduction

Imagine a world in which everything is the same; people are identical in all respects. They wear identical clothes; they eat the same meals; they are all the same height from birth; they all go to the same school with identical teachers, identical lessons and identical facilities; they all go on holiday in the same month; they all do the same job; they all live in identical houses; and the sun shines every day. They do not have sex as we know it since there are no sexes so everyone self-reproduces at the age of 30; their gardens have the same plants and the soil is exactly the same no matter whose garden; they all die on their 75th birthdays and are all buried in the same wooden boxes in identical plots of land. They are all equally clever and they all have identical personalities. Their genetic make-up never varies. Mathematically speaking all of these characteristics are constants. If this world seems less than ideal then have we got news for you – you need statistics. Only in a world of standardisation would you not need statistics – in a richly varying world statistics is essential.

If nothing varies, then everything that is to be known about people could be guessed from information obtained from a single person. No problems would arise in generalising since what is true of Sandra Green is true of everyone else – they're all called Sandra Green after all. Fortunately, the world is not like that. Variability is an essential characteristic of life and the social world in which we exist. The sheer quantity of variability has to be tamed when trying to make statements about the real world. Statistics is largely about making sense of variability.

Statistical techniques perform three main functions:

1. They provide ways of summarising the information that we collect from a multitude of sources. Statistics is partly about tabulating your research information or data as clearly and effectively as possible. As such it merely describes the information collected. This is achieved using tables and diagrams summarising data and simple formulae which turn fairly complex data into simple indexes that describe numerically the main features of the data.

This branch of statistics is called *descriptive statistics* for very obvious reasons – it describes the information you collect as accurately and succinctly as possible. The first few chapters of this book are largely devoted to descriptive statistics.

2. Another branch of statistics is far less familiar to most of us: *inferential statistics*. This branch of statistics is really about economy of effort in research. There was a time when in order to find out about people, for example, everyone in the country would be contacted in order to collect information. This is done today when the government conducts a *census* of everyone in order to find out about the population of the country at a particular time. This is an enormous and time-consuming operation that cannot be conducted with any great frequency. But most of us are familiar with using relatively small *samples* in order to approximate the information that one would get by studying everybody. This is common in public opinion surveying where the answers of a sample of 1000 or so people may be used, say, to predict the outcome of a national election. Granted that sometimes samples can be misleading, nevertheless it is the principle of sampling that is important. *Inferential statistics* is about the confidence with which we can generalise from a sample to the entire population.

3. The amount of data that a researcher can collect is potentially massive. Some statistical techniques enable the researcher to clarify trends in vast quantities of data using a number of powerful methods. Data simplification, data exploration or data reduction are among the names given to the process. Whatever the name the objective is the same – to make sense of large amounts of data that otherwise would be much too confusing. These *data exploration techniques* are mainly dealt with in later chapters.

1.2   Variables and measurement

The concept of a *variable* is basic but vitally important in statistics. It is also as easy as pie. A *variable is merely anything that varies and can be measured*. These measurements need *not* correspond very well with everyday notions of measurement such as weight, distance, and temperature. So the sex of people is a variable since it can be measured as either male or female – and sex varies between people. Similarly, eye colour is a variable because a set of people will include some with brown eyes, some with blue eyes and some with green eyes. Thus measurement can involve merely categorisation. Clinical psychologists might use different diagnostic categories such as schizophrenia, manic-depression and anxiety in research. These diagnostic categories constitute a variable since they are different mental and emotional problems to which people can be allocated. Such categorisation techniques are an important type of measurement in statistics.

Another type of measurement in statistics is more directly akin to everyday concepts of measurement in which numerical values are provided. These *numerical* values are assigned to variables such as weight, length, distance, temperature and the like – for example, 10 kilometres or 30 degrees. These numerical values are called *scores*. In psychological research many variables are measured and *quantified* in much the same way. Good examples are the many tests and scales used to assess intelligence, personality, attitudes and mental abilities. In most of these, people are assigned a number (or score) in order to describe, for example, how neurotic or how extraverted an individual is. Psychologists will speak of a person having an IQ of 112 or 93, for example, or they will say an individual has a low score of 6 on a measure of psychoticism. Usually these numbers are used as if they corresponded exactly to other forms of measurement such as weight or length. For these, we can make statements such as that a person has a weight of 60 kilograms or is 1.3 metres tall.

1.3   The major types of measurement

Traditionally, statistics textbooks for psychologists emphasise different types of measurement – usually using the phrase *scales of measurement*. However, *for virtually all practical purposes there are only two different types of measurement in statistics*. These have already been discussed, but to stress the point:

1. *Score/numerical measurement.* This is the assignment of a *numerical* value to a measurement. This includes most physical and psychological measures. In psychological jargon these numerical measurements are called *scores*. We could record the IQ scores of five people as in Table 1.1. Each of the numerical values in the table indicates the named individual's *score* on the variable IQ. It is a simple point, but note that the numbers contain information that someone with an IQ of 150 has a higher intelligence than someone with an IQ of 80. In other words, the numbers *quantify* the variable.

2. *Nominal/category measurement.* This is merely deciding to which category of a variable a particular case belongs. So, if we were measuring a person's job or occupation, we would have to decide whether or not he or she was a lorry driver, a professor of sociology, a debt collector, and so forth. This is called *nominal* measurement since usually the categories are described in words and, especially, given names. Thus the category 'lorry driver' is a name or verbal description of what sort of case should be placed in that category.

Table 1.1 **IQ scores of five named individuals**

Individual	IQ score
Stan	80
Mavis	130
Sanjit	150
Sharon	145
Peter	105

Table 1.2 **Frequencies of different occupations**

Occupational category	Number or frequency in set
Lorry drivers	27
Sociology professors	10
Debt collectors	15
Other occupations	48

Notice that there are no numbers involved in the process of categorisation as such. A person is either a lorry driver or not. *However, you need to be warned of a possible confusion that can occur.* If you have 100 people whose occupations are known you might wish to count how many are lorry drivers, how many are professors of sociology, and so forth. These counts could be entered into a data table like Table 1.2. Notice that the numbers this time merely correspond to a count of the *frequency* or number of cases falling into each of the four occupational categories. *They are not scores*, but frequencies. The numbers do not correspond to a single measurement but are the aggregate of many separate (nominal) measurements.

The distinction between numerical scores and frequencies is important so always take care to check whether what appear to be numerical scores in a table are not actually frequencies.

Make a habit of mentally labelling variables as numerical scores or nominal categories. Doing so is a big step forward in thinking statistically. This is all you really need to know about types of measurement. However, you should be aware that others use more complex systems. Read the following section to learn more about scales of measurement.

Formal measurement theory

You may find it unnecessary to learn the contents of this section in detail. However, it does contain terms with which you ought to be familiar since other people might make reference to them.

Many psychologists speak of four different scales of measurement. Conceptually they are distinct. Nevertheless, for most practical situations in psychologists' use of statistics the nominal category versus numerical scores distinction discussed above is sufficient.

The four 'theoretical' scales of measurement are as follows. Numbers 2, 3 and 4 are different types of *numerical* scores.

1. **Nominal** categorisation. This is the placing of cases into *named* categories – nominal clearly refers to names. It is exactly the same as our nominal measurement or categorisation process.

2. **Ordinal** (or rank) measurement. The assumption here is that the values of the numerical scores tell us little else other than which is the smallest, the next smallest and so forth up to the largest. In other words, we can place the scores in *order* (hence ordinal) from the smallest to the largest. It is sometimes called rank measurement since we can assign ranks to the first, second, third, fourth, fifth, etc. in order from the smallest to the largest numerical value. These ranks have the numerical value 1, 2, 3, 4, 5, etc. You will see examples of this later in the book, especially in Chapters 7 and 18. However, few psychologists collect data directly as ranks.

3. **Interval** or equal-interval measurement. The basic idea here is that in some cases the intervals between numbers on a numerical scale are equal in size. Thus, if we measure distance on a scale of centimetres then the distance between 0 and 1 centimetre on our scale is exactly the same as the difference between 4 and 5 centimetres or between 11 and 12 centimetres on that scale. This is obvious for some standard physical measurements such as temperature.

4. **Ratio** measurement. This is exactly the same as interval scale measurement with one important proviso. A ratio scale of measurement has an absolute zero point that is measured as 0. Most physical measurements such as distance and weight have zero points that are absolute. Thus zero on a tape measure is the smallest distance one can have – there is no distance between two coincident points. With this sort of scale of measurement it is possible to work out ratios between measures. So, for example, a town that is 20 kilometres away is twice as far away as a town that is only 10 kilometres away. A building that is 15 metres high is half the height of a building that is 30 metres high. (Not all physical measures have a zero that is absolute zero – this applies particularly to several measures of temperature. Temperatures measured in degrees Celsius or Fahrenheit have points that are labelled as zero. However, these zero points do not correspond to the lowest possible temperature you can have. It is then meaningless to say, for example, that it is twice as hot if the temperature is 20 degrees Celsius than if it were 10 degrees Celsius.)

It is very difficult to apply the last three types of measure to psychological measurements with certainty. Since most psychological scores do not have any directly observable physical basis, it is impossible to decide whether they consist of equal intervals or have an absolute zero. For many years this problem caused great controversy and confusion among psychologists. For the most part, much current usage of statistics in psychology ignores the distinctions between the three different types of numerical scores. This has the support of many statisticians. On the other hand, some psychologists prefer to emphasise that some data are best regarded as rankable and lack the qualities which are characteristic of interval/ratio data. They are more likely to use the statistical techniques to be found in Chapter 18 and the ranking correlation coefficient (Chapter 7) than others. In other words, for precisely the same data, different psychologists will adopt different statistical techniques. Usually this will make little difference to the outcomes of their statistical analyses. In general, it will cause you few, if any, problems if you ignore the three subdivisions of numerical score measurement in your practical use of statistics. The exceptions to this are discussed in Chapters 7 and 18. Since psychologists rarely if ever collect data in the form of ranks, Chapters 2 to 6 are unaffected by such considerations.

1.4   Notes and recommendations

- ■ Always ask yourself what sort of measurement it is you are considering – is it a numerical score on a variable or is it putting individuals into categories?
- ■ Never assume that a number is necessarily a numerical score. Without checking, it could be a *frequency* of observations in a named category.
- ■ Clarity of thinking is a virtue in statistics – you will rarely be expected to demonstrate great creativity in your statistical work. Understanding precisely the meaning of terms is a positive advantage in statistics.

Chapter 2

Describing variables

Tables and diagrams

Preparation

Remind yourself what a variable is from Chapter 1. Similarly, if you are still not sure of the nominal (categorisation) form of measurement and the use of numerical scores in measurement then revise these too.

2.1 Introduction

You probably know a lot more about statistics than you think. The mass media regularly feature statistical tables and diagrams; children become familiar with statistical tables and diagrams at school. Skill with these methods is essential because researchers collect large amounts of data from numerous people. If we asked 100 people their age, sex, marital status (divorced, married, single, etc.), their number of children and their occupation this would yield 500 separate pieces of information. Although this is small fry compared with much research, it is not very helpful to present these 500 measurements in your research report. Such unprocessed information is called *raw data*. Statistical analysis has to be more than describing the raw ingredients. It requires structuring data in ways that *effectively communicate* the major trends. If you fail to structure your data, you may as well just give the reader copies of your questionnaires or observation schedules to interpret themselves.

There are very few rules regulating the production of tables and diagrams in statistics so long as they are clear and concise; they need to communicate quickly the important trends in the data. There is absolutely no point in using tables and diagrams that do not ease the task of communication. Probably the best way of deciding whether your tables and diagrams do their job well is to ask other people to decipher what they mean. Tables which are unclear to other people are generally useless.

The distinction between nominal (category) data and numerical scores discussed in the previous chapter is important in terms of the appropriate tables and diagrams to use.

Design consideration   One of the easiest mistakes to make in research is to allow participants in your research to give more than one answer to a question. So, for example, if you ask people to name their favourite television programme and allow each person more than one answer you will find that the data can be very tricky to analyse thoroughly. Take our word for it for now: statistics in general do not handle multiple responses very well. Certainly it is possible to draw up tables and diagrams but some of the more advanced statistical procedures become difficult to apply. You will sometimes read comments to the effect that the totals in a table exceed the number of participants in the research. This is because the researcher has allowed multiple responses to a single variable. So only allow the participants in your research to give one piece of data for each variable you are measuring to avoid digging a pit for yourself. If you plan your data analysis in detail before you collect your data you should be able to anticipate any difficulties.

2.2   Choosing tables and diagrams

So long as you are able to decide whether your data are either numerical scores or nominal (category) data, there are few other choices to be made since the available tables and diagrams are essentially dependent upon this distinction.

Tables and diagrams for nominal (category) data

One of the main characteristics of tables and diagrams for nominal (category) data is that they have to show the *frequencies* of cases in each category used. While there may be as many categories as you wish, it is *not* the function of statistical analysis to communicate all of the data's detail; the task is to identify the major trends. For example, imagine you are researching the public's attitudes towards private health care. If you ask participants in your research their occupations then you might find that they mention tens if not hundreds of different job titles – newsagents, homemakers, company executives and so forth. Simply counting the frequencies with which different job titles are mentioned results in a vast number of categories. You need to think of relevant and meaningful ways of reducing this vast number into a smaller number of much broader categories that might reveal important trends. For example, since the research is about a health issue you might wish to form a category made up of those involved in health work – some might be dentists, some nurses, some doctors, some paramedics, and so forth. Instead of keeping these as different categories, they might be combined into a category 'health worker'. There are no hard-and-fast rules

Table 2.1 **Occupational status of participants in the research expressed as frequencies and percentage frequencies**

Occupation	Frequency	Percentage frequency
Nuns	17	21.25
Nursery teachers	3	3.75
Television presenters	23	28.75
Students	20	25.00
Other	17	21.25

about combining to form broader categories. The following might be useful rules of thumb:

1. Keep your number of categories low, especially when you have only small numbers of participants in your research.

2. Try to make your 'combined' categories meaningful and sensible in the light of the purposes of your research. It would be nonsense, for example, to categorise jobs by the letter of the alphabet with which they start – nurses, nuns, nursery teachers and national footballers. All of these have jobs beginning with the same letter but it is very difficult to see any other common thread which allows them to be combined meaningfully.

In terms of drawing tables, all we do is to list the categories we have chosen and give the frequency of cases that fall into each of the categories (Table 2.1).

The frequencies are presented in two ways in this table – *simple* frequencies and *percentage* frequencies. A percentage frequency is merely the frequency expressed as a percentage of the total of the frequencies (or total number of cases, usually).

Notice also that one of the categories is called 'other'. This consists of those cases which do not fit into any of the main categories. It is, in other words, a 'rag bag' category or miscellany. Generally, all other things being equal, it is best to have a small number of cases in the 'other' category.

Calculation 2.1

Percentage frequencies

Many readers will not need this, but if you are a little rusty with simple maths, it might be helpful.

The percentage frequency for a particular category, say for students, is the frequency in that category expressed as a percentage of the total frequencies in the data table.

Step 1 What is the category frequency? For students in Table 2.1:

Category frequency $_{[students]}$ = 20

Step 2 Add up all of the frequencies in Table 2.1:

Total frequencies = Nuns +Nursery teachers + TV presenters + Students + Other

= 17 + 3 + 23+ 20 + 17
= 80

Step 3

$$\text{Percentage frequency }_{[students]} = \frac{\text{Category frequency }_{[students]} \times 100}{\text{Total frequencies}}$$

$$= \frac{20 \times 100}{80}$$

$$= \frac{2000}{80}$$

$$= 25\%$$

One advantage of using computers is that they enable experimentation with different schemes of categorising data in order to decide which is best for your purposes. In this you would use initially narrow categories for coding your data. Then you can tell the computer which of these to combine into broader categories.

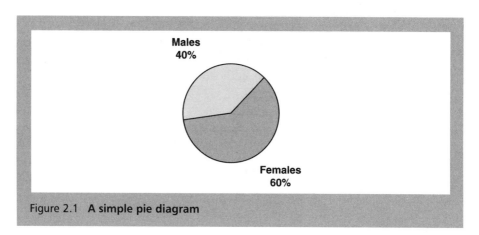

Figure 2.1 **A simple pie diagram**

Sometimes it is preferable to turn frequency tables into diagrams. Good diagrams are quickly understood and add variety to the presentation. The main types of diagram for nominal (category) data are *pie diagrams* and *bar charts*. A pie diagram is a very familiar form of presentation – it simply expresses each category as a slice of a pie which represents all cases (see Figure 2.1).

Notice that the *number* of slices is small – a multitude of slices can be confusing. Each slice is clearly marked with its category name, and the percentage frequency in each category also appears.

Calculation 2.2

Slices for a pie diagram

There is nothing difficult in constructing a pie diagram. Our recommendation is that you turn each of your frequencies into a percentage frequency. Since there are 360 degrees in a circle, if you multiply each percentage frequency by 3.6 you will obtain the angle (in degrees) of the slice of the pie which you need to mark out. In order to create the diagram you will require a protractor to measure the angles. However, graph packages for use on the computer would be standard at any university or college and do an impressive job.

In Table 2.1, 25.00% of cases were students. In order to turn this into the correct angle for the slice of the pie you simply need to multiply 25.00 by 3.6 to give an angle of 90 degrees.

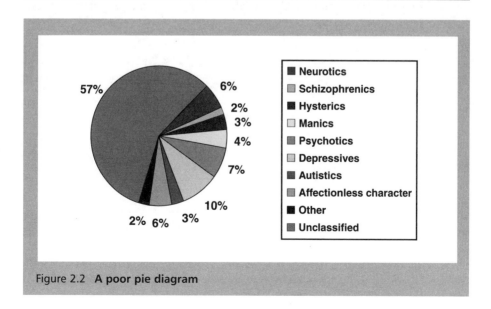

Figure 2.2 **A poor pie diagram**

Figure 2.2 shows a *bad* example of a pie diagram for purposes of comparison. There are several problems with this pie diagram:

1. There are too many small slices identified by different shading patterns and the legend takes time to decode.

2. It is not too easily seen what each slice concerns and the relative sizes of the slices are difficult to judge. We have the size of the slices around the figure and a separate legend or key to identify the components to help cope with the overcrowding problem. In other words, too many categories have resulted in a diagram which is far from easy to read – a cardinal sin in any statistical diagram.

A simple frequency table might be more effective in this case.

Another very familiar form of statistical diagram for nominal (category) data is the *bar chart*. Again these are very common in the media. Basically they are diagrams in which bars represent the size of each category. An example is shown in Figure 2.3.

The relative lengths (or heights) of the bars quickly reveal the main trends in the data. With a bar chart there is very little to remember other than that the bars have a standard space separating them. The spaces indicate that the categories are not in a numerical order; they are frequencies of categories, *not* scores.

It is hard to go wrong with a bar chart (that is not a challenge!) so long as you remember the following:

1. The heights of the bars represent frequencies (number of cases) in a category.

2. Each bar should be clearly labelled as to the category it represents.

3. Too many bars make bar charts hard to follow.

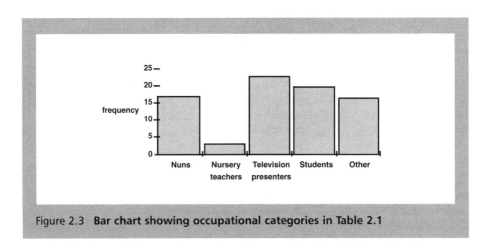

Figure 2.3 **Bar chart showing occupational categories in Table 2.1**

4. Avoid having *many* empty or near-empty categories which represent very few cases. Generally, the information about substantial categories is the most important. (Small categories can be combined together as an 'other' category.)

5. Nevertheless, if *important* categories have very few entries then this needs recording. So, for example, a researcher who is particularly interested in opportunities for women surveys people in top management and finds very few women employed in such jobs. It is important to draw attention to this in the bar chart of males and females in top management. Once again, there are no hard-and-fast rules to guide you – common sense will take you a long way.

6. Make sure that the vertical axis (the heights of the bars) is clearly marked as being frequencies or percentage frequencies.

7. The bars should be of equal width.

In newspapers and on television you are likely to come across a variant of the bar chart called the *pictogram*. In this, the bars of the bar chart are replaced by varying sized drawings of something eye-catching to do with your categories. Thus, pictures of men or women of varying heights, for example, replace the bars. Pictograms are rarely used in professional presentations. The main reason is that pictures of things get wider as well as taller as they increase in size. This can misrepresent the relative sizes of the categories, given that readers forget that it is only the height of the picture which counts.

Tables and diagrams for numerical score data

One crucial consideration when deciding what tables and diagrams to use for score data is the number of separate scores recorded for the variable in question. This can vary markedly. So, for example, age in the general population can range from newly born to over 100 years of age. If we merely recorded ages to the nearest whole year then a table or diagram may have entries for 100 different

Table 2.2 **Ages expressed as age bands**

Age range	Frequency
0–9 years	19
10–19 years	33
20–29 years	17
30–39 years	22
40–49 years	17
50 years and over	3

ages. Such a table or diagram would look horrendous. If we recorded age to the nearest month, then we could multiply this number of ages by twelve! Such scores can be grouped into bands or ranges of scores to allow effective tabulation (Table 2.2).

Many psychological variables have a much smaller range of numerical values. So, for example, it is fairly common to use questions which pre-specify just a few response alternatives. The so-called Likert-type questionnaire item is a good case in point. Typically this looks something like this:

Statistics is my favourite university subject:

Strongly agree	*Agree*	*Neither agree nor disagree*	*Disagree*	*Strongly disagree*

Participants completing this questionnaire circle the response alternative which best fits their personal opinion. It is conventional in this type of research to code these different response alternatives on a five-point scale from one to five. Thus strongly agree might be coded 1, neither agree nor disagree 3, and strongly disagree 5. This scale therefore has only five alternative values. Because of this small number of alternative answers, a table based on this question will be relatively simple. Indeed, if students are not too keen on statistics, you may well find that they select only the disagree and strongly disagree categories.

Tabulating such data is quite straightforward. Indeed you can merely report the numbers or frequencies of replies for each of the different categories or scores as in Table 2.3.

A *histogram* might be the best form of statistical diagram to represent these data. At first sight histograms look very much like bar charts but without gaps between the bars. This is because the histogram does not represent distinct unrelated categories but different points on a *numerical* measurement scale. So a histogram of the above data might look like Figure 2.4.

But what if your data have numerous different possible values of the variable in question? One common difficulty for most psychological research is that the number of respondents tends to be small. The large number of possible different scores on the variable is therefore shared between very few respondents. Tables and diagrams should present major features of your data in a simple and easily

Table 2.3 **Distribution of students' attitudes towards statistics**

Response category	Value	Frequency
Strongly agree	1	17
Agree	2	14
Neither agree nor disagree	3	6
Disagree	4	2
Strongly disagree	5	1

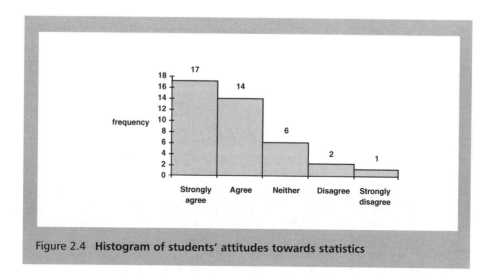

Figure 2.4   **Histogram of students' attitudes towards statistics**

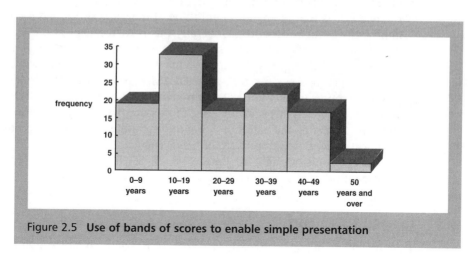

Figure 2.5   **Use of bands of scores to enable simple presentation**

assimilated form. So sometimes you will have to use *bands of scores* rather than individual score values just as you did for Table 2.2 above. So if we asked 100 people their ages we could categorise their replies into bands such as 0–9 years, 10–19 years, 30–39 years, 40–49 years and a final category of those 50 years and over. By using bands we reduce the risk of empty parts of the table and allow any trends to become clear (Figure 2.5).

    How one chooses the bands to use is an important question. The answer is a bit of luck and judgement and a lot of trial and error. It is very time consuming to rejig the ranges of the bands when one is analysing the data by hand. One big advantage of computers is that they will recode your scores into bands repeatedly until you

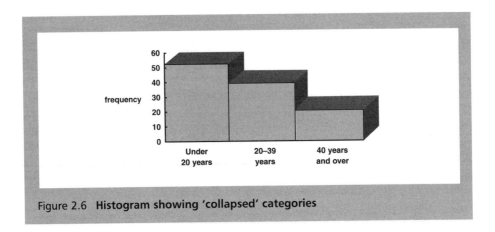

Figure 2.6 **Histogram showing 'collapsed' categories**

have tables which seem to do the job as well as possible. The criterion is still whether the table communicates information effectively.

The one rule is that the bands ought to be of the same size – that is cover, for example, equal ranges of scores. Generally this is easy except at the upper and lower ends of the distribution. Perhaps you wish to use 'over 70' as your upper range. This, in modern practice, can be done as a bar of the same width as the others, but must be very carefully marked. (Strictly speaking the width of the band should represent the range of scores involved and the height reduced in the light of this. However, this is rarely done in modern psychological statistics.)

One might redefine the bands of scores and generate another histogram based on identical data but a different set of bands (Figure 2.6).

It requires some thought to decide which of the diagrams is best for a particular purpose. There are no hard-and-fast rules.

2.3   Errors to avoid

There are a few mistakes that you can make in drawing up tables and diagrams:

1. *Do not* forget to head the table or diagram with a succinct description of what it concerns. You will notice that we have done our best throughout this chapter to supply each table and diagram with a clear title.

2. Label everything on the table or diagram as clearly as possible. What this means is that you have to mark your bar charts and histograms in a way that tells the reader what each bar means. Then you must indicate what the height of the bar refers to – probably either frequency or percentage frequency.

Note that this chapter has concentrated on describing a *single* variable as clearly as possible. In Chapter 6, methods of making tables and diagrams showing the relationships between two or more variables are described.

2.4   Notes and recommendations

■ Try to make your tables and diagrams useful. It is not usually their purpose to record the data as you collected it in your research. Of course you can list your data in the appendix of projects that you carry out, but this is not useful as a way of illustrating trends. It is part of a researcher's job to make the data accessible to the reader in a structured form that is easily understood by the reader.

■ Especially when using computers, it is very easy to generate *useless* tables and diagrams. This is usually because computer analysis encourages you not to examine your raw data in any detail. This implies that you should always regard your first analyses as tentative and merely a step towards something more ideal.

■ If a table is not clear to you, it is unlikely to be any clearer to anyone else.

■ Check each table and diagram for clear and full labelling of each part. Especially, check that frequencies are clearly marked as such.

■ Check that there is a clear, helpful title to each table and diagram.

Chapter 3

Describing variables numerically

Averages, variation and spread

Preparation
Revise the meaning of nominal (category) data and numerical score data.

3.1 Introduction

Tables and diagrams take up a lot of space. It can be more efficient to use numerical indexes to describe the distributions of variables. For this reason, you will find relatively few pie charts and the like in published research. One numerical index is familiar to everyone – the numerical average (or arithmetic mean). Large amounts of data can be described adequately using just a few numerical indexes.

Table 3.1 **Two different sets of scores**

Variable A scores	Variable B scores
2	27
2	29
3	35
3	40
3	41
4	42
4	45
4	45
4	49
4	49
5	49
5	
5	

What are the major features of data that we might attempt to summarise in this way? Look at the two different sets of scores in Table 3.1. The major differences between these two sets of data are:

1. The sets of scores differ substantially in terms of their typical value – in one case the scores are relatively large (variable B); in the other case the scores are much smaller (variable A).
2. The sets of scores differ in their spread or variability – one set (variable B) seems to have more spread or a greater variability than the other.
3. If we plot these two sets of scores as histograms then we also find that the shapes of the distributions differ markedly. Variable A is much steeper and less spread out than variable B.

Each of these different features of a set of scores can be described using various indexes. They do *not* generally apply to nominal (category) variables.

3.2   Typical scores: mean, median and mode

Researchers sometimes speak about the *central tendency* of a set of scores. By this they are raising the issue of what are the most typical and likely scores in the distribution of measurements. We could speak of the average score but that can mislead us into thinking that the arithmetic mean is the average score when it is just one of several possibilities. There are three main measures of the typical scores: the *arithmetic mean*, the *mode* and the *median*. These are quite distinct concepts but generally simple enough in themselves.

The arithmetic mean

The arithmetic mean is calculated by summing all of the scores in a distribution and dividing by the number of scores. This is the everyday concept of average. In statistical notation we can express this mean as follows:

$$\overline{X}_{[\text{mean}]} = \frac{\Sigma\, X_{[\text{scores}]}}{N_{[\text{number of scores}]}}$$

As this is the first statistical formula we have presented, you should take very careful note of what each symbol means:

X is the statistical symbol for a score
Σ is the summation or sigma sign
ΣX means add up all of the scores X
N is the number of scores
$\overline{X}$ is the statistical symbol for the arithmetic mean of a set of scores

We have added a few comments in small square brackets [just like this]. Although mathematicians may not like them very much, you might find they help you to interpret a formula a little more quickly.

Calculation 3.1

The numerical or arithmetic mean

To illustrate the calculation of the arithmetic mean we can use the following six scores:

$$X_1 = 7$$
$$X_2 = 5$$
$$X_3 = 4$$
$$X_4 = 7$$
$$X_5 = 7$$
$$X_6 = 5$$

The subscripts following the Xs above define a particular score.

$$\overline{X}_{[mean]} = \frac{\Sigma\, X_{[scores]}}{N_{[number\ of\ scores]}}$$

$$\overline{X} = \frac{X_1 + X_2 + X_3 + X_4 + X_5 + X_6}{N}$$

$$= \frac{7 + 5 + 4 + 7 + 7 + 5}{6}$$

$$= \frac{35}{6}$$

$$= 5.83$$

Although you probably do not need the formula to work out the arithmetic mean, it is useful at this stage to make sure that you understand how to decode the symbols. It is a simple example but contains several of the important elements of statistical formulae. It is good preparation to go through the calculation using the formula.

The mode

The mode is the most frequently occurring category of score. It is merely the most common score or most frequent category of scores. In other words, you can

Table 3.2 **Frequencies of scores**

Score	Frequency (*f*)
4	1
5	2
6	0
7	3

Table 3.3 **A bimodel frequency distribution**

Score	Frequency (*f*)
3	1
4	2
5	3
6	1
7	3
8	1

apply the mode to any category data and not just scores. In the above example where the scores were 7,5,4,7,7,5 we could represent the scores in terms of their frequencies of occurrence (Table 3.2).

Frequencies are often represented as *f* in statistics. It is very easy to see in this example that the most frequently occurring score is 7 with a frequency of 3. So the mode of this distribution is 7.

If we take the slightly different set of scores 7, 5, 4, 7, 7, 5, 3, 4, 6, 8, 5, the frequency distribution of these scores is shown in Table 3.3. Here there is no single mode since scores 5 and 7 jointly have the highest frequency of 3. This sort of distribution is called *bimodal* and the two modes are 5 and 7. The general term *multimodal* implies that a frequency distribution has several modes.

The mode is the only measure in this chapter that applies to nominal (category) data as well as numerical score data.

The median

The median is the middle score of a set if they are organised from the smallest to the largest. Thus the scores 7, 5, 4, 7, 7, 5, 3, 4, 6, 8, 5 become 3, 4, 4, 5, 5, 5, 6, 7, 7, 7, 8 when put in order from the smallest to the largest. Since there are 11 scores and the median is the middle score from the smallest to the largest, the median has to be the sixth score, i.e. 5.

With odd numbers of scores all of which are different, the median is easily calculated since there is a single score that corresponds to the middle score in the set of scores. However, if there is an even number of all different scores in the set then sometimes the mid-point will not be a single score but two scores. So if you have 12 different scores placed in order from smallest to largest, the median will be somewhere between the sixth and seventh score from smallest. There is no such score, of course, by definition – the 6.5th score just does not exist. What we could do in these circumstances is to take the average of the sixth and seventh scores to give us an estimate of the median.

For the distribution of 40 scores shown in Table 3.4, the middle score from the smallest is somewhere between the 20th and 21st scores. Thus the median is somewhere between score 5 (the 20th score) and score 6 (the 21st score). One could give the average of these two as the median score – that is, the median is 5.5. For most purposes this is good enough.

You may find that computer programs give different values from this. The computer program is making adjustments since there may be several identical scores near the median but you need only a fraction of them to reach your mid-point score. So in the above example the 21st score comes in score category 6 although there are actually eight scores in that category. So in order to get that extra score we need take only one-eighth of score category 6. One-eighth equals 0.125 so the estimated median equals 5.125. To be frank, it is difficult to think of many circumstances in which this level of precision about the value of the median is required in psychological statistics. You ought to regard this feature of computer output as a bonus and adopt the simpler method for your hand calculations.

Table 3.4 **Frequency distribution of 40 scores**

Score	Frequency (f)
1	1
2	2
3	4
4	6
5	7
6	8
7	6
8	3
9	2
10	1
11	0
12	1

3.3   Comparison of mean, median and mode

Usually the mean, median and mode will give different values of the central tendency when applied to the same set of scores. It is only when a distribution is perfectly symmetrical *and* the distribution peaks in the middle that they coincide completely. Regard big differences between the mean, median and mode as a sign that your distribution of scores is rather asymmetrical or lopsided.

Distributions of scores do not have to be perfectly symmetrical for statistical analysis but it tends to make some calculations a little more accurate. It is difficult to say how much lack of symmetry there can be without it becoming a serious problem. There is more about this later, especially in Chapter 18 and Appendix A which makes some suggestions about how to test for asymmetry. This is done relatively rarely in our experience.

3.4   The spread of scores: variability

The concept of variability is essential in statistics. Variability is a non-technical term and is related to (but is *not* identical with) the statistical term *variance*. Variance is nothing more nor less than a mathematical formula that serves as a useful indicator of variability. But it is not the only way of assessing variability.

The following set of ages of twelve university students can be used to illustrate some different ways of measuring variability in our data:

| 18 years | 21 years | 23 years | 18 years | 19 years | 19 years |
| 19 years | 33 years | 18 years | 19 years | 19 years | 20 years |

These twelve students vary in age from 18 to 33 years. In other words, the range covers a 15-year period. The interval from youngest to oldest (or tallest to shortest, or fattest to thinnest) is called the *range* – a useful statistical concept. As a *statistical* concept, range is *always* expressed as a single number such as 20 centimetres and *never* as an interval, say, from 15 to 25 centimetres.

One trouble with range is that it can be heavily influenced by extreme cases. Thus the 33-year-old student in the above set of ages is having a big influence on the range of ages of the students. This is because he or she is much older than most of the students. For this reason, the *interquartile range* has advantages. To calculate the interquartile range we split the age distribution into quarters and take the range of the middle two quarters (or middle 50%), ignoring the extreme quarters. Since we have 12 students, we delete the three youngest (the three 18-year-olds) and the three oldest (aged 33, 23 and 21). This leaves us with the middle two quarters (the middle 50%) which includes five 19-year-olds and one 20-year-old. The range of this middle two quarters, or the interquartile range, is one year (from 19 years to 20 years). The interquartile range is sometimes a better indicator of the variability of, say, age than the full range because extreme ages are excluded.

Table 3.5 Deviations from the mean

Score – mean	Deviation from mean
18 – 20.5	–2.5
21 – 20.5	0.5
23 – 20.5	2.5
18 – 20.5	–2.5
19 – 20.5	–1.5
19 – 20.5	–1.5
19 – 20.5	–1.5
33 – 20.5	12.5
18 – 20.5	–2.5
19 – 20.5	–1.5
19 – 20.5	–1.5
20 – 20.5	–0.5

Useful as the range is, a lot of information is ignored. It does not take into account all of the scores in the set, merely the extreme ones. For this reason, measures of spread or variability have been developed which include the extent to which each of the scores in the set differs from the mean score of the set.

One such measure is the *mean deviation*. To calculate this we have to work out the mean of the set of scores and then how much each score in the set differs from that mean. These deviations are then added up, ignoring the negative signs, to give the total of deviations from the mean. Finally we can divide by the number of scores to give the average or mean deviation from the mean of the set of scores. If we take the ages of the students listed above, we find that the total of the ages is 18 + 21 + 23 + 18 + 19 + 19 + 19 + 33 + 18 + 19 + 19 + 20 = 246. Divide this total by 12 and we get the average age in the set to be 20.5 years. Now if we subtract 20.5 years from each of the student's ages we get the figures in Table 3.5.

The average amount of deviation from the mean (ignoring the sign) is known as the mean deviation (for the above deviations this would give a value of 2.6 years). Although frequently mentioned in statistical textbooks it has no practical applications in psychological statistics and is best forgotten. However, there is a very closely related concept, *variance*, that is much more useful and has widespread and extensive applications. Variance is calculated in an almost identical way to mean deviation but for one thing. When we draw up a table to calculate the variance, we *square* each deviation from the mean before summing the total of these squared deviations as shown in Table 3.6.

The total of the squared deviations from the mean is 193. If we divide this by the number of scores (12), it gives us the value of the variance, which equals 16.08 in this case.

Table 3.6 **Squared deviations from the mean**

Score – mean	Deviation from mean	Square of deviation from mean
18 – 20.5	–2.5	6.25
21 – 20.5	0.5	0.25
23 – 20.5	2.5	6.25
18 – 20.5	–2.5	6.25
19 – 20.5	–1.5	2.25
19 – 20.5	–1.5	2.25
19 – 20.5	–1.5	2.25
33 – 20.5	12.5	156.25
18 – 20.5	–2.5	6.25
19 – 20.5	–1.5	2.25
19 – 20.5	–1.5	2.25
20 – 20.5	–0.5	0.25
	Total = 0	Total = 193

Expressing the concept as a formula:

$$\text{Variance} = \frac{\Sigma\,(X - \bar{X})^2}{N}$$

The above formula defines what variance is – it is the *defining formula*. The calculation of variance above corresponds to this formula. However, in statistics there are often quicker ways of doing calculations. These quicker methods involve *computational formulae*. The computational formula for variance is important and worth memorising as it occurs in many contexts.

Standard deviation (see Chapter 5) is a concept which computationally is very closely related to variance. Indeed, many textbooks deal with them at one and the same time. Unfortunately, this tends in our view to confuse two very distinct concepts and adds nothing to clarity.

Calculation 3.2

Variance using the computational formula

The computational formula for variance speeds the calculation since it saves having to calculate the mean of the set of scores and subtract this mean from each of the scores. The formula is:

$$\text{Variance}_{\text{[computational formula]}} = \frac{\Sigma X^2 - \frac{(\Sigma X)^2}{N}}{N}$$

Take care with elements of this formula:

X	= the general symbol for each member of a set of scores
Σ	= sigma or the summation sign, i.e. add up all the things which follow
ΣX^2	= the sum of the square of each of the scores
$(\Sigma X)^2$	= sum all the scores and square that total
N	= the number of scores

Step 1 Applying this formula to our set of scores, it is useful to draw up a table (Table 3.7) consisting of our scores and some of the steps in the computation. N (number of scores) equals 12.

Table 3.7 **A set of scores and their squares for use in the computing formula for variance**

Score X	Squared score X^2
18	324
21	441
23	529
18	324
19	361
19	361
19	361
33	1089
18	324
19	361
19	361
20	400

$$\Sigma X = 246 \qquad \Sigma X^2 = 5236$$
$$(\Sigma X)^2 = 246^2 = 60{,}516$$

Step 2 Substituting these values in the computational formula:

$$\text{Variance}_{\text{[computational formula]}} = \frac{\Sigma X^2 - \frac{(\Sigma X)^2}{N}}{N}$$

$$\text{Variance} = \frac{5236 - \frac{60{,}516}{12}}{12}$$

$$= \frac{5236 - 5043}{12}$$

$$= \frac{193}{12}$$

$$= 16.08$$

Interpreting the results Variance is difficult to interpret in isolation from other information about the data since it is dependent on the measurement in question. Measures which are based on a wide numerical scale for the scores will tend to have higher variance than measures based on a narrow scale. Thus if the range of scores is only 10 then the variance is likely to be less than if the range of scores is 100. Frequently variance is treated comparatively – that is, variances of different groups of people are compared (see Chapter 19).

Reporting the results Usually variance is routinely reported in tables which summarise a variable or a number of variables along with other statistics such as the mean and range. This is shown in Table 3.8.

Table 3.8 **Illustrating the table for descriptive statistics**

Variable	N	Mean	Variance	Range
Age	12	20.50 years	16.08	15 years

There is a concept called the *variance estimate* (or estimated variance) which is closely related to variance. The difference is that the variance estimate is your best guess as to the variance of a population of scores *if* you only have the data from a small set of scores from that population on which to base your estimate. The variance estimate is described in Chapter 11. It involves a slight amendment to the variance formula in that instead of dividing by N one divides by $N - 1$.
    The formula for the estimated variance is:

$$\text{Estimated variance} = \frac{\Sigma X^2 - \frac{(\Sigma X)^2}{N}}{N - 1}$$

Some psychologists prefer to use this formula in all practical circumstances. Similarly, some textbooks and some computer programs give you calculations based on the above formula rather than the one we have used in Calculation 3.2. Since virtually all statistical analyses in psychology are based on samples and we normally wish to generalise from these samples to all cases, then the estimated variance is likely to be used in practice. Hence it is reasonable to use the estimated variance as the general formula for variance. The drawback to this is that if we are merely describing the data, this practice is theoretically imprecise.

3.5 Notes and recommendations

■ Because they are routine ways of summarising the typical score and the spread of a set of scores, it is important always to report the following information for each of your variables:

- mean, median and mode
- range and variance
- number of scores in the set of scores.

■ *The above does not apply to nominal categories*. For these, the frequency of cases in each category exhausts the main possibilities.

■ It is worth trying to memorise the definitional and computational formulae for variance. You will be surprised how often these formulae appear in statistics.

■ When using a computer, look carefully for variables that have zero variance. They can cause problems and generally ought to be omitted from your analyses (see Chapter 7). Normally the computer will not compute the calculations you ask for in these circumstances. The difficulty is that if all the scores of a variable are the same, it is impossible to calculate many statistical formulae. If you are calculating by hand, variables with all the scores the same are easier to spot.

Chapter 4

Shapes of distributions of scores

Preparation
Be clear about numerical scores and how they can be classified into ranges of scores (Chapter 2).

The final important characteristic of sets of scores is the particular shape of their distribution. It is useful for a researcher to be able to describe this shape succinctly. Obviously it is possible to find virtually any shape of distribution amongst the multitude of variables that could be measured. So, intuitively, it seems unrealistic to seek to describe just a few different shapes. But there are some advantages in doing so, as we shall see.

4.1 Histograms and frequency curves

Most of us have very little difficulty in understanding histograms; we know that they are plots of the frequency of scores (the vertical dimension) against a numerical scale (the horizontal dimension). Figure 4.1 is an example of a histogram based on a relatively small set of scores. This histogram has quite severe steps from bar to bar. In other words, it is quite angular and not a smooth shape at all. Part of the reason for this is that the horizontal numerical scale moves along in discrete steps, so resulting in this pattern. Things would be different if we measured on a *continuous scale* on which every possible score could be represented to the smallest fraction. For example, we might decide to measure people's heights in centimetres to the nearest whole centimetre. But we know that heights do not really conform to this set of discrete steps or points; people who measure 120 centimetres actually differ in height by up to a centimetre from each other. Height can be measured in fractions of centimetres, not just whole centimetres. In other words height is a continuous measurement with infinitesimally small steps between measures so long as we have sufficiently precise measuring instruments.

So a histogram of heights measured in centimetre units is at best an approximation to reality. Within each of the blocks of the histogram is a possible

Figure 4.1   **Histogram showing steep steps**

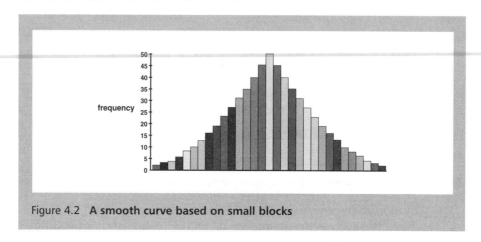

Figure 4.2   **A smooth curve based on small blocks**

multitude of smaller steps. For this reason, it is conventional when drawing frequency curves for theoretical purposes to smooth out the blocks to a continuous curve. In essence this is like taking much finer and precise measurements and redrawing the histogram. Instead of doing this literally we approximate it by drawing a smooth curve through imaginary sets of extremely small steps. When this is done our histogram is 'miraculously' turned into a continuous unstepped curve (Figure 4.2).

A frequency curve can, of course, be of virtually any shape but one shape in particular is of concern in psychological statistics – the normal curve.

4.2   The normal curve

The normal curve describes a particular shape of the frequency curve. Although this shape is defined by a formula and can be described mathematically, for most purposes it is sufficient to regard it as a symmetrical bell-shape (Figure 4.3).

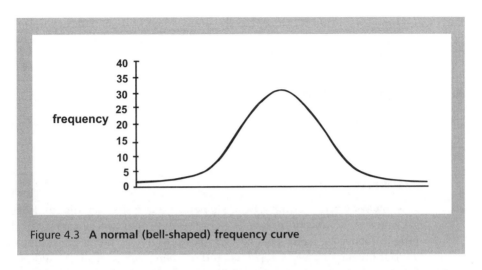

Figure 4.3   **A normal (bell-shaped) frequency curve**

It is called the 'normal' curve because it was once believed that distributions in the natural world correspond to this shape. Even though it turns out that the normal curve is not universal, it is important because many distributions are more-or-less this shape – at least sufficiently so for most practical purposes. The crucial reason for its use in statistics is that theoreticians developed many statistical techniques on the assumption that the distributions of scores were bell-shaped or normal. It so happens that these assumptions which are useful in the development of statistical techniques have little bearing on their day-to-day application. The techniques may generally be applied to data which are only very roughly bell-shaped without too much inaccuracy. In run-of-the-mill psycho-logical statistics, the question of whether a distribution is normal or bell-shaped is relatively unimportant. Exceptions to this will be mentioned as appropriate in later chapters.

Design consideration   One thing which may trouble you is the question of how precisely your data need fit this normal or bell-shaped ideal. Is it possible to depart much from the ideal without causing problems? The short answer is that usually a lot of deviation is possible without it affecting things too much. So, in the present context, you should not worry too much if the mean, median and mode do differ somewhat; for practical purposes you can disregard deviations from the ideal distribution, especially when dealing with about 30 or more scores. Unfortunately, all of this involves a degree of subjective judgement since there are no useful ways of assessing what is an acceptable amount of deviation from the ideal when faced with the small amounts of data that student projects often involve.

Don't forget that for the perfectly symmetrical, bell-shaped (normal) curve the values of the mean, median and mode are identical. Disparities between the three are indications that you have an asymmetrical curve.

4.3   Distorted curves

The main concepts which deal with distortions in the normal curve are *skewness* and *kurtosis*.

Skewness

It is always worth examining the shape of your frequency distributions. Gross skewness is the exception to our rule-of-thumb that non-normality of data has little influence on statistical analyses. By skewness we mean the extent to which your frequency curve is lopsided rather than symmetrical. A mid-point of a frequency curve may be skewed either to the left or to the right of the range of scores (Figures 4.4 and 4.5).

Figure 4.4   **Negative skew**

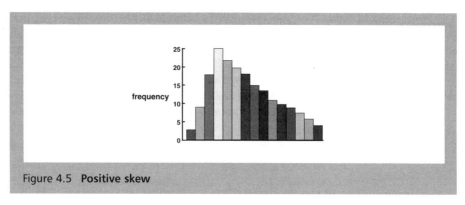

Figure 4.5   **Positive skew**

There are special terms for left-handed and right-handed skew:

■ *Negative skew*:
  – more scores are to the left of the mode than to the right;
  – the mean and median are smaller than the mode.
■ *Positive skew:*
  – more scores are to the right of the mode than to the left;
  – the mean and median are bigger than the mode.

There is also an index of the amount of skew shown in your set of scores. With hand-calculated data analyses the best approach is usually to look at your frequency curve. With computer analyses the ease of obtaining the index of skewness makes more formal methods unnecessary. The index of skewness is positive for a positive skew and negative for a negative skew. Appendix A explains how to test for skewness in your data.

Kurtosis (or steepness/shallowness)

Some symmetrical curves may look rather like the normal bell-shaped curve except that they are excessively steep or excessively flat compared to the mathematically defined normal bell-shaped curve (Figures 4.6 and 4.7).

Kurtosis is the term used to identify the degree of steepness or shallowness of a distribution. There are technical words for different types of curve:

■ a steep curve is called leptokurtic
■ a normal curve is called mesokurtic
■ a flat curve is called platykurtic.

Although they are terms beloved of statistics book writers, since the terms mean nothing more than steep, middling and flat there seems to be good reason to drop the Greek words in favour of everyday English.

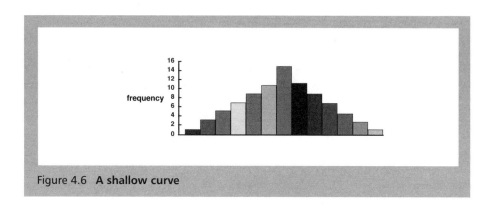

Figure 4.6 **A shallow curve**

Figure 4.7 **A steep curve**

It is possible to obtain indexes of the amount of shallowness or steepness of your distribution compared with the mathematically defined normal distribution. These are probably most useful as part of a computer analysis. For most purposes an inspection of the frequency curve of your data is sufficient in hand analyses. Knowing what the index means should help you cope with computer output; quite simply:

■ a positive value of kurtosis means that the curve is steep

■ a zero value of kurtosis means that the curve is middling

■ a negative value of kurtosis means that the curve is flat.

Steepness and shallowness have little or no bearing on the statistical techniques you use to analyse your data, quite unlike skewness.

Figure 4.8 **A bimodal frequency histogram**

4.4   Other frequency curves

Bimodal and multimodal frequency distributions

Of course, there is no rule that says that frequency curves have to peak in the middle and tail off to the left and right. As we have already explained, it is perfectly possible to have a frequency distribution with twin peaks (or even multiple peaks). Such twin-peaked distributions are called *bimodal* since they have two modes – most frequently occurring scores. Such a frequency curve might look like Figure 4.8.

Cumulative frequency curves

There are any number of different ways of presenting a single set of data. Take, for example, the 50 scores in Table 4.1 for a measure of extraversion obtained from airline pilots.

One way of tabulating these extraversion scores is simply to count the number of pilots scoring at each value of extraversion from 1 to 5. This could be presented in several forms, for example Table 4.2, Table 4.3 and Figure 4.9.

Table 4.1   **Extraversion scores of 50 airline pilots**

3	5	5	4	4	5	5	3	5	2
1	2	5	3	2	1	2	3	3	3
4	2	5	5	4	2	4	5	1	5
5	3	3	4	1	4	2	5	1	2
3	2	5	4	2	1	2	3	4	1

Table 4.2   **Frequency table based on data in Table 4.1**

Number scoring 1	7
Number scoring 2	11
Number scoring 3	10
Number scoring 4	9
Number scoring 5	13

Table 4.3   **Alternative layout for data in Table 4.1**

Number of pilots scoring				
1	2	3	4	5
7	11	10	9	13

Table 4.4 Cumulative frequency distribution of pilots'
extraversion scores from Table 4.1

Score range	Cumulative frequency	Cumulative percentage frequency
1	7	14%
2 or less	18	36%
3 or less	28	56%
4 or less	37	74%
5 or less	50	100%

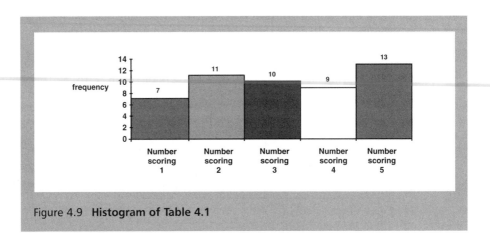

Figure 4.9 **Histogram of Table 4.1**

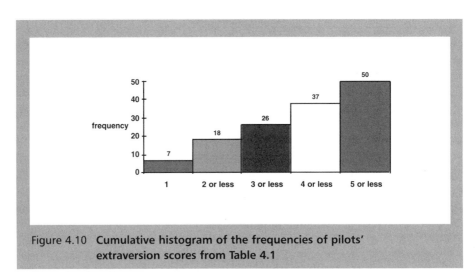

Figure 4.10 **Cumulative histogram of the frequencies of pilots'
extraversion scores from Table 4.1**

Table 4.5 **Alternative style of cumulative frequency distribution of pilots' extraversion scores from Table 4.1**

		Number of pilots scoring		
1	**2 or less**	**3 or less**	**4 or less**	**5 or less**
7	18	28	37	50

Exactly the same distribution of scores could be represented using a *cumulative* frequency distribution. A simple frequency distribution merely indicates the number of people who achieved any particular score. A cumulative frequency distribution gives the number scoring, say, one, two or less, three or less, four or less, and five or less. In other words, the frequencies accumulate. Examples of cumulative frequency distributions are given in Table 4.4, Table 4.5 and Figure 4.10. Cumulative frequencies can be given also as cumulative percentage frequencies in which the frequencies are expressed as percentages and these percentages accumulated. This is shown in Table 4.4.

There is nothing difficult about cumulative frequencies – but you must label such tables and diagrams clearly or they can be very misleading.

Percentiles

Percentiles are merely a form of cumulative frequency distribution, but instead of being expressed in terms of accumulating scores from lowest to highest, the categorisation is in terms of whole numbers of percentages of people. In other words, the percentile is the score which a given percentage of scores equal or exceed. You do not necessarily have to report every percentage point and units of 10 might suffice for some purposes. Such a distribution would look something like Table 4.6.

The table shows that 10% of scores are equal to 7 or less and 80% of scores are equal to 61 or less. Note that the 50th percentile corresponds to the median score.

Percentiles are commonly used in standardisation tables of psychological tests and measures. For these it is often very useful to be able to describe a person's standing compared with the set of individuals on which the test or measure was initially researched. Thus if a particular person's neuroticism score is described as being at the 90th percentile it means that they are more neurotic than about 90% of people. In other words, percentiles are a quick method of expressing a person's score relative to those of others.

In order to calculate the percentiles for any data it is first necessary to produce a table of cumulative percentage frequencies. This table is then examined to find the score which cuts off, for example, the bottom 10%, the bottom 20%, the bottom 30% etc. of scores. It should be obvious that calculating percentiles in this way is actually easier if there is a large number of scores so that the cut-off points can be found precisely. Generally speaking, percentiles are used in psychological tests and measures that have been standardised on large numbers of people.

Table 4.6 **Example of percentiles**

Percentile	Score
10th	7
20th	9
30th	14
40th	20
50th	39
60th	45
70th	50
80th	61
90th	70
100th	78

4.5 Notes and recommendations

■ The most important concept in this chapter is that of the normal curve or normal distribution. It is worth extra effort to memorise the idea that the normal curve is a bell-shaped symmetrical curve.

■ Be a little wary if you find that your scores on a variable are very *skewed* since this can lose precision in certain statistical analyses.

Chapter 5

Standard deviation

The standard unit of measurement in statistics

Preparation

Make sure you know the meaning of variables, scores, Σ and scales of measurement – especially nominal, interval and ratio (Chapter 1).

5.1 Introduction

Measurement ideally uses standard or universal units. It would be really stupid if, when we ask people how far it is to the nearest railway station, one person says 347 cow's lengths, another says 150 poodle jumps, and a third person says three times the distance between my doctor's house and my dentist's home. If you ask us how hot it was on midsummer's day you would be pretty annoyed if one of us said 27 degrees Howitt and the other said 530 degrees Cramer. We measure in standard units such as centimetres, degrees Celsius, kilograms, and so forth. The advantages of doing so are obvious: standard units of measurement allow us to communicate easily, precisely and effectively with other people.

It is much the same in statistics – the trouble is the perplexing variety of types of units possible because of the universality of statistics in many research disciplines. Some variables are measured in physical ways such as metres and kilograms. Others use more abstract units of measurement such as scores on an intelligence test or a personality inventory. Although it would be nice if statisticians had a standard unit of measurement, it is not intuitively obvious what this should be.

5.2 Theoretical background

Imagine a 30 centimetre rule – it will be marked in one centimetre units from zero centimetres to 30 centimetres (Figure 5.1). The standard unit of measurement here is the centimetre. But you could have a different sort of rule in which instead of the scale being from 0 to 30 centimetres, the mid-point of the scale is 0 and the scale is marked as $-15, -14, -13, \ldots, -1, 0, +1, \ldots, +13, +14, +15$ centimetres. This rule is in essence marked in deviation units (Figure 5.2).

Figure 5.1 **A 30 centimetre rule**

Figure 5.2 **A 30 centimetre rule using deviation units**

The two rules use the same unit of measurement (the centimetre) but the deviation rule is marked with 0 in the middle, not at the left-hand side. In other words, the mid-point of the scale is marked as 0 deviation (from the mid-point). The standard deviation is similar to this rule in so far as it is based on *distances or deviations* from the average or mid-point.

As it is the standard unit of measurement in statistics, it is a pity that statisticians chose to call it standard deviation rather than 'standard statistical unit'. The latter phrase would better describe what it is. In contrast to a lot of measurements such as metres and kilograms, the standard deviation corresponds to no single standard of measurement that can be defined in *absolute terms* against a physical entity locked in a vault somewhere.

The standard deviation of a set of scores is measured *relative* to all of the scores in that set. Put as simply as possible, *the standard deviation is the 'average' amount by which scores differ from the mean or average score.* Now this is an odd idea – basing your standard measure on a set of scores rather than on an absolute standard. Nevertheless, it is an important concept to grasp. Don't jump ahead at this stage – there are a couple of twists in the logic yet. Perhaps you are imagining that if the scores were 4, 6, 3 and 7 then the mean is 20 divided by 4 (the number of scores), or 5. Each of the four scores deviates from the average by a certain amount – for example, 7 deviates from the mean of 5 by just 2. The sum of the deviations of our four scores from the mean of 5 is $1 + 1 + 2 + 2$ which equals 6. Surely, then, the standard deviation is 6 divided by 4, which equals 1.5?

But this is *not* how statisticians work out the average deviation for their standard unit. Such an approach might seem logical but it turns out to be not very useful in practice. Instead *standard deviation uses a different type of average which most mortals would not even recognise as an average.*

The big difference is that standard deviation is calculated as the average *squared* deviation. What this implies is that instead of taking our four deviation scores $(1 + 1 + 2 + 2)$ we square each of them $(1^2 + 1^2 + 2^2 + 2^2)$ which gives $1 + 1 + 4 + 4 = 10$. If we divide this total deviation of 10 by the number of scores (4), this gives a value of 2.5. However, this is still not quite the end of the story since *we then have to calculate the square root of this peculiar average deviation from the mean.* Thus we take the 2.5 and work out its square root – that is, 1.58. In words, *the standard deviation is the square root of the average squared deviation from the mean.*

And that really is it – honest. It is a pity that one of the most important concepts in statistics is less than intuitively obvious, but there we are. To summarise:

1. The standard deviation is the standard unit of measurement in statistics.
2. The standard deviation is simply the 'average' amount that the scores on a variable deviate (or differ) from the mean of the set of scores. In essence, the standard deviation is the average deviation from the mean. Think of it like this since most of us will have little difficulty grasping it in these terms. Its peculiarities can be safely ignored for most purposes.
3. Although the standard deviation is an average, it is not the sort of average which most of us are used to. However, it is of greater use in statistical applications than any other way of calculating the average deviation from the mean.

The standard deviation gives greater numerical emphasis to scores which depart by larger amounts from the mean. The reason is that it involves *squared* deviations from the mean which give disproportionately more emphasis to larger deviations.

It should be stressed that the *standard deviation is not a unit-free measure.* If we measured a set of people's heights in centimetres, the standard deviation of their heights would also be a certain number of *centimetres.* If we measured 50 people's intelligences using an intelligence test, the standard deviation would be a certain number of IQ points. It might help you to remember this, although most people would merely say or write things like 'the standard deviation of height was 4.5' without mentioning the units of measurement.

Calculation 5.1

Standard deviation

The defining formula for standard deviation is as follows:

$$\text{Standard deviation} = \sqrt{\frac{\Sigma(X - \overline{X})^2}{N}}$$

or the computationally quicker formula is:

$$\text{Standard deviation} = \sqrt{\frac{\Sigma X^2 - \frac{(\Sigma X)^2}{N}}{N}}$$

Table 5.1 **Steps in the calculation of the standard deviation**

Scores (*X*) (age in years)	Scores squared (*X²*)
20	400
25	625
19	361
35	1225
19	361
17	289
15	225
30	900
27	729
$\Sigma X = 207$	$\Sigma X^2 = 5115$

Table 5.1 lists the ages of nine students (N = number of scores = 9) and shows steps in calculating the standard deviation. Substituting these values in the standard deviation formula:

$$\text{Standard deviation} = \sqrt{\frac{\Sigma X^2 - \frac{(\Sigma X)^2}{N}}{N}}$$

$$= \sqrt{\frac{5115 - \frac{(207)^2}{9}}{9}}$$

$$= \sqrt{\frac{5115 - 4761}{9}}$$

$$= \sqrt{\frac{354}{9}}$$

$$= \sqrt{39.3333}$$

$$= 6.27 \text{ years}$$

(You may have spotted that the standard deviation is simply the square root of the variance.)

Interpreting the results Like variance, standard deviation is difficult to interpret without other information about the data. Standard deviation is merely a sort of average deviation from the mean. Its size will depend on the scale of the measurement in question. The bigger the units of the scale, the bigger the standard deviation is likely to be.

Reporting the results Usually standard deviation is routinely reported in tables which summarise a variable or a number of variables along with other statistics such as the mean and range. This is shown in Table 5.2.

Table 5.2 **Illustrating the table for descriptive statistics**

Variable	*N*	Mean	Range	Standard deviation
Age	9	23.00 years	20.00 years	6.27 years

The standard deviation is important in statistics for many reasons. The most important is that the *size* of the standard deviation is an indicator of how much variability there is in the scores for a particular variable. The bigger the standard deviation the more spread there is in the scores. However, this is merely to use standard deviation as a substitute for its close relative variance.

In this chapter the standard deviation is discussed as a descriptive statistic; that is, it is used like the mean and median, for example, to characterise important features of a set of scores. Be careful to distinguish this from the *estimated* standard deviation which is discussed in Chapter 11. Estimated standard deviation is your best guess as to the standard deviation of a population of scores based on information known about only a small subset or sample of scores from that population. Estimated standard deviation involves a modification to the standard deviation formula so that the estimate is better – the formula is modified to read *N*–1 instead of just *N*.

The formula for the estimated standard deviation is:

$$\text{Estimated standard deviation} = \sqrt{\frac{\Sigma X^2 - \frac{(\Sigma X)^2}{N}}{N-1}}$$

If you wish, this formula could be used in all of your calculations of standard deviation. Some textbooks and some computer programs give you calculations based on the above formula in all circumstances. Since virtually all statistical analyses in psychology are based on samples and we normally wish to generalise from these samples to all cases then there is good justification for this practice. The downside is that if we are describing the data rather than generalising from them then the formula is theoretically a little imprecise.

5.3   Measuring the number of standard deviations – the z-score

Given that one of the aims of statisticians is to make life as simple as possible for themselves, they try to use the minimum number of concepts possible. Expressing standard statistical units in terms of standard deviations is just one step towards trying to express many measures in a consistent way. Another way of achieving consistency is to express all scores in terms of a *number* of standard deviations. That is, we can abandon the original units of measurements almost entirely if all scores are re-expressed as a number of standard deviations.

It is a bit like calculating all weights in terms of kilograms or all distances in terms of metres. So, for example, since there are 2.2 pounds in a kilogram, something which weighs 10 pounds converts to 4.5 kilograms. We simply divide the number of pounds weight by the number of pounds in a kilogram in order to express our weight in pounds in terms of our standard unit of weight, the kilogram.

It is very much like this in statistics. If we know that the size of the standard deviation is, say, 7, we know that a score which is 21 above the mean score is 21/7 or three standard deviations above the mean. A score which is 14 below the mean is 14/7 or two standard deviations below the mean. So, once the size of the standard deviation is known, all scores can be re-expressed in terms of the *number* of standard deviations they are from the mean. One big advantage of this is that unlike other standard units of measurement such as distance and weight, the *number* of standard deviations will apply no matter what the variable being measured is. Thus it is equally applicable if we are measuring time, anxiety, depression, height or any other variable. So *the number of standard deviations is a universal scale* of measurement. But note the stress on the *number* of standard deviations.

Despite sounding a bit space-age and ultra-modern, the *z-score* is nothing other than the *number* of standard deviations a particular score lies above or below the mean of the set of scores – precisely the concept just discussed. So in order to work out the z-score for a particular score (X) on a variable we also need to know the mean of the set of scores on that variable and the value of the standard deviation of that set of scores. Sometimes it is referred to as the *standard score* since it allows all scores to be expressed in a standard form.

Calculation 5.2

Converting a score into a z-score

To convert the age of a 32-year-old to a z-score, given that the mean of the set of ages is 40 years and the standard deviation of age is 6 years, just apply the following formula:

$$z\text{-score} = \frac{X - \overline{X}}{\text{sd}}$$

where X stands for a particular score, $\overline{X}$ is the mean of the set of scores, and sd stands for standard deviation.

The z-score of any age (e.g. 32) can be obtained as follows:

$$z\text{-score}_{\text{[of a 32-year-old]}} = \frac{32 - 40}{6} = \frac{-8}{6} = -1.33$$

The value of –1.33 means that:

1. A 32-year-old is 1.33 standard deviations from the mean age of 40 for this set of age scores.

2. The minus sign simply means that the 32-year-old is younger (lower) than the mean age for the set of age scores. A plus sign (or no sign) would mean that the person is older (higher) than the mean age of 40 years.

Interpreting the results   There is little to be added about interpreting the z-score since it is defined by the formula as the number of standard deviations a score is from the mean score. Generally speaking, the larger the z-score (either positive or negative) the more atypical a score is of the typical score in the data. A z-score of about 2 or more is fairly rare.

Reporting the results   As z-scores are scores they can be presented as you would any other score using tables or diagrams. Usually there is no point in reporting the mean of a set of z-scores since this will be 0.00 if calculated for all of the cases.

5.4   A use of z-scores

So z-scores are merely scores expressed in terms of the *number* of standard statistical units of measurement (standard deviations) they are from the mean of the set of scores. One big advantage of using these standard units of measurement is that variables measured in terms of many different units of measurement can be compared with each other and even combined.

A good example of this comes from a student project (Szostak, 1995). The researcher was interested in the amount of anxiety that child tennis players exhibited and its effect on their performance (serving faults) in competitive situations as compared with practice. One consideration was the amount of commitment that parents demonstrated to their children's tennis. Rather than base this simply on the extent to which parents claimed to be involved, she asked parents the amount of money they spent on their child's tennis, the amount of time they spent on their child's tennis, and so forth:

1. How much money do you spend *per week* on your child's *tennis coaching*?
2. How much money do you spend *per year* on your child's *tennis equipment*?
3. How much money do you spend *per year* on your child's *tennis clothing*?
4. How many *miles per week* on average do you spend travelling to tennis events?
5. How many *hours per week* on average do you spend watching your child *play tennis*?
6. How many *LTA tournaments* does your child participate in *per year*?

This is quite straightforward information to collect but it causes difficulties in analysing the data. The student wanted to combine these six different measures of commitment to give an overall commitment score for each parent. However, the six items are based on radically different units of measurement – time, money and so forth. Her solution was simply to turn each parent's score on each of the questionnaire items into a z-score. This involves only the labour of working out the mean and standard deviation of the answers to each questionnaire and then turning each score into a z-score. These six z-scores are then added (including the + or – signs) to give a total score on the amount of commitment by each parent, which could be a positive or negative value since z-scores can be + or –.

This was an excellent strategy since this measure of parental commitment was the best predictor of a child performing poorly in competitive situations; the more parental commitment the worse the child does in real matches compared with practice.

There are plenty of other uses of the standard deviation in statistics as we shall see.

5.5   The standard normal distribution

There is a remaining important use of standard deviation. Although it should now be obvious that there are some advantages in converting scores into standard units of measurement, you might get the impression that, in the end, the scores themselves on a variable contain information which the z-score does not fully capture. In particular, if one looks at a distribution of the original scores, it is possible to have a good idea of how a particular individual scores relative to other people. So, for example, if you know the distribution of weights in a set of people, it should be possible to say something about the weight of a particular person relative to other people. A histogram giving the weights of 38 children in a school class allows us to compare a child with a weight of say 42 kilograms with the rest of the class (Figure 5.3).

We can see that a child of 42 kilograms is in the top four of the distribution – that is, in about the top 10% of the weight distribution. Counting the frequencies in the histogram tells us the percentage of the part of the distribution the child

Figure 5.3   **Distribution of weights in a set of children**

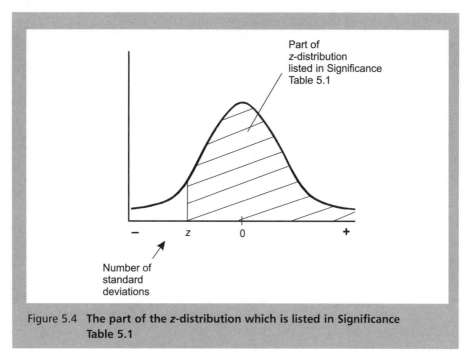

Figure 5.4   **The part of the z-distribution which is listed in Significance Table 5.1**

falls in. We can also work out that 34 out of 38 (about 90%) of the class are lighter than this particular child.

Surely this cannot be done if we work with standard deviations? In fact it is relatively straightforward to do so since there are ready-made tables to tell us precisely how a particular score (expressed as a z-score or number of standard deviations from the mean) compares with other scores. This is achieved by using

Significance Table 5.1 **The standard normal z-distribution: this gives the percentage of z-scores which are higher than the tabled values**

z-score	Percentage of scores higher than this particular z-score	z-score	Percentage of scores higher than this particular z-score
−4.00	99.997%	0.00	50.00%
−3.00	99.87%	+0.10	46.02%
−2.90	99.81%	+0.20	42.07%
−2.80	99.74%	+0.30	38.21%
−2.70	99.65%	+0.40	34.46%
−2.60	99.53%	+0.50	30.85%
−2.50	99.38%	+0.60	27.43%
−2.40	99.18%	+0.70	24.20%
−2.30	98.93%	+0.80	21.19%
−2.20	98.61%	+0.90	18.41%
−2.10	98.21%	+1.00	15.87%
−2.00	97.72%	+1.10	13.57%
−1.96	97.50%	+1.20	11.51%
		+1.30	9.68%
SCORES ABOVE THIS POINT ARE IN THE		+1.40	8.08%
EXTREME 5% OF SCORES IN EITHER		+1.50	6.68%
DIRECTION FROM THE MEAN (I.E. THE		+1.60	5.48%
EXTREME 2.5% BELOW THE MEAN)			
−1.90	97.13%	SCORES BELOW THIS POINT ARE IN THE	
−1.80	96.41%	EXTREME 5% ABOVE THE MEAN	
−1.70	95.54%	+1.64	5.00%
−1.64	95.00%	+1.70	4.46%
		+1.80	3.59%
SCORES ABOVE THIS POINT ARE IN THE		+1.90	2.87%
EXTREME 5% BELOW THE MEAN			
−1.60	94.52%	SCORES BELOW THIS POINT ARE IN THE	
−1.50	93.32%	EXTREME 5% OF SCORES IN EITHER	
−1.40	91.92%	DIRECTION FROM THE MEAN (I.E. THE	
−1.30	90.32%	EXTREME 2.5% ABOVE THE MEAN)	
−1.20	88.49%	+1.96	2.50%
−1.10	86.43%	+2.00	2.28%
−1.00	84.13%	+2.10	1.79%
−0.90	81.59%	+2.20	1.39%
−0.80	78.81%	+2.30	1.07%
−0.70	75.80%	+2.40	0.82%
−0.60	72.57%	+2.50	0.62%
−0.50	69.15%	+2.60	0.47%
−0.40	65.54%	+2.70	0.35%
−0.30	61.79%	+2.80	0.26%
−0.20	57.93%	+2.90	0.19%
−0.10	53.98%	+3.00	0.13%
0.00	50.00%	+4.00	0.0003%

a commonly available table which gives the frequency curve of z-scores assuming that this distribution is bell-shaped or normal. This table is known as either the standard normal distribution or the z-distribution. To be frank, some versions of the table are rather complicated but we have opted for the simplest and most generally useful possible. Many statistical tables are known as *tables of significance* for reasons which will become more apparent later on.

Significance Table 5.1 gives the percentage number of scores which will be higher than a score with a given z-score. Basically this means that the table gives the proportion of the frequency distribution of z-scores which lie in the shaded portions in the example shown in Figure 5.4. The table assumes that the distribution of scores is normal or bell-shaped. The table usually works sufficiently well even if the distribution departs somewhat from the normal shape.

Calculation 5.3

Using the table of the standard normal distribution

Significance Table 5.1 is easy to use. Imagine that you have the IQs of a set of 250 people. The mean $(\overline{X})$ of these IQs is 100 and you calculate that the standard deviation (sd) is 15. You could use this information to calculate the z-score of Darren Jones who scored 90 on the test:

$$z\text{-score} = \frac{X - \overline{X}}{\text{sd}}$$

$$= \frac{90 - 100}{15} = \frac{-10}{15} = -0.67 = -0.7 \text{ (to 1 decimal place)}$$

Taking a z-score of -0.7, Significance Table 5.1 tells us that 75.80% of people in the set would have IQs equal to or greater than Darren's. In other words, he is not particularly intelligent. If the z-score of Natalie Smith is $+2.0$ then this would mean that only 2.28% of scores are equal to or higher than Natalie's – she's very bright.

Of course, you could use the table to calculate the proportion of people with *lower* IQs than Darren and Natalie. Since the total amount of scores is 100%, we can calculate that there are 100% − 75.80% = 24.20% of people with IQs equal to or smaller than his. For Natalie, there are 100% − 2.28% = 97.72% of scores equal to or lower than hers.

More about Significance Table 5.1

Significance Table 5.1 is just about as simple as we could make it. It is not quite the same as similar tables in other books:

1. We have given negative as well as positive values of z-scores.

2. We have only given z-scores to 1 decimal place with minor exceptions.

3. We have given percentages – many other versions of the table give *proportions* out of 1. In order to convert the values in Significance Table 5.1 into proportions, simply divide the percentage by 100 and delete the % sign.

4. We have introduced a number of 'cut-off points' or zones into the table. These basically isolate extreme parts of the distribution of z-scores and identify those z-scores which come into the extreme 5% of the distribution. If you like, these are the exceptionally high and exceptionally low z-scores. The importance of this might not be obvious right now but will be clearer later on. The extreme zones are described as 'significant'. We have indicated the extreme 5% in either direction (that is, the extreme 2.5% above and below the mean) as well as the extreme 5% in a particular direction.

5.6   An important feature of z-scores

By using z-scores the researcher is able to say an enormous amount about a distribution of scores extremely succinctly. If we present the following information:

■ the mean of a distribution

■ the standard deviation of the distribution

■ that the distribution is roughly bell-shaped or normal

then we can use this information to make very clear statements about the relative position of any score on the variable in question. In other words, rather than present an entire frequency distribution, these three pieces of information are virtually all that is required. Indeed, the third assumption is rarely mentioned since in most applications it makes very little difference.

5.7   Notes and recommendations

■ Do not despair if you have problems in understanding standard deviation; it is one of the most abstract ideas in statistics but so fundamental that it cannot be avoided. It can take some time to absorb completely.

■ Remember that the standard deviation is a sort of average deviation from the mean and you will not go far wrong.

■ Remember that using z-scores is simply a way of putting variables on a standard unit of measurement irrespective of special characteristics of that variable.

■ Remember that virtually any numerical score variable can be summarised using the standard deviation and that virtually any measurement can be expressed as a z-score. The main exception to its use is measurements which are in *nominal* categories like occupation or eye colour. Certainly if a score is *interval or ratio* in nature, standard deviation and z-scores are appropriate.

Chapter 6

Relationships between two or more variables

Diagrams and tables

Preparation

You should be aware of the meaning of variables, scores and the different scales of measurement, especially the difference between nominal (category) measurement and numerical scores.

6.1 Introduction

Although it is fundamental and important to be able to describe the characteristics of each variable in your research both diagrammatically and numerically, *interrelationships* between variables are more characteristic of research in most areas of psychology and the social sciences. Public opinion polling is the most common use of single-variable statistics that most of us come across. Opinion pollsters ask a whole series of questions about political leaders and voting intentions which are generally reported separately. However, researchers often report relationships between two variables. So, for example, if one asks whether the voting intentions of men and women differ it is really to enquire whether there is a relationship between the variable 'sex' and the variable 'voting intention'. Similarly, if one asks whether the popularity of the President of the USA changed over time, this really implies that there may be a relationship between the variable 'time' and the variable 'popularity of the President'. Many of these questions seem so familiar to us that we regard them almost as common sense. Given this, we should not have any great difficulty in understanding the concept of interrelationships among variables.

Interrelationships between variables form the bedrock of virtually all psychological research. It is rare in psychology to have research questions which require data from only one variable at a time. Much of psychology concerns explanations of why things happen – what causes what – which clearly is about relationships between variables. This chapter describes some of the main graphical and tabular methods for presenting interrelationships between variables. Diagrams and tables often overlap in function as will become apparent in the following discussion.

Table 6.1 **Types of relationships based on nominal categories and numerical scores**

	Variable X = numerical scores	Variable X = nominal categories
Variable Y = numerical scores	Type A	Type C
Variable Y = nominal categories	Type C	Type B

6.2 The principles of diagrammatic and tabular presentation

Choosing appropriate techniques to show relationships between two variables requires an understanding of the difference between nominal category data and numerical score data. If we are considering the interrelationships between *two* variables (X and Y) then the types of variable involved are as shown in Table 6.1.

Once you have decided to which category your pair of variables belongs, it is easy to suggest appropriate descriptive statistics. We have classified different situations as Type A, Type B and Type C. Thus Type B has both variables measured on the nominal category scale of measurement.

6.3 Type A: both variables numerical scores

Where both variables take the form of numerical scores, generally the best form of graphical presentation is the *scattergram* or scatterplot. This is a sort of graph in which the values on one variable are plotted against the values on the other variable. The most familiar form of graph is one which plots a variable against time. These are very familiar from newspapers, especially the financial sections (see Figure 6.1).

Time is no different, statistically speaking, from a wide range of other numerical scores. Figure 6.2 is an example of a scattergram from a psychological study. You will see that the essential features remain the same. In Figure 6.2, the point marked with an arrow represents a case whose score on the X-variable is 8 and whose score on the Y-variable is 120. It is sometimes possible to see that the points of a scattergram fall more or less on a straight line. This line through the points of a scattergram is called the *regression line*. Figure 6.2 includes the regression line for the points of the scattergram.

One complication you sometimes come across is where several points on the scattergram overlap completely. In these circumstances you may well see a number next to a point which corresponds to the number of overlapping points at that position on the scattergram.

In line with general mathematical notation, the horizontal axis or horizontal dimension is described as the X-axis and the vertical axis or vertical dimension is

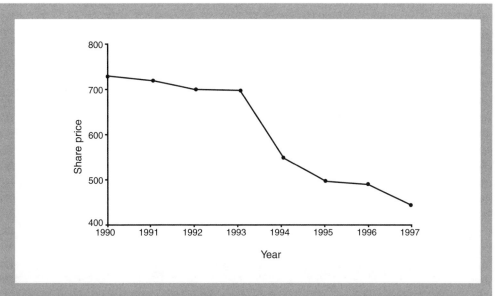

Figure 6.1 **The dramatic fall in share prices in the Timeshare Office Company**

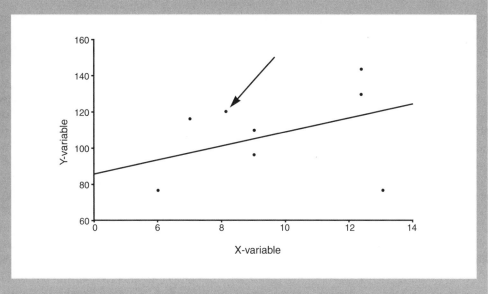

Figure 6.2 **A scattergram showing the relationship between two variables**

Table 6.2 **Use of bands of scores to tabulate the relationship between two numerical score variables**

		Variable Y				
		1–5	6–10	11–15	16–20	21–25
Variable X	0–9	15	7	6	3	4
	10–19	7	12	3	5	4
	20–29	4	9	19	8	4
	30–39	1	3	2	22	3
	40–49	3	2	3	19	25

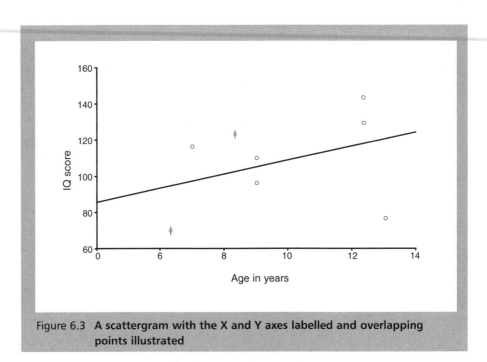

Figure 6.3 **A scattergram with the X and Y axes labelled and overlapping points illustrated**

called the Y-axis. It is helpful if you remember to label one set of scores the *X* scores since these belong on the horizontal axis, and the other set of scores the *Y* scores because these belong on the vertical axis (Figure 6.3).

In Figure 6.3, overlapping points are marked not with a number but with lines around the point on the scattergram. These are called 'sunflowers' – the number of 'petals' is the number of cases overlapping at the same point. So if there are two 'petals' then there are *two* people with the same pattern of scores on the two variables. If there are three 'petals' then *three* people have exactly the same pattern of scores on the two variables. Another way of indicating overlaps is simply to put the *number* of overlaps next to the scattergraph point.

Apart from cumbersomely listing all of your pairs of scores, it is often difficult to think of a succinct way of presenting data from pairs of numerical scores in tabular form. The main possibility is to categorise each of your score variables into 'bands' of scores and express the data in terms of *frequencies* of occurrence in these bands; a table like Table 6.2 might be appropriate.

Such tables are known as 'crosstabulation' or 'contingency' tables. In Table 6.2 there does seem to be a relationship between Variable X and Variable Y. People with low scores on Variable X also tend to get low scores on Variable Y. High scorers on Variable X also tend to score highly on Variable Y. However, the trend in the table is less easily discerned than in the equivalent scattergram.

6.4   Type B: both variables nominal categories

Where both variables are in nominal categories it is necessary to report the frequencies in all of the possible groupings of the variables. If you have more than a few nominal categories, the tables or diagrams can be too big.

Take the imaginary data shown in Table 6.3 on relationship between a person's sex and whether they have been hospitalised at any time in their life for a psychiatric reason. These data are ideal for certain sorts of tables and diagrams because *there are few categories of each variable*. Thus a suitable table for summarising these data might look like Table 6.4 – it is called a contingency or crosstabulation table.

The numbers (frequencies) in each category are instantly obvious from this table. You might prefer to express the table in percentages rather than frequencies,

Table 6.3   **Sex and whether previously hospitalised for a set of 89 people**

Person	Sex	Previously hospitalised
1	Male	Yes
2	Male	No
3	Male	No
4	Male	Yes
5	Male	No
. . .	. . .	. . .
85	Female	Yes
86	Female	Yes
87	Female	No
88	Female	No
89	Female	Yes

Table 6.4 **Crosstabulation table of sex against hospitalisation**

	Male	Female
Previously hospitalised	$f = 20$	$f = 25$
Not previously hospitalised	$f = 30$	$f = 14$

Table 6.5 **Crosstabulation table with all frequencies expressed as a percentage of the total number of frequencies**

	Male	Female
Previously hospitalised	22.5%	28.1%
Not previously hospitalised	33.7%	15.7%

Table 6.6 **Crosstabulation table with hospitalisation expressed as a percentage of the male and female frequencies taken separately**

	Male	Female
Previously hospitalised	40.0%	64.1%
Not previously hospitalised	60.0%	35.9%

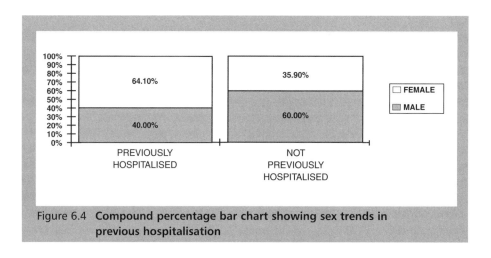

Figure 6.4 **Compound percentage bar chart showing sex trends in previous hospitalisation**

Figure 6.5 **How *not* to do a compound bar chart**

but some thought needs to go into the choice of percentages. For example, you could express the frequencies as percentages of the total of males and females (Table 6.5).

You probably think that Table 6.5 is not much of an improvement in clarity. An alternative is to express the frequencies as percentages of males *and* percentages of females (Table 6.6). By presenting the percentages based on males and females separately, it is easier to see the trend for females to have had a previous psychiatric history relatively more frequently than males.

The same data can be expressed as a *compound bar chart*. In a compound bar chart information is given about the subcategories based on a pair of variables. Figure 6.4 shows one example in which the proportions are expressed as percentages of the males and females separately.

The golden rule for such data is to ensure that the number of categories is manageable. In particular, avoid having too many empty or near-empty categories. The compound bar chart shown in Figure 6.5 is a particularly bad example and is *not to be copied*. This chart fails any reasonable clarity test and is too complex to decipher quickly.

6.5 Type C: one variable nominal categories, the other numerical scores

This final type of situation offers a wide variety of ways of presenting the relationships between variables. We have examined the compound bar chart so it is not surprising to find that there is also a *compound histogram*. To be effective, a compound histogram needs to consist of:

■ a small number of categories for the nominal category variable, and

■ a few *ranges* for the numerical scores.

Table 6.7 Crosstabulation table of anxiety against type of industry

	Frequency of anxiety score			
	0–3	4–7	8–11	12–15
Low-tech industry	7	18	3	1
High-tech industry	17	7	0	0

Table 6.8 Comparison of the statistical characteristics of anxiety in two different types of industry

	Mean	Median	Mode	Inter quartile range	Variance
High-tech industry	3.5	3.9	3	2.3–4.2	2.2
Low-tech industry	5.3	4.7	6	3.9–6.3	3.2

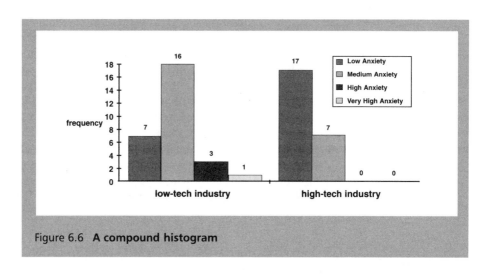

Figure 6.6 **A compound histogram**

So, for example, if we wish to plot the relationship between managers' anxiety scores and whether they are managers in a high-tech or a low-tech industry, we might create a compound histogram like Figure 6.6 in which there are only two values of the nominal variable (high-tech and low-tech) and four bands of anxiety score (low anxiety, medium anxiety, high anxiety and very high anxiety).

An alternative way of presenting such data is to use a crosstabulation table as in Table 6.7. Instead, however, it is almost as easy to draw up a table (Table 6.8)

which gives the mean, median, mode, etc., for the anxiety scores of the two different groups.

6.6   Notes and recommendations

■ Never assume that your tables and diagrams are good enough at the first attempt. They could probably be improved with a little care and adjustment.

■ Do not forget that tables and diagrams are there to present clearly the major trends in your data (or lack of them). There is not much point in having tables and diagrams which do not clarify your data.

■ Your tables and diagrams are not means of tabulating your unprocessed data. If you need to present your data in full then most of the methods to be found in this chapter will not help you much.

■ Labelling tables and diagrams clearly and succinctly is an important part of the task – without clear titling and labelling you are probably wasting your time.

Chapter 7

Correlation coefficients

Pearson correlation and Spearman's rho

Preparation
Revise variance (Chapter 3) and the use of the scattergram to show the relationship between two variables (Chapter 6).

7.1 Introduction

Although the scattergram is an important statistical tool for showing relationships between two variables, it is space consuming. For many purposes it is more convenient to have the main features of the scattergram expressed as a single numerical index – the *correlation coefficient*. This is merely a numerical index which summarises some, but not all, of the key features of a scattergram. The commonest correlation coefficient is the *Pearson correlation*, also known more grandly and obscurely as the Pearson product moment correlation coefficient. It includes two major pieces of information:

1. The closeness of the fit of the points of a scattergram to the best-fitting straight line through those points.

2. Information about whether the slope of the scattergram is positive or negative.

It therefore omits other information such as the scales of measurement of the two variables and specific information about individuals.

The correlation coefficient thus neatly summarises a great deal of information about a scattergram. It is especially useful when you have several variables which would involve drawing numerous scattergrams, one for each pair of variables. It most certainly does not replace the scattergram entirely but merely helps you to present your findings rather more concisely than other methods. Indeed, we recommend that you draw a scattergram for every correlation coefficient you calculate even if that scattergram is not intended for inclusion in your report.

Although the correlation coefficient is a basic descriptive statistic, it is elaborated in a number of sophisticated forms such as partial correlation, multiple correlation and factor analysis. It is of paramount importance in many forms of research, especially survey, questionnaire and similar forms of research.

7.2 Principles of the correlation coefficient

The correlation coefficient basically takes the following form:

$$r \text{ [correlation coefficient]} = \begin{array}{l} +1.00 \\ \text{or} \quad 0.00 \\ \text{or} \quad -1.00 \\ \text{or} \quad 0.30 \\ \text{or} \quad -0.72, \text{etc.} \end{array}$$

So a correlation coefficient consists of two parts:

1. A positive or negative sign (although for positive values the sign is frequently omitted).
2. Any numerical value in the range of 0.00 to 1.00.

The + or – sign tells us something important about the slope of the regression line (i.e. the best-fitting straight line through the points on the scattergram). A positive value means that the slope is *from the bottom left to the top right* of the scattergram (Figure 7.1). On the other hand, if the sign is negative (–) then the slope of the straight line goes *from upper left to lower right* on the scattergram (Figure 7.2).

The numerical value of the correlation coefficient (0.50, 0.42, etc.) is an index of how close the points on the scattergram fit the best-fitting straight line.

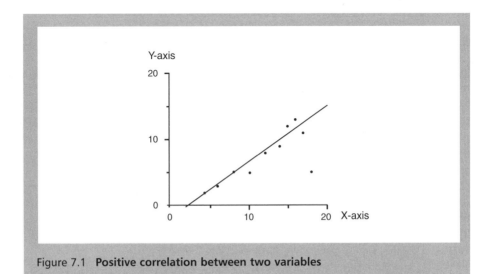

Figure 7.1 **Positive correlation between two variables**

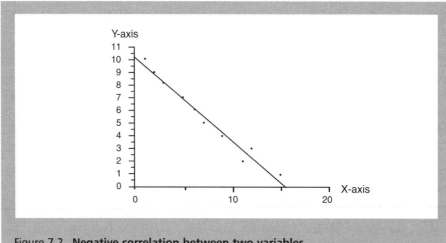

Figure 7.2 **Negative correlation between two variables**

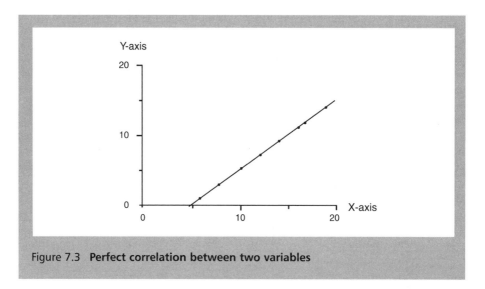

Figure 7.3 **Perfect correlation between two variables**

A value of 1.00 means that the points of the scattergram all lie exactly on the best-fitting straight line (Figure 7.3), unless that line is perfectly vertical or perfectly horizontal, in which case it means that there is no variation in the scores on one of the variables and so no correlation can be calculated.

A value of 0.00 means that the points of the scattergram are randomly scattered around the straight line. It is purely a matter of luck if any of them actually touch the straight line (Figure 7.4). In this case the best-fitting straight line for the scattergram could be virtually any line you arbitrarily decide to draw

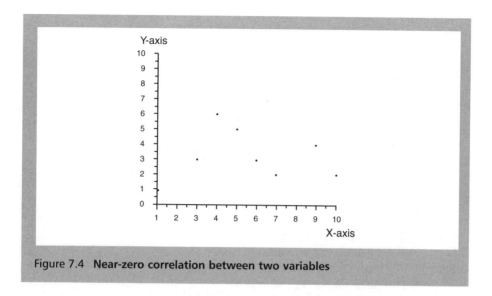

Figure 7.4   **Near-zero correlation between two variables**

through the points. Conventionally it is drawn as a horizontal line, but any other angle of slope would do just as well since there is no discernible trend in the relationship between the two variables on the scattergram.

A value of 0.50 would mean that although the points on the scattergram are generally close to the best-fitting straight line, there is considerable spread of these points around that straight line.

The correlation coefficient is merely an index of the amount of variance of the scattergram points from the straight line. However, it is calculated in such a way that the *maximum* variance around that straight line results in a correlation of zero. In other words, the closer the relationship between the two variables, the higher is the correlation coefficient, up to a maximum value of 1.00.

To summarise, the components of the correlation coefficient are the sign (+ or –), which indicates the direction of the slope, and a numerical value which indicates how much variation there is around the best-fitting straight line through the points (i.e. the higher the numerical value the closer the fit).

Covariance

The actual computation of the correlation coefficient involves little more than an elaboration of the formula for variance:

$$\text{Variance} = \frac{\Sigma\,(X - \overline{X})^2}{N}$$

If you wished (you will see why in a moment), the formula for variance could be re-expressed as:

$$\text{Variance} = \frac{\Sigma \; X - \overline{X}) \; (X - \overline{X})}{N}$$

All we have done is to expand the formula so as not to use the square sign. (A square is simply a number multiplied by itself.)

In the formula for the correlation coefficient we use something called the *covariance*. This is almost exactly the same as the formula for variance, but instead of multiplying scores by themselves we multiply the score on one variable (X) by the score on the second variable (Y):

$$\text{Covariance}_{\text{[of Variable X with Variable Y]}} = \frac{\Sigma \; (X - \overline{X}) \; (Y - \overline{Y})}{N}$$

where:

X = scores on Variable X
$\overline{X}$ = mean score on Variable X
Y = scores on Variable Y
$\overline{Y}$ = mean score on Variable Y
N = number of pairs of scores

We get a large positive value of covariance if there is a strong positive relationship between the two variables, and a big negative value if there is a strong negative relationship between the two variables. If there is no relationship between the variables then the covariance is zero. Notice that unlike variance the covariance can take positive or negative values.

However, the size of the covariance is affected by the size of the variances of the two separate variables involved. The larger the variances, the larger is the covariance, potentially. Obviously this would make comparisons difficult. So the covariance is adjusted by dividing by the square root of the product of the variances of the two separate variables. (Because N, the number of pairs of scores, in the variance and covariance formulae can be cancelled out in the correlation formula, the usual formula includes no division by the number of scores.) Once this adjustment is made to the covariance formula, we have the formula for the correlation coefficient:

$$r_{\text{[correlation coefficient]}} = \frac{\Sigma \; (X - \overline{X}) \; (Y - \overline{Y})}{\sqrt{\Sigma \; (X - \overline{X})^2} \; \sqrt{\Sigma \; (Y - \overline{Y})^2}}$$

The lower part of the formula actually gives the largest possible value of the covariance of the two variables – that is, the theoretical covariance if the two variables lay perfectly on the straight line through the scattergram. Dividing the covariance by the maximum value it could take (if there were no spread of points away from the straight line through the scattergram) ensures that the correlation coefficient can never be greater than 1.00. The covariance formula also contains the necessary sign to indicate the slope of the relationship.

A slightly quicker computational formula which does not involve the calculation of the mean scores directly is as follows:

$$r \text{ [correlation coefficient]} = \frac{\Sigma XY - \dfrac{\Sigma X \, \Sigma Y}{N}}{\sqrt{\left(\Sigma X^2 - \dfrac{(\Sigma X)^2}{N}\right)\left(\Sigma Y^2 - \dfrac{(\Sigma Y)^2}{N}\right)}}$$

The resemblance of parts of this formula to the computational formula for variance should be fairly obvious. This is not surprising as the correlation coefficient is a measure of the *lack* of variation around a straight line through the scattergram.

Calculation 7.1

The Pearson correlation coefficient

Our data for this calculation come from scores on the relationship between mathematical ability and musical ability for a group of 10 children (Table 7.1).

Table 7.1   **Scores on musical and mathematical ability for 10 children**

Individual	Music score	Mathematics score
Angela	2	8
Arthur	6	3
Peter	4	9
Mike	5	7
Barbara	7	2
Jane	7	3
Jean	2	9
Ruth	3	8
Alan	5	6
Theresa	4	7

It is always sound practice to draw the scattergram for any correlation coefficient you are calculating. For these data, the scattergram will be like Figure 7.5. Notice that the slope of the scattergram is negative, as one could have deduced from the tendency for those who score highly on mathematical ability to have low scores on musical ability. You can also see not only that a straight line is a pretty good way of describing the trends in the points on the scattergram but that the points fit the straight line reasonably well. Thus we should expect a fairly high negative correlation from the correlation coefficient.

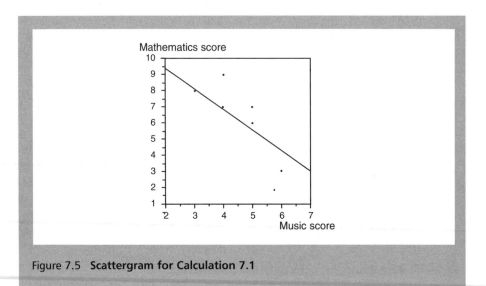

Figure 7.5 Scattergram for Calculation 7.1

Step 1 Set the scores out in a table (Table 7.2) and follow the calculations as shown. Here N is the number of *pairs* of scores, i.e. 10.

Table 7.2 **Essential steps in the calculation of the correlation coefficient**

X score (music)	Y score (mathematics)	X^2	Y^2	$X \times Y$
2	8	4	64	16
6	3	36	9	18
4	9	16	81	36
5	7	25	49	35
7	2	49	4	14
7	3	49	9	21
2	9	4	81	18
3	8	9	64	24
5	6	25	36	30
4	7	16	49	28
$\Sigma X = 45$	$\Sigma Y = 62$	$\Sigma X^2 = 233$	$\Sigma Y^2 = 446$	$\Sigma XY = 240$

Step 2 Substitute the values from Table 7.2 in the formula:

$$r_{\text{[correlation coefficient]}} = \frac{\Sigma XY - \dfrac{\Sigma X \, \Sigma Y}{N}}{\sqrt{\left(\Sigma X^2 - \dfrac{(\Sigma X)^2}{N}\right)\left(\Sigma Y^2 - \dfrac{(\Sigma Y)^2}{N}\right)}}$$

$$= \frac{240 - \dfrac{45 \times 62}{10}}{\sqrt{\left(233 - \dfrac{45^2}{10}\right)\left(446 - \dfrac{62^2}{10}\right)}}$$

$$= \frac{240 - \dfrac{2790}{10}}{\sqrt{\left(233 - \dfrac{2025}{10}\right)\left(446 - \dfrac{3844}{10}\right)}}$$

$$= \frac{240 - 279}{\sqrt{(233 - 202.5)\,(446 - 384.4)}}$$

$$= \frac{-39}{\sqrt{30.5 \times 61.6}}$$

$$= \frac{-39}{\sqrt{1878.8}}$$

$$= \frac{-39}{43.35}$$

$$= -0.90$$

Interpreting the results   So the value obtained for the correlation coefficient equals –0.90. This value is in line with what we suggested about the scattergram which serves as a rough check on our calculation. There is a very substantial negative relationship between mathematical and musical ability. In other words, the good mathematicians tended to be the poor musicians and vice versa. It is not claimed that they are good at music *because* they are poor at mathematics but merely that there is an inverse association between the two.

Reporting the results   Normally when reporting a correlation coefficient it is usual to report its statistical significance. The meaning of statistical significance is explained in Chapters 9 and 10 and especially Calculation 10.1. You could ignore Chapter 8 and proceed directly to these chapters. However, the important point for now is to remember that statistical significance is invariably reported with the value of the correlation coefficient.

   We would write something like: 'It was found that musical ability was inversely related to mathematical ability. The Pearson correlation coefficient was –0.9 which is statistically significant at the 5% level with a sample size of

10.' The information in the final sentence will not be informative to you until you have studied Chapters 9 and 10.

7.3   Some rules to check out

1. You should make sure that a straight line is the best fit to the scattergram points. If the best-fitting line is a *curve* such as in Figure 7.6 then you should not use the Pearson correlation coefficient. The reason for this is that the Pearson correlation assumes a straight line which is a gross distortion if you have a curved (curvilinear) relationship.

2. Make sure that your scattergram does not contain a few extreme cases which are unduly influencing the correlation coefficient (Figure 7.7). In this diagram you can see that the points at the top left of the scattergram are responsible for the apparent negative correlation between the two variables. Your eyes probably suggest that for virtually all the points on the scattergram there is no relationship at all. You could in these circumstances eliminate the 'outliers' (i.e. extreme, highly influential points) and recalculate the correlation coefficient based on the remaining, more typical group of scores. If the correlation remains significant with the same sign as before then your interpretation of your data is likely to remain broadly unchanged. However, there needs to be good reason for deleting the 'outliers'; this should not be done simply because the data as they stand do not support your ideas. It may be that something unusual had happened – perhaps an outlier arose from the responses of a slightly deaf person who could not hear the researcher's instructions, for example.

Design consideration It is typically argued that a correlation does not prove causality. Because two variables are related to each other is not reason to say anything other than that they are related. Statistical analysis is basically incapable of proving that one variable influenced the other variable directly. Questions such as whether one variable affected the other are addressed primarily through the nature of your research design and not through the statistical analysis as such. Conventionally psychologists have turned to laboratory experiments in which variables could be systematically manipulated by the researcher in order to be able to enhance their confidence in making causal interpretations about relationships between variables.

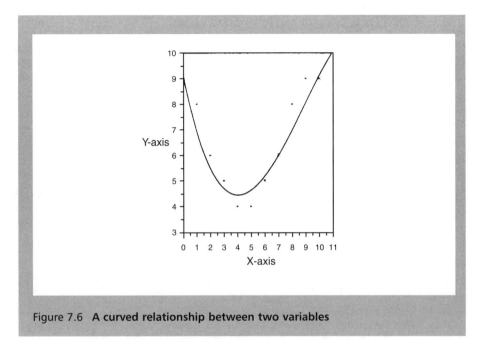

Figure 7.6 **A curved relationship between two variables**

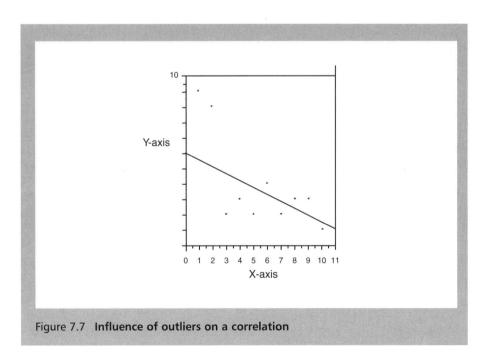

Figure 7.7 **Influence of outliers on a correlation**

7.4   Coefficient of determination

The correlation coefficient is an index of how much variance two variables have in common. However, you need to square the correlation coefficient in order to know precisely how much variance is shared. The squared correlation coefficient is also known as the *coefficient of determination*.

The proportion of variance shared by two variables whose correlation coefficient is 0.5 equals 0.5^2 or 0.25. This is a proportion out of 1 so as a percentage it is $0.25 \times 100\% = 25\%$. A correlation coefficient of 0.8 means that $0.8^2 \times 100\%$ or 64% of the variance is shared. A correlation coefficient of 1.00 means that $1.00^2 \times \square$ 100% = 100% of the variance is shared. Since the coefficient of determination is based on *squaring* the correlation coefficient, it should be obvious that the amount of variance shared by the two variables declines increasingly rapidly as the correlation coefficient gets smaller (Table 7.3).

Table 7.3   **Variance shared by two variables**

Correlation coefficient	Variance shared by two variables
1.00	100%
0.90	81%
0.80	64%
0.70	49%
0.60	36%
0.50	25%
0.40	16%
0.30	9%
0.20	4%
0.10	1%
0.00	0%

7.5   Significance testing

Some readers who have previously studied statistics a little will be familiar with the notion of significance testing and might be wondering why this has not been dealt with for the correlation coefficient. The answer is that we will be dealing with it, but not until Chapter 10. In the present chapter we are merely presenting the correlation coefficient as a descriptive statistic which numerically summarises a scattergram between two variables. For those of you who wish to understand significance testing for the correlation coefficient, simply skip Chapter 8 on regression for now and proceed to Chapters 9 and 10.

7.6   Spearman's rho – another correlation coefficient

> Spearman's rho is often written as r_s. We have not used this symbol in the following discussion although it is common in textbooks.

The Pearson correlation coefficient is the dominant correlation index in psychological statistics. There is another called *Spearman's rho* which is not very different – practically identical, in truth. Instead of taking the scores directly from your data, the scores on a variable are ranked from smallest to largest. That is, the smallest score on Variable X is given rank 1, the second smallest score on Variable X is given rank 2, and so forth. The smallest score on Variable Y is given rank 1, the second smallest score on Variable Y is given rank 2, etc. Then Spearman's rho is calculated like the Pearson correlation coefficient between the two sets of ranks as if the ranks were scores. A special procedure is used to deal with *tied ranks*, as follows.

Table 7.4   Ranking of a set of scores when tied (equal) scores are involved

Scores	4	5	5	6	7	8	9	9	9	10
Ranks	1	2.5	2.5	4	5	6	8	8	8	10

Sometimes certain scores on a variable are identical. There might be two or three people who scored 7 on Variable X, for example. This situation is described as *tied scores* or *tied ranks*. The question is what to do about them. The conventional answer in psychological statistics is to pretend first of all that the tied scores can be separated by fractional amounts. Then we allocate the appropriate ranks to these 'separated' scores but give each of the tied scores the average rank that they would have received if they could have been separated (Table 7.4).

The two scores of 5 are each given the rank 2.5 because if they were slightly different they would have been given ranks 2 and 3 respectively. But they cannot be separated and so we average the ranks as follows:

$$\frac{2+3}{2} = 2.5$$

This average of the two ranks corresponds to what we entered into Table 7.4.

There are three scores of 9 which would have been allocated the ranks 7, 8, and 9 if the scores had been slightly different from each other. These three ranks are averaged to give an average rank of 8 which is entered as the rank for each of the three tied scores in Table 7.4.

There is a special computational formula (see Calculation 7.3 later in this chapter) which can be used which is quicker than applying the conventional Pearson correlation formula to data in the form of ranks. It is nothing other than a special case of the Pearson correlation formula. Most statistics textbooks provide this formula for routine use. Unfortunately this formula is only accurate when you have absolutely no tied ranks at all – otherwise it gives a slightly wrong answer. As tied ranks are common in psychological research it is dubious whether there is anything to be gained in using the special Spearman's rho computational formula as opposed to the Pearson correlation coefficient applied to the ranks.

You may wonder why we have bothered to turn the scores into ranks before calculating the correlation coefficient. The reason is that ranks are commonly used in psychological statistics when the distributions of scores on a variable are markedly unsymmetrical and do not approximate (even poorly) a normal distribution. In the past it was quite fashionable to use rankings of scores instead of the scores themselves but we would suggest that you avoid ranking if possible. Use ranks only when your data seem extremely distorted from a normal distribution. We realise that others may argue differently. The reasons for this are explained in Chapter 18.

Calculation 7.2

Spearman's rho with or without tied ranks

We could apply the Spearman rho correlation to the data on the relationship between mathematical ability and musical ability for a group of 10 children which we used previously. But we must rank the two sets of scores before applying the normal Pearson correlation formula since there are tied ranks (see Table 7.5). In our calculation, N is the number of *pairs* of ranks, i.e. 10.

We then substitute the totals in the computational formula for the Pearson correlation coefficient, although now we call it Spearman's rho:

$$r_{[\text{Spearman's rho}]} = \frac{\Sigma X_r Y_r - \frac{\Sigma X_r \, \Sigma Y_r}{N}}{\sqrt{\left(\Sigma X_r^2 - \frac{(\Sigma X_r)^2}{N}\right)\left(\Sigma Y_r^2 - \frac{(\Sigma Y_r)^2}{N}\right)}}$$

$$= \frac{230.5 - \left(\frac{55 \times 55}{10}\right)}{\sqrt{\left(383 - \frac{55^2}{10}\right)\left(383 - \frac{55^2}{10}\right)}}$$

$$= \frac{230.5 - 302.5}{\sqrt{(383 - 302.5)(383 - 302.5)}}$$

$$= \frac{-72.00}{\sqrt{(80.5)(80.5)}}$$

$$= \frac{-72.00}{80.5}$$

$$= -0.89$$

Table 7.5 **Steps in the calculation of Spearman's rho correlation coefficient**

Person	Maths score X score	Music score Y score	Maths rank X_r	Maths rank squared X_r^2	Music rank Y_r	Music rank squared Y_r^2	Maths rank × music rank $X_r \times Y_r$
1	8	2	7.5	56.25	1.5	2.25	11.25
2	3	6	2.5	6.25	8	64.00	20.00
3	9	4	9.5	90.25	4.5	20.25	42.75
4	7	5	5.5	30.25	6.5	42.25	35.75
5	2	7	1	1.00	9.5	90.25	9.50
6	3	7	2.5	6.25	9.5	90.25	23.75
7	9	2	9.5	90.25	1.5	2.25	14.25
8	8	3	7.5	56.25	3	9.00	22.50
9	6	5	4	16.00	6.5	42.25	26.00
10	7	4	5.5	30.25	4.5	20.25	24.75
			ΣX_r = 55	ΣX_r^2 = 383	ΣY_r = 55	ΣY_r^2 = 383	$\Sigma X_r Y_r$ = 230.50

Interpreting the results So, Spearman's rho gives a substantial negative correlation just as we would expect from these data. You can interpret the Spearman correlation coefficient more or less in the same way as the Pearson correlation coefficient so long as you remember that it is calculated using ranks.

It so happens in this case that the Spearman coefficient gives virtually the same numerical value as Pearson's applied to the same data. *This is fortuitous. Usually there is a discrepancy between the two.*

Reporting the results Just as with the Pearson correlation (Calculation 7.1), when reporting the Spearman's rho correlation coefficient it is normal to report the statistical significance of the coefficient. The meaning of statistical significance is explained in Chapters 9 and 10 and especially Calculation 10.2. Proceed to these chapters for a discussion of statistical significance. The most important thing for the time being is to remember that statistical significance is almost invariably reported with the value of the correlation coefficient.

We would write up the results something like: 'It was found that musical ability was inversely related to mathematical ability. The value of Spearman's rho correlation coefficient was –0.89 which is statistically significant at the 5% level with a sample size of 10.' The last sentence will not mean much until Chapters 9 and 10 have been studied.

We referred earlier to a special computational formula which could be used to calculate Spearman's rho when there are no ties. There seems little point in learning this formula, since a lack of tied ranks is not characteristic of psychological data. You may as well simply use the method of Calculation 7.2 irrespective of whether there are ties or not. For those who want to save a little time when there are no tied ranks, the procedure of Calculation 7.3 may be used.

Calculation 7.3

Spearman's rho where there are no tied ranks

The formula used in this computation applies only when there are no tied scores. If there are any, the formula becomes increasingly inaccurate and the procedure of Calculation 7.2 should be applied. However, many psychologists use the formula whether or not there are tied ranks, despite the inaccuracy problem.

For illustrative purposes we will use the same data on maths ability and musical ability despite there being ties, as listed in Table 7.6. Once again, $N = 10$.

$$r_{[\text{Spearman's rho}]} = 1 - \frac{6\Sigma D^2}{N\,(N^2 - 1)}$$

$$= 1 - \frac{6 \times 305}{10\,(10^2 - 1)}$$

$$= 1 - \frac{1830}{10 \times (100 - 1)}$$

$$= 1 - \frac{1830}{10 \times 99}$$

$$= 1 - \frac{1830}{990}$$

$$= 1 - 1.848$$

$$= -0.848$$

$$= -0.85 \text{ to 2 decimal places}$$

Table 7.6 **Steps in the calculation of Spearman's rho correlation coefficient using the speedy formula**

Person	Maths score	Music score	Maths rank	Music rank	Maths rank – music rank	Square of previous column
	X score	Y score	X_r	Y_r	D (difference)	D^2
1	8	2	7.5	1.5	6.0	36.00
2	3	6	2.5	8	–5.5	30.25
3	9	4	9.5	4.5	5	25.00
4	7	5	5.5	6.5	–1.0	1.00
5	2	7	1	9.5	–8.5	72.25
6	3	7	2.5	9.5	–7.0	49.00
7	9	2	9.5	1.5	8.0	64.00
8	8	3	7.5	3	4.5	20.25
9	6	5	4	6.5	–2.5	6.25
10	7	4	5.5	4.5	1.0	1.00
						$\Sigma D^2 = 305$

Interpreting the results It should be noted that this value of Spearman's rho is a little different from its correct value (–0.89) as we calculated it in Calculation 7.2. The reason for this difference is the inaccuracy of the speedy formula when there are tied scores. Although the difference is not major, you are strongly recommended not to incorporate this error. Otherwise the interpretation of the negative correlation is the same as we have previously discussed.

Reporting the results   As with the Pearson correlation (Calculation 7.1), when reporting the Spearman's rho correlation coefficient we would report the statistical significance of the coefficient. The meaning of statistical significance is explained in Chapters 9 and 10 and especially Calculation 10.2. Ignore Chapter 8 and proceed directly to these chapters for an explanation. However, the important point for now is to remember that statistical significance is invariably reported with the value of the correlation coefficient.

We would write up the results something along the lines of the following: 'It was found that musical ability was inversely related to mathematical ability. The value of Spearman's rho correlation coefficient was –0.85 which is statistically significant at the 5% level with a sample size of 10.' The last sentence will not mean much until Chapters 9 and 10 have been studied.

7.7   An example from the literature

Pearson correlation coefficients are extremely common in published research. They can be found in a variety of contexts so choosing a typical example is virtually meaningless. The correlation coefficient is sometimes used as an indicator of the validity of a psychological test. So it might be used to indicate the relationship between a test of intelligence and children's performance in school. The test is a valid predictor of school performance if there is a substantial correlation between the test score and school performance.

The correlation coefficient is also very useful as an indicator of the reliability of a psychological test. This might mean the extent to which people's scores on the test are consistent over time. You can use the correlation coefficient to indicate whether those who perform well now on the test also performed well a year ago. For example, Gillis (1980) in the manual accompanying the Child Anxiety Scale indicates that he retested 127 US schoolchildren in the first to third grades immediately after the initial testing. The reliability coefficients (test–retest reliability) or the correlation coefficients between the two testings were:

Grade 1 = 0.82
Grade 2 = 0.85
Grade 3 = 0.92

A sample of children retested after a week had a retest reliability coefficient of 0.81. It is clear from this that the reliability of the measure is good. This means that the children scoring the most highly one week also tend to get the highest scores the next week. It does not mean that the scores are identical from week to week – only that the relative scores are the same.

Practically all reliability and validity coefficients used in psychological testing are variants on much the same theme and are rarely much more complex than the correlation coefficient itself.

7.8   Notes and recommendations

Most of the major points have been covered already. But they bear repetition:

- Check the scattergram for your correlation coefficient for signs of a nonlinear relationship – if you find one you should not be using the Pearson correlation coefficient. In these circumstances you should use coefficient eta (η) which is designed for curvilinear relationships. However, eta is a relatively obscure statistic. It is mentioned again in Chapter 31.

- Check the scattergram for outliers which may spuriously be producing a correlation when overwhelmingly the scattergram says that there is a poor relationship.

- Examine the scattergram to see whether there is a positive or negative slope to the scatter and form a general impression of whether the correlation is good (the points fit the straight line well) or poor (the points are very widely scattered around the straight line). Obviously you will become more skilled at this with experience but it is useful as a rough computational check among other things.

- Before concluding your analysis, check out Chapter 10 to decide whether or not to generalise from your set of data.

Chapter 8

Regression
Prediction with precision

Preparation
You should have a working knowledge about the scattergram (Chapter 6) of the relationship between two variables and understand the correlation coefficient (Chapter 7).

8.1 Introduction

Regression, like the correlation coefficient, numerically describes important features of a scattergram relating two variables. However, it does it in a different way from the correlation coefficient. Among its important uses is that it allows the researcher to make predictions (for example, when choosing the best applicant for a job on the basis of an aptitude or ability test).

Assume that research has shown that a simple test of manual dexterity is capable of distinguishing between the better and not-so-good assembly workers in a precision components factory. Manual dexterity is a *predictor* variable and

Table 8.1 **Manual dexterity and number of units produced per hour**

Manual dexterity score	Number of units produced per hour
56	17
19	6
78	23
92	22
16	9
23	10
29	13
60	20
50	16
35	19

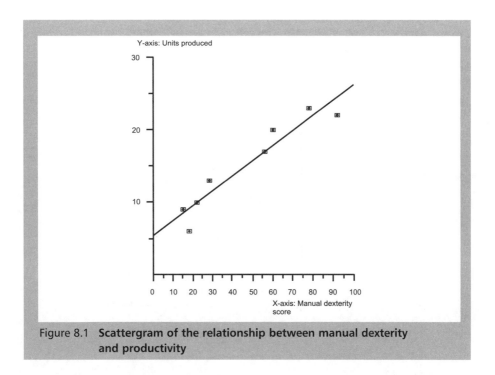

Figure 8.1 **Scattergram of the relationship between manual dexterity and productivity**

job performance the *criterion* variable. So it should be possible to predict which applicants are likely to be the more productive employees from scores on this easily administered test of manual dexterity. Using the test might be a lot cheaper than employing people who do not make the grade. Imaginary data for such a study are shown in Table 8.1.

The scattergram (Figure 8.1) shows imaginary data on the relationship between scores on the manual dexterity test and the number of units per hour the employee produces in the components factory. Notice that we have made scores on the manual dexterity test the horizontal dimension (X-axis) and the number of units produced per hour the vertical dimension (Y-axis).

In regression in order to keep the number of formulae to the minimum, *the horizontal dimension (X-axis) should always be used to represent the variable from which the prediction is being made, and the vertical dimension (Y-axis) should always represent what is being predicted.*

It is clear from the scattergram that the number of units produced by workers is fairly closely related to scores on the manual dexterity test. If we draw a straight line as best we can through the points on the scattergram, this line could be used as a basis for making predictions about the most likely score on work productivity from the aptitude test score of manual dexterity. This line through the points on a scattergram is called the *regression line*. In order to predict the likeliest number of units per hour corresponding to a score of 70 on the manual

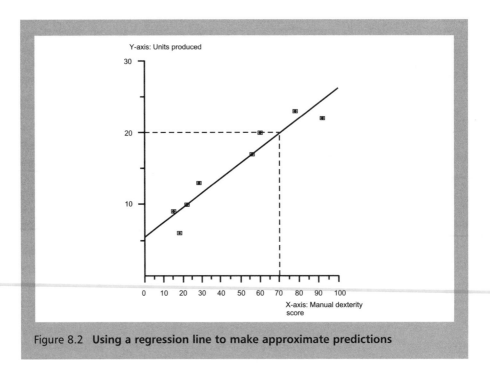

Figure 8.2 **Using a regression line to make approximate predictions**

dexterity test, we simply draw a right angle from the score 70 on the horizontal axis (manual dexterity test score) to the regression line, and then a right angle from the vertical axis to meet this point. In this way we can find the productivity score which best corresponds to a particular manual dexterity score (Figure 8.2). Estimating from this scattergram and regression line, it appears that the best prediction from a manual dexterity score of 70 is a productivity rate of about 19 or 20.

There is only one major problem with this procedure – the prediction depends on the particular line drawn through the points on the scattergram. You might draw a somewhat different line from the one we did. Subjective factors such as these are not desirable and it would be better to have a method which was not affected in this way. So mathematical ways of determining the regression line have been developed. Fortunately, the computations are generally straightforward.

8.2   Theoretical background and regression equations

The line through a set of points on a scattergram is called the regression line. In order to establish an objective criterion, the regression line is chosen which gives the closest fit to the points on the scattergram. In other words, the procedure ensures that there is a minimum sum of distances of the regression line to the points in the scattergram. So, in theory, one could keep trying different possible regression lines until one is found which has the minimum deviation of the points from it.

The sum of the deviations (Σd) of the scattergram points from the regression line should be minimal. Actually, the precise criterion is the sum of the *squared* deviations. This is known as the *least squares solution*. But it would be really tedious work drawing different regression lines then calculating the sum of the squared deviations for each of these in order to decide which regression line has the smallest sum of squared deviations. Fortunately things are not done like that and trial-and-error is not involved at all. The formulae for regression do all of that work for you.

In order to specify the regression line for any scattergram, you quantify two things:

1. The point at which the regression line cuts the vertical axis – this is a number of units of measurement from the zero point of the vertical axis. It can take a positive or negative value, denoting whether the vertical axis is cut above or below its zero point. It is normally denoted in regression as point *a* or the *intercept*.

2. The *slope* of the regression line or, in other words, the gradient of the best-fitting line through the points on the scattergram. Just as with the correlation coefficient, this slope may be positive in the sense that it goes up from

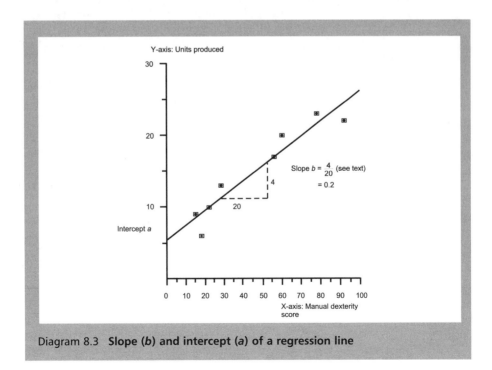

Diagram 8.3 **Slope (*b*) and intercept (*a*) of a regression line**

bottom left to top right or it can be negative in that it goes downwards from top left to bottom right. The slope is normally denoted by the letter b.

The intercept and slope are both shown in Figure 8.3. To work out the slope, we have drawn a horizontal dashed line from $X = 30$ to $X = 50$ (length 20) and a vertical dashed line up to the regression line (length about 4 up the Y-axis). The slope b is the increase (+) or decrease (−) of the units produced (in this case +4) divided by the increase in the manual dexterity score (in this case 20), i.e. +0.2.

The slope is simply the number of units that the regression line moves up the vertical axis for each unit it moves along the horizontal axis. In other words, you mark a single step along the horizontal axis and work out how much increase this represents on the vertical axis. So, for example, if you read that the slope of a scattergram is 2.00, this means that for every increase of 1.00 on the horizontal axis (X-axis) there is an increase of 2.00 on the vertical axis (Y-axis). If there is a slope of −0.5 then this means that for every increase of 1 on the horizontal axis (X-axis) there is a *decrease* of 0.5 on the vertical axis (Y-axis).

In our example, for every increase of 1 in the manual dexterity score, there is an increase of 0.2 (more accurately, 0.21) in the job performance measure (units produced per hour). We have estimated this value from the scattergram – it may not be exactly the answer that we would have obtained had we used mathematically more precise methods. This increase defines the slope. (Note that you do not work with angles, merely distances on the vertical and horizontal axes.)

Fortunately, the application of two relatively simple formulae (see Calculation 8.1) provides all the information we need to calculate the slope and the intercept. A third formula is used to make our predictions from the horizontal axis to the vertical axis.

The major differences between correlation and regression are:

1. Regression retains the original units of measurement so direct comparisons between regression analyses based on different variables are difficult. Correlation coefficients can readily be compared as they are essentially on a standardised measurement scale and free of the original units of measurement.

2. The correlation coefficient does *not* specify the slope of a scattergram. Correlation indicates the amount of spread or variability of the points around the regression line in the scattergram.

Design consideration There are always two regression lines between two variables: that from which Variable A is predicted from Variable B, and that from which Variable B is predicted from Variable A. They almost invariably have different slopes. However, life is made simpler if we always have the predictor on the horizontal axis and the criterion to be predicted on the vertical axis. You need to be careful what you are trying to predict and from what.

In other words, correlation and regression have somewhat different functions despite their close similarities.

Calculation 8.1

Regression equations

To facilitate comparison, we will take the data used in the computation of the correlation coefficient (Chapter 7). The data concern the relationship between mathematical and musical ability for a group of 10 individuals. The 10 scores need to be set out in a table like Table 8.2 and the various intermediate calculations carried out. However, it is important with regression to make the X scores the predictor variable; the Y scores are the criterion variable. N is the number of *pairs* of scores, i.e. 10. (Strictly speaking the Y^2 and ΣY^2 calculations are not necessary for regression but are included here because they highlight the similarities between the correlation and regression calculations.)

Table 8.2 **Important steps in calculating the regression equation**

Person	Maths score X score	Music score Y score	X^2	Y^2	XY
1	8	2	64	4	16
2	3	6	9	36	18
3	9	4	81	16	36
4	7	5	49	25	35
5	2	7	4	49	14
6	3	7	9	49	21
7	9	2	81	4	18
8	8	3	64	9	24
9	6	5	36	25	30
10	7	4	49	16	28
	ΣX = 62	ΣY = 45	ΣX^2 = 446	ΣY^2 = 233	ΣXY = 240

The slope (b) of the regression line is given by the following formula:

$$b = \frac{\Sigma XY - \left(\frac{\Sigma X \Sigma Y}{N}\right)}{\Sigma X^2 - \frac{(\Sigma X)^2}{N}}$$

Thus, substituting the values from the table in the above formula:

$$b_{[slope]} = \frac{240 - \left(\dfrac{62 \times 45}{10}\right)}{446 - \dfrac{(62)^2}{10}}$$

$$= \frac{240 - \dfrac{2790}{10}}{446 - \dfrac{3844}{10}}$$

$$= \frac{240 - 279}{446 - 384.4}$$

$$= \frac{-39}{61.6}$$

$$= -0.63$$

This tells us that the slope of the regression line is negative – it moves downwards from top left to bottom right. Furthermore, for every unit one moves along the horizontal axis, the regression line moves 0.63 units *down* the vertical axis since in this case it is a *negative* slope.

We can now substitute in the following formula to get the cutting point or intercept (a) of the regression line on the vertical axis:

$$a_{[intercept\ on\ vertical\ axis]} = \frac{\Sigma Y - b\Sigma X}{N}$$

$$= \frac{45 - (-0.63 \times 62)}{10}$$

$$= \frac{45 - (-39.06)}{10}$$

$$= \frac{84.06}{10}$$

$$= 8.41$$

This value for a is the point on the vertical axis (musical ability) cut by the regression line.

If one wishes to predict the most likely score on the vertical axis from a particular score on the horizontal axis, one simply substitutes the appropriate values in the following formula:

$$Y_{[predicted\ score]} = a_{[intercept]} + b_{[slope]} \times X_{[known\ score]}$$

Thus if we wished to predict musical ability for a score of 8 on mathematical ability, given that we know the slope (*b*) is –0.63 and the intercept is 8.41, we simply substitute these values in the formula:

$$Y_{\text{[predicted score]}} = a_{\text{[intercept]}} + b_{\text{[slope]}} \times X_{\text{[known score]}}$$
$$= 8.41 + (-0.63 \times 8)$$
$$= 8.41 + (-5.04)$$
$$= 3.37$$

This is the *best* prediction – it does not mean that people with a score of 8 on mathematical ability inevitably get a score of 3.37 on musical ability. It is just our most intelligent estimate.

Interpreting the results The proper interpretation of the regression equations depends on the scattergram between the two variables showing a more-or-less linear (i.e. straight line) trend. If it does not show this, then the interpretation of the regression calculations for the slope and intercept will be misleading since the method assumes a straight line. Curvilinear relationships (see Chapter 7) are difficult to handle mathematically.

If the scattergram reveals a linear relationship, then the interpretation of the regression equations is simple as the formulae merely describe the scattergram mathematically.

Reporting the results This regression analysis could be reported as follows: 'Because of the negative correlation between mathematical and musical abilities, it was possible to carry out a regression analysis to predict musical ability from mathematical ability. The slope of the regression of mathematical ability on musical ability (*b*) is –0.63 and the intercept (*a*) is 8.41.'

Design consideration The use of regression in prediction is a fraught issue not because of the statistical methods but because of the characteristics of the data used. In particular, note that our predictions about job performance are based on data from the people already in the job. So, for example, those with the best manual dexterity might have developed these skills on the job rather than having them when they were interviewed. Thus it may not be that manual dexterity determines job performance but that they are both influenced by other (unknown) factors. Similarly, if we found that age was a negative predictor of how quickly people get promoted in a banking corporation, this may simply reflect a bias against older people in the profession rather than greater ability of younger people.

8.3   Standard error: how accurate are the predicted score and the regression equations?

You may prefer to leave studying the following material until you have had the opportunity to study Chapter 11.

The accuracy of the predicted score on the criterion is dependent on the closeness of the scattergram points to the regression line; if there is a strong correlation between the variables there is little error in the prediction. Examining the scattergram between two variables will give you an idea of the variability around the regression line and hence the precision of the estimated or predicted scores.

Statisticians prefer to calculate what they call the standard error to indicate how certain one can be about aspects of regression such as the prediction, the intercept or cut-off points, and the slope. A standard error is much the same as the standard deviation except it applies to the means of samples rather than individual scores. So the standard error of something is the average deviation of sample means from the mean of the sample means. Don't worry too much if you don't quite understand the concept yet, since we come back to it in Chapters 11 and 12. *Just regard standard error of an estimate as the average amount by which an estimate is likely to be wrong.* As you might expect, since this is statistics, the average is calculated in an unexpected way, as it was for the standard deviation, which is little different.

> Standard error is discussed again in later chapters. Superficially, it may appear to be quite different from the ideas in this chapter. However, remember that whenever we use any characteristic of a sample as the basis for estimating the characteristic of a population, we are likely to be wrong to some extent. The standard error is merely the average amount by which the characteristics of *samples* from the population differ from the characteristic of the *whole* population.

Although the formulae for calculating the standard errors of the various aspects of the regression line are readily available, they add considerably to the computational labour involved in regression, so we recommend that you use a computer to relieve you of this computational chore.

The main standard errors involved in regression are:

1. The one for your predicted (or estimated) value on the criterion (this is known as the standard error of the estimate of y).
2. The one for the slope of the regression line (b).
3. The one for the intercept on the vertical axis (a).

Don't forget that the formulae for calculating these standard errors merely give you the average amount by which your estimate is wrong.

It might be more useful to estimate the likely range within which the true value of the prediction, slope or intercept is likely to fall. In other words, to be able to say that, for example, the predicted score on the criterion variable is likely to be between 2.7 and 3.3. In statistics, this likely range of the true value is known as the *confidence interval*. Actually there are several confidence intervals depending on how confident you wish to be that you have included the true value – the interval is obviously going to be wider if you wish to be *very* confident rather than just confident. In statistics one would routinely use the 95% confidence interval. This 95% confidence interval indicates the range of values within which the true value will fall 95% of the time. That is, we are likely to be wrong only 5% of times.

The following is a rule of thumb which is accurate enough for your purposes for now. Multiply the standard error by two. This gives you the amount which you need to *add and subtract* from the estimated value to cut off the middle 95% of the possible values – that is the 95% confidence interval. In other words, if the estimated value of the criterion (Y-variable) is 6.00 and the standard error of this estimate is 0.26, then the 95% confidence interval is 6.00 plus or minus (2×0.26) which is 6.00 plus or minus 0.52. This gives us a 95% confidence interval of 5.48 to 6.52. Thus it is almost certain that the person's score will actually fall in the range of 5.48 to 6.52 although the most likely value is 6.00.

Exactly the same applies to the other aspects of regression. If the slope is 2.00 with a standard error of 0.10, then the 95% confidence interval is 2.00 plus or minus 2×0.10, which gives a confidence interval of 1.80 to 2.20.

The use of confidence intervals is not as common as it ought to be despite the fact that it gives us a realistic assessment of the precision of our estimates.

The above calculations of confidence intervals are approximate if you have fewer than about 30 pairs of scores. If you have between 16 and 29 pairs of scores the calculation will be more accurate if you multiply by 2.1 rather than 2.0. If you have between 12 and 15 pairs of scores then multiplying by 2.2 would improve the accuracy of the calculation. With fewer than 12 pairs the method gets a little more inaccurate. When you have become more knowledgeable about statistics, you could obtain precise confidence intervals by multiplying your standard error by the appropriate value of t from Significance Table 12.1 (Chapter 12). The appropriate value is in the row headed 'Degrees of freedom', corresponding to your number of pairs of scores minus 2 under the column for the 5% significance level (i.e. if you have 10 pairs of scores then you would multiply by 2.31).

8.4   Notes and recommendations

■ Drawing the scattergram will invariably illuminate the trends in your data and strongly hint at the broad features of the regression calculations. It will also provide a visual check on your computations.

■ These regression procedures assume that the best-fitting regression line is a straight line. If it looks as if the regression line ought to be curved or curvilinear, do not apply these numerical methods. Of course, even if a relationship is curvilinear you could use the curved-line scattergram to make graphically based predictions.

■ It may be that you have more than one predictor variable that you wish to use – if so, look at Chapter 28 on multiple regression.

Part 2

Significance testing

Chapter 9

Samples and populations

Generalising and inferring

Preparation

This chapter introduces some important new ideas. They can be understood by anyone with a general familiarity with Chapters 1–8.

Most research in psychology relies on just a small sample of data from which general statements are made. The terms *sample* and *population* are familiar to most of us, although the fine detail may be a little obscure. So far we have mainly discussed *sets* of data. This was deliberate since *everything that we have discussed in previous chapters is applicable to either samples or populations*. The next stage is to understand how we can use a sample of scores to make general statements or draw general conclusions that apply well beyond that sample. This is a branch of statistics called *inferential* statistics because it is about drawing inferences about all scores in the population from just a sample of those scores.

9.1 Theoretical considerations

We need to be careful when defining our terms. A *sample* is fairly obvious – it is just a small number of scores selected from the entirety of scores. A *population* is the entire set of scores. In other words, a sample is a small set or a subset taken from the full set or population of scores.

You need to notice some special features of the terminology we have used. We have mentioned a population of *scores* and a sample of *scores*. In other words, population and sample refer to scores on a variable. We do not deal with a population of people or even a sample of people. So, in statistical terms, all of the people living in Scotland do not constitute a population. Similarly, all of the people working in clothing factories in France or all of the goats on the Isle of Capri are not *statistical* populations. They may be populations for geographers or for everyday purposes, but they are not statistical populations. A statistical population is merely *all* of the scores on a particular variable.

This notion can take a little getting used to. However, there is another feature of statistical populations that can cause confusion. In some cases all of the scores are potentially obtainable, for example the ages of students entering psychology degree courses in a particular year. However, often the population of scores is infinite and otherwise impossible to specify. An example of this might be the amount of time people take to react to an auditory signal in a laboratory. The number of possible measures of reaction time in these circumstances is bounded only by time and resources. No one could actually find out the population of scores other than by taking measurement after measurement – and then there is always another measurement to be taken. The notion of population in statistics is much more of a conceptual tool than something objective. Normally a psychologist will only have a few scores (his or her sample) and no direct knowledge of what all the scores or the population of scores are.

Thus the sample is usually known about in detail in research whereas the population generally is unknown. But the real question is what can we possibly say about the population based on our knowledge of this limited entity, the sample? Quite a lot. The use of sampling in public opinion polls, for example, is so familiar that we should need little convincing of the value of samples. Samples may only approximate the characteristics of the population but generally we accept that they are sufficient to base decisions on.

If we know nothing about the population other than the characteristics of a sample drawn from that population of scores, our best guess or inference about the characteristics of the population is the characteristics of the sample from that population. It does not necessarily have to be particularly precise since an informed guess has to be better than nothing. So, in general, if we know nothing else, our best guess as to the mean of the population is the mean of the sample, our best guess as to the mode of the population is the mode of the sample, and our best guess as to the variance of the population is the variance of the sample. It is a case of beggars not being able to be choosers.

In statistical inference, it is generally assumed that samples are drawn *at random* from the population. Such samples are called *random samples* from the population. The concept of randomness is sometimes misunderstood. Randomness is not the same as arbitrariness, informality, haphazardness or any other term that suggests a casual approach to drawing samples. A random sample of scores from a population entails selecting scores in such a way that each and every score in the population has an equal chance of being selected. In other words, a random sample favours the selection of no particular scores in the population. Although it is not difficult to draw a random sample, it does require a systematic approach. Any old sample you choose because you like the look of it is not a random sample.

There are a number of ways of drawing a random sample. Here are just a few:

1. Put the information about each member of the population on a slip of paper, put all of the slips into a hat, close your eyes, give the slips a long stir with

your hand and finally bring one slip out of the hat. This slip is the first member of the sample; repeat the process to get the second, third and subsequent members of the sample. *Technically the slip of paper should be returned to the container after being selected so it may be selected again. However, this is not done, largely because with a large population it would make little difference to the outcome.*

2. Number each member of the population. Then press the appropriate randomisation button on your scientific calculator to generate a random number. If it is not one of the numbers in your population, ignore it and press the button again. The member of the population corresponding to this number becomes a member of the sample. Computer programs are also available for generating random numbers.

3. Low-tech researchers might use the random number tables found in many statistics textbooks. Essentially what you do is choose a random starting point in the table (a pin is recommended) and then choose numbers using a predetermined formula. For example, you could take the first three numbers after the pin, then a gap of seven numbers and then the three numbers following this, then a gap of seven numbers and then the three numbers following this, etc.

Do not laugh at these procedures – they are valid and convenient ways of choosing random samples.

9.2 The characteristics of random samples

In Table 9.1 there is a population of 100 scores – the mode is 2, the median is 6.00, and the mean is 5.52. Have a go at drawing random samples of, say, five

Table 9.1 **A population of 100 scores**

7	5	11	3	4	3	5	8	9	1
9	4	0	2	2	2	9	11	7	12
4	8	2	9	7	0	8	0	8	10
10	7	4	6	6	2	2	1	12	2
2	5	6	7	10	6	6	2	1	9
3	4	2	4	9	7	5	1	6	4
5	7	12	2	8	8	3	4	6	5
9	2	6	0	7	7	5	9	10	8
6	1	7	12	3	5	2	7	2	7
2	2	8	11	4	5	8	6	4	6

Table 9.2 **Means of 40 samples each of five scores taken at random from the population in Table 9.1**

2.20	5.60	4.80	5.00	8.40	6.80	4.60	6.60
4.00	3.00	5.00	5.60	8.80	5.60	4.60	6.80
3.00	8.20	8.20	3.80	5.40	6.00	4.80	5.20
3.20	5.20	3.00	5.00	5.40	4.80	6.00	7.40
5.00	2.00	3.60	4.60	5.60	4.60	4.40	6.00

scores from this population. Repeat the process until you have a lot of sets (or samples) of scores. For each sample calculate any of the statistics just mentioned – the mean is a particularly useful statistic.

We have drawn 40 samples from this population at random using a random sampling procedure from a computer program. The means of each of the 40 samples are shown in Table 9.2. It is noticeable that these means vary quite considerably. However, if we plot them graphically we find that sample means close to the population mean of 5.52 are relatively common. The average of the sample means is 5.20 which is close to the population mean. The minimum sample mean is 2.00 and the maximum is 8.80; these contrast with minimum and maximum values of 0 and 12 in the population. Sample means very different from this population mean become relatively uncommon the further away they go from the population mean.

We could calculate the standard deviation of these 40 sample means by entering each mean into the standard deviation formula:

$$\text{Standard deviation} = \sqrt{\frac{\Sigma X^2 - \frac{(\Sigma X)^2}{N}}{N}}$$

This gives us a standard deviation of sample means of 1.60. The standard deviation of sample means has a technical name, although the basic concept differs only in that it deals with means of samples and not scores. The special term is *standard error*.

So, in general, it would seem that sample means are a pretty good estimate of population means although not absolutely necessarily so.

All of this was based on samples of size 5. Table 9.3 shows the results of exactly the same exercise with samples of size 20.

Much the same trends appear with these larger samples but for the following:

1. The spread of the sample means is reduced somewhat and they appear to cluster closer to the population mean. The minimum value is 4.25 and the maximum value is 6.85. The overall mean of these samples is 5.33, close to the population mean of 5.52.

Table 9.3 **Means of 40 samples each of size 20 taken at random from the population in Table 9.1**

4.50	5.70	5.90	5.15	4.25	5.25	5.60	5.00
5.35	5.90	6.85	5.55	5.30	5.60	5.70	4.55
6.35	6.30	4.40	5.25	4.65	5.30	4.80	5.65
4.85	5.35	5.70	4.35	5.25	5.10	6.45	5.05
5.50	6.15	5.65	5.05	5.15	5.10	4.65	4.95

2. The standard deviation of these means (i.e. the standard error) of larger samples is smaller. For Table 9.3 the standard deviation is 0.60.

3. The distribution of sample means is a steeper curve than for the smaller samples.

The conclusion of all this is that the larger sample size produces better estimates of the mean of the population. For statistics, this verges on common sense.

Great emphasis is placed on the extreme samples in a distribution. We have seen that samples from the above population differ from the population mean by varying amounts, that the majority of samples are close to that mean, and that the bigger the sample the closer to the population mean it is likely to be. There is a neat trick in statistics by which we try to define which sample means are very unlikely to occur through random sampling. It is true that in theory just about any sample mean is possible in random sampling, but those very different from the population mean are relatively rare. In statistics the extreme 5% of these samples are of special interest. Statisticians identify the extreme 2.5% of means on each side of the population mean for special consideration. Two 2.5s make 5%. These extreme samples come in the zone of relative rarity and are termed *significant*. Significance in statistics really means that we have a sample with characteristics very different from those of the population from which it was drawn. Significance at the 5% level of confidence merely means falling into the 5% of samples which are most different from the population. These extremes are, as we have seen, dependent on the size of sample being used.

9.3 Confidence intervals

There is another idea that is fundamental to some branches of statistics – *confidence interval of the mean*. In public opinion surveys you often read of the margin of error being a certain percentage. The margin of error is simply the amount for, say, voting intention which defines the middle 95% most likely sample means. This is expressed relative to the obtained sample mean. So when public opinion pollsters say that the margin of error is a certain percentage they are telling us the cut-off points from the obtained percentage which would include the middle 95% of sample means. The confidence interval in more general statistics is the range of means that cuts off the extreme 5% of sample means. So the 95% confidence interval merely gives the range of sample means which occupies the middle 95% of the distribution of sample means. The confidence interval will be larger for smaller samples, all other things being equal.

Finally, a little more jargon. The correct term for characteristics of samples such as their means, standard deviations, ranges and so forth is *statistics*. The same characteristics of populations are called *parameters*. In other words, you use the statistics from samples to estimate or infer the parameters of the population from which the sample came.

9.4   Notes and recommendations

- The material in this chapter is not immediately applicable to research. Regard it as a conceptual basis for the understanding of inferential statistics.

- You need to be a little patient since the implications of this chapter will not be appreciated until later.

Chapter 10

Statistical significance for the correlation coefficient

A practical introduction to statistical inference

Preparation

You must be familiar with correlation coefficients (Chapter 7) and populations and samples (Chapter 9).

Researchers have correlated two variables for a sample of 20 people. They obtained a correlation coefficient of 0.56. The problem is that they wish to generalise beyond this sample and make statements about the trends in the data which apply more widely. However, their analyses are based on just a small sample which might not be characteristic of the trends in the population.

10.1 Theoretical considerations

We can all sympathise with these researchers. The reason why they are concerned is straightforward. Imagine that Table 10.1 contains the *population* of pairs of scores. Overall, the correlation between the two variables in this population is 0.00. That is, there is absolutely no relationship between Variable X and Variable Y in the population.

What happens, though, if we draw many samples of, say, eight pairs of scores at random from this population and calculate the correlation coefficients for *each* sample? Some of the correlation coefficients are indeed more-or-less zero but a few are substantially different from zero as we can see from Table 10.2. Plotted on a histogram, the distribution of these correlation coefficients looks like Figure 10.1. It is more-or-less a normal distribution with a mean correlation of zero and most of the correlations being close to that zero point. However, some of the correlation coefficients are substantially different from 0.00. This shows that even where there is zero relationship between the two variables in the population, random samples can appear to have correlations which depart from 0.00.

Just about anything is possible in samples although only certain things are likely. Consequently, we try to stipulate which are the *likely* correlations in

Table 10.1 **An imaginary population of 60 pairs of scores with zero correlation between the pairs**

Pair	Variable X	Variable Y	Pair	Variable X	Variable Y	Pair	Variable X	Variable Y
01	14	12	02	5	11	03	12	5
04	3	13	05	14	9	06	10	14
07	5	12	08	17	17	09	4	8
10	15	5	11	3	3	12	19	12
13	16	7	14	14	9	15	12	13
16	13	8	17	15	11	18	15	7
19	12	17	20	11	14	21	5	13
22	12	11	23	11	9	24	15	14
25	5	12	26	15	9	27	12	13
28	6	13	29	14	7	30	18	13
31	12	1	32	19	12	33	12	19
34	11	14	35	12	17	36	13	9
37	14	12	38	15	5	39	18	13
40	17	11	41	3	12	42	16	9
43	16	12	44	11	9	45	18	2
46	12	14	47	12	14	48	15	11
49	16	12	50	12	14	51	8	14
52	5	11	53	7	8	54	16	8
55	13	13	56	12	15	57	18	2
58	3	1	59	7	8	60	11	6

samples of a given size and which are the *unlikely* ones (if the population correlation is zero). Actually all we say is that correlations in the *middle* 95% of the distribution of samples are likely if the population correlation is zero. Correlations in the extreme 5% (usually the extreme 2.5% in each direction) are unlikely in these circumstances. These are arbitrary cut-off points, but they are conventional in statistics and have long antecedents. It is also not an unreasonable cut-off for most purposes to suggest that if a sample has only a 1 in 20 chance of occurring then it is unlikely to represent the population value.

If a correlation is in the extreme 5% of the distribution of samples from a *population* where the correlation is zero, it is deemed *statistically significant*. We

Table 10.2   **Two hundred correlation coefficients obtained by repeatedly random sampling eight pairs of scores from Table 10.1**

−0.56	−0.30	0.36	0.54	−0.27	0.05	−0.33	−0.19	0.54	0.18
−0.54	0.11	0.25	−0.15	−0.57	−0.31	−0.24	0.17	−0.69	−0.19
−0.53	0.68	−0.22	−0.22	−0.26	−0.42	0.08	−0.30	−0.41	0.29
−0.45	−0.09	−0.06	−0.30	−0.72	−0.53	0.04	−0.66	0.65	−0.53
−0.39	−0.21	0.07	−0.80	−0.68	0.08	0.13	0.76	−0.04	0.18
−0.36	−0.19	0.29	0.24	0.38	−0.55	−0.40	0.50	−0.09	−0.30
−0.30	−0.56	0.68	−0.14	0.35	−0.28	0.56	−0.38	−0.16	0.15
−0.29	−0.23	−0.42	−0.27	0.01	0.43	0.01	−0.33	−0.20	0.49
−0.26	−0.41	−0.09	0.00	0.54	0.17	0.34	0.52	−0.11	0.67
−0.26	−0.16	−0.70	0.00	−0.17	0.40	0.03	−0.02	0.35	−0.01
−0.23	0.03	0.30	−0.52	−0.05	−0.26	−0.32	−0.37	−0.51	0.18
−0.20	−0.17	−0.43	−0.39	0.37	0.23	−0.10	0.32	0.02	0.52
−0.18	0.38	0.45	−0.50	−0.58	0.28	−0.34	−0.28	0.24	0.53
−0.17	−0.02	−0.34	−0.23	−0.54	0.25	−0.71	0.72	0.03	−0.13
−0.08	−0.30	−0.06	−0.10	−0.65	0.27	−0.04	0.32	−0.52	−0.42
−0.04	0.59	−0.29	−0.31	0.48	−0.48	0.02	−0.30	0.81	−0.23
0.10	−0.12	−0.51	−0.19	0.08	0.18	−0.27	−0.67	−0.69	0.50
0.15	−0.54	−0.15	0.05	0.01	0.52	0.19	0.19	0.07	0.27
0.34	−0.44	−0.11	−0.21	−0.02	−0.07	0.17	−0.30	−0.06	−0.49
0.57	−0.10	−0.23	0.01	−0.09	−0.27	0.22	−0.28	0.43	−0.34

should be sitting up and taking notice if this happens. In other words, statistical significance merely signals the statistically unusual or unlikely. In the above example, by examining Table 10.2 we find that the correlations 0.81, 0.76, 0.72, 0.68 and 0.68 and −0.80, −0.72, −0.71, −0.70, and −0.69 are in the extreme 5% of correlations away from zero. This extreme 5% is made up of the extreme 2.5% positive correlations and the extreme 2.5% negative correlations. Therefore, a correlation of between 0.68 and 1.00 or −0.69 and −1.00 is in the extreme 5% of correlations. This is the range which we describe as statistically significant. Statistical significance simply means that our sample falls in the relatively extreme part of the distribution of samples obtained if the null hypothesis (see next section) of no relationship between the two variables is true.

Figure 10.1 **Distribution of correlation coefficients presented in Table 10.2**

These ranges of significant correlations mentioned above only apply to samples of size eight. A different size of sample from the same population results in a different spread of correlations obtained from repeated sampling. The spread is bigger if the samples are smaller and less if the samples are larger. In other words, there is more variation in the distribution of samples with small sample sizes than with larger ones.

On the face of things, all of this is merely a theoretical meandering of little value. We have assumed that the population correlation is zero. A major difficulty is that we are normally unaware of the population correlation since our information is based solely on a sample which may or may not represent the population very well. However, it is not quite the futile exercise it appears. Some information provided by a sample can be used to infer or estimate the characteristics of the population. For one thing, information about the variability or variance of the scores in the sample is used *to estimate the variability of scores in the population.*

10.2 Back to the real world: the null hypothesis

There is another vitally important concept in statistics – the hypothesis. Hypotheses in psychological statistics are usually presented as antithetical pairs – the *null hypothesis* and its corresponding *alternative hypothesis*:

1. The *null hypothesis* is in essence a statement that there is no relationship between two variables. The following are all examples of null hypotheses:

    (a) There is no relationship between brain size and intelligence.
    (b) There is no relationship between gender and income.
    (c) There is no relationship between baldness and virility.
    (d) There is no relationship between children's self-esteem and that of their parent of the same sex.

    (e) There is no relationship between ageing and memory loss.

    (f) There is no relationship between the amount of carrots eaten and ability to see in the dark.

2.   The *alternative hypothesis* simply states that there is a relationship between two variables. In its simplest forms the alternative hypothesis says only this:

    (a) There is a relationship between the number of years of education people have and their income.

    (b) There is a relationship between people's sex and how much they talk about their emotional problems.

    (c) There is a relationship between people's mental instability and their artistic creativity.

    (d) There is a relationship between abuse in childhood and later psychological problems.

    (e) There is a relationship between birth order and social dominance.

    (f) There is a relationship between the degree of similarity of couples and their sexual attraction for each other.

So the difference between null and alternative hypotheses is merely the word 'no'. Of course, sometimes psychologists dress their hypotheses up in fancier language than this but the basic principle is unchanged. (Actually there is a complication – directional hypotheses – but these are dealt with in Chapter 17.)

The statistical reason for using the null hypothesis and alternative hypothesis is that they *clarify* the populations in statistical analyses. *In statistics, inferences are based on the characteristics of the population as defined by the null hypothesis.* Invariably the populations defined by the null hypothesis are ones in which there is no relation between a pair of variables. Thus, the population defined by the null hypothesis is one where the correlation between the two variables under consideration is 0.00. The characteristics of a sample can be used to assess whether it is likely that the correlation for the sample comes from a population in which the correlation is zero.

So the basic trick is to use certain of the characteristics of a sample together with the notion of the null hypothesis to define the characteristics of a population. Other characteristics of the sample are then used to estimate the likelihood that this sample comes from this particular population. To repeat and summarise:

1.   The null hypothesis is used to define a population in which there is no relation between two variables.

2.   Other characteristics, especially the variability of this population, are estimated or inferred from the known sample.

It is then possible to decide whether or not it is likely that the sample comes from this population defined by the null hypothesis. If it is *unlikely* that the sample comes from the null hypothesis-based population, the possibility that the null hypothesis is true is rejected. Instead the view that the alternative hypothesis is true is accepted. That is, the alternative hypothesis that there really is a relationship is preferred. This is the same thing as saying that we can safely generalise from our sample.

10.3 Pearson's correlation coefficient again

The null hypothesis for research involving the correlation coefficient is that there is *no* relationship between the two variables. In other words, the null hypothesis implies that the correlation coefficient between two variables is 0.00 in the population (defined by the null hypothesis). So what if, in a sample of 10 pairs of scores, the correlation is 0.94 as for the data in Table 10.3?

Is it likely that such a correlation would occur in a sample if it actually came from a population where the true correlation is zero? We are back to our basic problem of how likely it is that a correlation of 0.94 would occur if really there is no correlation in the population. We need to plot the distribution of correlations in random samples of 10 pairs drawn from this population. Unfortunately we do not have the population of scores, only a sample of scores. However, statisticians can use the variability of this sample of scores to estimate the variability in the population. Then the likely distribution of correlations in repeated samples of a given size drawn from the population with this amount of variability can be calculated. Mere mortals like ourselves do not have to get actively involved in this since it is fairly easy to capitalise on statisticians' efforts. They have provided tables which neatly summarise a great deal of hard work on their part.

Tables are available which, for any given size of sample, tell you the minimum size of a correlation coefficient which cuts the middle 95% of correlations from the extreme 5% of correlations (assuming the null hypothesis is true in the population). These cut-off points are usually called *critical values*:

1. If the sample's correlation is in the middle 95% of correlations then we accept the null hypothesis that there is no relationship between the two variables.

Table 10.3 **A sample of 10 pairs of scores**

Pair number	*X* score	*Y* score
1	5	4
2	2	1
3	7	8
4	5	6
5	0	2
6	1	0
7	4	3
8	2	2
9	8	9
10	6	7

2. However, if the correlation in the sample is in the extreme 5% of correlations then the alternative hypothesis is accepted (that there is a relationship between the two variables).

Significance Table 10.1 reveals that for a sample size of 10, a correlation has to be between −0.63 and −1.00 *or* between 0.63 and 1.00 to be sufficiently large as to be in the extreme 5% of correlations which support the alternative hypothesis. Correlations closer to 0.00 than these come in the middle 95% which are held to support the null hypothesis.

Significance Table 10.1   **5% significance values of the Pearson correlation coefficient (two-tailed test)**

Your value must be in the listed ranges for your sample size to be significant at the 5% level (i.e. to accept the hypothesis).

If your required sample size is not listed, then take the nearest *smaller* sample size. Alternatively, extrapolate from listed values.

Sample size	Significant at 5% level Accept hypothesis
5	−0.88 to −1.00 *or* +0.88 to +1.00
6	−0.81 to −1.00 *or* +0.81 to +1.00
7	−0.75 to −1.00 *or* +0.75 to +1.00
8	−0.71 to −1.00 *or* +0.71 to +1.00
9	−0.67 to −1.00 *or* +0.67 to +1.00
10	−0.63 to −1.00 *or* +0.63 to +1.00
11	−0.60 to −1.00 *or* +0.60 to +1.00
12	−0.58 to −1.00 *or* +0.58 to +1.00
13	−0.55 to −1.00 *or* +0.55 to +1.00
14	−0.53 to −1.00 *or* +0.53 to +1.00
15	−0.51 to −1.00 *or* +0.51 to +1.00
16	−0.50 to −1.00 or +0.50 to +1.00
17	−0.48 to −1.00 or +0.48 to +1.00
18	−0.47 to −1.00 or +0.47 to +1.00
19	−0.46 to −1.00 or +0.46 to +1.00
20	−0.44 to −1.00 or +0.44 to +1.00
25	−0.40 to −1.00 or +0.40 to +1.00
30	−0.36 to −1.00 or +0.36 to +1.00
40	−0.31 to −1.00 or +0.31 to +1.00
50	−0.28 to −1.00 or +0.28 to +1.00
60	−0.25 to −1.00 or +0.25 to +1.00
100	−0.20 to −1.00 or +0.20 to +1.00

An extended and conventional version of this table is to be found in Appendix C.

Calculation 10.1

Statistical significance of a Pearson correlation coefficient

Having calculated your value of the Pearson correlation coefficient, make a note of the sample size and consult Significance Table 10.1. In the example in Chapter 7 (Calculation 7.1), the correlation between mathematical scores and musical scores was found to be –0.90 with a sample size of 10. If this correlation is in the range of correlations listed as being in the extreme 5% of correlations for this sample size, the correlation is described as being statistically significant at the 5% level of significance.

Interpreting the results In this case, since our obtained value of the correlation coefficient is in the significant range of the correlation coefficient (–0.63 to –1.00 and 0.63 to 1.00), we reject the null hypothesis in favour of the alternative hypothesis that there is a relationship between mathematical and musical scores.

Reporting the results In our report of the study we would conclude by writing something to the following effect: 'There is a negative correlation of –0.90 between mathematical and musical scores which is statistically significant at the 5% level with a sample size of 10.'

The terms *Type 1 error* and *Type 2 error* frequently appear in statistics textbooks although they are relatively uncommon in reports and other publications. They refer to the risk that no matter what decision you make in statistics there is always a chance that you will be making the wrong decision.

A Type 1 error is deciding that the null hypothesis is false when it is actually true. A Type 2 error is deciding that the null hypothesis is true when it is actually false. Powerful statistical tests are those in which there is less chance of a Type 2 error.

Unfortunately, the terms are not particularly useful in the everyday application of statistics where it is hard enough making a decision let alone worrying about the chance that you have made a wrong decision. Given that statistics deals with probabilities and not certainties, there is always a chance that any decision you make is wrong.

10.4 The Spearman's rho correlation coefficient

If you followed our advice in Chapter 7 to use the standard Pearson correlation coefficient formula on the ranked scores instead of using the Spearman rho formula (Calculation 7.3) then the significance of your calculation should be assessed using Significance Table 10.1. This is the approach used by standard computer packages such as SPSS. However, assuming that you used the Spearman rho formula in Calculation 7.2, especially if there are tied scores, then Significance Table 10.2 should be used.

Significance Table 10.2   **5% significance values of the Spearman correlation coefficient (two-tailed test)**

Your value must be in the listed ranges for your sample size to be significant at the 5% level (i.e. to accept the hypothesis).

If your required sample size is not listed, then take the nearest *smaller* sample size. Alternatively, extrapolate from listed values.

Sample size	Significant at 5% level Accept hypothesis						
5			−1.00	or	+1.00		
6	−0.89	to	−1.00	or	+0.89	to	+1.00
7	−0.79	to	−1.00	or	+0.79	to	+1.00
8	−0.74	to	−1.00	or	+0.74	to	+1.00
9	−0.68	to	−1.00	or	+0.68	to	+1.00
10	−0.65	to	−1.00	or	+0.65	to	+1.00
11	−0.62	to	−1.00	or	+0.62	to	+1.00
12	−0.59	to	−1.00	or	+0.59	to	+1.00
13	−0.57	to	−1.00	or	+0.57	to	+1.00
14	−0.55	to	−1.00	or	+0.55	to	+1.00
15	−0.52	to	−1.00	or	+0.52	to	+1.00
16	−0.51	to	−1.00	or	+0.51	to	+1.00
17	−0.49	to	−1.00	or	+0.49	to	+1.00
18	−0.48	to	−1.00	or	+0.48	to	+1.00
19	−0.46	to	−1.00	or	+0.46	to	+1.00
20	−0.45	to	−1.00	or	+0.45	to	+1.00
25	−0.40	to	−1.00	or	+0.40	to	+1.00
30	−0.36	to	−1.00	or	+0.36	to	+1.00
40	−0.31	to	−1.00	or	+0.31	to	+1.00
50	−0.28	to	−1.00	or	+0.28	to	+1.00
60	−0.26	to	−1.00	or	+0.26	to	+1.00
100	−0.20	to	−1.00	or	+0.20	to	+1.00

An extended and conventional version of this table is to be found in Appendix D.

Calculation 10.2

Statistical significance of Spearman's rho correlation coefficient

In Chapter 7 (Calculation 7.2) we calculated Spearman's rho correlation coefficient between mathematical score and musical score. The correlation was found to be –0.89 with a sample size of 10. Significance Table 10.2 reveals that in order to be significant at the 5% level with a sample size of 10, correlations have to be in the range 0.65 to 1.00 *or* –0.65 to –1.00.

Interpreting the results Since our obtained value of the Spearman's rho correlation coefficient is in the range of significant correlations we accept the alternative hypothesis that mathematical and musical scores are (inversely) related and reject the null hypothesis.

Reporting the results We can report a significant correlation: 'There is a negative correlation of –0.89 between mathematical and musical scores which is statistically significant at the 5% level with a sample size of 10.'

10.5 Notes and recommendations

■ There is nothing complex in the calculation of statistical significance for the correlation coefficients. However, statistical tables normally do not include every sample size. When a particular sample size is missing you can simply use the nearest (lower) tabulated value. Alternatively you could extrapolate from the nearest tabulated value above and the nearest tabulated value below your actual sample size.

■ It is a bad mistake to report a correlation without indicating whether it is statistically significant.

■ Chapter 16 explains how to report your significance levels in a more succinct form. Try to employ this sort of style as it eases the writing of research reports and looks professional.

■ Beware that some statistical textbooks provide significance tables which are distributed by degrees of freedom rather than sample size. For any given sample size, the degrees of freedom are *two* less. Thus, for a sample size of 10, the degrees of freedom are 10 – 2, or 8.

Chapter 11

Standard error

The standard deviation of the means of samples

Preparation
Review z-scores and standard deviation (Chapter 5) and sampling from populations (Chapter 9).

Most psychological research involves the use of samples drawn from a particular population. Just what are the characteristics of samples drawn from a population? In theory, it is possible to draw samples with virtually any mean score if we randomly sample from a population of scores. So is it possible to make any generalisations about the characteristics of randomly drawn samples from a population?

Standard error is one way of summarising the diversity of sample means drawn from a population. This chapter explains the concept of standard error. However, the practical use of standard error in psychological research will not become obvious until the next two chapters which deal with the *t*-tests. Nevertheless, it is essential to understand standard error before moving on to its practical applications.

11.1 Theoretical considerations

Table 11.1 contains a population of 25 scores with a mean of 4.20. We have selected, at random, samples of four scores until we have 20 samples. These are arbitrary decisions for illustrative purposes. For each of these 20 samples the mean has been calculated giving 20 separate sample means. They are shown in Table 11.2.

The distribution of the sample means is called a *sampling distribution*. Clearly, in Table 11.2 the 20 sample means differ to varying degrees from each other and from the population mean of 4.20. In fact the average of the sample means is

Table 11.1   **A population of 25 scores**

5	7	9	4	6
2	6	3	2	7
1	7	5	4	3
3	6	1	2	4
2	5	3	3	4

Table 11.2   **Means of 20 samples each of four scores taken at random from the population of 25 scores in Table 11.1**

3.75	6.00	4.00	4.25
3.00	3.75	4.50	3.50
4.50	3.00	4.25	2.50
3.50	5.00	3.00	4.25
4.00	3.00	4.50	5.75

4.00. The standard deviation of these 20 sample means is 0.89. This was calculated using the normal formula for the standard deviation (see Calculation 5.1). There is a special name for the standard deviation formula when it is applied to a set of sample means – the *standard error*. Therefore the standard error is 0.89. The implication of this is that the standard error is directly comparable to the standard deviation. Consequently, the standard error is simply the average deviation of sample means from the mean of the sample means. Although this is clumsy to write down or say, it captures the essence of standard error effectively. (The average of sample means, if you have a lot of samples, will be more-or-less identical to the mean of the population. Thus, it is more usual to refer to the population mean rather than the average of sample means.)

If we sampled from the population of scores in Table 11.1 but using a different sample size, say samples of 12, we would get a rather different sampling distribution. In general, all other things being equal, the standard error of the means of bigger samples is less than that of smaller sized samples. This is merely a slightly convoluted way of supporting the commonsense belief that larger samples are more precise estimates of the characteristics of populations than are smaller samples. In other words, we tend to be more convinced by large samples than small samples.

A frequency curve of the means of samples drawn from a population will tend to get taller and narrower as the sample size involved increases. It also tends to be normal in shape, i.e. bell-shaped. The more normal (bell-shaped) the population of scores on which the sampling is done, the more normal (bell-shaped) the frequency curve of the sample means.

11.2 Estimated standard deviation and standard error

The difficulty with the concept of standard error is that we rarely have information about anything other than a sample taken from the population. This might suggest that the standard error is unknowable. After all, if we only have a single sample mean, how on earth can we calculate the standard error? There is only one sample mean which obviously cannot vary from itself. Fortunately we can estimate the standard error from the characteristics of a sample of scores. The first stage in doing this involves estimating the *population* standard deviation from the standard deviation of a *sample* taken from that population. There is a relatively easy way of using the standard deviation of a sample of scores in order to estimate the standard deviation of the population. The formula is:

$$\text{Estimated standard deviation} = \sqrt{\frac{\Sigma X^2 - \frac{(\Sigma X)^2}{N}}{N-1}}$$

The above formula is exactly the same as the standard deviation computational formula given in Chapter 5 with one difference. You will see in the lower half of the formula the term $N - 1$. In our previous version of the formula, N occurred rather than $N - 1$. The point is that if we know the scores in a sample, we can use them to estimate the standard deviation of the scores in the population.

You may be wondering about the $N - 1$ in the above formula. The reason is that if we try to extrapolate the standard deviation of the whole population directly from the standard deviation of a sample from this population, we get things somewhat wrong. However, this is easily corrected by adjusting the standard deviation by dividing by $N - 1$ instead of N. The adjusted standard deviation formula gives the *estimated* standard deviation. We can also estimate the variance of the population from the characteristics of the sample:

$$\text{Estimated variance} = \frac{\Sigma X^2 - \frac{(\Sigma X)^2}{N}}{N-1}$$

These formulae for estimated standard deviation and estimated variance apply when you are using a sample to estimate the characteristics of a population. However, some researchers also use these estimating formulae (in which you divide by N – 1) in place of the variance and standard deviation formulae (in which you divide by N) when dealing with populations. Generally this makes little difference in practice since psychologists are usually working with samples and trying to estimate the characteristics of the population.

The term $N - 1$ is called the *degrees of freedom.*

There is a second step in estimating the standard error from the characteristics of a sample. The standard error involves sample *means*, not the *scores* involved in the standard deviation and estimated standard deviation. How does one move from scores to sample means? Fortunately a very simple relationship exists between the standard deviation of a population of scores and the standard error of samples of scores taken from that population. The standard error is obtained by dividing the population standard deviation by the *square root* of the sample size involved. This implies that the standard deviation of large samples taken from the population of scores is smaller than the standard deviation of small samples taken from the population. The formula is basically the same whether we are using the standard deviation of a known population or the estimated standard deviation of a population based on the standard deviation of a sample.

$$\text{(Estimated) standard error} = \frac{\text{(Estimated) standard deviation of population}}{\sqrt{N}}$$

Obviously it is possible to combine the (estimated) standard deviation and the (estimated) standard error formulae:

$$\text{(Estimated) standard error} = \frac{\sqrt{\dfrac{\Sigma X^2 - \dfrac{(\Sigma X)^2}{N}}{N - 1}}}{\sqrt{N}}$$

Calculation 11.1

Estimated standard error of sample means from scores for a single sample from the population

The following is a sample of six scores taken at random from the population: 5, 7, 3, 6, 4, 5.

Table 11.3 **Steps in calculating the standard error**

X (scores)	X^2 (squared scores)
5	25
7	49
3	9
6	36
4	16
5	25
$\Sigma X = 30$	$\Sigma X^2 = 160$

Step 1 Using this information we can estimate the standard error of samples of size 6 taken from the same population. Taking our six scores (X), we need to produce Table 11.3, where $N = 6$.

Step 2 Substitute these values in the standard error formula:

$$\text{(Estimated) standard error} = \cfrac{\sqrt{\cfrac{\Sigma X^2 - \cfrac{(\Sigma X)^2}{N}}{N-1}}}{\sqrt{N}}$$

$$= \cfrac{\sqrt{\cfrac{160 - \cfrac{30^2}{6}}{6-1}}}{\sqrt{6}}$$

$$= \cfrac{\sqrt{\cfrac{160 - \cfrac{900}{6}}{5}}}{2.449}$$

$$= \cfrac{\sqrt{\cfrac{160 - 150}{5}}}{2.449}$$

$$= \cfrac{\sqrt{\cfrac{10}{5}}}{2.449}$$

$$= \cfrac{\sqrt{2}}{2.449}$$

$$= \cfrac{1.414}{2.449}$$

$$= 0.58$$

Interpreting the results Roughly speaking, this suggests that on average sample means differ from the population mean by 0.58.

Reporting the results Standard error is not routinely reported although sometimes it is seen. It is no more informative than the standard deviation which is more likely to be included in reports. Many psychologists report the variance or standard deviation instead since this is just as informative descriptive statistics as the standard error.

The term standard *error* is used because it is the standard or average amount by which you would be wrong if you tried to estimate the mean of the population from the mean of a sample from that population.

11.3 Notes and recommendations

■ The standard error is often reported in computer output and in research publications. Very much like standard deviation, it can be used as an indicator of the variability in one's data. Variables with different standard errors essentially have different variances so long as the number of scores is the same for the two variables.

■ Standard error is almost always really *estimated* standard error in psychological statistics. However, usually this estimate is referred to simply as the standard error. This is a pity since it loses sight of the true nature of standard error.

Chapter 12

The *t*-test

Comparing two samples of correlated/related scores

Preparation

Review z-scores and standard deviation (Chapter 5) and standard error (Chapter 11).

12.1 Introduction

Many research projects involve comparisons between two groups of scores. Each group of scores is a sample from a population of scores. There is a test called the related (correlated) *t*-test which compares the means of two *related* samples of scores to see whether the means differ significantly. The meaning of related samples can be illustrated by the following examples:

1. People's scores on a psychological test of creativity are measured at two different points in time in order to see if any improvement has taken place (see Table 12.1). Notice that we have mentioned individuals by name to stress that they are being measured twice – they are *not* different individuals in the two conditions. Also, some of the data have been omitted.

Table 12.1 **Creativity scores measured at two different times**

	1 March	**Six months later**
Sam	17	19
Jack	14	17
. . .	. . .	. . .
Karl	12	19
Shahida	19	25
Mandy	10	13
Mean	$\overline{X}_1 = 15.09$	$\overline{X}_2 = 18.36$

Table 12.2 **Time of day and memory performance scores**

	Morning	**Afternoon**
Rebecca	9	15
Sharon	16	23
. . .	. . .	. . .
Neil	18	24
Mean	$\overline{X}_1 = 17.3$	$\overline{X}_2 = 22.1$

Table 12.3 **Reaction time in seconds for drug and no-drug conditions**

	'Nogloom'	**Placebo**
Jenny	0.27	0.25
David	0.15	0.18
. . .	. . .	. . .
Mean	$\overline{X}_1 = 0.22$	$\overline{X}_2 = 0.16$

2. A group of students' memory test scores are measured in the morning and in the afternoon in order to see whether memory is affected by time of day (Table 12.2).

3. A group of participants in an experiment are assessed in terms of their reaction time to a coloured light when they have taken the anti-depressant drug 'Nogloom' and when they have taken an inert control tablet (placebo) (see Table 12.3).

In each of the above experiments, the researcher wishes to know whether the means of the two conditions differ from each other. The question is whether the mean scores in the two conditions are sufficiently different from each other that they fall in the extreme 5% of cases. If they do, this allows us to generalise from the research findings. In other words, are the two means significantly different from each other?

The key characteristics of all of the above studies is that a group of participants is measured twice on a single variable in slightly different conditions or circumstances. So in the above studies, creativity has been measured twice, memory has been measured twice and reaction time has been measured twice. In other words, they are *repeated measures designs* for the obvious reason that participants have been measured more than once on the same variable. Repeated measures designs are also called *related measures designs* and *correlated scores designs*.

Design consideration   Repeated measures designs of the sort described in this chapter can be problematic. For example, since the participants in the research are measured under both the experimental and control conditions, it could be that their experiences in the experimental condition affect the way they behave in the control condition. Many of the problems can be overcome by *counterbalancing* conditions. By this we mean that a random selection of half of the participants in the research are put through the experimental condition first; the other half are put through the control condition first.

In our opening paragraph we mentioned the related (correlated) *t*-test. There are in fact two versions of the *t*-test – a correlated/related and an uncorrelated/unrelated samples version. The latter is more likely to be of use to you simply because unrelated designs are more common in psychological statistics. However, the correlated/related *t*-test is substantially simpler to understand and is useful as a learning aid prior to tackling the more difficult unrelated *t*-test, which is described in Chapter 13.

Design consideration   It is also possible to have a related design if you take pairs of subjects *matched* to be as similar as possible on factors which might be related to their scores on the dependent variable. So pairs of participants might be matched on sex and age so that each member of the pair in question is of the same sex and age group (or as close as possible). One member of the pair would be assigned at *random* to one experimental condition, the other member to the other experimental condition. Using the effects of time of day on memory research question (Table 12.2), the arrangement for a matched pairs or matched subjects design might be as in Table 12.4.

Table 12.4   **A matched pairs design testing memory score**

Matched pairs	Morning score	Afternoon score
Both male and under 20	16	17
Both female and under 20	21	25
Both male and over 20	14	20
Both female and over 20	10	14

The purpose of matching, like using the same person twice, is to reduce the influence of unwanted variables on the comparisons.

12.2 Dependent and independent variables

The scores in Tables 12.1–12.3 are scores on the *dependent variable*. They include the variables creativity, memory and reaction time in the above experiments.

However, there is another variable – the *independent variable*. This refers to the various conditions in which the measurements are being taken. In Table 12.1 measurements are being taken at two different points in time – on 1 March and six months later. The alternative hypothesis is that there *is* a relationship between the independent variable 'time of measurement' and the dependent variable 'creativity score'. Obviously, it is being assumed that creativity scores are *dependent* on the variable time.

12.3 Some basic revision

A z-score is simply the number of standard deviations a score is away from the mean of the set of scores. The formula is:

$$z\text{-score} = \frac{X - \overline{X}}{\text{sd}}$$

where X is a particular score, $\overline{X}$ is the mean of the set of scores, and sd is the standard deviation of the set of scores.

Remember, once you have obtained the z-score, it is possible to use the table of the standard normal distribution (z-distribution) (Significance Table 12.1) to identify the relative position of the particular score compared to the rest of the set.

12.4 Theoretical considerations

As we have seen, the most important theoretical concept with any inferential statistical test is the null hypothesis. This states that there is *no* relationship between the two variables in the research. In the previous example the independent variable is time of day and the dependent variable is memory. The null hypothesis is that there is no relation between the independent variable time and the dependent variable memory. This implies, by definition, that the two samples, according to the null hypothesis, come from the same population. In other words, in the final analysis the overall trend is for pairs of samples drawn from this population to have identical means. However, that is the trend over many pairs of samples. The means of some pairs of samples will differ somewhat from each other simply because samples from even the same population tend to vary. Little differences will be more common than big differences.

Another important concept is that of the *t*-distribution. This is a theoretical statistical distribution which is similar to the z-distribution discussed in Chapter 5. There is also a *t*-score which is similar to the z-score. The *t*-score is based on analogous logic to the z-score. The major difference is that the *t*-score involves *standard error* and not standard deviation. As we saw in the previous chapter, the standard error is nothing other than the standard deviation of a set of sample means. Using the *z*-distribution, it is possible to work out the standing of any score relative to the rest of the set of scores. Exactly the same applies where one has the standard error of a set of sample means. One can calculate the relative extent to which a particular sample mean differs from the average sample mean. (The average sample mean with many samples will be the same as the mean of the population, so normally the population mean is referred to rather than the average of sample means.) The key formulae are as follows:

$$z = \frac{\text{Particular score} - \text{Sample mean of scores}}{\text{Standard deviation of scores}}$$

$$t = \frac{\text{Particular sample mean} - \text{Average of sample means}}{\text{Standard error of sample means}}$$

or

$$t = \frac{\text{Particular sample mean} - \text{Population mean}}{\text{Standard error of sample means}}$$

As you can see, the form of each of these formulae is identical.

Both *z*- and *t*- refer to standard distributions which are symmetrical and bell-shaped. The *z*-distribution is a normal distribution – the standard normal distribution. Similarly, the *t*-distribution is also a normal distribution when large sample sizes are involved. In fact *z*- and *t*- are identical in these circumstances. As the sample size gets smaller, however, the *t*-distribution becomes a decidedly flatter distribution. Significance Table 12.1 is a table of the *t*-distribution which reports the value of the *t*-score needed to put a sample mean outside the middle 95% of sample means and into the extreme 5% of sample means that are held to be unlikely or *statistically significant* sample means. Notice that the table of the *t*-distribution is structured according to the *degrees of freedom*. Usually this is the sample size minus one if a single sample is used to *estimate* the standard error, otherwise it may be different.

The *t*-test can be applied to the data on the above population. Assume that for a given population, the population mean is 1.0. We have estimated the standard error by taking a known sample of 10 scores, calculating its estimated standard deviation and dividing by the square root of the sample size. All of these stages are combined in the following formula which was discussed in Chapter 11:

$$\text{(Estimated) standard error} = \frac{\sqrt{\dfrac{\Sigma X^2 - \dfrac{(\Sigma X)^2}{N}}{N-1}}}{\sqrt{N}}$$

This has given the (estimated) standard error to be 2.5. We can calculate if a sample with a mean of 8.0 ($N = 10$) is statistically unusual. We simply apply the t-test formula to the information we have:

$$t = \frac{\text{Particular sample mean} - \text{Population mean}}{\text{Standard error of sample means}}$$

$$= \frac{8.0 - 1.0}{2.5}$$

$$= \frac{7.0}{2.5}$$

$$= 2.8$$

In other words, our sample mean is actually 2.8 standard errors *above* the average sample mean (i.e. population mean) of 1.0.

We can now use Significance Table 12.1. This table is distributed according to the number of degrees of freedom involved in the estimation of the population standard deviation. Since the sample size on which this estimate was based is 10, the degrees of freedom are 1 less than 10, i.e. $N - 1 = 9$ degrees of freedom. Significance Table 12.1 tells us that we need a t-score of 2.26 or more to place our particular sample mean in the extreme 5% of sample means drawn from the population. Our obtained t-score was 2.8. This means that our sample mean is within the extreme 5% of sample means, i.e. that it is statistically significantly different from the average of sample means drawn from this particular population.

Wonderful! But what has this got to do with our research problem which we set out at the beginning of this chapter? The above is simply about a single sample compared with a multitude of samples. What we need to know is whether or not *two* sample means are sufficiently different from each other that we can say that the difference is statistically significant. There is just one remaining statistical trick that statisticians employ in these circumstances. That is, *the two samples of scores are turned into a single sample by subtracting one set of scores from the other*. We calculate the difference between a person's score in one sample and their score in the other sample. This leaves us with a sample of difference scores (D) which constitutes the single sample we need. In other words, the standard error of a single sample is sufficient theory.

The stylised data in Table 12.5 show just what is done. The difference scores in the final column are the single sample of scores which we use in our standard error formula. For this particular sample of difference scores the mean is 4.0. According to the null hypothesis, the general trend should be zero difference between the two samples – that is, the mean of the difference scores would be zero if the sample reflected precisely the null hypothesis. Once again we are reliant on the null hypothesis to tell us what the population characteristics are. Since the null hypothesis has it that there is no difference between the *samples*,

Table 12.5 **Basic rearrangement of data for the related samples *t*-test**

Person	Sample 1 (X_1)	Sample 2 (X_2)	Difference $X_1 - X_2 = D$
A	9	5	4
B	7	2	5
C	7	3	4
D	11	6	5
E	7	5	2

there should be zero difference in the population, that is, the average difference score should be 0. (Since the difference between sample means under the null hypothesis that the two samples do not differ is zero by definition, this means that the population mean should be zero. In other words we can delete the population mean from the formula for *t*-scores.) We would of course expect some samples of difference scores to be above or below zero by varying amounts. The question is whether a mean difference of 4.0 is sufficiently different from zero to be statistically significant. If it comes in the middle 95% of the distribution of sample means then we accept the null hypothesis. If it comes in the extreme 5% then we describe it as significant and reject the null hypothesis in favour of the alternative hypothesis. We achieve this by using the *t*-test formula applied to the sample of difference scores. We then test the significance of *t* by comparing it to the values in Significance Table 12.1. For a sample of four, since the degrees of freedom are $N - 1$ which equals 3, the table tells us that we need a *t*-score of 3.18 at the minimum to put our sample mean in the significant extreme 5% of the distribution of sample means.

Calculation 12.1

The related/correlated samples *t*-test

The data are taken from an imaginary study which looked at the relationship between age of an infant and the amount of eye contact it makes with its mother. The infants were six months old and nine months old at the time of testing – age is the independent variable. The dependent variable is the number of one-minute segments during which the infant made any eye contact with its mother over a ten-minute session. The null hypothesis is that there is no relation between age and eye contact. The data are given in Table 12.6 which includes the difference between the six-month and nine-month scores as well as the square of this difference. The number of cases, N, is the number of difference scores, i.e. 8.

Table 12.6 **Steps in calculating the related/correlated samples *t*-test (number of one-minute segments with eye contact)**

Subject	Six months X_1	Nine months X_2	Difference $D = X_1 - X_2$	Difference^2 D^2
Baby Clara	3	7	−4	16
Baby Martin	5	6	−1	1
Baby Sally	5	3	2	4
Baby Angie	4	8	−4	16
Baby Trevor	3	5	−2	4
Baby Sam	7	9	−2	4
Baby Bobby	8	7	1	1
Baby Sid	7	9	−2	4
Sums of columns	ΣX_1 $= 42$	ΣX_2 $= 54$	ΣD $= -12$	ΣD^2 $= 50$
Means of columns	$\overline{X_1}$ $= 5.25$	$\overline{X_2}$ $= 6.75$	$\overline{D}$ $= -1.5$	

We can clearly see from Table 12.6 that the nine-month-old babies are spending more periods in eye contact with their mothers, on average, than they did when they were six months old. The average difference in eye contact is 1.5. The question remains, however, whether this difference is statistically significant.

Step 1 The formula for the standard error of the difference (*D*) scores is as follows. It is exactly as for Calculation 11.1 except that we have substituted *D* for *X*.

$$\text{Standard error} = \frac{\sqrt{\dfrac{\Sigma D^2 - \dfrac{(\Sigma D)^2}{N}}{N-1}}}{\sqrt{N}}$$

Substituting the values from Table 12.6:

$$= \frac{\sqrt{\dfrac{50 - \dfrac{-12^2}{8}}{8-1}}}{\sqrt{8}}$$

$$= \frac{\sqrt{\dfrac{50 - \dfrac{144}{8}}{7}}}{2.828}$$

$$= \sqrt{\dfrac{\dfrac{50-18}{7}}{2.828}}$$

$$= \sqrt{\dfrac{\dfrac{32}{7}}{2.828}}$$

$$= \dfrac{\sqrt{4.571}}{2.828}$$

$$= \dfrac{2.138}{2.828}$$

$$= 0.756$$

Step 2 We can now enter our previously calculated values in the following formula:

$$t\text{-score} = \dfrac{\overline{D}}{\text{se}}$$

where $\overline{D}$ is the average difference score and se is the standard error

$$t\text{-score} = \dfrac{-1.5}{0.756}$$

$$= -1.98$$

Step 3 If we look up this *t*-score in Significance Table 12.1 for $N - 1 = 7$ degrees of freedom, we find that we need a *t*-value of 2.37 or more (or –2.37 or less) to put our sample mean in the extreme 5% of sample means. In other words, our sample mean of –1.5 is in the middle 95% of sample means which are held to be statistically not significant. In these circumstances we prefer to believe that the null hypothesis is true. In other words, there is no significant difference between the babies' scores at six and nine months.

Interpreting the results Check the mean scores for the two conditions in order to understand which age group has the highest levels of eye contact. Although eye contact was greater at nine months, the *t*-test is not significant which indicates that the difference between the two ages was not sufficient to allow us to conclude that the two groups truly differ from each other.

Reporting the results We would write something along the lines of the following in our report: 'Eye contact was slightly higher at nine months ($\overline{X} = 6.75$) than at six months ($\overline{X} = 5.25$). However, the difference did not support the hypothesis that eye contact differs in six-month and nine-month-old babies since the obtained value of a t of -2.37 is not statistically significant at the 5% level.'

An alternative way of putting this is as follows: 'Eye contact was slightly higher at nine months ($\overline{X} = 6.75$) than at six months ($\overline{X} = 5.25$). However, the difference did not support the hypothesis that the amount of eye contact differs at six months and nine months at the 5% level of significance ($t = -2.37$, df $= 7, p > 0.05$).'

The material in the brackets simply gives the statistic used (the t-test), its value (2.37), the degrees of freedom (7) and the level of significance which is more than that required for the 5% level ($p > 0.05$). Chapter 16 explains this in greater detail.

Warning comment

The distribution of the difference scores should not be markedly skewed if the t-test is to be used. Appendix A explains how to test for significant skewness. If the distribution of difference scores is markedly skewed, you might wish to consider the use of the Wilcoxon Matched Pairs Test (Chapter 18, Calculation 18.2).

12.5 Cautionary note

Many psychologists act as if they believe that it is the design of the research which determines whether you should use a related test. Related designs are those, after all, in which people serve in both research conditions. It is assumed that there is a correlation between subjects' scores in the two conditions. What if there is no correlation between the two samples of scores? The standard error becomes relatively large compared to the number of degrees of freedom so your research is less likely to be statistically significant (especially if the samples are small). So while trying to control for unwanted sources of error, if there is no correlation between the scores in the two conditions of the study, the researcher may simply reduce the likelihood of achieving statistical significance. The reason is that the researcher may have obtained non-significant findings simply because (a) they have reduced the error degrees of freedom, which therefore (b) increases the error estimate, thereby (c) reducing the significance level perhaps to non-significance. Some computer programs print out the correlation between the two variables as part of the correlated t-test output. If this correlation is not significant then you might be wise to think again about your test of significance. This situation is particularly likely to occur where you are using a matching procedure (as opposed to having the same people in both conditions). Unless your matching variables actually do correlate with the dependent variable, the matching can have no effect on reducing the error variance.

Significance Table 12.1   **5% significance values of related *t* (two-tailed test)**

Your value must be in the listed ranges for your degrees of freedom to be significant at the 5% level (i.e. to accept the hypothesis).

If your required degrees of freedom are not listed, then take the nearest *smaller* listed values. Appendix E gives a fuller and conventional version of this table. Refer to this if you need a more precise value of *t*.

'More extreme' means that, for example, values in the ranges of +3.18 to infinity or −3.18 to (minus) infinity are statistically significant with 3 degrees of freedom.

Degrees of freedom (always $N - 1$ for related *t*-test)	Significant at 5% level Accept hypothesis
3	±3.18 or more extreme
4	±2.78 or more extreme
5	±2.57 or more extreme
6	±2.45 or more extreme
7	±2.37 or more extreme
8	±2.31 or more extreme
9	±2.26 or more extreme
10	±2.23 or more extreme
11	±2.20 or more extreme
12	±2.18 or more extreme
13	±2.16 or more extreme
14	±2.15 or more extreme
15	±2.13 or more extreme
18	±2.10 or more extreme
20	±2.09 or more extreme
25	±2.06 or more extreme
30	±2.04 or more extreme
40	±2.02 or more extreme
60	±2.00 or more extreme
100	±1.98 or more extreme
∞	±1.96 or more extreme

In the previous calculation, we found no significant change in eye contact in older compared with younger babies. It is worth examining the correlation between the two sets of scores to see if the assumption of correlation is fulfilled. The correlation is 0.42 but we need a correlation of 0.71 or greater to be statistically significant. In other words the correlated scores do not really correlate – certainly not significantly. Even applying the uncorrelated version of the *t*-test described in the next chapter makes no difference. It still leaves the difference between the two age samples non-significant. We are not for one minute suggesting that if a related t-test fails to achieve significance you should replace it by an unrelated t-test, merely that you risk ignoring trends in your data which may be important. The most practical implication is that matching variables should relate to the dependent variable, otherwise there is no point in matching in the first place.

12.6 Notes and recommendations

■ The related or correlated t-test is merely a special case of the one-way analysis of variance for related samples (Chapter 21). Although it is frequently used in psychological research it tells us nothing more than the equivalent analysis of variance would do. Since the analysis of variance is generally a more flexible statistic allowing any number of groups of scores to be compared, it might be your preferred statistic. However, the common occurrence of the t-test in psychological research means that you need to have some idea about what it is.

■ The related t-test assumes that the distribution of the difference scores is not markedly skewed. If it is then the test may be unacceptably inaccurate. Appendix A explains how to test for skewness.

■ If you compare many pairs of samples with each other in the same study using the t-test, you should consult Chapter 23 to find out about appropriate significance levels. There are better ways of making multiple comparisons, as they are called, but with appropriate adjustment to the critical values for significance, multiple t-tests can be justified.

■ If you find that your related t-test is not significant, it could be that your two samples of scores are not correlated thus not meeting the assumptions of the related t-test.

■ The t-table presented in this chapter applies whenever we have estimated the standard error from the characteristics of a sample. However, if we had actually known the population standard deviation and consequently the standard error was the actual standard error and not an estimate, we should not use the t-distribution table. In these rare (virtually unknown) circumstances, the distribution of the t-score formula is that for the z-scores.

■ Although the correlated t-test can be used to compare any pairs of scores, it does not always make sense to do so. For example, you could use the correlated t-test to compare the weights and heights of people to see if the weight mean and the height mean differ. Unfortunately, it is a rather stupid thing to do since the numerical values involved relate to radically different things which are not comparable with each other. It is the comparison which is nonsensical in this case. The statistical test is not to blame. On the other hand, one could compare a sample of people's weights at different points in time quite meaningfully.

Chapter 13

The *t*-test

Comparing two samples of unrelated/uncorrelated scores

Preparation
This chapter will be easier if you have mastered the related t-test of Chapter 12. Revise dependent and independent variables from that chapter.

The *t*-test described in this chapter has various names. The unrelated *t*-test, the uncorrelated scores *t*-test and the independent samples *t*-test are the most common variants. It is also known as the Student *t*-test after its inventor who used the pen-name Student.

13.1 Introduction

Often researchers compare two groups of scores from *two* separate groups of individuals to assess whether the average score of one group is higher than that of the other group. The possible research topics involved in such comparisons are limitless:

1. One might wish to compare an experimental group with a control group. For example, do volunteer women who are randomly assigned to a sexually abstinent condition have more erotic dreams than those in the sexually active control group? The independent variable is sexual activity (which has two levels – sexually abstinent and sexually active) and the dependent variable is the number of erotic dreams in a month (see Table 13.1). The independent variable differentiates the two groups being compared. In the present example this is the amount of sexual activity (sexually abstinent versus sexually active). The dependent variable is the variable which might be influenced by

Table 13.1   **Number of erotic dreams per month in experimental and control groups**

Experimental group: sexually abstinent	Control group: sexually active
17	10
14	12
16	7

Table 13.2   **Decision time (seconds) in experienced and inexperienced managers**

Experienced managers	Inexperienced managers
24	167
32	133
27	74

Table 13.3   **Number of times bullied in a year in schools with different discipline policies**

Strict policy	Counselling
8	12
5	1
2	3

the independent variable. These variables correspond to the scores given in the main body of the table (i.e. number of erotic dreams).

2.   A group of experienced managers may be compared with a group of inexperienced managers in terms of the amount of time which they take to make complex decisions. The independent variable is experience in management (which has two levels – experienced versus inexperienced) and the dependent variable is decision-making time (Table 13.2).

3.   A researcher might compare the amount of bullying in two schools, one with a strict and punitive policy and the other with a policy of counselling on discipline infringements. A sample of children from each school is interviewed and the number of times they have been bullied in the previous school year obtained. The independent variable is policy on discipline (which has two levels – strict versus counselling); and the dependent variable is the number of times a child has been bullied in the previous school year (see Table 13.3).

The basic requirements for the unrelated/uncorrelated scores *t*-test are straightforward enough – two groups of scores coming from two distinct groups of people. The scores should be roughly similar in terms of the shapes of their distributions. Ideally both distributions should be bell-shaped and symmetrical. However, there can be marked deviance from this ideal and the test will remain sufficiently accurate.

The *t*-test is the name of a statistical technique which examines whether the two groups of scores have significantly *different* means – in other words, how likely is it that there could be a difference between the two groups as big as the one obtained if there is no difference in reality in the population?

13.2 Theoretical considerations

The basic theoretical assumption underlying the use of the *t*-test involves the characteristics of the null hypothesis. We explained null hypotheses in Chapter 10. The following explanation uses the same format for null hypotheses as we used in that chapter.

Null hypotheses are statements that there is no relationship between two variables. The two variables in question at the moment are the independent and dependent variables. *This is another way of saying that there is no difference between the means of the two groups (i.e. columns) of scores.* The simplest null hypotheses for the above three studies are:

1. There is no relationship between sexual activity and the number of erotic dreams that women have.

2. Managerial experience is not related to speed of complex decision making.

3. The disciplinary style of a school is not related to the amount of bullying.

The alternative hypotheses to these null hypotheses can be obtained by simply deleting *no* or *not* from each of the above. Notice that the above way of writing the null hypothesis is relatively streamlined compared with what you often read in books and journals. So do not be surprised if you come across null hypotheses expressed in much more clumsy language such as:

4. Women who abstain from sex will have the same number of erotic dreams as women who are sexually active.

5. Erotic dreams do not occur at different frequencies in sexually active and sexually inactive women.

Styles 4 and 5 tend to obscure the fact that null hypotheses are fundamentally similar irrespective of the type of research under consideration.

The erotic dreams experiment will be used to illustrate the theoretical issues. There are two different samples of scores defined by the independent variable – one for the sexually abstinent group and the other for the sexually active group. The scores in Table 13.4 are the numbers of sexual dreams that each woman

Table 13.4 **Possible data from the sexual activity and erotic dreams experiment (dreams per seven days)**

Subject	Sexually abstinent condition	Subject	Sexually active condition
Lindsay	6	Janice	2
Claudine	7	Jennifer	5
Sharon	7	Joanne	4
Natalie	8	Anne-Marie	5
Sarah	9	Helen	6
Wendy	10	Amanda	6
Ruth	8	Sophie	5
Angela	9		

Table 13.5 **Imaginary population of scores for erotic dreams study**

Experimental group: sexually abstinent	Control group: sexually active
8	6
7	8
6	7
7	4
5	6
5	9
2	10
3	6
6	4
7	7
7	9
9	8
8	7
7	5
4	2
6	3
10	6
9	7
7	8
5	7
4	6
6	7
7	5
8	5
6	7

in the study has in a seven-day period. We can see that, on average, the sexually active women have fewer erotic dreams. Does this reflect a generalisable (significant) difference? The data might be as in Table 13.4. Apart from suggesting that Wendy's fantasy life is wonderful, the table indicates that sexual abstinence leads to an increase in erotic dreams.

The *null hypothesis* suggests that the scores in the two samples come from the same population since it claims that there is no relationship between the independent and dependent variables. That is, for all intents and purposes, the two samples can be construed as coming from a single population of scores; there is no difference between them due to the independent variable. Any differences between samples drawn from this null-hypothesis-defined population are due to chance factors rather than a true relationship between the independent and dependent variables. Table 13.5 is an imaginary population of scores from this null-hypothesis-defined population on the dependent variable 'number of erotic dreams'. The table also indicates whether the score is that of a sexually abstinent woman or a sexually active one. If the two columns of scores are examined carefully, there are no differences between the two sets of scores. In other words, they have the same average scores. Statistically, all of the scores in Table 13.5 can be regarded as coming from the same population. There is no relationship between sexual activity and the number of erotic dreams.

Given that the two samples (sexually abstinent and sexually active) come from the same population of scores on erotic dreams, in general we would expect no difference between pairs of samples drawn at random from this single population. Of course, sampling always introduces a chance element so some pairs of samples would be different but mostly the differences will cluster around zero.

Table 13.6 **Random samples of scores from population in Table 13.5 to represent experimental and control conditions**

Experimental group: sexually abstinent	Control group: sexually active
4	5
5	5
10	10
7	9
7	7
5	7
7	8
9	6
9	2
8	
$\overline{X}_1 = 7.100$	$\overline{X}_2 = 6.556$

Table 13.7 **Forty pairs of random samples from the population in Table 13.5**

Experimental group: sexually abstinent $N = 10$	Control group: sexually active $N = 9$	Difference (column 1 – column 2)
6.100	6.444	–0.344
6.300	5.444	0.856
6.000	6.556	–0.556
6.400	6.778	–0.378
6.600	6.111	0.489
5.700	6.111	–0.411
6.700	6.111	0.589
6.300	5.667	0.633
6.400	6.667	–0.267
5.900	5.778	0.122
6.400	6.556	–0.156
6.360	6.444	–0.084
6.400	6.778	–0.378
6.200	6.222	–0.022
5.600	5.889	–0.289
6.100	6.222	–0.122
6.800	6.667	0.133
6.100	6.222	–0.122
6.900	6.000	0.900
7.200	5.889	1.311
5.800	7.333	–1.533
6.700	6.889	–0.189
6.200	6.000	0.200
6.500	6.444	0.056
5.900	6.444	–0.544
6.000	6.333	–0.333
6.300	6.778	–0.478
6.100	5.778	0.322
6.000	6.000	0.000
6.000	6.667	–0.667
6.556	6.778	–0.222
6.700	5.778	0.922
5.600	7.000	–1.400
6.600	6.222	0.378
5.600	6.667	–1.067
5.900	7.222	–1.322
6.000	6.667	–0.667
7.000	6.556	0.444
6.400	6.556	–0.156
6.900	6.222	0.678

Overall, numerous pairs of samples will yield an *average* difference of zero. We are assuming that we consistently subtract the sexually active mean from the sexually abstinent mean (or vice versa – it does not matter so long as we always do the same thing) so that positive and negative differences cancel each other out.

Since in this case we know the population of scores under the null hypothesis, we could pick out samples of 10 scores at random from the population to represent the sexually abstinent sample and, say, nine scores from the population to represent the sexually active sample. (Obviously the sample sizes will vary and they do not have to be equal.) Any convenient randomisation procedure could be used to select the samples (e.g. computer generated, random number tables or numbers drawn from a hat). The two samples selected at random, together with their respective means, are listed in Table 13.6.

Examining Table 13.6, we can clearly see that there is a difference between the two sample means. This difference is $7.100 - 6.556 = 0.544$. This difference between the two sample means has been obtained despite the fact that we know that there is no relationship between the independent variable and the dependent variable in the null-hypothesis-defined population. This is the nature of the random sampling process.

We can repeat this experiment by drawing more pairs of samples of these sizes from the null-hypothesis-defined population. This is shown for 40 new pairs of variables in Table 13.7.

Many of the differences between the pairs of means in Table 13.7 are very close to zero. This is just as we would expect since the independent and dependent variables are not related. Nevertheless, the means of some pairs of samples are somewhat different. In Table 13.7, 95% of the differences between the two means come in the range 0.922 to –1.400. (Given the small number of samples we have used, it is not surprising that this range is not symmetrical. If we had taken large numbers of samples, we would have expected more symmetry. Furthermore, had we used normally distributed scores, the symmetry may have been better.) The middle 95% of the distribution of differences between pairs of sample means are held clearly to support the null hypothesis. The extreme 5% beyond this middle range are held more likely to support the alternative hypothesis.

The standard deviation of the 40 'difference' scores gives the standard error of the differences. Don't forget we are dealing with *sample* means so the term standard error is the correct one. The value of the standard error is 0.63. This is the 'average' amount by which the differences between sample means is likely to deviate from the population mean difference of zero.

13.3 Standard deviation and standard error

The trouble with all of the above is that it is abstract theory. Normally we know nothing for certain about the populations from which our samples come. Fortunately, quite a lot can be inferred about the population given the null hypothesis and information from the samples:

1. Since the null hypothesis states that there is no relationship between the independent and dependent variables in the population, it follows that there should be no systematic difference between the scores in the pair of samples. That is, the average difference between the two means should be zero over many pairs of samples.

2. We can use the scores in a sample to estimate the standard deviation of the scores in the population. However, if we use our usual standard deviation formula the estimate tends to be somewhat too low. Consequently we have to modify our standard deviation formula (Chapter 5) when estimating the standard deviation of the population. The change is minimal – the N in the bottom half of the formula is changed to $N - 1$:

$$\text{Estimated standard deviation} = \sqrt{\frac{\Sigma X^2 - \frac{(\Sigma X)^2}{N}}{N - 1}}$$

The net effect of this adjustment is to increase the estimated standard deviation in the population – the amount of adjustment is greatest if we are working with small sample sizes for which subtracting 1 is a big adjustment.

But this only gives us the estimated standard deviation of the *scores* in the population. We really need to know about the standard deviation (i.e. standard error) of sample means taken from that population. Remember, there is a simple formula which converts the estimated standard deviation of the population to the estimated standard error of sample means drawn from that population: we simply divide the estimated standard deviation by the square root of the sample size. It so happens that the computationally most useful way of working out the standard error is as follows:

$$\text{Standard error} = \frac{\sqrt{\frac{\Sigma X^2 - \frac{(\Sigma X)^2}{N}}{N - 1}}}{\sqrt{N}}$$

Still we have not finished because this is the estimated standard error of *sample means*; we want the estimated standard error of *differences between pairs of sample means*. It makes intuitive sense that the standard error of differences between pairs of sample means is likely to be the sum of the standard errors of the two samples. After all, the standard error is merely the average amount by which a sample mean differs from the population mean of zero. So the standard error of the differences between pairs of sample means drawn from a population should be the two separate standard errors combined.

Well, that is virtually the procedure. However, the two different standard errors are added together in a funny sort of way:

$$se_{\text{[of differences between sample means]}} = \sqrt{(se_1^2 + se_2^2)}$$

Finally, because the sample sizes used to estimate the two individual standard errors are not always the same, it is necessary to adjust the equation to account for this, otherwise you end up with the wrong answer. The computational formula for the estimated standard error of differences between pairs of sample means is as follows:

Standard error of differences between pairs of sample means

$$= \sqrt{\left(\frac{\left(\Sigma X_1^2 - \frac{(\Sigma X_1)^2}{N_1} \right) + \left(\Sigma X_2^2 - \frac{(\Sigma X_2)^2}{N_2} \right)}{N_1 + N_2 - 2} \right) \left(\frac{1}{N_1} + \frac{1}{N_2} \right)}$$

Although this looks appallingly complicated, the basic idea is fairly simple. It looks complex because of the adjustment for different sample sizes.

Now we simply use the *t*-test formula. The average difference between the pairs of sample means is zero assuming the null hypothesis to be true. The *t* formula is:

$$t = \frac{\text{Sample 1 mean} - \text{Sample 2 mean} - 0}{\text{Standard error of differences between sample means}}$$

or

$$t = \frac{\text{Difference between the two sample means} - 0}{\text{Standard error of differences between sample means}}$$

Since in the above formula the population mean of difference between pairs of sample means is always zero, we can omit it:

$$t = \frac{\text{Sample 1 mean} - \text{Sample 2 mean}}{\text{Standard error of differences between sample means}}$$

The formula expressed in full looks very complicated:

$$t = \frac{\overline{X}_1 - \overline{X}_2}{\sqrt{\left(\frac{\left(\Sigma X_1^2 - \frac{(\Sigma X_1)^2}{N_1} \right) + \left(\Sigma X_2^2 - \frac{(\Sigma X_2)^2}{N_2} \right)}{N_1 + N_2 - 2} \right) \left(\frac{1}{N_1} + \frac{1}{N_2} \right)}}$$

So *t* is the number of standard errors by which the difference between our two sample means differs from the population mean of zero. The distribution of *t* is rather like the distribution of *z* if you have a large sample – thus it approximates very closely the normal distribution. However, with smaller sample sizes the curve of *t* becomes increasingly flatter and more spread out than the normal curve. Consequently we need different *t*-distributions for different sample sizes.

Significance Table 13.1 gives values for the *t*-distributions. Notice that the distribution is dependent on the degrees of freedom which for this *t*-test is the total number of scores in the two samples combined minus 2.

Significance Table 13.1   **5% significance values of unrelated *t* (two-tailed test)**

Your value must be in the listed ranges for your degrees of freedom to be significant at the 5% level (i.e. to accept the hypothesis).

If your required degrees of freedom are not listed, then take the nearest *smaller* listed values. Appendix E gives a fuller and conventional version of this table. Refer to this if you need a precise value of *t*.

'More extreme' means that, for example, values in the ranges of +3.18 to infinity or –3.18 to (minus) infinity are statistically significant with 3 degrees of freedom.

Degrees of freedom (always $N - 2$ for unrelated *t*-test)	Significant at 5% level Accept hypothesis
3	±3.18 or more extreme
4	±2.78 or more extreme
5	±2.57 or more extreme
6	±2.45 or more extreme
7	±2.37 or more extreme
8	±2.31 or more extreme
9	±2.26 or more extreme
10	±2.23 or more extreme
11	±2.20 or more extreme
12	±2.18 or more extreme
13	±2.16 or more extreme
14	±2.15 or more extreme
15	±2.13 or more extreme
18	±2.10 or more extreme
20	±2.09 or more extreme
25	±2.06 or more extreme
30	±2.04 or more extreme
40	±2.02 or more extreme
60	±2.00 or more extreme
100	±1.98 or more extreme
∞	±1.96 or more extreme

Calculation 13.1

The unrelated (uncorrelated) *t*-test

The calculation of the unrelated *t*-test uses the following formula:

$$t = \frac{\overline{X}_1 - \overline{X}_2}{\sqrt{\left(\frac{\left(\Sigma X_1^2 - \frac{(\Sigma X_1)^2}{N_1}\right) + \left(\Sigma X_2^2 - \frac{(\Sigma X_2)^2}{N_2}\right)}{N_1 + N_2 - 2}\right)\left(\frac{1}{N_1} + \frac{1}{N_2}\right)}}$$

Horrific, isn't it? Probably the worst formula that you are likely to use in psychological statistics. However, it contains little new. It is probably best to break the formula down into its component calculations and take things step-by-step. However, if you prefer to try to work directly with the above formula do not let us stand in your way.

The data are from an imaginary study involving the emotionality of children from lone-parent and children from two-parent families. The independent variable is family type which has two levels – the lone-parent type and the two-parent type. The dependent variable is emotionality on a standard psychological measure – the higher the score on this test, the more emotional is the child. The data are listed in Table 13.8.

Table 13.8 **Emotionality scores in two-parent and lone-parent families**

Two-parent family X_1	**Lone-parent family** X_2
12	6
18	9
14	4
10	13
19	14
8	9
15	8
11	12
10	11
13	9
15	
16	

A key thing to note is that we have called the scores for the two-parent family condition X_1 and those for the lone-parent family condition X_2.

Step 1 Extend the data table by adding columns of squared scores, column totals, and sample sizes as in Table 13.9. The sample size for $X_1 = N_1 = 12$; the sample size for $X_2 = N_2 = 10$.

ΣX_1 = sum of scores for two-parent family sample
ΣX_1^2 = sum of squared scores for two-parent family sample
ΣX_2 = sum of scores for lone-parent family sample
ΣX_2^2 = sum of squared scores for lone-parent family sample

Table 13.9 Table 13.8 extended to include steps in the calculation

Two-parent family X_1	Square previous column X_1^2	Lone-parent family X_2	Square previous column X_2^2
12	144	6	36
18	324	9	81
14	196	4	16
10	100	13	169
19	361	14	196
8	64	9	81
15	225	8	64
11	121	12	144
10	100	11	121
13	169	9	81
15	225		
16	256		
$\Sigma X_1 = 161$	$\Sigma X_1^2 = 2285$	$\Sigma X_2 = 95$	$\Sigma X_2^2 = 989$

Step 2 Do each of the following calculations.

Calculation A:

$$A = \frac{\Sigma X_1}{N_1} - \frac{\Sigma X_2}{N_2}$$

$$= \frac{161}{12} - \frac{95}{10}$$

$$= 13.417 - 9.500$$

$$= 3.917$$

Calculation B:

$$B = \Sigma X_1^2 - \frac{(\Sigma X_1)^2}{N_1}$$

$$= 2285 - \frac{161^2}{12}$$

$$= 2285 - \frac{25,921}{12}$$

$$= 2285 - 2160.0833$$

$$= 124.9167$$

Calculation C:

$$C = \Sigma X_2^{\,2} - \frac{(\Sigma X_2)^2}{N_2}$$

$$= 989 - \frac{95^2}{10}$$

$$= 989 - \frac{9025}{10}$$

$$= 989 - 902.5$$

$$= 86.5$$

Calculation D:

$$D = N_1 + N_2 - 2$$

$$= 12 + 10 - 2$$

$$= 20$$

Calculation E:

$$E = \frac{1}{N_1} + \frac{1}{N_2}$$

$$= \frac{1}{12} + \frac{1}{10}$$

$$= 0.0833 + 0.1000$$

$$= 0.1833$$

Calculation F:

$$F = \left(\frac{B+C}{D}\right) \times E$$

$$= \left(\frac{124.9167 + 86.5000}{20}\right) \times 0.1833$$

$$= \left(\frac{211.4167}{20}\right) \times 0.1833$$

$$= 10.57083 \times 0.1833$$

$$= 1.938$$

Calculation G:

$$G = \sqrt{F}$$
$$= \sqrt{1.938}$$
$$= 1.392$$

Calculation t:

$$t = \frac{A}{G}$$
$$= \frac{3.917}{1.392}$$
$$= 2.81$$

Step 3 t is the t-score or the number of standard errors our sample data are away from the population mean of zero. We use Significance Table 13.1 to check the statistical significance of our value of 2.81 by checking against the row for degrees of freedom (i.e. $N_1 + N_2 - 2 = 20$ degrees of freedom). This table tells us that our value of t is in the extreme 5% of the distribution because it is larger than 2.09; so we reject the null hypothesis that family structure is unrelated to emotionality. Our study showed that emotionality is significantly greater in the two-parent family structure as opposed to the lone-parent family structure.

Interpreting the results Remember to check carefully the mean scores for both groups in order to know which of the two groups has the higher scores on the dependent variable. In our example, this shows that the greater emotionality was found in the children from the two-parent families. The significant value of the t-test means that we are reasonably safe to conclude that the two groups do differ in terms of their emotionality.

Reporting the results The statistical analysis could be reported in the following style: 'It was found that emotionality was significantly higher ($t = 2.81$, df $= 20$, $p < 0.05$) in the two-parent families ($\overline{X} = 13.42$) than in the lone-parent families ($\overline{X} = 9.50$).'

The material in the final brackets simply reports the significance test used (the t-test), its value (2.81), the degrees of freedom (df $= 20$) and that the value of t is statistically significant ($p < 0.05$). Chapter 16 explains the approach in greater detail.

13.4 Cautionary note

You should not use the t-test if your samples are markedly skewed, especially if they are skewed in opposite directions. Appendix A explains how to test for skewness. You might consider using the Mann–Whitney U-test in these circumstances (Chapter 18, Calculation 18.3).

13.5
Notes and recommendations

■ The *t*-test is commonly used in psychological research, so it is important that you have an idea of what it does. However, it is only a special case of the analysis of variance (Chapter 20) which is a much more flexible statistic. Given the analysis of variance's ability to handle any number of samples, you might prefer to use it instead of the *t*-test in most circumstances. To complicate matters, some use the *t*-test in the analysis of variance.

■ The *t*-test assumes that the variances of the two samples are similar so that they can be combined to yield an overall estimate. However, if the variances of the two samples are significantly different from each other, you should not use this version of the *t*-test. The way to see if two variances are dissimilar is to use the variance ratio test described in Chapter 18.

■ If you wish to use the *t*-test but find that you fall foul of this *F*-ratio requirement, there is a version of the *t*-test which does not assume equal variances. The best way of doing such *t*-tests is to use a computer package which applies both tests to the same data. Unfortunately the calculation for the degrees of freedom is a little complex (you can have fractions involved in the values) and it goes a little beyond reasonable hand calculations. The calculation details are provided in Blalock (1972).

Chapter 14

Chi-square

Differences between samples of frequency data

Preparation

Crosstabulation/contingency tables; samples and populations.

Often, chi-square is written as χ^2. However, we have avoided Greek letters as far as possible.

14.1 Introduction

If a researcher has several samples of data which involve *frequencies* rather than scores, a statistical test designed for frequency data must be used. The following are some examples of research of this sort:

1. Male and female schoolchildren are compared in terms of wanting to be psychologists when they leave school (Table 14.1).

2. The sexual orientations of a sample of religious men are compared with those of a non-religious sample (Table 14.2).

Table 14.1 **Relationship between sex and wanting to be a psychologist**

Intention	Male	Female
Wants to be a psychologist	$f = 17$	$f = 98$
Does not want to be a psychologist	$f = 67$	$f = 35$

Table 14.2 Relationship between sexual orientation and religion

Orientation	Religious	Non-religious
Heterosexual	57	105
Gay	13	27
Bisexual	8	17

Table 14.3 Relationship between doll choice and ethnicity

Choice	Black child	White child	Mixed-race child
Black doll	19	17	5
White doll	16	18	9

Table 14.4 Stylised table for chi-square

Category	Sample 1	Sample 2	Sample 3
Category 1	27	21	5
Category 2	19	20	19
Category 3	9	17	65

3. Choosing to play with either a black or a white doll in black and white children (Table 14.3).

In each of these examples, both variables consist of a relatively small number of categories. In other words, schematically each study approximates to the form shown in Table 14.4 in which the independent variable is the sample and the dependent variable consists of one of several categories.

The precise number of samples may vary from study to study and the number of categories of the dependent variable can be two or more. As a rule of thumb, *it is better to have just a few samples and a few categories*, since large tables can be difficult to interpret and generally require large numbers of participants or cases to be workable.

The 'cells' of Table 14.4 (called a *crosstabulation* or *contingency* table) contain the frequencies of individuals in that particular sample and that particular category. So the 'cell' which corresponds to sample 2 and category 3 contains the frequency 17. This means that in your data there are 17 cases in sample 2 which also fit category 3. In other words, a cell is the intersection of a row and a column.

The statistical question is whether the distribution of frequencies in the different samples is so varied that it is unlikely that these all come from the same population. As ever, this population is the one defined by the null hypothesis (which suggests that there is no relationship between the independent and dependent variables).

14.2 Theoretical issues

Imagine a research study in which children are asked to choose between two television programmes, one violent and the other non-violent. Some of the children have been in trouble at school for fighting and the others have not been in trouble. The researcher wants to know if there is a relationship between the violence of the preferred television programme and having been in trouble for fighting at school. The data might look something like Table 14.5.

We can see from Table 14.5 that the fighters (sample 1) are more likely to prefer the violent programme and the non-fighters (sample 2) are more likely to prefer the non-violent programme. The frequencies obtained in the research are known as the *observed* frequencies. This merely refers to the fact that we obtain them from our empirical *observations* (that is, the data).

Assume that both of the samples come from the same population of data in which there is no relationship between the dependent and independent variables. This implies that any differences between the samples are merely due to the chance fluctuations of sampling. A useful index of how much the samples differ from each other is based on how different each sample is from the population distribution defined by the null hypothesis. As ever, since we do not know the population directly in most research, we have to estimate its characteristics from the characteristics of samples.

With the chi-square test, we simply *add* together the frequencies for whatever number of samples we have. These sums are then used as an estimate of the distribution of the different categories in the population. Since differences between the samples under the null hypothesis are solely due to chance factors, by combining samples the best possible estimate of the characteristics of the population is obtained. In other words, we simply add together the characteristics of two or more samples to give us an estimate of the population distribution of the categories. The first stage of doing this is illustrated in Table 14.6.

Table 14.5 **Relationship between preferred TV programme and fighting**

Preference	Sample 1 Fighters	Sample 2 Non-fighters
Violent TV preferred	40	15
Non-violent TV preferred	30	70

Table 14.6 **Relationship between preferred TV programme and fighting including the marginal frequencies (column and row frequencies)**

Preference	Sample 1 Fighters	Sample 2 Non-fighters	Row frequencies
Violent TV preferred	40	15	55
Non-violent TV preferred	30	70	100
Column frequencies	70	85	Overall frequencies = 155

So in the null-hypothesis-defined population, we would expect 55 out of every 155 to prefer the violent programme and 100 out of 155 to prefer the non-violent programme. But we obtained 40 out of 70 preferring the violent programme in Sample 1, and 15 out of 85 preferring the violent programme in Sample 2. How do these figures match the expectations from the population defined by the null hypothesis? We need to calculate the expected frequencies of the cells in Table 14.6. This calculation is based on the assumption that the null hypothesis population frequencies are our best information as to the relative proportions preferring the violent and non-violent programmes if there truly was no difference between the samples.

Sample 1 contains 70 children; if the null hypothesis is true then we would expect 55 out of every 155 of these to prefer the violent programme. Thus our expected frequency of those preferring the violent programme in Sample 1 is:

$$70 \times \frac{55}{155} = 70 \times 0.354$$
$$= 24.84$$

Similarly, since we expect under the null hypothesis 100 out of every 155 to prefer the non-violent programme, then our expected frequency of those preferring the non-violent programme in sample 1 out of the 70 children in that sample is

$$70 \times \frac{100}{155} = 70 \times 0.645$$
$$= 45.16$$

Notice that the sum of the expected frequencies for sample 1 is the same as the number of children in that sample (24.84 + 45.16 = 70).

We can apply the same logic to sample 2 which contains 85 children. We expect that 55 out of every 155 will prefer the violent programme and 100 out of every 155 will prefer the non-violent programme. The expected frequency preferring the violent programme in sample 2 is:

$$85 \times \frac{55}{155} = 85 \times 0.354$$
$$= 30.16$$

Table 14.7 **Contingency table including both observed and expected frequencies**

Preference	Sample 1 Fighters	Sample 2 Non-fighters	Row frequencies
Violent TV preferred	Observed frequency = 40 *Expected frequency = 24.84*	Observed frequency = 15 *Expected frequency = 30.16*	55
Non-violent TV preferred	Observed frequency = 30 *Expected frequency = 45.16*	Observed frequency = 70 *Expected frequency = 54.84*	100
Column frequencies (i.e. sum of observed frequencies in column)	70	85	Overall frequencies = 155

The expected frequency preferring the non-violent programme in sample 2 is:

$$85 \times \frac{100}{155} = 85 \times 0.645$$
$$= 54.84$$

We can enter these expected frequencies (population frequencies under the null hypothesis) into our table of frequencies (Table 14.7).

The chi-square statistic is based on the differences between the observed and the expected frequencies. It should be fairly obvious that the greater the disparity between the observed frequencies and the population frequencies under the null hypothesis, the less likely is the null hypothesis to be true. Thus if the samples are very different from each other, the differences between the observed and expected frequencies will be large. Chi-square involves calculating the overall disparity between the observed and expected frequencies over all the cells in the table. To be precise, the chi-square formula involves the squared deviations over the expected frequencies, but this is merely a slight diversion to make our formula fit a convenient statistical distribution which is called chi-square. The calculated value of chi-square is then compared with a table of critical values of chi-square (Significance Table 14.1) in order to estimate the probability of obtaining our pattern of frequencies by chance (if the null hypothesis of no differences between the samples was true). This table is organised according to degrees of freedom, which is always (number of columns of data − 1) × (number of rows of data − 1). This would be (2 − 1) × (2 − 1) or 1 for Table 14.7.

Significance Table 14.1   **5% and 1% significance values of chi-square (two-tailed test)**

Your value must be in the listed ranges for your degrees of freedom to be significant at the 5% level (column 2) or the 1% level (column 3) (i.e. to accept the hypothesis).

Should you require more precise values than those listed below, these are to be found in the table in Appendix F.

Degrees of freedom	Significant at 5% level Accept hypothesis	Significant at 1% level Accept hypothesis
1	3.8 or more	6.7 or more
2	6.0 or more	9.2 or more
3	7.8 or more	11.3 or more
4	9.5 or more	13.3 or more
5	11.1 or more	15.1 or more
6	12.6 or more	16.8 or more
7	14.1 or more	18.5 or more
8	15.5 or more	20.1 or more
9	16.9 or more	21.7 or more
10	18.3 or more	23.2 or more
11	19.7 or more	24.7 or more
12	21.0 or more	26.2 or more

Calculation 14.1

Chi-square

The calculation of chi-square involves several relatively simple but repetitive calculations. For each cell in the chi-square table you calculate the following:

$$\frac{(\text{Observed frequency} - \text{Expected frequency})^2}{\text{Expected frequency}}$$

The only complication is that this small calculation is repeated for each of the cells in your crosstabulation or contingency table. The formula in full becomes:

$$\text{Chi-square} = \Sigma \frac{(O - E)^2}{E}$$

where O = observed frequency and E = expected frequency.

The following is an imaginary piece of research in which teenage boys and girls were asked to name their favourite type of television programme from a list of three: (1) soap operas, (2) crime dramas, and (3) neither of these. The researcher suspects that sex may be related to programme preference (Table 14.8).

Table 14.8 **Relationship between favourite type of TV programme and sex of respondent**

Respondents	Soap opera	Crime drama	Neither	Totals
Males	Observed = 27	Observed = 14	Observed = 19	Row 1 = 60
Females	Observed = 17	Observed = 33	Observed = 9	Row 2 = 59
Total	Column 1 = 44	Column 2 = 47	Column 3 = 28	Total = 119

We next need to calculate the expected frequencies for each of the cells in Table 14.8. One easy way of doing this is to multiply the row total and the column total for each particular cell and divide by the total number of observations (i.e. total frequencies). This is shown in Table 14.9.

Table 14.9 **Calculation of expected frequencies by multiplying appropriate row and column totals and then dividing by overall total**

Respondents	Soap opera	Crime drama	Neither	Total
Males	Observed = 27 *Expected = 60 ×* *44/119 = 22.185*	Observed = 14 *Expected = 60 ×* *47/119 = 23.697*	Observed = 19 *Expected = 60 ×* *28/119 = 14.118*	Row 1 = 60
Females	Observed = 17 *Expected = 59 ×* *44/119 = 21.815*	Observed = 33 *Expected = 59 ×* *47/119 = 23.303*	Observed = 9 *Expected = 59 ×* *28/119 = 13.882*	Row 2 = 59
Total	Column 1 = 44	Column 2 = 47	Column 3 = 28	Total = 119

We then simply substitute the above values in the chi-square formula:

$$\text{Chi-square} = \Sigma \frac{(O - E)^2}{E}$$

$$= \frac{(27 - 22.185)^2}{22.185} + \frac{(14 - 23.697)^2}{23.697} + \frac{(19 - 14.118)^2}{14.118} + \frac{(17 - 21.815)^2}{21.815} + \frac{(33 - 23.303)^2}{23.303} + \frac{(9 - 13.882)^2}{13.882}$$

$$= \frac{4.815^2}{22.185} + \frac{(-9.697)^2}{23.697} + \frac{4.882^2}{14.118} + \frac{(-4.815)^2}{21.815} + \frac{9.697^2}{23.303} + \frac{(-4.882)^2}{13.882}$$

$$= \frac{23.184}{22.185} + \frac{94.032}{23.697} + \frac{23.834}{14.118} + \frac{23.184}{21.815} + \frac{94.032}{23.303} + \frac{23.834}{13.882}$$

$$= 1.045 + 3.968 + 1.688 + 1.063 + 4.035 + 1.717$$

$$= 13.52$$

The degrees of freedom are (the number of columns – 1) × (the number of rows – 1) = (3 – 1) × (2 – 1) = 2 degrees of freedom.

We then check the table of the critical values of chi-square (Significance Table 14.1) in order to assess whether or not our samples differ amongst each other so much that they are unlikely to be produced by the population defined by the null hypothesis. The value must equal or exceed the tabulated value to be significant at the listed level of significance. Some tables will give you more degrees of freedom but you will be hard pressed to do a sensible chi-square that exceeds 12 degrees of freedom.

Interpreting the results Our value of chi-square is well in excess of the minimum value of 6.0 needed to be significant at the 5% level for 2 degrees of freedom, so we reject the hypothesis that the samples came from the population defined by the null hypothesis. Thus we accept the hypothesis that there is a relationship between television programme preferences and sex.

Only if you have a 2 × 2 chi-square is it possible to interpret the significance level of the chi-square directly in terms of the trends revealed in the data table. As we will see in Section 14.3, if we have a bigger chi-square than this (say 3 × 2 or 3 × 3) then a significant value of chi-square merely indicates that the samples are dissimilar to each other overall without stipulating which samples are different from each other.

Because the sample sizes generally differ in contingency tables, it is helpful to convert the frequencies in each cell to percentages of the relevant sample size at this stage. It is important though never to actually calculate chi-square itself on these percentages as you will obtain the wrong significance level if you do. It seems from Table 14.10 that males prefer soap operas more often than females do, females have a preference for crime drama, and males are more likely than females to say that they prefer another type of programme. Unfortunately, as things stand we are not able to say which of these trends are statistically significant unless we partition the chi-square as described in Section 14.3.

Reporting the results The results could be written up as follows: 'The value of chi-square was 13.52 which was significant at the 5% level with 2 degrees of freedom. Thus there is a sex difference in favourite type of TV programme. Compared with females, males were more likely to choose soap operas and less likely to choose crime dramas as their favourite programmes and more likely to prefer neither of these.'

However, as this table is bigger than a 2 × 2 table, it is advisable to partition the chi-squared as discussed in Section 14.3 in order to say which of these trends are statistically significant.

An alternative way of writing up the results is as follows: 'There was a significant gender difference in favourite type of TV programme (chi-square = 13.52, $df = 1$, $p < 0.05$). Compared with females, males were more likely to choose soap operas and less likely to choose crime dramas as their favourite programmes and more likely to prefer neither of these.' Chapter 16 explains how to report statistical significance in the shorter, professional way used in this version.

Table 14.10 Observed percentages in each sample based on the observed frequencies in Table 14.8

Respondents	Soap opera	Crime drama	Neither
Males	45.0	23.0	31.7
Females	28.8	55.9	15.3

14.3 Partitioning chi-square

There is no problem when the chi-square contingency table is just two columns and two rows. The chi-square in these circumstances tells you that your two samples are different from each other. But if you have, say, a 2 × 3 chi-square (e.g. you have two samples and three categories) then there is some uncertainty as to what a significant chi-square means – does it mean that all three samples are different from each other, that sample 1 and sample 2 are different, that sample 1 and sample 3 are different, or that sample 2 and sample 3 are different? In the television programmes example, although we obtained a significant overall chi-square, there is some doubt as to why we obtained this. The major differences between the sexes are between the soap opera and crime drama conditions rather than between the soap opera and the 'other' condition.

It is a perfectly respectable statistical procedure to break your large chi-square into a number of 2 × 2 chi-square tests to assess precisely where the significant differences lie. Thus in the TV programmes study you could generate *three* separate chi-squares from the 2 × 3 contingency table. These are illustrated in Table 14.11.

These three separate chi-squares each have just one degree of freedom (because they are 2 × 2 tables). If you calculate chi-square for each of these tables you hopefully should be able to decide precisely where the differences are between samples and conditions.

The only difficulty is the significance levels you use. Because you are doing three separate chi-squares, the normal significance level of 5% still operates but it is *divided between the three chi-squares* you have carried out. In other words we share the 5% between three to give us the 1.667% level for each – any of the three chi-squares would have to be significant at this level to be reported as being significant at the 5% level. Significance Table 14.2 gives the adjusted values of chi-square required to be significant at the 5% level (two-tailed test). Thus if you have three comparisons to make, the minimum value of chi-square that is significant is 5.73. The degrees of freedom for these comparisons will always be 1 as they are always based on 2 × 2 contingency tables.

14.4 Important warnings

Chi-square is rather less user-friendly than is warranted by its popularity among psychologists. The following are warning signs not to use chi-square or to take very great care:

Significance Table 14.2 **Chi-square 5% two-tailed significance values for 1–10 unplanned comparisons**

To use this table, simply look under the column for the number of separate comparisons you are making using chi-square. Your values of chi-square must equal or exceed the listed value to be significant at the 5% level with a two-tailed test.

Degree of freedom	Number of comparisons being made									
	1	2	3	4	5	6	7	8	9	10
1	3.84	5.02	5.73	6.24	6.64	6.96	7.24	7.48	7.69	7.88

Table 14.11 **Three partitioned sub-tables from the 2 × 3 contingency table (Table 14.8)**

(1) Soap Opera versus Crime Drama

Respondents	Soap opera	Crime drama	Totals
Males	27	14	Row 1 = 41
Females	17	33	Row 2 = 50
Totals	Column 1 = 44	Column 2 = 47	Total = 91

(2) Soap Opera versus Neither

Respondents	Soap opera	Neither	Totals
Males	27	19	Row 1 = 46
Females	17	9	Row 2 = 26
Totals	Column 1 = 44	Column 3 = 28	Total = 72

(3) Crime Drama versus Neither

Respondents	Crime drama	Neither	Totals
Males	14	19	Row 1 = 33
Females	33	9	Row 2 = 42
Totals	Column 2 = 47	Column 3 = 28	Total = 75

1. If the expected frequencies in any cell fall lower than 5 then chi-square becomes rather inaccurate. Some authors suggest that no more than one-fifth of values should be below 5 but this is a more generous criterion. Some computers automatically print an alternative to chi-square if this assumption is breached.

2. Never do chi-square on percentages or anything else other than frequencies.
3. Always check that your total of frequencies is equal to the number of participants in your research. Chi-square should not be applied where participants in the research are contributing more than one frequency each to the total of frequencies.

14.5 Alternatives to chi-square

The situation is only salvageable if your chi-square violates the expected cell frequencies rule – none should fall below 5. Even then you cannot always save the day. The alternatives are as follows:

1. If you have a 2 × 2 or a 2 × 3 chi-square table then you can use the Fisher Exact Probability Test which is not sensitive to small expected frequencies (see Calculation 14.2 below).
2. Apart from omitting very small samples or categories, sometimes you can save the day by combining samples and/or categories in order to avoid the small expected frequencies problem; by combining in this way you should increase the expected frequencies somewhat. So, for example, take the data set out in Table 14.12. It should be apparent that by combining two samples and/or two categories you are likely to increase the expected frequencies in the resulting chi-square table.

But you cannot simply combine categories or samples at a whim – the samples or categories have to be combined meaningfully. So if the research was on the relationship between the type of degree that students take and their hobbies, you might have the following categories and samples:

Category 1 – Socialising
Category 2 – Dancing
Category 3 – Stamp collecting
Sample 1 – English literature students
Sample 2 – Media studies students
Sample 3 – Physics students

Looking at these, it would seem reasonable to combine categories 1 and 2 and samples 1 and 2 since they seem to reflect rather similar things. No other combinations would seem appropriate. For example, it is hard to justify combining dancing and stamp collecting.

Table 14.12 **A 3 × 3 contingency table**

Sample	Category 1	Category 2	Category 3
Sample 1	10	6	14
Sample 2	3	12	4
Sample 3	4	2	5

Calculation 14.2

The Fisher Exact Probability Test

The Fisher Exact Probability Test is not usually presented in introductory statistics books. We will only give the calculation of a 2 × 2 Fisher Exact Probability Test although there is a version for 2 × 3 tables. The reason for its inclusion is that much student work for practicals and projects has very small sample sizes. As a consequence, the assumptions of the chi-square test are frequently broken. The Fisher Exact Probability Test is not subject to the same limitations as the chi-square and can be used when chi-square cannot. It is different from chi-square in that it calculates the exact probability rather than a critical value. Apart from that, a significant result is interpreted much as the equivalent chi-square would be, so we will not explain it further.

A number followed by ! is called a factorial. So 5! = 5 × 4 × 3 × 2 × 1 = 120. And 9! = 9 × 8 × 7 × 6 × 5 × 4 × 3 × 2 × 1 = 362,880. Easy enough but it can lead to rather big numbers which make the calculation awkward to handle. Table 14.13 list factorials up to 15.

The Fisher Exact Probability Test is applied to a 2 × 2 contingency table by extending the table to include the marginal row and column totals of frequencies as well as the overall total (see Table 14.14).

Table 14.13 **Factorials of numbers from 0 to 15**

Number	Factorial
0	1
1	1
2	2
3	6
4	24
5	120
6	720
7	5,040
8	40,320
9	362,880
10	3,628,800
11	39,916,800
12	479,001,600
13	6,227,020,800
14	87,178,291,200
15	1,307,674,368,000

Table 14.14 **Symbols for the Fisher exact probability**

	Column 1	Column 2	Row totals
Row 1	a	b	$W (= a + b)$
Row 2	c	d	$X (= c + d)$
Column totals	$Y (= a + c)$	$Z (= b + d)$	Overall total $= N$

The formula for the exact probability is as follows:

$$\text{Exact probability} = \frac{W!\ X!\ Y!\ Z!}{N!\ a!\ b!\ c!\ d!}$$

Imagine you have collected data on a small group of exceptionally gifted children. You find that some have 'photographic' memories and others do not. You wish to know if there is a relationship between sex of subject and having a photographic memory (Table 14.15).

Table 14.15 **Steps in calculating the Fisher exact probability**

Respondents	Photographic memory	No photographic memory	Row totals
Males	$a = 2$	$b = 7$	$W (= a + b) =$ 9
Females	$c = 4$	$d = 1$	$X (= c + d) =$ 5
Column totals	$Y (= a + c) = 6$	$Z (= b + d) = 8$	Overall total = 14

Substituting in the formula gives:

$$\text{Exact probability} = \frac{9!\ 5!\ 6!\ 8!}{14!\ 2!\ 7!\ 4!\ 1!}$$

The values of each of these factorials can be obtained from Table 14.13:

$$\text{Exact probability} = \frac{362{,}880 \times 120 \times 720 \times 40{,}320}{87{,}178{,}291{,}200 \times 2 \times 5040 \times 24 \times 1}$$

Unfortunately you will need a scientific calculator to do this calculation.

The alternative is to cancel wherever possible numbers in the upper part of the formula with those in the lower part:

$$\text{Exact probability} =$$

$$\frac{9 \times 8 \times 7 \times 6 \times 5 \times 4 \times 3 \times 2 \times 1 \times 5 \times 4 \times 3 \times 2 \times 1 \times 6 \times 5 \times 4 \times 3 \times 2 \times 1 \times 8 \times 7 \times 6 \times 5 \times 4 \times 3 \times 2 \times 1}{14 \times 13 \times 12 \times 11 \times 10 \times 9 \times 8 \times 7 \times 6 \times 5 \times 4 \times 3 \times 2 \times 1 \times 2 \times 1 \times 7 \times 6 \times 5 \times 4 \times 3 \times 2 \times 1 \times 4 \times 3 \times 2 \times 1 \times 1}$$

$$= \frac{5 \times 4 \times 3 \times 6 \times 5 \times 8}{14 \times 13 \times 12 \times 11 \times 10 \times 1}$$

$$= \frac{14,400}{240,240}$$

$$= 0.06$$

This is not our conventional two-tailed significance value. In order to approximate the conventional two-tailed significance value the significance level of 0.06 needs to be doubled to give the probability of 0.12.

Interpreting the results The two-tailed significance level is 0.12 which is not statistically significant at the 0.05 (or 5%) level. Thus we cannot reject the null hypothesis that the incidence of photographic memory is related to sex. It would be useful to convert the frequencies in Table 14.15 into percentages of the relevant sample size when interpreting these data as we have different numbers of males and females. Such a table would show that 80% of the females had photographic memories but only 22% of the males. Despite this, with such a small amount of data, the trend is not statistically significant.

Reporting the results The following would be an appropriate description: 'Although photographic memory was nearly four times more common in females than in males, this proved not to be statistically significant using the Fisher Exact Probability Test. The exact probability was 0.12 which is not significant at the 0.05 level. Thus we must reject the hypothesis that photographic memory is related to sex.'

   Alternatively we could write: 'Photographic memory was nearly four times more common in females than in males. However the difference was not statistically significant (Fisher, $p = 0.12$). Thus we must reject the hypothesis that photographic memory is related to sex.' This style of presenting statistical significance is explained in detail in Chapter 16.

Fisher Exact Probability Test for 2 × 3 tables

This is calculated in a very similar way as for the Fisher 2 × 2 test, the difference being simply the increased numbers of cells (Table 14.16). The formula for the 2 × 3 exact probability is as follows:

$$\text{Exact probability} = \frac{W! \ X! \ K! \ L! \ M!}{N! \ a! \ b! \ c! \ d! \ e! \ f!}$$

Remember to double the answer to give the two-tailed test value. The calculation should be easy enough although it can be even more cumbersome than for the 2 × 2 Fisher Exact Probability Test.

Table 14.16 **Stages in the calculation of a 2 × 3 Fisher Exact Probability Test**

	Column 1	Column 2	Column 3	Row totals
Row 1	a	b	c	W $(= a + b + c)$
Row 2	d	e	f	X $(= d + e + f)$
Column totals	$K (= a + d)$	$L (= b + e)$	$M (= c + f)$	Overall total $= N$

14.6 Chi-square and known populations

Sometimes but rarely in research we know the distribution in the population. If the population distribution of frequencies is known then it is possible to employ the 'single sample' chi-square. Usually the population frequencies are known as relative frequencies or percentages. So, for example, if you wished to know the likelihood of getting a sample of 40 university psychology students in which there are 30 female and 10 male students *if* you know that the population of psychology students is 90% female and 10% male, you simply use the latter proportions to calculate the expected frequencies of females and males in a sample of 40. If the sample were to reflect the population then 90% of the 40 should be female and 10% male. So the expected frequencies are 40 × 90/100 for females and 40 × 10/100 for males = 36 females and 4 males. These are then entered into the chi-square formula, but note that there are only two cells. The degrees of freedom for the one-sample chi-square is the number of cells minus 1 (i.e. $2 - 1 = 1$).

Calculation 14.3

The one-sample chi-square

The research question is whether a sample of 80 babies of a certain age in foster care show the same level of smiling to their carer as a population of babies of the same age assessed on a developmental test. On this developmental test 50% of babies at this age show clear evidence of the smiling response, 40% clearly show no evidence, and for 10% it is impossible to make a judgement. This is the population from which the foster babies are considered to be a sample. It is found that 35 clearly showed evidence of smiling, 40 showed no clear evidence of smiling and the remaining 5 were impossible to classify (Table 14.17).

We can use the population distribution to work out the expected frequency in the sample of 80 if this sample precisely matched the population. Thus 50% of the 80 (= 40) should be clear smilers, 40% of the 80 (= 32) should be clear non-smilers, and 10% of the 80 (= 8) should be impossible to classify. Table 14.16 gives the expected frequencies (i.e. population-based) and observed frequencies (i.e. sample-based).

These observed and expected frequencies are entered into the usual chi-square formula. The only difference is that the degrees of freedom are not quite the same – they are the number of conditions minus 1 (i.e. $3 - 1 = 2$ in the above example):

$$\text{Chi-square} = \Sigma \frac{(O - E)^2}{E}$$

$$= \frac{(35 - 40)^2}{40} + \frac{(40 - 32)^2}{32} + \frac{(5 - 8)^2}{8}$$

$$= \frac{(-5)^2}{40} + \frac{8^2}{32} + \frac{(-3)^2}{8}$$

$$= \frac{25}{40} + \frac{64}{32} + \frac{9}{8}$$

$$= 0.625 + 2.000 + 1.125$$

$$= 3.75$$

Table 14.17 **Data for a one-sample chi-square**

	Clear smilers	**Clear non-smilers**	**Impossible to classify**
Observed frequency	35	40	5
Expected frequency	40	32	8

But from Significance Table 14.1 we can see that this value of chi-square is far below the critical value of 6.0 required to be significant at the 5% level. Thus the sample of foster babies is not significantly different from the population of babies in terms of their smiling response.

Interpreting the results A significant value of the one-sample chi-square means that the distribution over the various categories departs markedly from that of the known population. That is, the sample is significantly different from the population and is unlikely to come from that population. In our example, however, the sample does not differ significantly from the population. This shows that smiling behaviour in our sample of babies is no different from that of the population of babies. For the one-sample chi-square, it is sufficient to compare the observed frequencies with the expected frequencies (which are the population values). In our example, there seems to be little difference between the sample and the population values.

Reporting the results The following would summarise the findings of this study effectively: 'It was possible to compare smiling behaviour in babies in foster care with population values of known smiling behaviour on a standard developmental test. A one-sample chi-square test yielded a chi-square value of 3.75 which was not statistically significant with 2 degrees of freedom. Thus it can be concluded that the fostered babies were no different in terms of smiling behaviour from the general population of babies of this age.'

Alternatively, one could write: 'It was found that smiling behaviour in babies in foster care was not different from population figures obtained from a standard developmental test (chi-square = 3.75, df = 2, p ns). Thus it can be concluded that the fostered babies were no different in terms of smiling behaviour from the general population of babies of this age.' This style of reporting statistical significance is discussed in greater detail in Chapter 16.

14.7 Chi-square for related samples – the McNemar Test

It is possible to use chi-square to compare *related* samples of frequencies. Essentially this involves arranging the data in such a way that the chi-square contingency table only includes two categories: those who change from the first to the second occasion. For example, data are collected on whether or not teenage students wish to go to university; following a careers talk favouring university education the same informants are asked again whether they wish to go to university. The data can be tabulated as in Table 14.18.

We can see from this table that although some students did not change their minds as a consequence of the talk (30 wanted to go to university before the talk and did not change their minds, 32 did not want to go to university before the talk and did not change their minds), some students did change. Fifty changed their minds and wanted to go to university following the talk and 10 changed their minds and did not want to go to university after the talk.

The McNemar Test simply uses the data on those who changed; non-changers are ignored. The logic of the test is that if the talk did not actually affect the teenagers, just as many would change their minds in one direction after the talk as change their minds in the other direction. That is, 50% should change towards wanting to go to university and 50% should change against wanting to go to university, *if the talk had no effect*. We simply create a new table (Table 14.19) which only includes changers and calculate chi-square on the basis that the null hypothesis of no effect would suggest that 50% of the changers should change in each direction.

Table 14.18 **Illustrative data for the McNemar Test**

	Before talk 'yes'	**Before talk 'no'**
After talk 'yes'	30	50
After talk 'no'	10	32

Table 14.19 **Table of those who changed in a positive or negative direction based on Table 14.18**

	Positive changers	Negative changers
Observed frequency	50	10
Expected frequency	30	30

The calculation is now exactly like that for the one-sample chi-square. This gives us a chi-square value of 26.67 with 1 degree of freedom (since there are two conditions). This is very significant when checked against the critical values in Significance Table 14.1. Thus there appears to be more change towards wanting to go to university following the careers talk than change towards not wanting to go to university.

Yates's correction

A slightly outmoded statistical procedure when the expected frequencies in chi-square are small is to apply Yates's correction. This is intended to make such data fit the theoretical chi-square distribution a little better. In essence all you do is to subtract 0.5 from each (observed frequency – expected frequency) in the chi-square formula prior to squaring that difference. With large expected frequencies this has virtually no effect. With small tables, it obviously reduces the size of chi-square and therefore its statistical significance. We have opted for not using it in our calculations. Really it is a matter of personal choice as far as convention goes.

Example from the literature

In a study of the selection of prison officers, Crighton and Towl (1994) found the relationship shown in Table 14.20 between the ethnicity of the candidate and whether or not they were selected during the recruitment process.

The interpretation of this table is that there is no significant relationship ($p =$ ns) between selection and ethnicity. In other words, the table does not provide evidence of a selection bias in favour of white applicants, for example. While this is not an unreasonable conclusion based on the data if we ignore the small numbers of ethnic minority applicants, the statistical analysis itself is not appropriate. In particular, if you calculate the expected frequencies for the four cells you will find that 50% of the expected frequencies are less than 5, thus a rule has been violated. The Fisher Exact Probability Test would be better for these data.

Table 14.20 **Relationship between ethnicity and selection**

	Selected	Not selected
Ethnic minority	1	3
Ethnic majority	17	45
Chi-square = 0.43; p = ns		

14.8 Notes and recommendations

- Avoid as far as possible designing research with a multiplicity of categories and samples for chi-square. Large chi-squares with many cells are often difficult to interpret without numerous sub-analyses.

- Always make sure that your chi-square is carried out on frequencies and that each participant contributes only one to the total frequencies.

- Check for expected frequencies under 5; if you have any then take one of the escape routes described above if possible.

Recommended further reading

Maxwell, A.E. (1961). *Analysing Qualitative Data*. London: Methuen.

Chapter 15

Probability

Preparation
General familiarity with previous chapters.

15.1 Introduction

From time to time, researchers need to be able to calculate the probabilities associated with certain patterns of events. One of us remembers that as a student in class we carried out an experiment based on newspaper reports of a Russian study in which people appeared to be able to recognise colours through their finger-tips. So we designed an experiment in which a blindfolded person felt different colours in random order. Most of us did not do very well but some in the class seemed excellent. The media somehow heard about the study and a particularly good identifier in our experiment quickly took part in a live TV demonstration of her skills. She was appallingly bad at the task this time.

The reason why she was bad on television was that she had no special skills in the first place. It had been merely a matter of chance that she had done well in the laboratory. On the television programme, chance was not on her side and she turned out to be as bad as the rest of us. Actually, this reflects a commonly referred to phenomenon called *regression to the mean*. Choose a person (or group) because of their especially high (or, alternatively, especially low) scores and they will tend to score closer to the mean on the next administration of the test or measurement. This is because the test or measure is to a degree unreliable and by choosing exceptional scores you have to an extent capitalised on chance factors. With a completely unreliable test or measure, the reversion towards the mean will be dramatic. In our colour experiment the student did badly on TV because she had been selected totally on the basis of a criterion that was fundamentally unreliable – that is completely at random.

Similar problems occur in any investigation of individual paranormal or psychic powers. For example, a spiritual medium who addresses a crowd of 500 people is doing nothing spectacular if in Britain she claims to be speaking to a dead relative of someone and that relative is Mary or Martha or Margaret. The chances of someone in the 500 having such a relative are very high.

15.2 The principles of probability

When any of us use a test of significance we are utilising probability theory. This is because most statistical tests are based on it. Our working knowledge of probability in most branches of psychology does not have to be very great for us to function well. We have been using probability in previous chapters on significance testing when we talked about the 5% level of significance, the 1% level of significance, and the 95% confidence intervals. Basically what we meant by a 5% level of significance is that a particular event (or outcome) would occur on five occasions out of 100. Although we have adopted the percentage system of reporting probabilities in this book, statisticians would normally not write of a 5% probability. Instead they would express it as being out of a *single* event rather than 100 events. Thus:

- 0.05 (or just .05) is an alternative way of writing 5%
- 0.10 (or .10) is an alternative way of writing 10%
- 1.00 is an alternative way of writing 100%.

The difficulty for some of us with this alternative, more formal, way of writing probability is that it leaves everything in decimals that does not appeal to the less mathematically skilled. However, you should be aware of the alternative notation since it appears in many research reports. Furthermore, much computer output can give probabilities to several decimal places which can be confusing. For example, what does a probability of 0.00001 mean? The answer is one chance in 100,000 or a 0.001% probability ($\frac{1}{100,000} \times 100 = 0.001\%$).

There are two rules of probability with which psychologists ought to be familiar. They are the *addition rule* and the *multiplication rule*.

1. The *addition rule* is quite straightforward. It merely states that for a number of mutually exclusive outcomes the sum of their probabilities adds up to 1.00. So if you have a set of 150 people of which 100 are women and 50 are men, the probability of picking a woman at random is 100/150 or 0.667. The probability of picking a man at random is 50/150 or 0.333. However, the probability of picking either a man or a woman at random is 0.667 + 0.333 or 1.00. In other words, it is certain that you will pick either a man or a woman. The assumption is that the categories or outcomes are mutually exclusive, meaning that a person cannot be in both the man and woman categories. Being a man excludes that person from also being a woman. In statistical probability theory, one of the two possible outcomes is usually denoted p and the other is denoted q, so $p + q = 1.00$. Outcomes that are not mutually exclusive include, for example, the categories man and young since a person could be a man and young.

2. The *multiplication rule* is about a set of events. It can be illustrated by our set of 150 men and women in which 100 are women and 50 are men. Again the

assumption is that the categories or outcomes are mutually exclusive. We could ask how likely it is that the first five people that we pick at random will all be women, given that the probability of choosing a woman on a single occasion is 0.667. The answer is that we multiply the probability associated with the first person being a woman by the probability that the second person will be a woman by the probability that the third person will be a woman by the probability that the fourth person will be a woman by the probability that the fifth person will be a woman:

Probability of all five being women $= p \times p \times p \times p \times p$

$$= 0.667 \times 0.667 \times 0.667 \times 0.667 \times 0.667$$
$$= 0.13$$

Therefore there is a 13% probability (0.13) that we will choose a sample of five women at random. That is not a particularly rare outcome. However, picking a sample of all men from our set of men and women is much rarer:

Probability of all five being men $= q \times q \times q \times q \times q$

$$= 0.333 \times 0.333 \times 0.333 \times 0.333 \times 0.333$$
$$= 0.004$$

Therefore there is a 0.4% probability (0.004) of choosing all men.

The multiplication rule as stated here assumes that once a person is selected for inclusion in the sample, he or she is replaced in the population and possibly selected again. This is called random sampling with replacement. However, normally we do not do this in psychological research, though if the population is big then not replacing the individual back into the population has negligible influence on the outcome. Virtually all statistical analyses assume replacement but it does not matter that people are usually not selected more than once for a study in psychological research.

15.3 Implications

Such theoretical considerations concerning probability theory have a number of implications for research. They ought to be carefully noted.

1. *Repeated significance testing* within the same study. It is tempting to carry out several statistical tests on data. Usually we find that a portion of these tests are statistically significant at the 5% level whereas a number are not. Indeed, even if there were absolutely no trends in the population, we would expect, by chance, 5% of our comparisons to be significant at the 5% level. This is the meaning of statistical significance, after all. The more statistical comparisons we make on our data the more significant findings we would expect. If we did 20 comparisons we would expect one significant finding

even if there are no trends in the population. In order to cope with this, the correct procedure is to make the statistical significance more stringent the more tests of significance we do. So if we did two tests then our significance level per test should be 5%/2 or 2.5%; if we did four comparisons our significance level would be 5%/4 or 1.25% significance per test. In other words, we simply divide the 5% significance level by the number of tests we are doing. Although this is the proper thing to do, few psychological reports actually do it. However, the consequence of not doing this is to find more significant findings than you should.

2. *Significance testing across different studies.* An application of the multiplication rule in assessing the value of replicating research shows the dramatic increase in significance that this can achieve. Replication means the essential repeating of a study at a later date and possibly in radically different circumstances such as other locations. Imagine that the significance level achieved in the original study is 5% ($p = 0.05$). If one finds the same significance level in the replication the probability of two studies producing this level of significance by chance is $p \times p$ or $0.05 \times 0.05 = 0.0025$ or 0.25%. This considerably enhances our confidence that the findings of the research are not the result of chance factors but reflect significant trends.

Calculation 15.1

The addition rule

A psychologist wishes to calculate the chance expectations of marks on a multiple choice test of general knowledge. Since a person could get some answers correct simply by sticking a pin into the answer paper, there has to be a minimum score below which the individual is doing no better than chance. If each question has four response alternatives then one would expect that by chance a person could get one in four or one-quarter of the answers correct. That is intuitively obvious. But what if some questions have three alternative answers and others have four alternative answers? This is not quite so obvious but we simply apply the law of addition and add together the probabilities of being correct for all of the questions on the paper. This entails adding together probabilities of 0.33 and 0.25 since there are three or four alternative answers. So if there are 10 questions with three alternative answers and five questions with four alternative answers, the number of answers correct by chance is $(10 \times 0.33) + (5 \times 0.25)$ $= 3.3 + 1.25 = 4.55$.

Calculation 15.2

The multiplication rule

A psychologist studies a pair of twins who have been brought up separately and who have never met. The psychologist is surprised to find that the twins are alike on seven out of ten different characteristics. These characteristics are:

(a) They both marry women younger than themselves (0.9).

(b) They both marry brunettes (0.7).

(c) They both drive (0.7).

(d) They both swim (0.6).

(e) They have spent time in hospital (0.8).

(f) They both take foreign holidays (0.5).

(g) They both part their hair on the left (0.9).

However, they are different in the following ways:

(h) One attends church (0.4) and the other does not.

(i) One has a doctorate (0.03) and the other does not.

(j) One smokes (0.3) and the other does not.

The similarities between the two men are impressive if it is exceptional for two randomly selected men to be similar on each of the items. The probabilities of each of the outcomes are presented in brackets above. These probabilities are the proportions of men in the general population demonstrating these characteristics. For many of the characteristics it seems quite likely that they will be similar. So two men taken at random from the general population are most likely to marry a younger woman. Since the probability of marrying a younger woman is 0.9, the probability of any two men marrying younger women is $0.9 \times 0.9 = 0.81$. The probability of two men taken at random both being drivers is $0.7 \times 0.7 = 0.49$. In fact the ten characteristics listed above are shared by randomly selected pairs of men with the following probabilities:

(a) $0.9 \times 0.9 = 0.81$

(b) $0.7 \times 0.7 = 0.49$

(c) $0.7 \times 0.7 = 0.49$

(d) $0.6 \times 0.6 = 0.36$

(e) $0.8 \times 0.8 = 0.64$

(f) $0.5 \times 0.5 = 0.25$

(g) $0.9 \times 0.9 = 0.81$

(h) $0.4 \times 0.4 = 0.16$

(i) $0.03 \times 0.03 = 0.0009$

(j) $0.3 \times 0.3 = 0.09$

The sum of these probabilities is 4.10. Clearly the pair of twins are more alike than we might expect on the basis of chance. However, it might be that we would get a different answer if instead of taking the general population of men, we took men of the same age as the twins.

15.4 Notes and recommendations

■ Although probability theory is of crucial importance for mathematical statisticians, psychologists generally rely on an intuitive approach to the topic. That may be laziness on their part, but we have kept the coverage of probability minimal given the scope of this book. It can also be very deterring to anyone not too mathematically inclined. If you need to know more, especially if you need to estimate precisely the likelihood of a particular pattern or sequence of events occurring, we suggest that you consult books such as Kerlinger (1986) for more complete accounts of mathematical probability theory.

■ However, it is important to avoid basic mistakes such as repeated significance testing on the same data without adjusting your significance levels to allow for the multitude of tests. This is not necessary for tests designed for multiple testing such as those for the analysis of variance, some of which we discuss later (Chapter 23), as the adjustment is built in.

Chapter 16

Reporting significance levels succinctly

Preparation

You need to know about testing significance from Chapter 11 onwards.

16.1 Introduction

So far, the reporting of statistical significance in this book has been a relatively clumsy and long-winded affair. In contrast, a glance at any psychology journal will suggest that precious little space is devoted to reporting significance. Detailed expositions of the statistical significance of your analyses have no place in professional reports. Researchers can make life much simpler for themselves by adopting the 'standard' style of reporting statistical significance. Clarity is one great benefit; another is the loss of wordiness.

Although the 'standard' approach to reporting statistical significance does vary slightly, there is little difficulty with this. At a minimum, the following should be mentioned when reporting statistical significance:

1. The statistical distribution used (e.g. F, chi, r, z, t, etc.).
2. The degrees of freedom (df). Alternatively, for some statistical techniques you may report the sample size (N).
3. The value of the calculation (e.g. the value of your z-score or your chi-square).
4. The probability or significance level. Sometimes 'not significant', 'not sig.' or 'ns' is used.
5. If you have a one-tailed hypothesis then this should be also mentioned. Otherwise a two-tailed hypothesis is assumed. You can also state that you are using a two-tailed test. This is most useful when you have several analyses and some are one-tailed and others are two-tailed.

16.2 Shortened forms

In research reports, comments such as the following are to be found:

■ The hypothesis that drunks slur their words was supported ($t = 2.88$, degrees of freedom = 97, $p < 0.01$).

■ There was a trend for drunks to slur their words more than sober people ($t = 2.88$, df = 97, sig. = 1%).

■ The null hypothesis that drunks do not slur their words more than sober people was rejected ($t = 2.88$, degrees of freedom = 97, $p = 0.01$).

■ The analysis supported the hypothesis since drunks tended to slur their words the most often ($t(97) = 2.88$, $p = 0.01$, two-tailed test).

■ The hypothesis that drunks slur their words was accepted ($t(97) = 2.88$, $p = 0.005$, 1-tail).

All of the above say more-or-less the same thing. The symbol t indicates that the t-test was used. The symbol < indicates that your probability level is even smaller than the given value. Thus $p < 0.01$ means that the probability is, say, 0.008 or 0.005. That is, the test is statistically significant at better than the reported level of 0.01. Sometimes, the degrees of freedom are put in brackets after the symbol for the statistical test used, as in $t(97) = 2.88$. In all of the above examples, the hypothesis was supported and the null hypothesis rejected.

The following are examples of what might be written if the hypothesis was not supported by your data:

■ The hypothesis that drunks slur their words was rejected ($t = 0.56$, degrees of freedom = 97, $p > .05$).

■ Drunks and sober people did not differ in their average rates of slurring their speech ($t = 0.56$, df = 97, not sig.).

■ The hypothesis that drunks slur their words was rejected in favour of the null hypothesis ($t = 0.56$, df = 97, $p > 0.05$, not significant).

The last three statements mean much the same. The symbol > means that your probability is greater than the listed value. It is used to indicate that your calculation is not statistically significant at the stated level.

Notice throughout this chapter that the reported significance levels are not standardised on the 5% level of significance. It is possible, especially with computers, to obtain much more exact values of probability than the critical values used in tables of significance. While there is nothing at all technically wrong with using the more precise values if you have them to hand, there is one objection. Statistical significance can become a holy grail in statistics, supporting the view 'the smaller the probability the better'. Although significance is important, the size of the trends in your data is even more crucial. A significant result with a strong trend is the ideal which is not obtained simply by exploring the minutiae of probability.

One thing causes a lot of confusion in the significance levels given by computers. Sometimes values like $p < 0.0000$ are listed. All that this means is that the probability level for the statistical test is less than 0.0001. In other words the significance level might be, say, 0.00003 or 0.0000004. These are very significant findings, statistically speaking. We would recommend that you report them slightly differently in your writings. Values such as 0.0001 or 0.001 are clearer to some readers. So change your final 0 in the string of zeros to 1.

16.3 Examples from the published literature

Example 1

' ... a post hoc comparison was carried out between means of the adult molesters' and adult control groups' ratings using Student's t-test. A significant $(t(49) = 2.96, p < 0.001)$ difference was found between the two groups.' (Johnston and Johnston, 1986, p. 643)

The above excerpt is fairly typical of the ways in which psychologists summarise the results of their research. To the practised eye, it is not too difficult to decipher. However, some difficulties can be caused to the novice statistician. A little patience at first will help a lot. The extract contains the following major pieces of information:

1. The statistical test used was the t-test. The authors mention it by name but it is also identified by the t mentioned in the brackets. However, the phrase 'Student's t-test' might be confusing. Student was the pen-name of a researcher at the Guinness Brewery who invented the t-test. It is quite redundant nowadays – the name Student, not Guinness!

2. The degrees of freedom are the (49) contained in the brackets. If you check the original paper you will find that the combined sample size is 51. It should be obvious, then, that this is an unrelated or uncorrelated t-test since the degrees of freedom are clearly $N - 2$ in this case.

3. The value of the t-test is 2.96.

4. The difference between the two groups is statistically significant at the 0.001 or 0.1% level of probability. This is shown by $p < 0.001$ in the above excerpt.

5. Post hoc merely means that the researchers decided to do the test after the data had been collected. They had not planned it prior to collecting the data.

6. No mention is made of whether this is a one-tailed or a two-tailed test so we would assume that it is a two-tailed significance level.

Obviously, there are a variety of ways of writing up the findings of any analysis. The following is a different way of saying much the same thing:

' ... a post hoc comparison between the means of the adult molesters' and adult control groups' ratings was significant $(t = 2.96, df = 49, p < 0.001)$.'

Example 2

'The relationship of gender of perpetrators and victims was examined. Perpetrators of female victims were more often male (13,900 of 24,947, 55.8%)

while perpetrators of males were more often female (10,977 of 21,373, 51.4%, $\chi^2(1) = 235.18, p < 0.001$).' (Rosenthal, 1988, p. 267)

The interpretation of this is as follows:

1. The chi-square test was used. χ^2 is the Greek symbol for chi-square.

2. The value of chi-square is 235.18.

3. It is statistically very significant as the probability level is less than 0.001 or less than 0.1%.

4. Chi-square is usually regarded as a directionless test. That is, the significance level reported is for a two-tailed test unless stated otherwise.

5. Although the significance level in this study seems impressive, just look at the sample sizes involved – over 46,000 children in total. The actual trends are relatively small – 55.8% versus 51.4%. This is a good example of when not to get excited about statistically significant findings.

An alternative way of saying much the same thing is:

'Female victims were offended against by males in 55.8% of cases ($N = 24,947$). For male victims, 51.4% of offenders were female ($N = 21,373$). Thus victims were more likely to be offended against by a member of the opposite sex (chi-square = 235.18, degrees of freedom = 1, $p < 0.1\%$).'

Example 3

'A 2×2 analysis of variance (ANOVA) with anger and sex of target as factors was conducted on the BP2 (after anger manipulation) scores. This analysis yielded a significant effect for anger, $F(1, 116) = 43.76, p < 0.004$, with angered subjects revealing a larger increase in arousal ($M = 6.01$) than the nonangered subjects ($M = 0.01$).' (Donnerstein, 1980, p. 273)

This should be readily deciphered as:

1. A two-way analysis of variance with two different levels of each independent variable. One of the independent variables is anger (angered and non-angered conditions are the categories). The other independent variable is sex of the target of aggression. Something called BP2 (whatever that may be – it turns out to be blood pressure) is the dependent variable.

2. The mean BP2 score for the angered condition was 6.01 and the mean for the non-angered condition was 0.01. The author is using M as the symbol of the sample mean.

3. The test of significance is the F-ratio test. We know this because this is an analysis of variance but also because the statistic is stated to be F.

4. The value of F, the variance ratio, equals 43.76.

5. There are 1 and 116 degrees of freedom for the F-ratio for the main effect of the variable anger. The 1 degree of freedom is because there are two

different levels of the variable anger (df = $c - 1$ or the number of columns of data minus one). The 116 degrees of freedom means that there must have been 120 participants in the experiment. The degrees of freedom for a main effect is N – number of cells = $120 - (2 \times 2) = 120 - 4 = 116$. All of this is clarified in Chapter 22.

6. The difference between the angered and non-angered conditions is statistically significant at the 0.4% level.

A slightly different style of describing these findings is:

'Blood pressure following the anger manipulation was included as the dependent variable on a 2 × 2 analysis of variance. The two independent variables were sex of the target of aggression and anger. There was a significant main effect for anger ($F = 43.76$, df = 1, 116, p < 0.4%). The greater mean increase in blood pressure was for the angered group (6.01) compared to the non-angered group (0.01).'

16.4 Notes and recommendations

■ Remember that the important pieces of information to report are:
 – the symbol for the statistic (t, T, r, etc.)
 – the value of the statistic for your analysis – two decimal places are enough
 – an indication of the degrees of freedom or the sample size involved (df =, N =)
 – the probability or significance level
 – whether a one-tailed test was used.

■ Sometimes you will see symbols for statistical techniques that you have never heard of. Do not panic since it is usually possible to work out the sense of what is going on. Certainly if you have details of the sort described in this chapter, you know that a test of significance is involved.

■ Using the approaches described in this chapter creates a good impression and ensures that you include pertinent information. However, standardise on one of the variants in your report. Eventually if you submit papers to a journal for consideration, you should check out that journal's method of reporting significance.

■ Some statistical tests are regarded as being directionless. That is, their use always implies a two-tailed test. This is true of chi-square and the analysis of variance. These tests can only be one-tailed if the degrees of freedom equal one. Otherwise, the test is two-tailed. Even when the degrees of freedom equal one, only use a one-tailed test if you are satisfied that you have reached the basic requirements of one-tailed testing (see Chapter 17).

Chapter 17

One-tailed versus two-tailed significance testing

Preparation

Revise the null hypothesis and alternative hypothesis (Chapter 10) and significance testing.

17.1 Introduction

Sometimes researchers are so confident about the likely outcome of their research that they make pretty strong predictions about the relationship between their independent and dependent variables. So, for example, rather than say that the *independent variable* age is correlated with verbal ability, the researcher predicts that the *independent variable* age is *positively* correlated with the *dependent variable* verbal ability. In other words, it is predicted that the older participants in the research will have better verbal skills. Equally the researcher might predict a *negative* relationship between the independent and dependent variables.

It is conventional in psychological statistics to treat such *directional* predictions differently from *non-directional* predictions. Normally psychologists speak of a directional prediction being one-tailed whereas a non-directional prediction is two-tailed. The crucial point is that if you have a directional prediction (one-tailed test) the critical values of the significance test become slightly different.

In order to carry out a one-tailed test you need to be satisfied that you have met the criteria for one-tailed testing. These, as we will see, are rather stringent. In our experience, many one-tailed hypotheses put forward by students are little more than hunches and certainly not based on the required strong past-research or strong theory. In these circumstances it is unwise and wrong to carry out one-tailed testing. It would be best to regard the alternative hypothesis as non-directional and choose two-tailed significance testing exactly as we have done so far in this book. One-tailed testing is a contentious issue and you may be confronted with different points of view; some authorities reject it although it is fairly commonplace in psychological research.

17.2 Theoretical considerations

If we take a directional alternative hypothesis (such as that intelligence correlates positively with level of education) then it is necessary to revise our understanding of the null hypothesis somewhat. (The same is true if the directional alternative hypothesis suggests a negative relationship between the two variables.) In the case of the positively worded alternative hypothesis, the null hypothesis is:

Intelligence does not correlate *positively* with level of education.

Our previous style of null hypothesis would have left out the word *positively*. There are two different circumstances which support the null hypothesis that intelligence does not correlate *positively* with level of education:

If intelligence *does not correlate* at all with level of education, *or*
If intelligence correlates *negatively* with level of education.

That is, it is only research which shows a *positive* correlation between intelligence and education which supports the directional hypothesis – if we found an extreme negative correlation between intelligence and education this would lead to the rejection of the alternative hypothesis just as would zero or near-zero relationships. Because, in a sense, the dice is loaded against the directional alternative hypothesis, it is conventional to argue that we should not use the extremes of the sampling distribution in both directions for our test of significance for the directional hypothesis. Instead we should take the extreme samples in the positive direction (if it is positively worded) or the extreme samples in the negative direction (if it is negatively worded). In other words, our extreme 5% of samples which we define as significant should all be from one side of the sampling distribution, not 2.5% on each side as we would have done previously (see Figure 17.1).

Because the 5% of extreme samples, which are defined as significant, are all on the same side of the distribution, you need a smaller value of your significance test to be in that extreme 5%. Part of the attraction of directional or one-tailed significance tests of this sort is that basically you can get the same level of significance with a smaller sample or smaller trend than would be required for a two-tailed test. Essentially the probability level can be halved – what would be significant at the 5% level with a two-tailed test is significant at the 2.5% level with a one-tailed test.

There is a big proviso to this. If you predicted a positive relationship but found what would normally be a significant negative relationship, with a one-tailed test you ought to ignore that negative relationship – it merely supports the null hypothesis. The temptation is, however, to ignore your original directional alternative hypothesis and pretend that you had not predicted the direction. Given that significant results are at a premium in psychology and are much more likely to get published, it is not surprising that psychologists seeking to publish their research might be tempted to 'adjust' their hypotheses slightly.

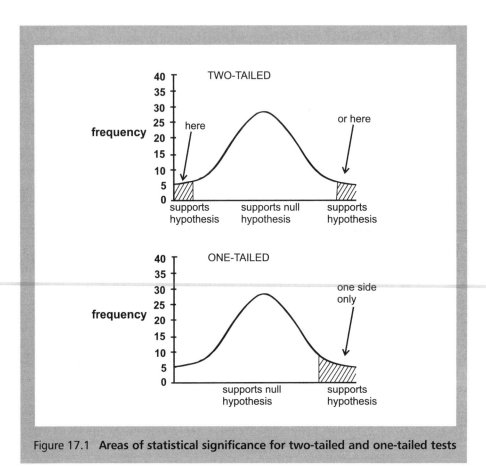

Figure 17.1　**Areas of statistical significance for two-tailed and one-tailed tests**

It is noteworthy that the research literature contains very few tests of significance of directional hypotheses which are rejected when the trend in the data is strongly (and significantly with a two-tailed test) in the opposite direction to that predicted. The only example we know of was written by one of us.

17.3 Further requirements

There are a number of other rules which are supposed to be followed if one is to use a directional hypothesis. These include:

1. The prediction is based on strong and well researched theory and not on a whim or intuition.

2. The prediction is based on previous similar research demonstrating consistent trends in the predicted direction.

3. One should make the above predictions in advance of any information about the trends in the data about which the prediction is to be made. That is, for

example, you do not look at your scattergrams and then predict the direction of the correlation between your variables. That would be manifestly cheating but a 'good' way otherwise of getting significant results with a one-tailed test when they would not quite reach significance with a two-tailed test.

There is another practical problem in the use of directional hypotheses. That is, if you have *more than two groups* of scores it is often very difficult to decide what the predicting trends between the groups would be. For this reason, many statistical techniques are commonly regarded as directionless when you have more than two groups of scores or subjects. This applies to techniques such as chi-square, the analysis of variance and other related tests.

Although this is clearly a controversial area, you will probably find that as a student you rarely if ever have sufficient justification for employing a one-tailed test. As you might have gathered, most of these criteria for selecting a one-tailed test are to a degree subjective which makes the use of one-tailed tests less objective than might be expected. We would recommend that you choose a two-tailed or directionless test unless there is a pressing and convincing reason to do otherwise. Otherwise the danger of loading things in favour of significant results is too great.

In addition to two-tailed critical values, the significance tables in the appendices give the one-tailed values where these are appropriate.

17.4 Notes and recommendations

■ Routinely make your alternative hypotheses two-tailed or directionless. This is especially the case when the implications of your research are of practical or policy significance. However, this may not be ideal if you are testing theoretical predictions when the direction of the hypothesis might be important. Nevertheless, it is a moot point whether you should take advantage of the 'less stringent' significance requirements of a one-tailed test.

■ If you believe that the well established theoretical or empirical bases for predicting the direction of the outcomes are strong enough, then still be a little cautious about employing one-tailed tests. In particular, do not formulate your hypothesis *after* collecting or viewing your data.

■ You cannot be faulted for using two-tailed tests since they are less likely to show significant relationships. Thus they are described as being statistically more conservative. Student research often does not arise out of previous research or theory. Often the research is initiated before earlier research and theory have been reviewed. In these circumstances one-tailed tests are not warranted.

Chapter 18

Ranking tests

Nonparametric statistics

Preparation
Be aware of the t-tests for related and unrelated samples. Revise ranking (Chapter 7).

18.1 Introduction

From time to time any researcher will be faced with the distinction between parametric and nonparametric significance tests. The difference is quite straightforward. Many statistical techniques require that the details are known or estimates can be made of the characteristics of the population. These are known as *parametric* tests (a parameter is a characteristic of a population). Almost invariably, as we have seen, the population is the population defined by the null hypothesis. Generally speaking, the numerical scores we used had to roughly approximate the normal (bell-shaped) distribution in order for our decisions to be precise. The reason for this is that the statistician's theoretical assumptions, when developing the test, included the normal distribution of the data. It is widely accepted that the assumption of a bell-shaped or normal distribution of scores is a very broad criterion and that the distribution of scores on a variable would have to be very lopsided (skewed) in order for the outcomes to be seriously out of line. Appendix A explains how to test for such skewness.

But what if assumptions such as that of symmetry are so badly violated that the use of the test seems somewhat unacceptable? One traditional alternative approach is called *nonparametric* testing because it makes few or no assumptions about the distribution in the population. Many nonparametric tests of significance are based on rankings given to the original numerical scores – it is unusual for researchers to collect their data in the form of ranks in the first place.

Conventionally these tests for ranks are regarded as relatively easy computations for students – this is part of their appeal. Up to a point this can be true, but the difficulties are as follows:

1. They become disproportionately cumbersome with increasing amounts of data.

2. They also suffer from the difficulty that many psychological data are gathered using rather restricted ranges of scores. This often results in the same values appearing several times in a set of data. The tests based on ranks also become cumbersome with increased tied scores and, consequently, somewhat inaccurate.

3. Worst of all, the variety and flexibility of these nonparametric statistical techniques is nowhere as great as for parametric statistics. For this reason it is generally best to err towards using parametric statistics in our opinion. Certainly current research practice seems to increasingly disfavour nonparametric statistics.

18.2 Theoretical considerations

Ranking merely involves the ordering of a set of scores from the smallest to the largest. The smallest score is given the rank 1, the second smallest score is given the rank 2, the fiftieth smallest score is given the rank 50 and so on.

Since many nonparametric statistical techniques use ranks, the question is raised why this is so. The answer is very much the same as the reason for using the normal distribution as the basis for parametric statistics – it provides a standard distribution of scores with standard characteristics. It is much the same for the tests based on ranks. Although there are incalculable varieties in samples of data, for any given number of scores the ranks are always the same. So the ranks of 10 scores which represent the IQs of the 10 greatest geniuses of all time are exactly the same as the ranks for the scores on introversion of the 10 members of the local stamp collectors' club: 1, 2, 3, 4, 5, 6, 7, 8, 9 and 10.

Since all sets of 10 scores use exactly the same set of ranks, this considerably eases the statistician's calculations of the distribution of the ranks under the null hypothesis that there is no relationship between pairs of variables. Instead of an infinite variety of 10 scores, there is just this one set of 10 ranks on which to do one's calculations. Only sample size makes a difference to the ranks, not the precise numerical values of the scores themselves.

18.3 Nonparametric statistical tests

There is an extensive battery of nonparametric tests although many are interchangeable with each other or rather obscure with very limited applications. In this chapter we will consider only a small number of tests which you may come across during your university courses or general reading. We have discussed chi-square (for frequencies) and Spearman's rho (for correlations) elsewhere in this book. The nonparametric tests discussed in this chapter are usually applicable in very much the same experimental designs as the parametric tests we have discussed elsewhere (see Table 18.1).

Table 18.1 **Similar parametric and nonparametric tests**

Parametric test	Nonparametric equivalent
Related t-test	Wilcoxon Matched Pairs Test
	Sign test
Unrelated t-test	Mann–Whitney U-test

Tests for related samples

Two nonparametric tests are familiar in the literature – the sign test (which is not based on ranks) and the Wilcoxon Matched Pairs Test (which is based on ranks). Because they would apply to data for the related t-test, we will use the data for the worked example in Chapter 12 to illustrate the application of both of these tests.

Calculation 18.1

The sign test

The sign test is like the related t-test in that it takes the differences between the two related samples of scores. However, instead of considering the *size* of the difference, the sign test merely uses the *sign* of the difference. In other words, it loses a lot of the information inherent in the size of the difference.

Step 1 Delete from the analysis any case which has identical scores for both variables. They are ignored in the sign test. Take the second group of scores away from the first group (Table 18.2). Remember to include the sign of the difference (+ or –).

Table 18.2 **Steps in the calculation of the sign test**

Subject	Six months X_1	Nine months X_2	Difference $D = X_1 - X_2$
Baby Clara	3	7	−4
Baby Martin	5	6	−1
Baby Sally	5	3	+2
Baby Angie	4	8	−4
Baby Trevor	3	5	−2
Baby Sam	7	9	−2
Baby Bobby	8	7	+1
Baby Sid	7	9	−2

Significance Table 18.1   **5% significance values for the sign test giving values of T (the smaller of the sums of signs) (two-tailed test)**

Your value must be in the listed ranges for your sample size to be significant at the 5% level (i.e. to accept the hypothesis). An extended table is to be found in Appendix G.

Number of pairs of scores (ignoring any tied pairs)	Significant at 5% level Accept hypothesis
6–8	0 only
9–11	0 to 1
12–14	0 to 2
15–16	0 to 3
17–19	0 to 4
20–22	0 to 5
23–24	0 to 6
25	0 to 7
26–28	0 to 8
29–30	0 to 9
31–33	0 to 10
34–35	0 to 11
36–38	0 to 12
39–40	0 to 13
41–42	0 to 14
43–45	0 to 15
46–47	0 to 16
48–49	0 to 17
50	0 to 18

Step 2 Count the *number* of scores which are positively signed and then count the *number* of scores which are negatively signed. (Don't forget that zero differences are ignored in the sign test.)

Step 3 Take whichever is the smaller number – the number of positive signs or the number of negative signs.

Step 4 Look up the significance of this smaller number in Significance Table 18.1. You need to find the row which contains the *sum* of the positive and negative signs (i.e. ignoring zero differences). Your value has to be in the tabulated range to be statistically significant.

In our example, there are 6 negative and 2 positive signs; 2 is the smaller number. The sum of positive and negative signs is 8. Significance Table 18.1 gives the significant values of the smaller number of signs as 0 only. Therefore our value is not statistically unusual and we accept the null hypothesis.

It would be a good approximation to use the one-sample chi-square formula (Calculation 14.3), given that you would expect equal numbers of positive and negative differences under the null hypothesis that 'the two samples do not differ'. That is, the distributions of the sign test and the McNemar Test (Section 14.7) for the significance of changes are the same.

Interpreting the results The mean scores for eye contact at six months and nine months need to be checked in order to know what the trend is in the data. Although eye contact was greater at nine months, the sign test is not significant which means that we should accept the null hypothesis of no differences in eye contact at the two ages.

Reporting the result The following could be written: 'Eye contact was higher at nine months ($\overline{X} = 6.75$) than at six months ($\overline{X} = 5.25$). However, this difference was insufficient to cause us to reject the null hypothesis that the amount of eye contact is the same at six months and nine months of age (sign test, $n = 8, p$ ns).'

The calculation steps for the Wilcoxon Matched Pairs (or Signed Ranks) Test are similar. However, this test retains a little more information from the original scores by ranking the differences.

Calculation 18.2

The Wilcoxon Matched Pairs Test

The test is also known as the Wilcoxon Signed Ranks Test. It is similar to the sign test except that when we have obtained the difference score we rank-order the differences ignoring the sign of the difference.

Step 1 The difference scores are calculated and then ranked ignoring the sign of the difference (Table 18.3). Notice that where there are tied values of the differences, we have allocated the average of the ranks which would be given if it were possible to separate the scores. Thus the two difference scores which equal 1 are both given the rank 1.5 since if the scores did differ minutely one would be given the rank 1 and the other the rank 2. Take care: zero differences are ignored and are *not* ranked.

Step 2 The ranks of the differences can now have the sign of the difference reattached – we have used superscripts after the rank to identify this in Table 18.3.

Step 3 The sum of the positive ranks is calculated = 4.5 + 1.5 = 6. The sum of the negative ranks is calculated = 7.5 + 1.5 + 7.5 + 4.5 + 4.5 + 4.5 = 30.

Table 18.3 **Steps in the calculation of the Wilcoxon Matched Pairs Test**

Subject	Six months X_1	Nine months X_2	Difference $D = X_1 - X_2$	Rank of difference ignoring sign during ranking
Baby Clara	3	7	−4	7.5−
Baby Martin	5	6	−1	1.5−
Baby Sally	5	3	2	4.5+
Baby Angie	4	8	−4	7.5−
Baby Trevor	3	5	−2	4.5−
Baby Sam	7	9	−2	4.5−
Baby Bobby	8	7	1	1.5+
Baby Sid	7	9	−2	4.5−

Step 4 We then decide which is the smaller of the two sums of ranks – in this case it is 6. This is normally designated T.

Step 5 We then find the significance values of T (the smaller of the two sums of ranks) from Significance Table 18.2. This is structured in terms of the number of pairs of scores used in the calculation, which is 8 in the present case. The critical value for a two-tailed test at the 5% level is 4 or less. Our value is 6 which is not statistically significant.

If your sample size is larger than Significance Table 18.2 deals with, Appendix B1 explains how to test for significance.

Interpreting the results As always, it is important to examine the means of the two sets of scores in order to know what the trend in the data is. Although the amount of eye contact at nine months was greater than at six months, the Wilcoxon Matched Pairs Test failed to reach statistical significance so it is not possible to reject the null hypothesis of no differences in eye contact at the two ages.

Reporting the results The following gives a reasonably concise account of our findings: 'Eye contact was slightly higher at nine months ($\overline{X}$ = 6.75) than at six months ($\overline{X}$ = 5.25). However, this did not reach statistical significance so it was not possible to reject the null hypothesis that eye contact does not change between these ages ($T = 6, n = 8, p > 0.05$, ns).'

Generally speaking it is difficult to suggest circumstances in which the sign test is to be preferred over the Wilcoxon Matched Pairs Test. The latter uses more of the information contained within the data and so is more likely to detect significant differences where they exist.

Significance Table 18.2   **5% significance values for the Wilcoxon Matched Pairs Test (two-tailed test)**

Your value must be in the listed ranges for your sample size to be significant at the 5% level (i.e. to accept the hypothesis).

An extended and conventional significance table for the Wilcoxon Matched Pairs Test is to be found in Appendix H.

Number of pairs of scores (ignoring any tied pairs)	Significant at 5% level Accept hypothesis
6	0 to 1
7	0 to 2
8	0 to 4
9	0 to 6
10	0 to 8
11	0 to 11
12	0 to 14
13	0 to 17
14	0 to 21
15	0 to 25
16	0 to 30
17	0 to 35
18	0 to 40
19	0 to 46
20	0 to 52
21	0 to 59
22	0 to 66
23	0 to 74
24	0 to 81
25	0 to 90

The sign test can be applied in virtually any circumstance in which the expected population distribution under the null hypothesis is 50% of one outcome and 50% of another. In other words, the table of significance of the sign test can be used to check for departures from this 50/50 expectation.

Tests for unrelated samples

The major nonparametric test for differences between two groups of unrelated or uncorrelated scores is the Mann–Whitney U-test.

Calculation 18.3

The Mann–Whitney U-test

The most common nonparametric statistic for unrelated samples of scores is the Mann–Whitney U-test. This is used for similar research designs as the unrelated or uncorrelated scores t-test (Chapter 13). In other words, it can be used whenever you have two groups of scores which are independent of each other (i.e. they are usually based on different samples of people). We will use the identical data upon which we demonstrated the calculation of the unrelated/uncorrelated scores t-test (Chapter 13).

Step 1 Rank all of the scores from the smallest to the largest (Table 18.4). Scores which are equal are allocated the average of ranks that they would be given if there were tiny differences between the scores. *Be careful! All of your scores are ranked irrespective of the group they are in.* To avoid confusion, *use the first column for the larger group* of scores. If both groups are equal in size then either can be entered in the first column. Group size $N_1 = 12$ for the two-parent families and $N_2 = 10$ for the lone-parent families.

Step 2 Sum the ranks for the *larger* group of scores. This is R_1. (If the groups are equal in size then either can be selected.)

Step 3 The sum of ranks (R_1) of Group 1 (174.5) (the larger group) and its sample size N_1 ($N_1 = 12$) together with the sample size N_2 of Group 2 ($N_2 = 10$) are entered into the following formula which gives you the value of the statistic U:

$$U = (N_1 \times N_2) + \frac{N_1 \times (N_1 + 1)}{2} - R_1$$

$$= (12 \times 10) + \frac{12 \times (12 + 1)}{2} - 174.5$$

$$= 120 + \frac{12 \times 13}{2} - 174.5$$

$$= 120 + \frac{156}{2} - 174.5$$

$$= 120 + 78 - 174.5$$

$$= 198 - 174.5$$

$$= 23.5$$

Step 4 Check the significance of your value of U by consulting Significance Table 18.3. In order to use this table, you need to find your value of N_1 in the column headings and your value of N_2 in the row headings. (However, since the table is symmetrical it does not matter if you use the rows instead of the columns and vice versa.) The table gives the *two* ranges of values of U which are significant. Your value must be in *either* of these two ranges to be statistically significant. (Appendix B1 explains what to do if your sample size exceeds the largest value in the table.)

The table tells us that for sample sizes of 12 and 10, the ranges are 0 to 29 or 91 to 120. Our value of 23.5 therefore is significant at the 5% level. In other words, we reject the null hypothesis that the independent variable is unrelated to the dependent variable in favour of the view that family structure has an influence on scores of the dependent variable.

Interpreting the results   The means of the two groups of scores must be examined to know which of the two groups has the higher scores on the dependent variable. In our example, greater emotionality was found in the children from the two-parent families. The significant value of the Mann–Whitney U-test suggests that we are reasonably safe to conclude that the two groups do differ in terms of their emotionality.

Table 18.4   **Steps in the calculation of the Mann–Whitney U-test**

Two-parent families (X_1) (This column is for the larger group)	Rankings	Lone-parent families (X_2) (This column is for the smaller group	Rankings
12	12.5	6	2
18	21	9	6
14	16.5	4	1
10	8.5	13	14.5
19	22	14	16.5
8	3.5	9	6
15	18.5	8	3.5
11	10.5	12	12.5
10	8.5	11	10.5
13	14.5	9	6
15	18.5		
16	20		

$\Sigma R_1 = 174.5$
(note that this is
the sum of ranks
for the *larger* group)

Reporting the results   The statistical analysis could be reported in the following style: 'It was found that emotionality was significantly higher ($U = 23.5, n = 22, p < 0.05$) in the two-parent families ($\overline{X} = 13.42$) than in the lone-parent families ($\overline{X} = 9.50$).'

Significance Table 18.3   **5% significance values for the Mann–Whitney U-test (two-tailed test)**

Your value must be in the listed ranges for your sample sizes to be significant at the 5% level (i.e. to accept the hypothesis).

Sample size for smaller group	Sample size for larger group											
	5	6	7	8	9	10	11	12	13	14	15	20
5	0–2	0–3	0–5	0–6	0–7	0–8	0–9	0–11	0–12	0–13	0–14	0–20
	23–25	27–30	30–35	34–40	38–45	42–50	46–55	49–60	53–65	57–70	61–75	80–100
6	0–3	0–5	0–6	0–8	0–10	0–11	0–13	0–14	0–16	0–17	0–19	0–27
	27–30	31–36	36–42	40–48	44–54	49–60	53–66	58–72	62–78	67–84	71–90	93–120
7	0–5	0–6	0–8	0–10	0–12	0–14	0–16	0–18	0–20	0–22	0–24	0–34
	30–35	36–42	41–49	46–56	51–63	56–70	61–77	66–84	71–91	76–98	81–105	106–140
8	0–6	0–8	0–10	0–13	0–15	0–17	0–19	0–22	0–24	0–26	0–29	0–41
	34–40	40–48	46–56	51–64	57–72	63–80	69–88	74–96	80–104	86–112	91–120	119–160
9	0–7	0–10	0–12	0–15	0–17	0–20	0–23	0–26	0–28	0–31	0–34	0–48
	38–45	44–54	51–63	57–72	64–81	70–90	76–99	82–108	89–117	95–126	101–135	132–180
10	0–8	0–11	0–14	0–17	0–20	0–23	0–26	0–29	0–33	0–36	0–39	0–55
	42–50	49–60	56–70	63–80	70–90	77–100	84–110	91–120	97–130	104–140	111–150	145–200
11	0–9	0–13	0–16	0–19	0–23	0–26	0–30	0–33	0–37	0–40	0–44	0–62
	46–55	53–66	61–77	69–88	76–99	84–110	91–121	99–132	106–143	114–154	121–165	158–220
12	0–11	0–14	0–18	0–22	0–26	0–29	0–33	0–37	0–41	0–45	0–49	0–69
	49–60	58–72	66–84	74–96	82–108	91–120	99–132	107–144	115–156	123–168	131–180	171–240
13	0–12	0–16	0–20	0–24	0–28	0–33	0–37	0–41	0–45	0–50	0–54	0–76
	53–65	62–78	71–91	80–104	89–117	97–130	106–143	115–156	124–169	132–182	141–195	184–260
14	0–13	0–17	0–22	0–26	0–31	0–36	0–40	0–45	0–50	0–55	0–59	0–83
	57–70	67–84	76–98	86–112	95–126	104–140	114–154	123–168	132–182	141–196	151–210	197–280
15	0–14	0–19	0–24	0–29	0–34	0–39	0–44	0–49	0–54	0–59	0–64	0–90
	61–75	71–90	81–105	91–120	101–135	111–150	121–165	131–180	141–195	151–210	161–225	210–300
20	0–20	0–27	0–34	0–41	0–48	0–55	0–62	0–69	0–76	0–83	0–90	0–127
	80–100	93–120	106–140	119–160	132–180	145–200	158–220	171–240	184–260	197–280	210–300	273–400

The above table has been adapted and extended from Table I of R.P. Runyon and A. Haber (1989). *Fundamentals of Behavioral Statistics*. New York: McGraw-Hill. With the kind permission of the publisher.

18.4 Three or more groups of scores

The Kruskal–Wallis test and the Friedman test are essentially extensions of the Mann–Whitney U-test and the Wilcoxon Matched Pairs Test respectively. Appendix B2 gives information on how to calculate these nonparametric statistics.

18.5 Notes and recommendations

■ Often you will not require nonparametric tests of significance of the sort described in this chapter. The t-test will usually fit the task better.

■ Only when you have marked symmetry problems in your data will you require the nonparametric tests. But even then remember that a version of the unrelated t-test is available to cope with some aspects of the problem (Chapter 13).

■ The computations for the nonparametric tests may appear simpler. A big disadvantage is that when the sample sizes get large the problems in ranking escalate disproportionately.

■ Some professional psychologists tend to advocate nonparametric techniques for entirely outmoded reasons.

■ There is no guarantee that the nonparametric test will always do the job better when the assumptions of parametric tests are violated.

■ There are large sample formulae for the nonparametric tests reported here for when your sample sizes are too big for the printed tables of significance. However, by the time this point is reached the computation is getting clumsy and can be better handled by a computer; also the advantages of the nonparametric tests are very reduced.

Recommended further reading

Mariscuilo, L.A. and McSweeney, M. (1977). *Nonparametric and Distribution-free Methods for the Social Sciences*. Monterey, CA: Brooks/Cole.

Siegel, S. and Castellan, N.J. (1988). *Nonparametric Statistics for the Behavioral Sciences*. New York: McGraw-Hill.

Part 3

Introduction to analysis of variance

Chapter 19

The variance ratio test

The *F*-ratio to compare two variances

Preparation

Make sure that you understand variance and the variance estimate (Chapters 3 and 11). Familiarity with the t-test will help with some applications (Chapters 12 and 13).

19.1 The research problem

In a number of circumstances in research it is important to compare the variances of two samples of scores. The conventions of psychological research stress examining the sample *means* with each other. However, it is perfectly possible to find that despite the means of two groups being identical, their variances are radically different. Take the following simple experiment in which men and women are shown advertisements for tights, set out in Table 19.1. The dependent variable is the readers' degree of liking for the product rated on a

Table 19.1 **Data comparing men and women on ratings of tights**

Men	Women
5	1
4	6
4	7
3	2
5	6
4	7
3	5
6	7
5	2
5	6
	1
	2

scale from 1 to 7 (on which 1 means that they strongly disliked the advertisement and 7 means that they strongly liked the advertisement).

The big difference between the two groups is not in terms of their means – the men's mean is 4.4 whereas the women's mean is 4.3. This is a small and unimportant difference. What is more noticeable is that the women seem to be split into two camps. The women's scores tend to be large or small with little in the centre. There is more variance in the women's scores. Just how does one test to see whether the differences in variances are significant?

There are other circumstances in which we compare variances:

1. For the unrelated *t*-test, it is conventional to make sure that the two samples do not differ significantly in terms of their variances – if they do then it is better to opt for an 'unpooled' *t*-test (see Chapter 13).

2. Another major application is the analysis of variance in which variance estimates are compared (see Chapter 20).

The statistical test to use in all these circumstances is called the *F*-ratio test or the variance ratio test.

Significance Table 19.1   **5% significance values of the *F*-distribution for testing differences in variance estimates between two samples (two-tailed test)**

Your value has to equal or be larger than the tabulated value to be significant at the 5% level for a two-tailed test (i.e. to accept the hypothesis).

Additional values are to be found in Significance Tables 20.1, 21.1 or 22.1.

Degrees of freedom for smaller variance estimate (denominator)	Degrees of freedom for larger variance estimate (numerator)					
	5	7	10	20	50	∞
5	5.1 or more	4.9	4.7	4.6	4.4	4.4
6	4.4	4.1	4.1	3.9	3.8	3.7
7	4.0	3.8	3.6	3.4	3.3	3.2
8	3.7	3.5	3.3	3.2	3.0	2.9
10	3.3	3.1	3.0	2.8	2.6	2.5
12	3.1	2.9	2.8	2.5	2.4	2.3
15	2.9	2.7	2.6	2.3	2.2	2.1
20	2.7	2.5	2.4	2.1	2.0	1.8
30	2.5	2.3	2.2	1.9	1.8	1.6
50	2.4	2.2	2.0	1.8	1.6	1.4
100	2.3	2.1	1.9	1.7	1.5	1.3
∞	2.2	2.0	1.8	1.6	1.4	1.0

19.2 Theoretical issues and an application

The variance ratio simply compares two variances in order to test whether they come from the same population. In other words, are the differences between the variances simply the result of chance sampling fluctuations? Of course, since we are comparing samples from a population we need the variance estimate formula. In the simpler applications of the variance ratio test (*F*-ratio) the variance estimate involves using the sample size minus one $(N - 1)$ as the denominator (lower part) of the variance estimate formula. (This does not apply in quite the same way in the more advanced case of the analysis of variance, as we will see in Chapter 20 onwards.)

The variance ratio formula is as follows:

$$F = \frac{\text{Larger variance estimate}}{\text{Smaller variance estimate}}$$

There is a table of the *F*-distribution (Significance Table 19.1) which is organised according to the degrees of freedom of the two variance estimates.

Calculation 19.1

The variance ratio (*F*-ratio)

Imagine a very simple piece of clinical research which involves the administration of electroconvulsive therapy (ECT). There are two experimental conditions: in one case the electric current is passed through the left hemisphere of the brain and in the other case it is passed through the right hemisphere of the brain. The dependent variable is scores on a test of emotional stability

Table 19.2 **Emotional stability scores from a study of ECT to different hemispheres of the brain**

Left hemisphere	Right hemisphere
20	36
14	28
18	4
22	18
13	2
15	22
9	1
Mean = 15.9	Mean = 15.9

following treatment. Patients were assigned to one or other group at random. The scores following treatment were as listed in Table 19.2.

Quite clearly there is no difference in terms of the mean scores on emotional stability. Looking at the data, though, it looks as if ECT to the right hemisphere tends to push people to the extremes whereas ECT to the left hemisphere leaves a more compact distribution.

To calculate the variance ratio, the variance *estimates* of the two separate samples (left and right hemispheres) have to be calculated using the usual variance estimate formula. The following is the computational formula version of this:

$$\text{Estimated variance} = \frac{\Sigma X^2 - \dfrac{(\Sigma X)^2}{N}}{N - 1}$$

Step 1   Calculate the variance of the first group of scores (i.e. the left hemisphere group), as in Table 19.3. The sample size (number of scores) is $N_1 = 7$.

Table 19.3   **Step 1 in the calculation of the variance estimate**

X_1 = left hemisphere	X_1^2
20	400
14	196
18	324
22	484
13	169
15	225
9	81
$\Sigma X_1 = 111$	$\Sigma X_1^2 = 1879$

Substituting in the formula:

$$\text{Variance estimate}_{[\text{group 1}]} = \frac{\Sigma X_1^2 - \dfrac{(\Sigma X_1)^2}{N_1}}{N_1 - 1}$$

$$= \frac{1879 - \dfrac{111^2}{7}}{7 - 1}$$

$$= \frac{1879 - \dfrac{12{,}321}{7}}{6}$$

$$= \frac{1879 - 1760.143}{6}$$

$$= \frac{118.857}{6}$$

$$= 19.81 \text{ (degrees of freedom} = N_1 - 1 = 6)$$

Step 2 The variance estimate of the right hemisphere group is calculated using the standard computational formula as in Table 19.4. The sample size $N_2 = 7$.

Table 19.4 **Step 2 in the calculation of the variance estimate**

X_2 = right hemisphere	X_2^2
36	1296
28	784
4	16
18	324
2	4
22	484
1	1
$\Sigma X_2 = 111$	$\Sigma X_2^2 = 2909$

Substituting in the formula:

$$\text{Variance estimate}_{[group\ 2]} = \frac{\Sigma X_2^2 - \frac{(\Sigma X_2)^2}{N_2}}{N_2 - 1}$$

$$= \frac{2909 - \frac{111^2}{7}}{7 - 1}$$

$$= \frac{2909 - \frac{12{,}321}{7}}{6}$$

$$= \frac{2909 - 1760.143}{6}$$

$$= \frac{1148.857}{6}$$

$$= 191.48 \text{ (degrees of freedom} = N_2 - 1 = 6)$$

Step 3 The larger variance estimate is divided by the smaller:

$$F = \frac{\text{Larger variance estimate}}{\text{Smaller variance estimate}}$$

$$= \frac{191.48}{19.81}$$

$$= 9.67 \text{ (df larger variance estimate} = 6,$$
$$\text{df smaller variance estimate} = 6)$$

Step 4 We need to check whether or not a difference between the two variance estimates as large as this ratio implies would be likely if the samples came from the same population of scores. Significance Table 19.1 contains the critical values for the F-ratio. To use the table you find the intersection of the column for the degrees of freedom for the larger variance estimate and the degrees of freedom for the smaller variance estimate. Notice that the degrees of freedom we want are not listed for the numerator, so we take the next smaller listed value. Thus the table tells us we need a value of 4.39 at a minimum to be significant at the 5% level with a two-tailed test. Our calculated value of F is substantially in excess of the critical value. Thus we conclude that it is very unlikely that the two samples come from the same population of scores. We accept the hypothesis that the two sample variances are significantly different from each other.

Interpreting the results The interpretation of the F-ratio test is simply a matter of examining the two variance estimates to see which is the largest value. If the F-ratio is statistically significant then the larger of the variance estimates is significantly larger than the smaller one.

Reporting the results The results could be written up in the following terms: 'Despite there being no difference between the mean scores on emotionality following ECT to left and right brain hemispheres, the variance of emotionality was significantly higher for ECT to the right hemisphere ($F = 9.67$, df $= 6, 6$ $p < 0.05$). This suggests that ECT to the right hemisphere increases emotionality in some people but decreases it in others.'

19.3 Notes and recommendations

- Psychologists often fail to explore for differences in variances. It is good practice to routinely examine your data for them.
- The F-ratio is a necessary adjunct to applying the unrelated t-test correctly. Make sure that you check that the variances are indeed similar before using the t-test.
- Be very careful when you use the F-ratio in the analysis of variance (Chapter 20 onwards). The F-ratio in the analysis of variance is not quite the same. In this you do not always divide the larger variance estimate by the smaller variance estimate.

Chapter 20

Analysis of variance (ANOVA)

Introduction to the one-way unrelated or uncorrelated ANOVA

Preparation

It is pointless to start this chapter without a clear understanding of how to calculate the basic variance estimate formula and the computational formula for variance estimate. A working knowledge of the variance ratio test (F-ratio test) is also essential.

20.1 Introduction

Up to this point we have discussed research designs comparing the means of just *two* groups of scores. The analysis of variance (ANOVA) can do this but in addition can extend the comparison to three or more groups of scores. Analysis of variance takes many forms but is primarily used to analyse the results of experiments. Nevertheless, the simpler forms of ANOVA are routinely used in surveys and similar types of research. This chapter describes the one-way analysis of variance. This can be used whenever we wish to compare two or more groups in terms of their mean scores on a dependent variable. The scores must be independent (uncorrelated or unrelated). In other words each respondent contributes just one score to the statistical analysis. Stylistically, Table 20.1 is the sort of research design for which the (uncorrelated or unrelated) one-way analysis of variance is appropriate.

Table 20.1 **Stylised table of data for unrelated analysis of variance**

Group 1	Group 2	Group 3	Group 4
9	3	1	27
14	1	4	24
11	5	2	25
12	5	31	

The scores are those on the dependent variable. The groups are the independent variable. There are very few limitations on the research designs to which this is applicable:

1. It is possible to have any number of groups with the minimum being two.

2. The groups consist of independent samples of scores. For example the groups could be:

    (a) men versus women
    (b) an experimental versus one control group
    (c) four experimental groups and one control group
    (d) three different occupational types – managers, office personnel, and production workers.

3. The scores (the dependent variable) can be for virtually any variable. The main thing is that they are numerical scores suitable for calculating the mean and variance.

4. It is *not* necessary to have equal numbers of scores in each group. With other forms of analysis of variance, not having equal numbers can cause complications.

20.2 Some revision and some new material

You should be familiar with most of the following. Remember the formula for *variance*:

$$\text{Variance}_{[\text{definitional formula}]} = \frac{\Sigma (X - \overline{X})^2}{N}$$

If you wish to estimate the variance of a population from the variation in a sample from that population, you use the *variance estimate* formula which is:

$$\text{Variance estimate}_{[\text{definitional formula}]} = \frac{\Sigma (X - \overline{X})^2}{N - 1}$$

(By dividing by $N - 1$ we get an unbiased estimate of the population variance from the sample data.)

It is useful if you memorise the fact that the top part of the formula, i.e.

$$\Sigma (X - \overline{X})^2$$

is called the *sum of squares*. It is the sum of the squared deviations from the mean. The phrase 'sum of squares' occurs repeatedly in all forms of the analysis of variance so cannot be avoided.

The bottom part of the variance formula (N) or variance estimate formula ($N - 1$) is called in the analysis of variance the *degrees of freedom*. It is a little complex in that its calculation can vary. Nevertheless, memorising that the phrase 'degrees of freedom' refers to the bottom part of the variance formulae is a useful start.

We can rewrite the above formulae as *computational formulae*:

$$\text{Variance estimate}_{[\text{computational formula}]} = \frac{\Sigma X^2 - \frac{(\Sigma X)^2}{N}}{N-1}$$

20.3 Theoretical considerations

The analysis of variance involves very few new ideas. However, some basic concepts are used in a relatively novel way. Unfortunately, most textbooks confuse readers by presenting the analysis of variance rather obscurely. In particular, they use a variant of the computational formula for the calculation of the variance estimate which makes it very difficult to follow the logic of what is happening. This is a pity since the analysis of variance is relatively simple in many respects. The main problem is the number of steps which have to be coped with.

All measurement assumes that a score is made up of two components:

■   the 'true' value of the measurement

■   an 'error' component.

Most psychological measurements tend to have a large error component compared to the true component. Error results from all sorts of factors – tiredness, distraction, unclear instructions and so forth. Normally we cannot say precisely to what extent these factors influence our scores. It is further assumed that the 'true' and 'error' components add together to give the obtained scores (i.e. the data). So, for example, an obtained score of 15 might be made up of:

$$15_{[\text{obtained score}]} = 12_{[\text{true}]} + 3_{[\text{error}]}$$

or an obtained score of 20 might be made up as follows:

$$20 = 24 + (-4)$$

The error score may take a positive or negative value.

We have no certain knowledge about anything other than the obtained scores. *The true and error scores cannot be known directly. However, in some circumstances we can infer them through intelligent guesswork.*

In the analysis of variance, each score is separated into the two components – true scores and error scores. This is easier than it sounds. Look at Table 20.2 from some fictitious research. It is a study of the effects of two different hormones and an inert (placebo) control on depression scores in men.

Tables 20.3 and 20.4 give the best estimates possible of the 'true' scores and 'error' scores in Table 20.2. Try to work out the simple 'tricks' we have employed. All we did to produce these two new tables was the following:

Table 20.2 **Stylised table of data for unrelated analysis of variance with means**

Group 1 Hormone 1	Group 2 Hormone 2	Group 3 Placebo control
9	4	3
12	2	6
8	5	3
Mean = 9.667	Mean = 3.667	Mean = 4.000
		Overall mean = 5.778

Table 20.3 **'True' scores based on the data in Table 20.2**

Group 1 Hormone 1	Group 2 Hormone 2	Group 3 Placebo control
9.667	3.667	4.000
9.667	3.667	4.000
9.667	3.667	4.000
Mean = 9.667	Mean = 3.667	Mean = 4.000
		Overall mean = 5.778

Table 20.4 **'Error' scores based on the data in Table 20.2**

Group 1 Hormone 1	Group 2 Hormone 2	Group 3 Placebo control
−0.667	0.333	−1.000
2.333	−1.667	2.000
−1.667	1.333	−1.000
Mean = 0.000	Mean = 0.000	Mean = 0.000
		Overall mean = 0.000

1. In order to obtain a table of 'true' scores we have simply substituted the column mean for each group for the individual scores, the assumption being that the obtained scores deviate from the 'true' score because of the influence of varying amounts of error in the measurement. In statistical theory, error is assumed to be randomly distributed. Thus we have replaced all of the scores for Group 1 by the mean of 9.667. The column mean is simply the best estimate of what the 'true' score would be for the group if *we*

could get rid of the 'error' component. As all of the scores are the same, there is absolutely no error component in any of the conditions of Table 20.3. The assumption in this is that the variability within a column is due to error so the average score in a column is our best estimate of the 'true' score for that column. Notice that the column means are unchanged by this.

2. We have obtained the table of 'error' scores (Table 20.4) simply by subtracting the scores in the 'true' scores table (Table 20.3) away from the corresponding score in the original scores table (Table 20.2). What is not a 'true' score is an 'error' score by definition. Notice that the error scores show a mixture of positive and negative values, *and* that the sum of the error scores in each column (and the entire table for that matter) is zero. This is always the case with error scores and so constitutes an important check on your calculations. An alternative way of obtaining the error scores is to take the column (or group) mean away from each score in the original data table.

So what do we do now that we have the 'true' scores and 'error' scores? The two derived sets of scores – the 'true' and the 'error' scores – are used separately to estimate the variance of the population of scores from which they are samples. (That is, the calculated variance estimate for the 'true' scores is an estimate of the 'true' variation in the population, and the calculated variance estimate of the 'error' scores is an estimate of the 'error' variation in the population.) Remember, the null hypothesis for this research would suggest that differences between the three groups are due to error rather than real differences related to the influence of the independent variable. The null hypothesis suggests that both the 'true' and 'error' variance estimates are similar since they are both the result of error. *If the null hypothesis is correct*, the variance estimate derived from the 'true' scores should be no different from the variance estimate derived from the 'error' scores. After all, under the null hypothesis the variation in the 'true' scores is due to error anyway. *If the alternative hypothesis is correct*, then there should be rather more variation in the 'true' scores than is typical in the 'error' scores.

We calculate the variance estimate of the 'true' scores and then calculate the variance estimate for the 'error' scores. Next the two variance estimates are examined to see whether they are significantly different using the *F*-ratio test (the variance ratio test). This involves the following calculation:

$$F = \frac{\text{Variance estimate}_{[\text{of true scores}]}}{\text{Variance estimate}_{[\text{of error scores}]}}$$

(The error variance is always at the bottom in the analysis of variance. This is different from the *F*-ratio test described in the previous chapter. This is because we want to know if the variance estimate of the true scores is *bigger* than the variance estimate of the 'error' scores. It is of little interest if the error variance is bigger than the true variance estimate.)

Significance Table 20.1   5% significance values of the *F*-ratio for unrelated ANOVA

Your value has to equal or be larger than the tabulated value to be significant at the 5% level for a two-tailed test (i.e. to accept the hypothesis).

Additional values are to be found in Significance Table 19.1.

Degrees of freedom for error or within-cells mean square (or variance estimate)	Degrees of freedom for true or between-treatments mean square (or variance estimate)					
	1	2	3	4	5	∞
1	161 or more	200	216	225	230	254
2	18.5	19.0	19.2	19.3	19.3	19.5
3	10.1	9.6	9.3	9.1	9.0	8.5
4	7.7	6.9	6.6	6.4	6.3	5.6
5	6.6	5.8	5.4	5.2	5.1	4.4
6	6.0	5.1	4.8	4.5	4.4	3.7
7	5.6	4.7	4.4	4.1	4.0	3.2
8	5.3	4.5	4.1	3.8	3.7	2.9
9	5.1	4.3	3.9	3.6	3.5	2.7
10	5.0	4.1	3.7	3.5	3.3	2.5
13	4.7	3.8	3.4	3.2	3.0	2.2
15	4.5	3.7	3.3	3.1	2.9	2.1
20	4.4	3.5	3.1	2.9	2.7	1.8
30	4.2	3.3	2.9	2.7	2.5	1.6
60	4.0	3.2	2.8	2.5	2.4	1.4
∞	3.8	3.0	2.6	2.4	2.2	1.0

It is then a fairly straightforward matter to use Significance Table 20.1 for the *F*-distribution to decide whether or not these two variance estimates are significantly different from each other. We just need to be careful to use the appropriate numbers of degrees of freedom. The *F*-ratio calculation was demonstrated in Chapter 19. If the variance estimates are similar then the variance in 'true' scores is little different from the variance in the 'error' scores; since the estimated 'true' variance is much the same as the 'error' variance in this case, both can be regarded as 'error'. On the other hand, if the *F*-ratio is significant it means that the variation due to the 'true' scores is much greater than that due to 'error'; the 'true' scores represent reliable differences between groups rather than chance factors.

And that is just about it for the one-way analysis of variance. There is just one remaining issue: the *degrees of freedom*. If one were to work out the variance estimate of the original data in our study we would use the formula as given above:

$$\text{Variance estimate}_{[\text{original data}]} = \frac{\Sigma X^2 - \frac{(\Sigma X)^2}{N}}{N - 1}$$

where $N - 1$ is the number of degrees of freedom.

However, the calculation of the number of degrees of freedom varies in the analysis of variance (it is not always $N - 1$). With the 'true' and 'error' scores the degrees of freedom are a little more complex although easily calculated using formulae. But the idea of degrees of freedom can be understood at a more fundamental level with a little work.

20.4 Degrees of freedom

This section gives a detailed explanation of degrees of freedom. It might be convenient to ignore this section until you are a little more familiar with ANOVA.

Degrees of freedom refer to the distinct items of information contained in your data. By information we mean something which is new and not already known. For example, if we asked you what is the combined age of your two best friends and then asked you the age of the younger of the two, you would be crazy to accept a bet that we could tell you the age of your older best friend, the reason being that if you told us that the combined ages of your best friends was 37 years and that the younger was 16 years, any fool could work out that the older best friend must be 21 years. The age of your older best friend is contained within the first two pieces of information. The age of your older friend is redundant because you already know it from your previous information.

It is much the same sort of idea with degrees of freedom – which might be better termed the quantity of distinct information.

Table 20.5 'True' scores based on the data in Table 20.2

Group 1 Hormone 1	Group 2 Hormone 2	Group 3 Placebo control
9.667	3.667	4.000
9.667	3.667	4.000
9.667	3.667	4.000
Mean = 9.667	Mean = 3.667	Mean = 4.000
		Overall mean = 5.778

Table 20.6 **Insertion of arbitrary values in the first column**

Group 1	Group 2	Group 3
10.000	–	–
10.000	–	–
10.000	–	–
Mean = 10.000		
		Overall mean = 5.778

Table 20.7 **Insertion of arbitrary values in the second column**

Group 1	Group 2	Group 3
10.000	3.000	–
10.000	3.000	–
10.000	3.000	–
Mean = 10.000	Mean = 3.000	
		Overall mean = 5.778

Table 20.5 repeats the table of the 'true' scores that we calculated earlier as Table 20.3. The question is how many items of truly new information the table contains. You have to bear in mind that what we are looking at is the variance estimate of the scores which is basically their variation around the overall mean of 5.778. Don't forget that the overall mean of 5.778 is our best estimate of the population mean under the null hypothesis that the groups do not differ.

Just how many of the scores in this table are we able to alter and still obtain this same overall mean of 5.778? For this table, we simply start scrubbing out the scores one-by-one and putting in any value we like. So *if we start with the first person in Group 1* we can arbitrarily set his or her score to 10.000 (or any other score you can think of). But, once we have done so, each score in Group 1 has to be changed to 10.000 because the columns of the 'true' score table have to have identical entries. Thus the first column has to look like the column in Table 20.6 (the dashes represent parts of the table we have not dealt with yet).

We have been free to vary just one score so far. We can now move on to the Group 2 column. Here we can arbitrarily put in a score of 3.000 to replace the first entry. Once we do this then the remaining two scores in the column have to be the same because this is the nature of 'true' tables – all the scores in a column have to be identical (Table 20.7).

Thus so far we have managed to vary only two scores independently. We can now move on to Group 3. We could start by entering, say, 5.000 to replace the

Table 20.8 Forced insertion of a particular value in the third column because of the requirement that the overall mean is 5.778

Group 1	Group 2	Group 3
10.000	3.000	4.333
10.000	3.000	4.333
10.000	3.000	4.333
Mean = 10.000	Mean = 3.000	Mean = 4.333
		Overall mean = 5.778

Table 20.9 'Error' scores based on the data in Table 20.2

Group 1	Group 2	Group 3
−0.667	0.333	−1.000
2.333	−1.667	2.000
−1.667	1.333	−1.000
Mean = 0.000	Mean = 0.000	Mean = 0.000
		Overall mean = 0.000

first score but there is a problem. The overall mean has to end up as 5.778 and the number 5.000 will not allow this to happen given that all of the scores in Group 3 would have to be 5.000. There is only one number which can be put in the Group 3 column which will give an overall mean of 5.778, that is 4.333 (Table 20.8).

We have not increased the number of scores we were free to vary by changing Group 3 – we have changed the scores but we had no freedom other than to put one particular score in their place.

Thus we have varied only *two* scores in the 'true' scores table – notice that this is one less than the number of groups we have. We speak of *the 'true' scores having two degrees of freedom*.

It is a similar process with the error table. The requirements this time are (a) that the column averages equal zero and (b) that the overall average equals zero. This is because they are error scores which must produce these characteristics – if they do not they cannot be error scores. Just how many of the scores can we vary this time and keep within these limitations? (We have 'adjusted' the column means to ignore a tiny amount of rounding error.)

The answer is six scores (Table 20.9). The first *two* scores in each group can be varied to any values you like. However, having done this the value of the third score has to be fixed in order that the column mean equals zero. Since there are three equal-size groups then there are *six degrees of freedom for the error table* in this case.

Just in case you are wondering, for the *original data* table the degrees of freedom correspond to the number of scores minus one. This is because there are no individual column constraints – the only constraint is that the overall mean has to be 5.778. The lack of column constraints means that the first eight scores could be given any value you like and only the final score is fixed by the requirement that the overall mean is 5.778. In other words, the variance estimate for the original data table uses $N - 1$ as the denominator – thus the formula is the usual variance estimate formula for a sample of scores.

Also note that the degrees of freedom for the 'error' and 'true' scores tables add up to $N - 1$.

Quick formulae for degrees of freedom

Anyone who has difficulty with the above explanation of degrees of freedom should take heart. Few of us would bother to work out the degrees of freedom from first principles. It is much easier to use simple formulae. For the one-way analysis of variance using unrelated samples, the degrees of freedom are as follows:

N = Number of scores in the table
Degrees of freedom$_{[original\ data]}$ = $N - 1$
Degrees of freedom$_{['true'\ scores]}$ = Number of columns – 1
Degrees of freedom$_{['error'\ scores]}$ = N – Number of columns

This is not cheating – most textbooks ignore the meaning of degrees of freedom and merely give the formulae anyway.

Calculation 20.1

Unrelated/uncorrelated one-way analysis of variance

Step-by-step, the following is the calculation of the analysis of variance.

Step 1 Draw up your data table using the format shown in Table 20.10. The degrees of freedom for this table is the number of scores minus one = $9 - 1 = 8$.

Table 20.10 **Data table for an unrelated analysis of variance**

Group 1 Hormone 1	Group 2 Hormone 2	Group 3 Placebo control
9	4	3
12	2	6
8	5	3
Mean = 9.667	Mean = 3.667	Mean = 4.000
		Overall mean = 5.778

Although this is not absolutely necessary you can calculate the variance estimate of your data table as a computational check – the sum of squares for the data table should equal the total of the sums of squares for the separate components. Thus, adding together the true and error sums of squares should give the total sum of squares for the data table. Similarly, the data degrees of freedom should equal the total of the true and error degrees of freedom. We will use the computational formula:

$$\text{Variance estimate}_{\text{[original data]}} = \frac{\Sigma X^2 - \frac{(\Sigma X)^2}{N}}{df}$$

ΣX^2 means square each of the scores and then sum these individual calculations:

$$
\begin{aligned}
\Sigma X^2 &= 9^2 + 4^2 + 3^2 + 12^2 + 2^2 + 6^2 + 8^2 + 5^2 + 3^2 \\
&= 81 + 16 + 9 + 144 + 4 + 36 + 64 + 25 + 9 \\
&= 388
\end{aligned}
$$

$(\Sigma X)^2$ means add up all of the scores and then square the total:

$$
\begin{aligned}
(\Sigma X)^2 &= (9 + 4 + 3 + 12 + 2 + 6 + 8 + 5 + 3)^2 \\
&= (52)^2 \\
&= 2704
\end{aligned}
$$

The number of scores, N, equals 9. The degrees of freedom (df) equals $N - 1 = 9 - 1 = 8$. Substituting in the formula:

$$\text{Variance estimate}_{\text{[original data]}} = \frac{\Sigma X^2 - \frac{(\Sigma X)^2}{N}}{df}$$

$$= \frac{388 - \frac{2704}{9}}{8}$$

$$= \frac{388 - 300.444}{8}$$

$$= \frac{87.556}{8}$$

$$= 10.944$$

Step 2 Draw up Table 20.11 of 'true' scores by replacing the scores in each column by the column mean.

Table 20.11   'True' scores based on the data in Table 20.10

Group 1	Group 2	Group 3
9.667	3.667	4.000
9.667	3.667	4.000
9.667	3.667	4.000
Mean = 9.667	Mean = 3.667	Mean = 4.000
		Overall mean = 5.778

$$\Sigma X^2 = 9.667^2 + 3.667^2 + 4.000^2 + 9.667^2 + 3.667^2 + 4.000^2 + 9.667^2 + 3.667^2 + 4.000^2$$

$$= 93.451 + 13.447 + 16.000 + 93.451 + 13.447 + 16.000 + 93.451 + 13.447 + 16.000$$

$$= 368.694$$

$$(\Sigma X)^2 = (9.667 + 3.667 + 4.000 + 9.667 + 3.667 + 4.000 + 9.667 + 3.667 + 4.000)^2$$

$$= (52.000)^2$$

$$= 2704$$

The number of scores, N, equals 9. The degrees of freedom (df) are given by:

$$\text{Degrees of freedom}_{[\text{true scores}]} = \text{Number of columns} - 1$$

$$= 3 - 1$$

$$= 2$$

We can now substitute in the formula:

$$\text{Variance estimate}_{[\text{true scores}]} = \frac{\Sigma X^2 - \dfrac{(\Sigma X)^2}{N}}{df}$$

$$= \frac{368.694 - \dfrac{2704}{9}}{2}$$

$$= \frac{368.694 - 300.444}{2}$$

$$= \frac{68.250}{2}$$

$$= 34.125$$

Table 20.12 'Error' scores based on the data in Table 20.10

Group 1	Group 2	Group 3
−0.667	0.333	−1.000
2.333	−1.667	2.000
−1.667	1.333	−1.000
Mean = 0.000	Mean = 0.000	Mean = 0.000
		Overall mean = 0.000

Step 3 Draw up the table of the 'error' scores (Table 20.12) by subtracting the 'true' scores table from the original data table (Table 20.10). Remember all you have to do is to take the corresponding scores in the two tables when doing this subtraction. The alternative is to take the appropriate column mean away from each score in your data table.

$$\text{Variance estimate}_{[\text{original data}]} = \frac{\Sigma X^2 - \dfrac{(\Sigma X)^2}{N}}{df}$$

$$\Sigma X^2 = (-0.667)^2 + 0.333^2 + (-1.000)^2 + 2.333^2 + (-1.667)^2 + 2.000^2 + (-1.667)^2 + 1.333^2 + (-1.000)^2$$

$$= 0.445 + 0.111 + 1.000 + 5.443 + 2.779 + 4.000 + 2.779 + 1.777 + 1.000$$

$$= 19.334$$

$$(\Sigma X)^2 = [(-0.667) + 0.333 + (-1.000) + 2.333 + (-1.667) + 2.000 + (-1.667) + 1.333 + (-1.000)]^2$$

$$= 0$$

The number of scores, N, equals 9. The degrees of freedom (df) equals N minus the number of columns, i.e. $9 - 3 = 6$. We can now substitute in the above formula:

$$\text{Variance estimate}_{[\text{error}]} = \frac{\Sigma X^2 - \dfrac{(\Sigma X)^2}{N}}{df}$$

$$= \frac{19.334 - \dfrac{0}{9}}{6}$$

$$= 3.222$$

Step 4 We can now work out the F-ratio by dividing the variance estimate$_{[\text{true scores}]}$ by the variance estimate$_{[\text{error scores}]}$:

$$F\text{-ratio} = \frac{\text{Variance estimate}_{[\text{true scores}]}}{\text{Variance estimate}_{[\text{error scores}]}}$$

$$= \frac{34.125}{3.222}$$

$$= 10.6 \text{ (degrees of freedom} = 2 \text{ for true and 6 for error)}$$

From Significance Table 20.1, we need a value of F of 5.1 or more to be significant at the 5% level of significance. Since our value of 10.6 is substantially larger than this, we can reject the null hypothesis and accept the hypothesis that the groups are significantly different from each other at the 5% level of significance.

20.5 The analysis of variance summary table

The analysis of variance calculation can get very complicated with complex experimental designs. In preparation for this, it is useful to get into the habit of recording your analysis in an analysis of variance summary table. This systematically records major aspects of the calculation. Table 20.13 is appropriate to the above analysis. Notice that the sums of squares for 'true' and 'error' added together are the same as the sum of squares of the original data (allowing for rounding errors). Don't forget that the sum of squares is simply the upper part of the variance estimate formula. Similarly the degrees of freedom of 'true' and 'error' scores added together give the degrees of freedom for the original data. The degrees of freedom are the lower part of the variance estimate formula.

In Table 20.13, we have used the terminology from our explanation. This is not quite standard in discussions regarding the analysis of variance. It is more usual to see the analysis of variance summary table in the form of Table 20.14 which uses slightly different terms.

Tables 20.13 and 20.14 are equivalent except for the terminology and the style of reporting significance levels:

1. 'Mean square' is analysis of variance terminology for variance estimate. Unfortunately the name 'mean square' loses track of the fact that it is an estimate and suggests that it is something new.

Table 20.13 **Analysis of variance summary table for unrelated ANOVAs**

Source of variation	Sum of squares	Degrees of freedom	Variance estimate	F-ratio	Probability
'True' scores	68.250	2	34.125	10.6	5%
'Error' scores	19.334	6	3.222		
Original data	87.556	8	10.944		

Table 20.14 **Analysis of variance summary table for unrelated ANOVAs using alternative terminology**

Source variation	Sum of squares	Degrees of freedom	Mean square	F-ratio
Between groups	68.250	2	34.125	10.6[a]
Within groups	19.334	6	3.222	
Total	87.556	8	10.944	

[a] Significant at 5% level.

2. 'Between' is another way of describing the variation due to the 'true' scores. The idea is that the variation of the 'true' scores is essentially the differences between the groups or experimental conditions. Sometimes these are called the 'treatments'.

3. 'Within' is just another way of describing the 'error' variation. It is called 'within' since the calculation of 'error' is based on the variation *within* a group or experimental condition.

4. Total is virtually self explanatory – it is the variation of the original scores which combine 'true' and 'error' components.

20.6 Quick calculation methods for ANOVA

The following step-by-step procedure describes the quick way for calculating the unrelated/uncorrelated one-way ANOVA by hand. This is less error prone than the conceptually more clear method described in Calculation 20.1 which often suffers from accumulated rounding errors. Statistics textbooks usually describe the quick formula method. It is based on the computational formula for the variance estimate (p. 111).

Calculation 20.2

One-way unrelated analysis of variance: quick method

The following calculation involves three different conditions (levels) of the independent variable. The method is easily adapted to any other number of conditions from a minimum of two.

Step 1 Draw up a data table using the format shown in Table 20.15. Calculate the totals for each column separately (i.e. T_1, T_2, T_3). (Notice that you are calculating totals rather than means with this method.) Remember that this table gives us the data on the influence of the independent variable (drug treatment, which has three levels – Hormone 1, Hormone 2 and Placebo control) on the dependent variable (depression).

1. Calculate the overall (or grand) total of the scores: $G = 9 + 12 + 8 + 4 + 2 + 5 + 3 + 6 + 3 = 52$, or simply add the column totals to obtain this value.
2. Calculate the number of scores: $N = 9$.
3. Insert the number of scores for each group (N_1, N_2 and N_3). In our example these are all 3 as the group sizes are equal, but this does not have to be so with the unrelated one-way analysis of variance.
4. Total degrees of freedom for the data table is: number of scores – 1 $= 9 - 1 = 8$.

Table 20.15 **Stylised data table for an unrelated analysis of variance**

Group 1 Hormone 1	Group 2 Hormone 2	Group 3 Placebo control
9	4	3
12	2	6
8	5	3
$N_1 = 3$	$N_2 = 3$	$N_3 = 3$
Total $= T_1 = 9 +12+8 = 29$	Total $= T_2 = 4+2+5 = 11$	Total $= T_3 = 3+6+3 = 12$

Step 2 Square each of the scores (X) and then sum all of these squared scores (i.e. to give the sum of squared scores or ΣX^2):

$$\Sigma X^2 = 9^2 + 12^2 + 8^2 + 4^2 + 2^2 + 5^1 + 3^2 + 6^2 + 3^2$$
$$= 81 + 144 + 64 + 16 + 4 + 25 + 9 + 36 + 9$$
$$= 388.000$$

Step 3 Calculate the 'correction factor' (G^2/N) by substituting the values of G and N previously obtained in steps 1 and 2. (The correction factor is merely part of the computational formula for the variance estimate (p. 111) expressed as (G^2/N) rather than (ΣX)^2/N.

$$\text{Correction factor} = \frac{G^2}{N} = \frac{52^2}{9} = \frac{2704}{9}$$
$$= 300.444$$

Step 4 The outcome of step 2 minus the outcome of step 3 gives the total sum of squares (SS$_{[total]}$) for the data table. It is equivalent to part of the computational formula for the calculation of the variance estimate (p. 111). Substituting the previously calculated values:

$$SS_{[total]} = \Sigma X^2 - \frac{G^2}{N}$$
$$= 388.000 - 300.444$$
$$= 87.556$$

Enter this value of the total sum of squares into an analysis of variance summary table such as Table 20.16.

Enter the degrees of freedom for the total sum of squares. This is always $N - 1$ or the number of scores $- 1 = 9 - 1 = 8$.

Step 5 The sum of squares between groups ($SS_{[between]}$) can be calculated as follows using the correction factor (from step 3) and the column totals (T_1 etc.) and cell sizes (n_1 etc.) from Table 20.15.

$$SS_{[between]} = \frac{T_1^2}{N_1} + \frac{T_2^2}{N_2} + \frac{T_3^2}{N_3} - \frac{G^2}{N}$$

$$= \frac{29^2}{3} + \frac{11^2}{3} + \frac{12^2}{3} - 300.44$$

$$= \frac{841}{3} + \frac{121}{3} + \frac{144}{3} - 300.44$$

$$= 280.333 + 40.333 + 48.000 - 300.444$$

$$= 368.666 - 300.444$$

$$= 68.222$$

The degrees of freedom between subjects is columns $- 1 = c - 1 = 3 - 1 = 2$. These values are entered in Table 20.16.

Step 6 Calculate the error (i.e. error or within) sum of squares ($SS_{[error]}$) by subtracting the between sum of squares from the total sum of squares:

$$SS_{[error]} = SS_{[total]} - SS_{[between]} = 87.566 - 68.222$$
$$= 19.344$$

The degrees of freedom for error are the number of scores minus the number of columns: $N - c = 9 - 3 = 6$. These values are entered in Table 20.16.

Step 7 The F-ratio is the between-groups mean square divided by the error mean square. This is $68.22/19.34 = 10.6$. This value can be checked against Significance Table 20.1. We need a value of F of 5.1 or more to be significant at the 5% level of significance with two degrees of freedom for the between groups mean square and six degrees of freedom for the error mean square. Thus our obtained F-ratio of 10.6 is statistically significant at the 5% level.

Interpreting the results The most important step in interpreting your data is simple. You need a table of the means for each of the conditions such as Table 20.17. It is obvious from this table that two of the cell means are fairly similar whereas the mean of Group 1 is relatively high. This would suggest to an experienced researcher that *if* the one-way analysis of variance is statistically significant, then a multiple-comparisons test (Chapter 23) is needed in order to test for significant differences between pairs of group means.

Reporting the results The results of this analysis could be written up as follows: 'The data were analysed using an unrelated one-way analysis of variance. It was found that there was a significant effect of the independent variable drug treatment on the dependent variable depression ($F = 10.59$, df = 2, 6, $p < 0.05$). The mean for the Hormone 1 group ($M = 9.67$) appears to indicate greater depression scores than for the Hormone 2 group ($M = 3.67$) and the placebo control ($M = 4.00$).'

Of course, you can use Appendix J to test for significance at other levels.
     In order to test whether the mean for Group 1 is significantly greater than for the other two groups, it is necessary to apply a multiple-comparisons test such as the Scheffe Test (Chapter 23) if the differences had not been predicted. The outcome of this should also be reported.

Table 20.16 **Analysis of variance summary table**

Source of variation	Sum of squares	Degrees of freedom	Mean square (variance estimate)	F-ratio
Between groups	68.222	2	34.111	$\dfrac{34.111}{3.222} = 10.59^a$
Error (within groups)	19.334	6	3.222	
Total	87.556	8	10.945	

[a] Significant at the 5% level.

We have given intermediary calculations for the F-ratio; these are not usually reported but may be helpful for calculation purposes.

Table 20.17 **Table of cell means**

Group 1 Hormone 1	Group 2 Hormone 2	Group 3 Placebo control
Mean = $M_1 = 9.67$	Mean = $M_2 = 3.67$	Mean = $M_3 = 4.00$

20.7 Notes and recommendations

■ The *t*-test is simply a special case of one-way ANOVA, so these tests can be used interchangeably when you have two groups of scores. They give identical significance levels.

■ Do not be too deterred by some of the strange terminology used in the analysis of variance. Words like treatments and levels of treatment merely reveal the agricultural origins of these statistical procedures; be warned that it gets worse. Levels of treatment simply refers to the number of different conditions for each independent variable. Thus if the independent variable has three different values it is said to have three different levels of the treatment.

■ The analysis of variance with just two conditions or sets of scores is relatively easy to interpret. You merely have to examine the difference between the means of the two conditions. It is not so easy where you have three or more groups. Your analysis may not be complete until you have employed a multiple comparisons procedure as in Chapter 23.

■ We have used computational procedures which are not identical to those in most textbooks. We have tried to explain the analysis of variance by referring to the basic notion of variance estimate. Virtually every textbook we have seen merely gives computational procedures alone. More typical calculation methods are also included in this book.

Chapter 21

Analysis of variance for correlated scores or repeated measures

Preparation

You need a good understanding of the unrelated/uncorrelated analysis of variance (Chapter 20). In addition, the difference between correlated/related samples and unrelated/uncorrelated samples (or repeated measures) should be revised.

> The analysis of variance reported in this chapter is also called the related, related scores, related samples, repeated measures and matched analysis of variance.

21.1 Introduction

Correlated or related research designs are held to be efficient forms of planning research. Generally these designs involve the same group of participants being assessed in two or more research conditions. The assumption is that by doing so many of the differences between people are 'allowed for' by having each person 'serve as their own control' – that is, appear in all of the research conditions.

The different sets of scores in the related or correlated analysis of variance are essentially different treatment conditions. We can describe them as either different levels of the treatment or different experimental conditions (Table 21.1).

The numerical scores are scores on the *dependent variable*. They can be any measures for which it is possible to calculate their means and variances meaningfully, in other words basically numerical scores. The treatments are the levels of the independent variable. There are very few limitations to the use of this research design:

1. It is possible to have any number of treatments with two being the minimum.

Table 21.1 **Stylised research design for the analysis of variance**

Case	Treatment 1	Treatment 2	Treatment 3	Treatment 4
Case 1 (John)	9	14	6	18
Case 2 (Heather)	7	12	9	15
Case 3 (Jane)	5	11	6	17
Case 4 (Tracy)	10	17	12	24
Case 5 (Paul)	8	15	7	19

Table 21.2 **Research design of IQ assessed sequentially over time**

Child	Age 5 years	Age 8 years	Age 10 years
John	120	125	130
Paula	93	90	100
Sharon	130	140	110
etc.			

Table 21.3 **Reaction time in seconds comparing two experimental conditions with two control conditions**

Subject	Four-letter words	Mild swear words	Neutral words	Nonsense syllables
Darren	0.3	0.5	0.2	0.2
Lisa	0.4	0.3	0.3	0.4
etc.				

2. The groups consist of related or correlated sets of scores, for example:
   (a) children's IQs assessed at the age of 5 years, then again at 8 years and finally at 10 years (Table 21.2)
   (b) two experimental conditions versus two control conditions so long as the same subjects are in each of the conditions. The research is a study of reaction time to recognising words. The two experimental conditions are very emotive words (four-letter words) and moderately emotive words (mild swear words). The two control conditions are using neutral words and using nonsense syllables; the dependent variable is reaction time (Table 21.3)
   (c) a group of weight watchers' weights before and after dieting. The dependent variable is their weight in pounds (Table 21.4).
3. It is necessary to have equal numbers of scores in each group since this is a related subjects or repeated measures design. Obviously in the above examples we have used small numbers of cases.

Table 21.4 **Weight in pounds before and after dieting**

Dieter	Before diet	After diet
Ben	130	120
Claudine	153	141
etc.		

Table 21.5 **Stylised ANOVA design using matched samples**

Matched set	Treatment 1	Treatment 2	Treatment 3	Treatment 4
Matched set 1	9	14	6	18
Matched set 2	7	12	9	15
Matched set 3	5	11	6	17
Matched set 4	10	17	12	24
Matched set 5	8	15	7	19

The related/correlated analysis of variance can also be applied when you have *matched sets* of people (Table 21.5). By this we mean that although there are different people in each of the treatment conditions, they are actually very similar. Each set is as alike as possible on specified variables such as age or intelligence. One member of each matched set is assigned at random to each of the treatment conditions. The variables forming the basis of the matching are believed or known to be correlated with the dependent variable. There is no point in matching if they are not. The purpose of matching is to reduce the amount of 'error' variation.

One advantage of using matched sets of people in experiments rather than the same person in several different treatment conditions is their lack of awareness of the other treatment conditions. That is, they only respond in one version of the experimental design and so cannot be affected by their ex-perience of the other conditions. Matching can be done on any variables you wish but it can get cumbersome if there are too many variables on which to match. So, for example, if you believed that age and sex were related to the dependent variable, you could control for these variables by using matched sets which contained people of the same sex and a very similar age. In this way variation due to sex and age is equally spread between the different treatments or conditions. Thus, Matched Set 1 might consist of four people matched in that they are all females in the age range 21–25 years. Each one of each of these is randomly assigned to one of the four treatment conditions. Matched Set 2 might consist of four males in the age range 16 to 20 years. Once again, one of each of these four people is randomly assigned to one of the four treatment conditions.

21.2 Theoretical considerations

It is a very small step from the uncorrelated to the correlated analysis of variance. All that is different in the correlated ANOVA is that the *error* scores are reduced (or adjusted) by removing from them the contribution made by *individual differences*. By an individual difference we mean the tendency of a particular person to score generally high or generally low irrespective of the research treatment or condition they are being tested in. So, for example, bright people will tend to score higher on tests involving intellectual skills no matter what the test is. Less bright people may tend to score relatively poorly no matter what the intellectual test is. In *uncorrelated* research designs there is no way of knowing the contribution of individual differences. In effect, the individual differences have to be lumped together with the rest of the variance which we have called error. But *repeated/related/correlated* designs allow us to subdivide the error variance into two sorts: (a) that which is explained (as individual differences), and (b) that which remains unexplained (or residual error variance). So far we have discussed error variance as if it were purely the result of chance factors but error variance is to some extent explicable in theory – the problem is that we do not know what causes it. If we can get an estimate of the contribution of an individual's particular characteristics to their scores in our research we should be able to revise the error scores so that they no longer contain any contribution from the individual difference of that participant. (Remember that individual differences are those characteristics of individuals which tend to encourage them to score generally high or generally low on the dependent variable.)

21.3 Examples

Once we have measured the same participant twice (or more) then it is possible to estimate the individual difference. Take the data from two individuals given in Table 21.6. Looking at these data we can see the participants' memory ability for both words and numbers. It is clear that Ann Jones tends to do better on these memory tasks irrespective of the precise nature of the task; John Smith generally does worse no matter what the task. Although both of them seem to do better on memory for numbers, this does not alter the tendency for Ann Jones to

Table 21.6 **Individual differences for two people**

Subject	Memory for words	Memory for numbers	Row mean
Ann Jones	17	20	18.5
John Smith	11	14	12.5
		Overall mean = 15.5	

Table 21.7 **Pain relief scores from a drugs experiment**

Participant	Aspirin	Product X	Placebo	Row mean
Bob Robertson	7	8	6	7.000
Mavis Fletcher	5	10	3	6.000
Bob Polansky	6	6	4	5.333
Ann Harrison	9	9	2	6.667
Bert Entwistle	3	7	5	5.000
Column mean	6.000	8.000	4.000	Overall mean = 6.000

generally do better. This is not measurement error but a general characteristic of Ann Jones. On average, Ann Jones tends to score six points above John Smith or three points above the overall mean of 15.5 and John Smith tends to score three points below the overall mean of 15.5. In other words, we can give a numerical value to their individual difference relative to the overall mean.

A physiological psychologist is researching the effects of different pain relieving drugs on the amount of relief from pain that people experience in a controlled trial. In one condition people are given aspirin, in another condition they are given the trial drug Product X, and in the third condition (the control condition) they are given a tablet which contains no active ingredient (this is known as a placebo). The amount of relief from pain experienced in these conditions is rated by each of the participants. The higher the score, the more pain relief. Just to be absolutely clear, participant 1 (Bob Robertson) gets a relief from pain score of 7 when given one aspirin, 8 when given Product X and 6 when given the inactive placebo tablet (Table 21.7). It is obvious that Bob Robertson tends to get the most relief from pain (the row mean for Bob is the highest there is) whereas Bert Entwistle tends to get the least relief from pain (his row mean is the lowest there is).

The related/correlated scores analysis of variance is different in that we make adjustments for these tendencies for individuals to typically score generally high or generally low or generally in the middle. We simply subtract each person's row mean from the table's overall mean of 6.000 to find the amount of adjustment needed to each person's score in order to 'eliminate' individual differences from the scores. Thus for Bob Robertson we need to add −1 (i.e. 6.000 − 7.000) to each of his scores in order to overcome the tendency of his scores to be 1.000 higher than the overall mean (i.e. average score in the table). Do not forget that adding −1 is the same as subtracting 1. Table 21.8 shows the amount of adjustment needed to everyone's scores in order to eliminate individual differences.

Apart from the adjustment for individual differences, the rest of the analysis of variance is much as in Chapter 20.

Table 21.8 **Amount of adjustment of Table 21.7 for individual differences**

Participant	Overall mean	Row mean	Adjustment needed to error scores to allow for individual differences (overall mean minus row mean)
Bob Robertson	6.000	7.000	−1.000
Mavis Fletcher	6.000	6.000	0.000
Bob Polansky	6.000	5.333	0.667
Ann Harrison	6.000	6.667	−0.667
Bert Entwistle	6.000	5.000	1.000

Calculation 21.1

Correlated samples analysis of variance

The end point of our calculations is the analysis of variance summary table (Table 21.9). Hopefully by the time we reach the end of our explanation you will understand all of the entries in this table.

Step 1 To begin, you need to tabulate your data. We will use the fictitious relief from pain experiment described above. This is given in Table 21.10.

If you wish you may calculate the variance estimate of this table using the standard variance estimate formula. As this is generally only a check on your calculations it is unnecessary for our present purposes since it contains nothing new. If you do the calculation then you should find that the sum of

Table 21.9 **Analysis of variance summary table**

Source of variation	Sum of squares	Degrees of freedom	Mean square (or variance estimate)	F-ratio	Probability (significance)
Between treatments (i.e. drugs)	40.00	2	20.00	5.10	5%
Between people (i.e. individual differences)	8.67	4	2.17		
Error (i.e. residual)	31.33	8	3.92		
Total	80.00	14			

Table 21.10 **Pain relief scores from a drugs experiment**

Participant	Aspirin	Product X	Placebo	Row mean
Rob Robertson	7	8	6	7.000
Mavis Fletcher	5	10	3	6.000
Bob Polansky	6	6	4	5.333
Ann Harrison	9	9	2	6.667
Bert Entwistle	3	7	5	5.000
Column mean	6.000	8.000	4.000	Overall mean = 6.000

Table 21.11 **'True' scores (obtained by replacing each score in a column by its column mean)**

Participant	Aspirin	Product X	Placebo	Row mean
Bob Robertson	6.000	8.000	4.000	6.000
Mavis Fletcher	6.000	8.000	4.000	6.000
Bob Polansky	6.000	8.000	4.000	6.000
Ann Harrison	6.000	8.000	4.000	6.000
Bert Entwistle	6.000	8.000	4.000	6.000
Column mean	6.000	8.000	4.000	Overall mean = 6.000

squares is 80 and the degrees of freedom 14 which would give a variance estimate value of 5.71 (i.e. 80 divided by 14). The first two pieces of information are entered into the analysis of variance summary table.

Step 2 We then produce a table of the 'true' scores. Remember that 'true' scores are usually called the 'between' or 'between groups' scores in analysis of variance. To do this we simply substitute the column mean for each of the individual scores in that column so leaving no variation within the column – the only variation is between the columns. The results are given in Table 21.11.

The estimated variance of these data can be calculated using the standard formula:

$$\text{Estimated variance}_{[\text{true/between scores}]} = \frac{\Sigma X^2 - \frac{(\Sigma X)^2}{N}}{df}$$

$$\Sigma X^2 = 6.000^2 + 8.000^2 + 4.000^2 + 6.000^2 + 8.000^2$$
$$+ 4.000^2 + 6.000^2 + 8.000^2 + 4.000^2 + 6.000^2$$
$$+ 8.000^2 + 4.000^2 + 6.000^2 + 8.000^2 + 4.000^2$$

$$= 36.000 + 64.000 + 16.000 + 36.000 + 64.000$$
$$+ 16.000 + 36.000 + 64.000 + 16.000 + 36.000$$
$$+ 64.000 + 16.000 + 36.000 + 64.000 + 16.000$$
$$= 580$$

$$(\Sigma X)^2 = (6.000 + 8.000 + 4.000 + 6.000 + 8.000$$
$$+ 4.000 + 6.000 + 8.000 + 4.000 + 6.000$$
$$+ 8.000 + 4.000 + 6.000 + 8.000 + 4.000)^2$$
$$= (90)^2$$
$$= 8100$$

The number of scores, N, equals 15. The degrees of freedom (df) equals the number of columns of data minus $1 = 3 - 1 = 2$. Substituting in the formula:

$$\text{Estimated variance}_{[\text{true/between scores}]} = \frac{\Sigma X^2 - \frac{(\Sigma X)^2}{N}}{df}$$

$$= \frac{580 - \frac{8100}{15}}{2}$$

$$= \frac{580 - 540}{2}$$

$$= \frac{40}{2}$$

$$= 20.00$$

Table 21.12 **'Error' scores (original data table minus true/between scores)**

Participant	Aspirin	Product X	Placebo	Row mean
Bob Robertson	1.000	0.000	2.000	1.000
Mavis Fletcher	−1.000	2.000	−1.000	0.000
Bob Polansky	0.000	−2.000	0.000	−0.667
Ann Harrison	3.000	1.000	−2.000	0.667
Bert Entwistle	−3.000	−1.000	1.000	−1.000
Column mean	0.000	0.000	0.000	Overall mean = 0.000

Table 21.13 'Residual (error)' scores (obtained by subtracting individual differences or row means from Table 21.12)

Participant	Aspirin	Product X	Placebo	Row mean
Bob Robertson	0.000	–1.000	1.000	0.000
Mavis Fletcher	–1.000	2.000	–1.000	0.000
Bob Polansky	0.667	–1.333	0.667	0.000
Ann Harrison	2.333	0.333	–2.667	0.000
Bert Entwistle	–2.000	0.000	2.000	0.000
Column mean	0.000	0.000	0.000	Overall mean = 0.000

Step 3 The error table is now calculated as an intermediate stage. As ever, this is done by subtracting the true/between scores from the scores in the original data table (see Table 21.12). Alternatively, we subtract the column mean from each of the scores in the data table.

This is essentially our table of 'error' scores but since the row means vary (Bert Entwistle's is –1.000 but Mavis Fletcher's is 0.000) then we still have to remove the effects of the individual differences. This we do simply by taking away the row mean from each of the error scores in the row. That is, we take 1.000 away from Bob Robertson's error scores, 0.000 from Mavis Fletcher's, –0.667 from Bob Polansky's, 0.667 from Ann Harrison's, and –1.000 from Bert Entwistle's. (Don't forget that subtracting a negative number is like adding a positive number.) This gives us a revised table of error scores without any individual differences. It is usually called the *residual* scores table in analysis of variance, but it is just a more refined set of error scores (Table 21.13).

Notice that both the column and row means now equal zero. This is because not only have the 'true' or between scores been removed from the table but the individual differences are now gone. We need to check out the degrees of freedom associated with this table. There are more constraints now because the row totals have to equal zero. Thus in the Aspirin column we can adjust four scores but the fifth score is fixed by the requirement that the mean equals zero. In the Product X condition we can again vary four scores. However, once we have made these changes, we cannot vary any of the scores in the placebo condition because the row means have to equal zero. In other words, there is a total of 8 degrees of freedom in the residual error scores.

The formula for the degrees of freedom is quite straightforward:

Degrees of freedom$_{[residual\ error\ scores]}$ =

(Number of columns of error scores – 1) × (Number of rows of error scores – 1)

The variance estimate of this residual error can be calculated using the standard formula:

$$\text{Variance estimate}_{\text{[residual error scores]}} = \frac{\Sigma X^2 - \dfrac{(\Sigma X)^2}{N}}{df}$$

$$
\begin{aligned}
\Sigma X^2 &= 0.000^2 + (-1.000)^2 + 1.000^2 + (-1.000)^2 + 2.000^2 \\
&\quad + (-1.000)^2 + 0.667^2 + (-1.333)^2 + 0.667^2 + 2.333^2 \\
&\quad + 0.333^2 + (-2.667)^2 + (-2.000)^2 + 0.000^2 + 2.000^2 \\
&= 0.000 + 1.000 + 1.000 + 1.000 + 4.000 \\
&\quad + 1.000 + 0.445 + 1.777 + 0.445 + 5.443 \\
&\quad + 0.111 + 7.113 + 4.000 + 0.000 + 4.000 \\
&= 31.334
\end{aligned}
$$

$$
\begin{aligned}
(\Sigma X)^2 &= [0.000 + (-1.000) + 1.000 + (-1.000) + 2.000 \\
&\quad + (-1.000) + 0.667 + (-1.333) + 0.667 + 2.333 \\
&\quad + 0.333 + (-2.667) + (-2.000) + 0.000 + 2.000]^2 \\
&= 0
\end{aligned}
$$

The number of scores, N, equals 15 as before. The degrees of freedom are given by:

$$
\begin{aligned}
\text{Degrees of freedom} &= (\text{Number of columns} - 1) \times (\text{Number of rows} - 1) \\
&= (3 - 1) \times (5 - 1) \\
&= 2 \times 4 \\
&= 8
\end{aligned}
$$

Substituting in the formula:

$$\text{Variance estimate}_{\text{[residual error scores]}} = \frac{\Sigma X^2 - \dfrac{(\Sigma X)^2}{N}}{df}$$

$$= \frac{31.334 - \dfrac{0}{15}}{8}$$

$$= \frac{31.334}{8}$$

$$= 3.92$$

Step 4 This is not absolutely necessary, but the conventional approach to correlated/repeated measures analysis of variance calculates the variance estimate of the individual differences. This is usually described as the between-people variance estimate or 'blocks' variance estimate. (The word 'blocks' originates from the days when the analysis of variance was confined to agricultural research. Different amounts of fertiliser would be put on a single area of land and the fertility of these different 'blocks' assessed. The analysis of variance contains many terms referring to its agricultural origins such as split plots, randomised plots, levels of treatment and so forth.)

If you wish to calculate the between-people (or individual differences) variance estimate, you need to draw up Table 21.14 which consists of the individual differences component in each score (this is obtained by the difference between the row means and the overall mean in the original data). In other words, it is a table of the amount of adjustment required to everyone's scores in order to remove the effect of their individual characteristics.

We calculate the variance estimate of this using the usual variance estimate formula for the analysis of variance. The degrees of freedom are constrained by the fact that the column means have to equal zero and that all the scores in the row are the same. In the end this means that the degrees of freedom for this table are the number of rows minus 1. We have five rows so therefore the number of degrees of freedom is 4.

The sum of squares for Table 21.14 is 8.67 and the degrees of freedom = 4, therefore the variance estimate is 8.67/4 = 2.17. These values can be entered in the analysis of variance summary table. (Strictly speaking this is another unnecessary stage in the calculation but it does provide a check on the accuracy of your calculations.)

Step 5 We can enter the calculations into an analysis of variance summary table. It might be more conventional to see an analysis of variance summary table written in the form shown in Table 21.15. Some calculations are unnecessary and we have omitted them.

Table 21.14 **Between-people (individual difference) scores (obtained by taking the difference between the row means and overall mean in the original data)**

Participant	Aspirin	Product X	Placebo	Row mean
Bob Robertson	1.000	1.000	1.000	1.000
Mavis Fletcher	0.000	0.000	0.000	0.000
Bob Polansky	−0.667	−0.667	−0.667	−0.667
Ann Harrison	0.667	0.667	0.667	0.667
Bert Entwistle	−1.000	−1.000	−1.000	−1.000
Column mean	0.000	0.000	0.000	Overall mean = 0.000

Table 21.15 Analysis of variance summary table

Source of variation	Sum of squares	Degrees of freedom	Mean square (or variance estimate)	F-ratio
Between treatments (i.e. drugs)	40.00	2	20.00	5.10[a]
Between people (i.e. individual differences)	8.67	4	2.17	–
Error (i.e. residual)	31.33	8	3.92	–
Total	80.00	14	–	–

[a] Significant at 5% level.

Notice that the total sum of squares (80.00) is the same as the sum of the individual components of this total (40.00 + 8.67 + 31.33) and this applies also to the degrees of freedom. This can provide a useful check on the accuracy of your calculations.

The most important part of the table is the F-ratio. This is the between-groups variance estimate divided by the error (residual) variance estimate. In other words, it is 20.00/3.92 = 5.10. The statistical significance of this value has been assessed by the use of Significance Table 21.1 (p. 218). With 2 degrees of freedom for between treatments and 8 for the error, a minimum F-ratio of 4.5 is needed to be statistically significant. Thus the obtained F-ratio of 5.10 is significant at the 5% level.

The significant probability value of 5% tells us that the variance in the between-groups scores is substantially greater than the error (residual) variance. Thus the null hypothesis that the drugs have no effect on the amount of relief from pain is rejected and the hypothesis that the drugs treatments have an effect at the 5% level of significance is accepted.

21.4 Quick method for calculating the correlated ANOVA

Calculation 21.1 gives a *conceptual* account of the calculation of the analysis of variance. It suffers from being somewhat laborious and prone to the cumulative effects of rounding which can produce slight errors. The following describes the usual calculation steps involved in the standard quick calculation method. The difficulty is that it gives little insight into what is actually happening with the analysis of variance. However, if you have mastered Calculation 21.1 then you might find it advantageous to try the following approach.

Calculation 21.2

Correlated samples analysis of variance: quick method

Step 1 Tabulate your data. We are using the fictitious relief from pain data given in Table 21.10 so that you may make comparisons with Calculation 21.1 if you wish. These data have been entered into Table 21.16. Certain additional calculations have been included such as the row total for each person in the study (i.e. P_1 etc.) and the column totals (i.e. C_1 etc.). The grand total or G is simply the sum of all of the scores in the table. Thus it could be calculated by adding all of the row totals or all of the column totals.

Table 21.16. **The data for the relief from pain study plus additional row and column totals**

Participant	Aspirin condition	Product X	Placebo	Row totals
Bob Robertson	7	8	6	$P_1 = 21$
Mavis Fletcher	5	10	3	$P_2 = 18$
Bob Polansky	6	6	4	$P_3 = 16$
Ann Harrison	9	9	2	$P_4 = 20$
Bert Entwistle	3	7	5	$P_5 = 15$
Column totals	$C_1 = 30$	$C_2 = 40$	$C_3 = 20$	Grand total = G = 90

Step 2 Calculate the square of each score to obtain the sum of squared scores $(\Sigma X^2_{[total]})$:

$$\Sigma X^2_{[total]} = 7^2 + 5^2 + 6^2 + 9^2 + 3^2 + 8^2 + 10^2 + 6^2 + 9^2 + 7^2 + 6^2 + 3^2 + 4^2 + 2^2 + 5^2$$

$$= 49 + 25 + 36 + 81 + 9 + 64 + 100 + 36 + 81 + 49 + 36 + 9 + 16 + 4 + 25$$

$$= 620$$

Step 3 Calculate the correction factor G^2/N:

$$\text{Correction factor} = \frac{G^2}{N} = \frac{90^2}{15} = \frac{8100}{15}$$

$$= 540.000$$

G is the grand total or total of all the scores. N is the number of scores. The correction factor is merely the equivalent of $(\Sigma X)^2/N$ in the calculation formula for the variance estimate (p. 111).

The following calculations should be entered into an analysis of variance summary table such as Table 21.17.

Step 4 Calculate the between people sum of squares. Refer to step 1 and Table 21.16 for the meaning and values of P_1^2 etc.:

$$SS_{[\text{between people}]} = \frac{P_1^2 + P_2^2 + P_3^2 + P_4^2 - P_5^2}{\text{Number of columns (i.e. conditions)}} - \frac{G^2}{N}$$

The number of columns of data is 3. Remember that the final part of the above formula after the minus sign is the correction factor which we calculated to equal 540.000 in step 3.

$$SS_{[\text{between people}]} = \frac{21^2 + 18^2 + 16^2 + 20^2 + 15^2}{3} - 540.000$$

$$= \frac{441 + 324 + 256 + 400 + 225}{3} - 540.000$$

$$= \frac{1646}{3} - 540.000$$

$$= 548.667 - 540.000$$

$$= 8.667$$

The degrees of freedom for the $SS_{[\text{between people}]}$ = the number of different people (in this case 5) $- 1 = 4$.

Step 5 Calculate the between-conditions sum of squares. Refer to step 1 and Table 21.16 for the meaning and values of C_1 etc. Remember that the correction factor has already been calculated to be 540.000 in step 2 so we can simply insert this value.

$$SS_{[\text{between conditions}]} = \frac{C_1^2 + C_2^2 + C_3^2}{\text{Number of rows (i.e. different people)}} - \frac{G^2}{N}$$

$$= \frac{30^2 + 40^2 + 20^2}{5} - 540.000$$

$$= \frac{900 + 1600 + 400}{5} - 540.00$$

$$= \frac{2900}{5} - 540.000$$

$$= 580.000 - 540.000$$

$$= 40.000$$

The degrees of freedom for the $SS_{[between\ conditions]}$ is the number of columns (i.e. conditions) minus one (i.e. $3 - 1 = 2$).

Step 6   Calculate the sum of squares for the error (i.e. residual error). This is based on the squares of the individual scores as calculated in step 2. All of the separate parts of the formula have already been calculated. Substitute these values from the earlier steps into the following formula:

$$SS_{[residual\ error]}$$

$$= \Sigma X^2_{total} - \frac{P_1^2 + P_2^2 + P_3^2 + P_4^2 + P_5^2}{\begin{matrix}\text{Number of columns}\\\text{(i.e. conditions)}\end{matrix}} - \frac{C_1^2 + C_2^2 + C_3^2}{\begin{matrix}\text{Number of rows}\\\text{(i.e. different people)}\end{matrix}} + \frac{G^2}{N}$$

$$= 620.000 - \frac{30^2 + 40^2 + 20^2}{5} - \frac{21^2 + 18^2 + 16^2 + 20^2 + 15^2}{3} + \frac{90^2}{15}$$

$$= 620.000 - 580.000 - 548.667 + 540.000$$

$$= 31.333$$

The degrees of freedom $SS_{[residual\ error]}$ = (number of conditions – 1) × (number of rows (or participants) – 1) = $(3 - 1) \times (5 - 1) = 8$.

Step 7   The essential calculations for the correlated/related one-way analysis of variance are now completed. The F-ratio in Table 21.17 is simply the between-treatments mean square divided by the (residual) error mean square. The interpretation of this table is exactly as for Calculation 21.1 since we have exactly the same ANOVA summary table. (Sometimes the two methods will produce slightly different answers because of the effects of rounding errors.) Use Significance Table 21.1 to check the minimum value to be statistically significant. The between-treatments degrees of freedom indicates the column to choose and the residual error degrees of freedom indicates the row to choose.

Interpretation of results   Remember that the interpretation of any data should be based first of all on an examination of cell means. Table 21.18 illustrates this for the present data. It is the pattern that you find in these which tells you just what the data say. The tests of significance merely confirm whether or not your interpretations can be generalised. The table of means seems to suggest that each of the groups is substantially different from any other.

Reporting the results   The results may be written up as follows: 'A related samples ANOVA was carried out on the data. It was found that there was a significant effect of the independent variable type of drug treatment on the dependent variable relief from pain ($F = 5.10$; $F = 2, 8$; $p < 0.05$). Product X produced the greatest relief from pain ($M = 8.00$), aspirin the next highest relief from pain (M = 6.00) and the inert placebo tablet the least relief from pain (M = 4.00). Thus it is clear that relief from pain was affected by the type of drug given.'

For a complete analysis of this data, also calculate exactly which of the three drug conditions were significantly different from each other. This involves multiple related t-tests (see Chapters 12 and 23) with the significance levels adjusted for the multiple comparisons made (pp. 263–4). It is usually recommended that you carry out this sort of analysis only if your F-ratio is statistically significant as in the above example.

Table 21.17 **Analysis of variance summary table for quick computation method**

Source of variation	Sum of squares	Degrees of freedom	Mean square (or variance estimate)	F-ratio
Between treatments (i.e drugs)	40.000	2	20.000	$\frac{20.000}{3.917} = 5.11^{a}$
Between people (i.e. individual differences)	8.667	4	2.167	–
Error (i.e. residual)	31.333	8	3.917	–
Total	80.000	14	–	–

[a] Significant at the 5% level.

Table 21.18 **Table of condition means**

Aspirin	Product X	Placebo
M_1 = 6.000	M_2 = 8.000	M_3 = 4.00

21.5 Notes and recommendations

■ Working out this analysis of variance by hand is quite time consuming and extremely repetitive. Computers will save most people time.

■ Do not be too deterred by some of the strange terminology used in the analysis of variance. Words like blocks, split-plots and levels of treatment have their origins in agricultural research, as does ANOVA.

■ The analysis of variance in cases in which you have just two conditions or sets of scores is relatively easy to interpret. It is not so easy where you have three or more groups; then your analysis is not complete until you have employed a multiple comparisons procedure as in Chapter 23.

Significance Table 21.1   **5% significance values of the *F*-ratio for related ANOVA (two-tailed test)**

Your value has to equal or be larger than the tabulated value to be significant at the 5% level for a two-tailed test (i.e. to accept the hypothesis).

Additional values are to be found in Significance Table 19.1.

Degrees of freedom for residual or residual error mean square (or variance estimate)	**Degrees of freedom for between-treatments mean square (or variance estimate)**					
	1	**2**	**3**	**4**	**5**	**∞**
1	161 or more	200	216	225	230	254
2	18.5	19.0	19.2	19.3	19.3	19.5
3	10.1	9.6	9.3	9.1	9.0	8.5
4	7.7	6.9	6.6	6.4	6.3	5.6
5	6.6	5.8	5.4	5.2	5.1	4.4
6	6.0	5.1	4.8	4.5	4.4	3.7
7	5.6	4.7	4.4	4.1	4.0	3.2
8	5.3	4.5	4.1	3.8	3.7	2.9
9	5.1	4.3	3.9	3.6	3.5	2.7
10	5.0	4.1	3.7	3.5	3.3	2.5
13	4.7	3.8	3.4	3.2	3.0	2.2
15	4.5	3.7	3.3	3.1	2.9	2.1
20	4.4	3.5	3.1	2.9	2.7	1.8
30	4.2	3.3	2.9	2.7	2.5	1.6
60	4.0	3.2	2.8	2.5	2.4	1.4
∞	3.8	3.0	2.6	2.4	2.2	1.0

Chapter 22

Two-way analysis of variance for unrelated/ uncorrelated scores

Two experiments for the price of one?

Preparation

Chapter 20 on the one-way analysis of variance contains material essential to the full understanding of this chapter.

22.1 Introduction

Often researchers wish to assess the influence of more than a single independent variable at a time in experiments. The one-way analysis of variance deals with a single independent variable which can have two or more levels. However, analysis of variance copes with several *independent* variables in a research design. These are known as multifactorial ANOVAs. The number of 'ways' is the number of independent variables. Thus a two-way analysis of variance allows two independent variables to be included, three-way analysis of variance allows three independent variables and five-way analysis of variance means that there are five independent variables. *There is only one dependent variable no matter how many 'ways' in each analysis of variance. If you have two or more *dependent* variables each of these will entail a separate analysis of variance. Although things can get very complicated conceptually, two-way analysis of variance is relatively straightforward and introduces just one major new concept – interaction.

In this chapter we will be concentrating on examples in which all of the scores are independent (uncorrelated). Each person therefore contributes just one score to the analysis. In other words, it is an *uncorrelated* design.

Generally speaking, the 'multivariate' analysis of variance is best suited to experimental research in which it is possible to allocate participants at random into the various conditions. Although this does not apply to the one-way analysis of variance, there are problems in using two-way and multi-way analyses of

Table 22.1 **Data for typical two-way analysis of variance: number of mistakes on video test**

| | Sleep deprivation | | |
	4 hours	12 hours	24 hours
Alcohol	16	18	22
	12	16	24
	17	25	32
No alcohol	11	13	12
	9	8	14
	12	11	12

variance in survey and other non-experimental research. The difficulty is that calculations become more complex if you do not have equal numbers of scores in each of the cells or conditions. This is difficult to arrange in surveys. (It is possible to work with unequal numbers of scores in the different conditions, or cells, but these procedures tend to be a little cumbersome for hand calculation – see Chapter 24.)

So a typical research design for a two-way analysis of variance is the effect of the *independent variables* alcohol *and* sleep deprivation on the *dependent variable* of people's comprehension of complex video material expressed in terms of the number of mistakes made on a test of understanding of the video material. The research design and data might look like that shown in Table 22.1.

In a sense one could regard this experiment conceptually as two separate experiments, one studying the effects of sleep deprivation and the other studying the effects of alcohol. The effects of each of the two independent variables are called the *main* effects. Additionally the analysis normally looks for *interactions* which are basically findings which cannot be explained on the basis of the distinctive effects of alcohol level and sleep deprivation acting in combination. For example, it could be that people do especially badly if they have been deprived of a lot of sleep *and* have been given alcohol. They do more badly than the additive effects of alcohol and sleep deprivation would predict. Interactions are about the effects of specific combinations of variables. We will return to the concept of interaction later.

In the analysis of variance we sometimes talk of the *levels of a treatment* – this is simply the number of values that any independent variable can take. In the above example, the alcohol variable has two different values – that is, there are two levels of the treatment or variable alcohol. There are three levels of the treatment or variable sleep deprivation. Sometimes, a two-way ANOVA is identified in terms of the numbers of levels of treatment for each of the independent variables. So a 2 × 3 ANOVA has two different levels of the first variable and three for the second variable. This corresponds to the above example.

22.2 Theoretical considerations

Much of the two-way analysis of variance is easy if it is remembered that it largely involves two separate 'one-way' analyses of variance as if there were two separate experiments. Imagine an experiment in which one group of subjects is given iron supplements in their diet to see if it has any effect on their depression levels. In the belief that women have a greater need for iron than men, the researchers included sex as their other independent variable. The data are given in Table 22.2.

Table 22.2 represents a 2 × 2 ANOVA. Comparing the four condition means (cell means), the depression scores for females not receiving the supplement seem rather higher than those of any other groups. In other words, it would appear that the lack of the iron supplement has more effect on women. Certain sex and iron supplement conditions in combination have a great effect on depression scores. This suggests an interaction. That is, particular cells in the analysis have much higher or lower scores than can be explained simply in terms of the sex trends or dietary supplement trends acting separately.

The assumption in the two-way analysis of variance is that the variation in Table 22.2 comes from four sources:

■ 'error', plus
■ the main effect of sex, plus
■ the main effect of iron supplement, plus
■ the interaction of sex and iron supplement.

The first three components above are dealt with exactly as they were in the one-way unrelated analysis of variance. The slight difference is that instead of calculating the variance estimate for one independent variable we now calculate

Table 22.2 **Data table for study of dietary supplements**

	Iron supplement		No iron supplement		
Males	3	Cell mean = 5.00	9	Cell mean = 7.00	Row mean = 6.00
	7		5		
	4		6		
	6		8		
Females	11	Cell mean = 9.00	19	Cell mean = 17.00	Row mean = 13.00
	7		16		
	10		18		
	8		15		
		Column mean = 7.00		Column mean = 12.00	Overall mean = 9.50

two variance estimates – one for each independent variable. However, the term main effect should not cause any confusion It is merely the effect of an independent variable acting alone as it would if the two-way design were turned into two separate one-way designs.

The interaction consists of any variation in the scores which is left after we have taken away the 'error' and main effects for the sex and iron supplements sub-experiments. That is, priority is given to finding main effects at the expense of interactions.

22.3 Steps in the analysis

Step 1

To produce an 'error' table we simply take our original data and subtract the cell mean from every score in the cell. Thus, for instance, we need to subtract 5.00 from each score in the cell for males receiving the iron supplement and 17.00 from each cell for the females not receiving the iron supplement, etc. In the present example the 'error' table is as in Table 22.3.

We calculate the 'error' variance estimate for this in the usual way. The formula, as ever, is:

$$\text{Variance estimate}_{[\text{'error'}]} = \frac{\Sigma X^2 - \frac{(\Sigma X)^2}{N}}{\text{df}}$$

The degrees of freedom (df), analogously to the one-way analysis of variance, is the number of scores minus the number of conditions or cells. This leaves 12 degrees of freedom (16 scores minus 4 conditions or cells).

Table 22.3 **'Error' scores for study of dietary supplements**

	Iron supplement		No iron supplement		
Males	3 – 5 = –2	Cell mean = 0.00	9 – 7 = 2	Cell mean = 0.00	Row mean = 0.00
	7 – 5 = 2		5 – 7 = –2		
	4 – 5 = –1		6 – 7 = –1		
	6 – 5 = 1		8 – 7 = 1		
Females	11 – 9 = 2	Cell mean = 0.00	19 – 17 = 2	Cell mean = 0.00	Row mean = 0.00
	7 – 9 = –2		16 – 17 = –1		
	10 – 9 = 1		18 – 17 = 1		
	8 – 9 = –1		15 – 17 = –2		
		Column mean = 0.00		Column mean = 0.00	Overall mean = 0.00

Step 2

To produce a table of the main effects for the iron supplement treatment, simply substitute the column means from the original data for each of the scores in the columns. The 'iron supplement' mean was 7.00 so each iron supplement score is changed to 7.00 thus eliminating any other source of variation. Similarly, the 'no iron supplement' mean was 12.00 so each score is changed to 12.00 (see Table 22.4).

The variance estimate of the above scores can be calculated using the usual variance estimate formula. The degrees of freedom are calculated in the familiar way – the number of columns minus one (i.e. df = 1).

Step 3

To produce a table of the main effect of sex, remember that the independent variable sex is tabulated as the rows (not the columns). In other words, we substitute the row mean for the males and the row mean for the females for the respective scores (Table 22.5).

The variance estimate of the above scores can be calculated with the usual variance estimate formula. Even the degrees of freedom are calculated in the usual way. However, *as the table is on its side* compared to our usual method, the degrees of freedom are the number of *rows* minus one in this case (2 – 1 or 1 degree of freedom).

Table 22.4 **Main effect scores for study of dietary supplements**

Iron supplement	No iron supplement	
7.00	12.00	Row mean = 9.50
7.00	12.00	
7.00	12.00	
7.00	12.00	
7.00	12.00	Row mean = 9.50
7.00	12.00	
7.00	12.00	
7.00	12.00	
Column mean = 7.00	Column mean = 12.00	Overall mean = 9.50

Table 22.5 **Main effect scores for study of dietary supplements**

Males	6.00	6.00	6.00	6.00	6.00	6.00	6.00	6.00	Row mean = 6.00
Females	13.00	13.00	13.00	13.00	13.00	13.00	13.00	13.00	Row mean = 13.00

The calculation of the main effects (variance estimates) for sex and the iron supplement follows exactly the same procedures as in the one-way analysis of variance.

Step 4

The remaining stage is to calculate the interaction. This is simply anything which is left over after we have eliminated 'error' and the main effects. So for any score, the interaction score is found by taking the score in your data and subtracting the 'error' score and the sex score and the iron supplement score.

Table 22.6 is our data table less the 'error' variance, in other words a table which replaces each score by its cell mean.

It is obvious that the row means for the males and females are not the same. The row mean for males is 6.00 and the row mean for females is 13.00. To get rid

Table 22.6 **Data table with 'error' removed**

	Iron supplement	No iron supplement	
Males	5.00	7.00	Row mean = 6.00
	5.00	7.00	
	5.00	7.00	
	5.00	7.00	
Females	9.00	17.00	Row mean = 13.00
	9.00	17.00	
	9.00	17.00	
	9.00	17.00	
	Column mean = 7.00	Column mean = 12.00	Overall mean = 9.50

Table 22.7 **Data table with 'error' and sex removed**

	Iron supplement	No iron supplement	
Males	−1.00	1.00	Row mean = 0.00
	−1.00	1.00	
	−1.00	1.00	
	−1.00	1.00	
Females	−4.00	4.00	Row mean = 0.00
	−4.00	4.00	
	−4.00	4.00	
	−4.00	4.00	
	Column mean = −2.50	Column mean = 2.50	Overall mean = 0.00

Table 22.8   Interaction table, i.e. data table with 'error', sex and iron supplement all removed

	Iron supplement	No iron supplement	
Males	1.5	−1.5	Row mean = 0.00
	1.5	−1.5	
	1.5	−1.5	
	1.5	−1.5	
Females	−1.5	1.5	Row mean = 0.00
	−1.5	1.5	
	−1.5	1.5	
	−1.5	1.5	
Column mean = 0.00	Column mean = 0.00	Overall mean = 0.00

of the sex effect we can subtract 6.00 from each male score and 13.00 from each female score in the previous table. The results of this simple subtraction are found in Table 22.7.

You can see that the male and female main effect has been taken into account since now both row means are zero. That is, there remains no variation due to sex. But you can see that there remains variation due to iron treatment. Those getting the supplement now score −2.50 on average and those not getting the iron treatment score +2.50. To remove the variation due to the iron treatment subtract −2.50 from the iron supplement column and 2.50 from the non-iron supplement column (Table 22.8). Do not forget that *subtracting a negative number is like adding a positive number*.

Looking at Table 22.8, although the column and row means are zero throughout, the scores in the cells are not. This shows that there still remains a certain amount of variation in the scores even after 'error' and the two main effects have been taken away. That is, there is an interaction, which may or may not be significant. We have to check this using the F-ratio test.

What the interaction table implies is that women *without* the iron supplement and men *with* the iron supplement are getting the higher scores on the dependent variable.

We can calculate the variance estimate for the interaction by using the usual formula. Degrees of freedom need to be considered. The degrees of freedom for the above table of the interaction is limited by:

■ all scores in the cells having to be equal (i.e. no 'error' variance)

■ all marginal means (i.e. row and column means) having to equal zero.

In other words, there can be only one degree of freedom in this case.

There is a general formula for the degrees of freedom of the interaction:

Degrees of freedom$_{[interaction]}$ = (Number of rows − 1) × (Number of columns − 1)

Since there are two rows and two columns in this case, the degrees of freedom are:

$$(2 - 1) \times (2 - 1) = 1 \times 1 = 1$$

Step 5

All of the stages in the calculation are entered into an analysis of variance summary table (Table 22.9).

Notice that there are several F-ratios because you need to know whether there is a significant effect of sex, a significant effect of the iron supplement and a significant interaction of the sex and iron supplement variables. In each case you divide the appropriate mean square by the 'error' mean square. If you wish to check your understanding of the processes involved, see if you can obtain the above table by going through the individual calculations.

The significant interaction indicates that some of the cells or conditions are getting exceptionally high or low scores which cannot be accounted for on the basis of the two main effects acting independently of each other. In this case, it would appear that females getting the iron supplement and males not getting the iron supplement are actually getting higher scores than sex or supplement acting separately and independently of each other would produce. In order to interpret an interaction you have to remember that the effects of the independent variables are separately removed from the table (i.e. the main effects are removed first). It is only after this has been done that the interaction is calculated. In other words, ANOVA gives priority to main effects and sometimes it can confuse interactions for main effects. Table 22.10 presents data from the present experiment in which the cell means have been altered to emphasise the lack of main effects.

Table 22.9 **Analysis of variance summary table**

Source of variation	Sums of squares	Degrees of freedom	Mean square	F-ratio
Main effects:				
Sex	196.00	1	196.00	58.96[a]
Iron supplement	100.00	1	100.00	30.00[a]
Interaction:				
Sex with iron supplement	36.00	1	36.00	10.81[a]
'Error'	40.00	12	3.33	–
Total (data)	372.00	15	–	–

[a] Significant at the 5% level.

Table 22.10 **Alternative data table showing different trends**

	Iron supplement	**No iron supplement**	
Males	Cell mean = 5.00	Cell mean = 5.00	Row mean = 5.00
Females	Cell mean = 5.00	Cell mean = 17.00	Row mean = 11.00
	Column mean = 5.00	Column mean = 11.00	

In this example, it is absolutely clear that all the variation in the cell means is to do with the female/no-supplement condition. All the other three cell means are identical at 5.00. Quite clearly the males and females in the iron supplement condition have exactly the same average score. Similarly, males in the iron supplement and no-supplement conditions are obtaining identical means. In other words, there seem to be no main effects at all. The females in the no-supplement condition are the only group getting exceptionally high scores.

This would suggest that there is an interaction but no main effects. However, if you do the analysis of variance on these data you will find that there are two main effects and an interaction! The reason for this is that the main effects are estimated before the interaction, so the exceptionally high row mean for females and the exceptionally high column mean for the no-supplement condition will lead to the interaction being mistaken for main effects as your ANOVA summary table might show significant main effects. So you need to examine your data with great care as you carry out your analysis of variance, otherwise you will observe main effects which are an artifact of the method and ignore interactions which are actually there! The analysis of variance may be tricky to execute but it can be even trickier for the novice to interpret properly – to be frank, many professional psychologists are unaware of the problems.

It is yet another example of the importance of close examination of the data alongside the statistical analysis itself.

Calculation 22.1

Two-way unrelated analysis of variance

Without a safety net we will attempt to analyse the sleep and alcohol experiment mentioned earlier. It is described as a 2 × 3 analysis of variance because one independent variable has two values and the other has three values (Table 22.11).

Table 22.11   **Data for sleep deprivation experiment: number of mistakes on video test**

	Sleep deprivation		
	4 hours	**12 hours**	**24 hours**
Alcohol	16	18	22
	12	16	24
	17	25	32
No alcohol	11	13	12
	9	8	14
	12	11	12

Table 22.12   **Data for sleep deprivation experiment with the addition of cell, column and row means**

	Sleep deprivation						
	4 hours		**12 hours**		**24 hours**		
Alcohol	16	Cell mean	18	Cell mean	22	Cell mean	Row mean
	12	= 15.000	16	= 19.667	24	= 26.000	= 20.222
	17		25		32		
No	11	Cell mean	13	Cell mean	12	Cell mean	Row mean
alcohol	9	= 10.667	8	= 10.667	14	= 12.667	= 11.333
	12		11		12		
		Column mean		Column mean		Column mean	Overall mean
		= 12.833		= 15.167		= 19.333	= 15.777

Step 1 (total variance estimate) We enter the row and column means as well as the means of each of the six cells (Table 22.12).

$$\text{Variance estimate}_{[\text{data}]} = \frac{\Sigma X^2 - \dfrac{(\Sigma X)^2}{N}}{df}$$

$$\Sigma X^2 = 16^2 + 18^2 + 22^2 + 12^2 + 16^2 + 24^2 + 17^2 + 25^2 + 32^2 + 11^2 + 13^2$$
$$+ 12^v + 9^2 + 8^2 + 14^2 + 12^2 + 11^2 + 12^2$$

$$= 256 + 324 + 484 + 144 + 256 + 576 + 289 + 625 + 1024 + 121$$
$$+ 169 + 144 + 81 + 64 + 196 + 144 + 121 + 144$$

$$= 5162$$

$$(\Sigma X)^2 = (16 + 18 + 22 + 12 + 16 + 24 + 17 + 25 + 32$$
$$+ 11 + 13 + 12 + 9 + 8 + 14 + 12 + 11 + 12)^2$$
$$= (284)^2$$
$$= 80{,}656$$

The number of scores, N, equals 18. The degrees of freedom (df) equals the number of scores minus one, i.e. 17. Substituting in the formula:

$$\text{Variance estimate}_{[data]} = \frac{\Sigma X^2 - \frac{(\Sigma X)^2}{N}}{df}$$

$$= \frac{5162 - \frac{80{,}656}{18}}{17}$$

$$= \frac{5162 - 4480.889}{17}$$

$$= \frac{681.111}{17}$$

$$= 40.065$$

The sum of squares here (i.e. 681.111) is called the *total* sum of squares in the ANOVA summary table. (Strictly speaking this calculation is unnecessary in that its only function is a computational check on your other calculations.)

Step 2 ('error' variance estimate) Subtract the cell mean from each of the scores in a cell to obtain the 'error' scores (Table 22.13).

Table 22.13 **'Error' scores**

| | Sleep deprivation | | | |
	4 hours	**12 hours**	**24 hours**	
Alcohol	1.000	−1.667	−4.000	Row mean
	−3.000	−3.667	−2.000	= 0.000
	2.000	5.333	6.000	
No alcohol	0.333	2.333	−0.667	Row mean
	−1.667	−2.667	1.333	= 0.000
	1.333	0.333	−0.667	
	Column mean = 0.000	Column mean = 0.000	Column mean = 0.000	Overall mean = 0.000

Apart from rounding errors, the cell means, the row means, the column means, and the overall mean are all zero – just as required of an 'error' table.

We calculate the 'error' variance estimate using the usual variance estimate formula:

$$\text{Variance estimate}_{[\text{'error' scores}]} = \frac{\Sigma X^2 - \dfrac{(\Sigma X)^2}{N}}{\text{df}}$$

$$\begin{aligned}
\Sigma X^2 &= 1.000^2 + (-1.667)^2 + (-4.000)^2 + (-3.000)^2 + (-3.667)^2 \\
&\quad + (-2.000)^2 + 2.000^2 + 5.333^2 + 6.000^2 + 0.333^2 + 2.333^2 \\
&\quad + (-0.667)^2 + (-1.667)^2 + (-2.667)^2 + 1.333^2 + 1.333^2 \\
&\quad + 0.333^2 + (-0.667)^2
\end{aligned}$$

$$\begin{aligned}
&= 1.000 + 2.779 + 16.000 + 9.000 + 13.447 + 4.000 + 4.000 \\
&\quad + 28.441 + 36.000 + 0.111 + 5.443 + 0.445 + 2.779 + 7.113 \\
&\quad + 1.777 + 1.777 + 0.111 + 0.445
\end{aligned}$$

$$= 134.668$$

$$\begin{aligned}
(\Sigma X)^2 &= [1.000 + (-1.667) + (-4.000) + (-3.000) + (-3.667) + (-2.000) \\
&\quad + 2.000 + 5.333 + 6.000 + 0.333 + 2.333 + (-0.667) + (-1.667) \\
&\quad + (-2.667) + 1.333 + 1.333 + 0.333 + (-0.667)]^2
\end{aligned}$$

$$= 0$$

(Notice that this latter calculation is unnecessary as it will always equal 0 for 'error' scores.) The number of scores, N, equals 18. The degrees of freedom, df, equals the number of scores minus the number of cells, i.e. $18 - 6 = 12$. We can now substitute these values in the formula:

$$\text{Variance estimate}_{[\text{'error' scores}]} = \frac{\Sigma X^2 - \dfrac{(\Sigma X)^2}{N}}{\text{df}}$$

$$= \frac{134.668 - \dfrac{0}{18}}{12}$$

$$= \frac{134.668}{12}$$

$$= 11.222$$

Table 22.14 **Scores due to sleep deprivation**

	Sleep deprivation	
4 hours	**12 hours**	**24 hours**
12.833	15.167	19.333
12.833	15.167	19.333
12.833	15.167	19.333
12.833	15.167	19.333
12.833	15.167	19.333
12.833	15.167	19.333
Column mean = 12.833	Column mean = 15.167	Column mean = 19.333

Step 3 (sleep deprivation variance estimate) We now derive our table containing the scores in the three sleep deprivation conditions (combining over alcohol and non-alcohol conditions) simply by replacing each score in the column by the column mean (Table 22.14).

$$\text{Variance estimate}_{[\text{'sleep deprivation' scores}]} = \frac{\Sigma X^2 - \dfrac{(\Sigma X)^2}{N}}{df}$$

$$
\begin{aligned}
\Sigma X^2 &= 12.833^2 + 15.167^2 + 19.333^2 + 12.833^2 + 15.167^2 + 19.333^2 \\
&\quad + 12.833^2 + 15.167^2 + 19.333^2 + 12.833^2 + 15.167^2 + 19.333^2 \\
&\quad + 12.833^2 + 15.167^2 + 19.333^2 + 12.833^2 + 15.167^2 + 19.333^2 \\
&= 164.686 + 230.038 + 373.765 + 164.686 + 230.038 + 373.765 \\
&\quad + 164.686 + 230.038 + 373.765 + 164.686 + 230.038 + 373.765 \\
&\quad + 164.686 + 230.038 + 373.765 + 164.686 + 230.038 + 373.765 \\
&= 4610.934
\end{aligned}
$$

$$
\begin{aligned}
(\Sigma X)^2 &= (12.833 + 15.167 + 19.333 + 12.833 + 15.167 + 19.333 + 12.833 \\
&\quad + 15.167 + 19.333 + 12.833 + 15.167 + 19.333 + 12.833 + 15.167 \\
&\quad + 19.333 + 12.833 + 15.167 + 19.333)^2 \\
&= 284^2 \\
&= 80{,}656
\end{aligned}
$$

The number of scores, N, equals 18. The degrees of freedom, df, equals the number of columns minus one, i.e. $3 - 1 = 2$. We can now substitute these values in the formula:

Table 22.15 **Scores due to alcohol effect alone**

Alcohol	20.222	20.222	20.222
	20.222	20.222	20.222
	20.222	20.222	20.222
No alcohol	11.333	11.333	11.333
	11.333	11.333	11.333
	11.333	11.333	11.333

$$\text{Variance estimate}_{\text{['sleep deprivation' scores]}} = \frac{\Sigma X^2 - \frac{(\Sigma X)^2}{N}}{df}$$

$$= \frac{4610.934 - \frac{80{,}656}{18}}{2}$$

$$= \frac{4610.934 - 4480.889}{2}$$

$$= \frac{130.045}{2}$$

$$= 65.023$$

Step 4 (alcohol variance estimate) The main effect for alcohol (or the table containing scores for the alcohol and no-alcohol comparison) is obtained by replacing each of the scores in the original data table by the row mean for alcohol or the row mean for no-alcohol as appropriate. In this way the sleep deprivation variable is ignored (Table 22.15).

The variance estimate of these 18 scores gives us the variance estimate for the independent variable alcohol. We calculate:

$$\text{Variance estimate}_{\text{['alcohol' scores]}} = \frac{\Sigma X^2 - \frac{(\Sigma X)^2}{N}}{df}$$

$$\Sigma X^2 = 20.222^2 + 20.222^2 + 20.222^2 + 20.222^2 + 20.222^2 + 20.222^2$$
$$+ 20.222^2 + 20.222^2 + 20.222^2 + 11.333^2 + 11.333^2 + 11.333^2$$
$$+ 11.333^2 + 11.333^2 + 11.333^2 + 11.333^2 + 11.333^2 + 11.333^2$$

$$= 408.929 + 408.929 + 408.929 + 408.929 + 408.929 + 408.929$$
$$+ 408.929 + 408.929 + 408.929 + 128.437 + 128.437 + 128.437$$

$$+ 128.437 + 128.437 + 128.437 + 128.437 + 128.437 + 128.437$$
$$= 4836.294$$

$$(\Sigma X)^2 = (20.222 + 20.222 + 20.222 + 20.222 + 20.222 + 20.222$$
$$+ 20.222 + 20.222 + 20.222 + 11.333 + 11.333 + 11.333$$
$$+ 11.333 + 11.333 + 11.333 + 11.333 + 11.333 + 11.333)^2$$
$$= (284)^2$$
$$= 80{,}656$$

The number of scores, N, equals 18. The degrees of freedom, df, equals the number of rows minus one, i.e. $2 - 1 = 1$. We can now substitute these values in the formula:

$$\text{Variance estimate}_{\text{['alcohol' scores]}} = \frac{\Sigma X^2 - \frac{(\Sigma X)^2}{N}}{df}$$

$$= \frac{4836.294 - \frac{80{,}656}{18}}{1}$$

$$= \frac{4836.294 - 4480.889}{1}$$

$$= \frac{355.405}{1}$$

$$= 355.405$$

Table 22.16 **Data minus 'error' (each data score replaced by its cell mean)**

| | Sleep deprivation | | | |
	4 hours	12 hours	24 hours	
Alcohol	15.000	19.667	26.000	Row mean
	15.000	19.667	26.000	= 20.222
	15.000	19.667	26.000	
No alcohol	10.667	10.667	12.667	Row mean
	10.667	10.667	12.667	= 11.333
	10.667	10.667	12.667	
	Column mean	Column mean	Column mean	Overall mean
	= 12.833	= 15.167	= 19.333	= 15.777

Table 22.17   **Data minus 'error' and alcohol effect (row mean subtracted from each score in Table 22.16)**

	Sleep deprivation			
	4 hours	12 hours	24 hours	
Alcohol	−5.222	−0.555	5.778	Row mean
	−5.222	−0.555	5.778	= 0.000
	−5.222	−0.555	5.778	
No alcohol	−0.666	−0.666	1.334	Row mean
	−0.666	−0.666	1.334	= 0.000
	−0.666	−0.666	1.334	
	Column mean	Column mean	Column mean	Overall mean
	= −2.944	= −0.611	= 3.556	= 0.000

Table 22.18   **Interaction table: data minus 'error', alcohol and sleep deprivation (column mean subtracted from each score in Table 22.17)**

	Sleep deprivation			
	4 hours	12 hours	24 hours	
Alcohol	−2.278	0.056	2.222	Row mean
	−2.278	0.056	2.222	= 0.000
	−2.278	0.056	2.222	
No alcohol	2.278	−0.056	−2.222	Row mean
	2.278	−0.056	−2.222	= 0.000
	2.278	−0.056	−2.222	
	Column mean	Column mean	Column mean	Overall mean
	= 0.000	= 0.000	= 0.000	= 0.000

Step 5 (interaction variance estimate) The final stage is to calculate the interaction. This is obtained by getting rid of 'error', getting rid of the effect of sleep deprivation and then getting rid of the effect of alcohol:

1. Remove 'error' by simply replacing our data scores by the cell mean (Table 22.16).
2. Remove the effect of the alcohol versus no-alcohol treatment. This is done simply by subtracting the row mean (20.222) from each of the alcohol scores and the row mean (11.333) from each of the no-alcohol scores (Table 22.17).

3. Remove the effect of sleep deprivation by subtracting the column mean for each sleep deprivation condition from the scores in the *previous table*. In other words *subtract* –2.944, –0.611 or 3.556 as appropriate. (Do not forget that subtracting a negative number is like adding the absolute value of that number.) This leaves us with the interaction (Table 22.18).

The variance estimate from the interaction is computed using the usual formula.

$$\text{Variance estimate}_{[\text{'interaction' scores}]} = \frac{\Sigma X^2 - \frac{(\Sigma X)^2}{N}}{df}$$

$$
\begin{aligned}
\Sigma X^2 = {} & (-2.278)^2 + 0.056^2 + 2.222^2 + (-2.278)^2 + 0.056^2 + 2.222^2 \\
& + (-2.278)^2 + 0.056^2 + 2.222^2 + 2.278^2 + (-0.056)^2 + (-2.222)^2 \\
& + 2.278^2 + (-0.056)^2 + (-2.222)^2 + 2.278^2 + (-0.056)^2 + (-2.222)^2
\end{aligned}
$$

$$
\begin{aligned}
= {} & 5.189 + 0.003 + 4.937 + 5.189 + 0.003 + 4.937 \\
& + 5.189 + 0.003 + 4.937 + 5.189 + 0.003 + 4.937 \\
& + 5.189 + 0.003 + 4.937 + 5.189 + 0.003 + 4.937
\end{aligned}
$$

$$= 60.774$$

$$
\begin{aligned}
(\Sigma X)^2 = {} & [\,(-2.278) + 0.056 + 2.222 + (-2.278) + 0.056 + 2.222 \\
& + (-2.278) + 0.056 + 2.222 + 2.278 + (-0.056) + (-2.222) \\
& + 2.278 + (-0.056) + (-2.222) + 2.278 + (-0.056) + (-2.222)\,]^2
\end{aligned}
$$

$$= 0$$

(This latter is an unnecessary calculation as it will always equal 0.) The number of scores, N, equals 18. The degrees of freedom, df, is given by the following formula:

$$
\begin{aligned}
df & = (\text{Number of rows} - 1) \times (\text{Number of columns} - 1) \\
& = (2 - 1) \times (3 - 1) \\
& = 1 \times 2 \\
& = 2
\end{aligned}
$$

We can now substitute the above values in the formula:

$$\text{'Variance estimate}_{[\text{'interaction' scores}]} = \frac{\Sigma X^2 - \frac{(\Sigma X)^2}{N}}{df}$$

$$= \frac{60.774 - \dfrac{0}{18}}{2}$$

$$= \frac{60.774 - 0}{2}$$

$$= \frac{60.774}{2}$$

$$= 30.387$$

Step 6 Table 22.19 is the analysis of variance summary table. The F-ratios are always the mean square of either one of the main effects or the interaction divided by the variance estimate (mean square) due to 'error'. The significance of each F-ratio is checked against Significance Table 22.1. Care must be taken to use the appropriate degrees of freedom. For error in this case it is 12, which means that alcohol (with one degree of freedom) must have an F-ratio of 4.8 or more to be significant at the 5% level. Sleep deprivation and the interaction need to have a value of 3.9 or more to be significant at the 5% level. Thus the interaction is not significant, but sleep deprivation is.

The interpretation of the analysis of variance summary table in this case appears to be quite straightforward:

1. Alcohol has a significant influence on the number of mistakes in the understanding of the video.

2. The amount of sleep deprivation has a significant influence on the number of mistakes in the understanding of the video.

Table 22.19 **Analysis of variance summary table**

Source of variation	Sums of squares	Degrees of freedom	Mean square	F-ratio
Main effects:				
Sleep deprivation	130.045	2	65.023	5.79[a]
Alcohol	355.405	1	355.405	31.67[a]
Interaction:				
Sleep deprivation with alcohol	60.774	2	30.387	2.71
'Error'	134.668	12	11.222	–
Total (data)	681.111[b]	17	–	–

[a] Significant at 5% level.
[b] This form of calculation has introduced some rounding errors

Significance Table 22.1 **5% significance values of the *F*-ratio for unrelated ANOVA**

Your value has to equal or be larger than the tabulated value to be significant at the
5% level for a two-tailed test (i.e. to accept the hypothesis).

Additional values are to be found in Significance Table 19.1.

Degrees of freedom for error or mean square (or variance estimate)	Degrees of freedom for between-treatments mean square (or variance estimate)					
	1	2	3	4	5	∞
1	161 or more 200		216	225	230	254
2	18.5	19.0	19.2	19.3	19.3	19.5
3	10.1	9.6	9.3	9.1	9.0	8.5
4	7.7	6.9	6.6	6.4	6.3	5.6
5	6.6	5.8	5.4	5.2	5.1	4.4
6	6.0	5.1	4.8	4.5	4.4	3.7
7	5.6	4.7	4.4	4.1	4.0	3.2
8	5.3	4.5	4.1	3.8	3.7	2.9
9	5.1	4.3	3.9	3.6	3.5	2.7
10	5.0	4.1	3.7	3.5	3.3	2.5
13	4.7	3.8	3.4	3.2	3.0	2.2
15	4.5	3.7	3.3	3.1	2.9	2.1
20	4.4	3.5	3.1	2.9	2.7	1.8
30	4.2	3.3	2.9	2.7	2.5	1.6
60	4.0	3.2	2.8	2.5	2.4	1.4
∞	3.8	3.0	2.6	2.4	2.2	1.0

3. There is apparently no significant interaction – that is, the differences
between the conditions are fully accounted for by alcohol and sleep
deprivation acting independently.

But this only tells us that there are significant differences; we have to check
the column and row means in order to say precisely which condition produces
the greatest number of mistakes. In other words, the analysis of variance
summary table has to be interpreted in the light of the original data table with
the column, row and cell means all entered.

Carefully checking the data suggests that the above interpretation is rather
too simplistic. It seems that sleep deprivation actually has little effect unless
the person has been taking alcohol. The high cell means are associated with
alcohol and sleep deprivation. In these circumstances, there is some doubt that
the main effects explanation is good enough.

We would conclude, in these circumstances, 'Although, in the ANOVA, only the main effects were significant, there is reason to think that the main effects are actually the results of the interaction between the main effects. Careful examination of the cell means suggests that especially high scores are associated with taking alcohol and undergoing higher amounts of sleep deprivation. In contrast, those in the no-alcohol condition were affected only to a much smaller extent by having high amounts of sleep deprivation.'

This is tricky for a student to write up since it requires a rather subtle interpretation of the data which might exceed the statistical skills of the readers of their work.

22.4 More on interactions

A conventional way of illustrating interactions is through the use of graphs such as those in Figures 22.1 and 22.2. These graphs deal with the sleep and alcohol study just analysed. Notice that the means are given for each of the cells of the two-way ANOVA. Thus the vertical axis is a numerical scale commensurate with

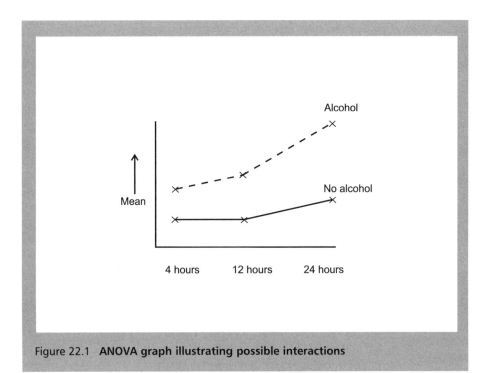

Figure 22.1   ANOVA graph illustrating possible interactions

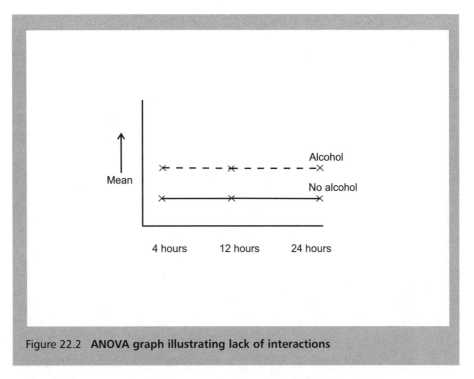

Figure 22.2   **ANOVA graph illustrating lack of interactions**

the scale of the dependent variable; the horizontal axis simply records the different levels of *one* of the independent variables. In order to indicate the different levels of the second independent variable, the different cell means for each level are joined together by a distinctively different line.

The main point to remember is that main effects are assumed to be effects which can be added directly to the scores in the columns or rows for that level of the main effect and that the effect is assumed to be common and equal in all of the cells involved. This implies that:

1. If there is *no* interaction, then the lines through the points should move more-or-less parallel to each other.

2. If there *is* an interaction, then the lines through the points will not be parallel; they may touch, move together or move apart.

Figure 22.2 illustrates the sort of pattern we might expect if there is no interaction between the independent variables. Figure 22.3 shows that it is possible for an interaction to involve the crossing of the lines through the points.

22.5 Calculation of two-way ANOVA using quick method

Calculation 22.1 gives a *conceptual* account of the two-way analysis of variance calculation. While it has the enormous advantage of showing precisely how your

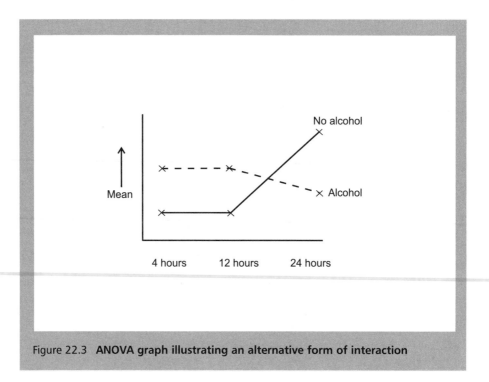

Figure 22.3   **ANOVA graph illustrating an alternative form of interaction**

data are being manipulated statistically, it is somewhat laborious and rounding errors can accumulate to give slightly imprecise results. The following calculation uses the computational formula for variance (p. 111) which saves some effort in the calculation. It gives little or no insight into how the analysis of variance works conceptually. Also remember that this calculation is appropriate only if you have equal numbers of scores in each cell. If not then you are far better off using a computer program which can cope easily with unequal sample sizes and is the preferred approach. If you wish to do a hand calculation, then the simplest procedure is to delete scores *at random* from the larger cells until each is the same size as the smallest cell.

Calculation 22.2

Two-way unrelated analysis of variance: quick method

Step 1   Enter your data into a table such as Table 22.20. These are the data given in Table 22.1 for the study into the effects of sleep deprivation and alcohol on errors on a video test with a few additions. These additions are:

■ the totals of scores in each cell (i.e. the cell totals or T_1 etc.)

■ the totals of scores in each row (i.e. the row totals or R_1 etc.)
■ the totals of scores in each column (i.e. the column totals or C_1 etc.)
■ the overall total of all of the scores (i.e. the grand total or G).

These additions are analogous to the calculations in Table 22.12 of the previous computational method. With the quick method we do not calculate the means, merely the totals.

Table 22.20 **Data for the two-way analysis of variance with added totals**

	4 hours	12 hours	24 hours	
		Sleep deprivation		
Alcohol	16	18	22	
	12	16	24	
	17	25	32	
	T_1 = Cell total = 45	T_2 = Cell total = 59	T_3 = Cell total = 78	R_1 = Row total = 182
No alcohol	11	13	12	
	9	8	14	
	12	11	12	
	T_4 = Cell total = 32	T_5 = Cell total = 32	T_6 = Cell total = 38	R_2 = Row total = 102

C_1 = Column total 77 C_2 = Column total = 91 C_3= Column total = 116 G = Grand total = 284

Step 2 Square each of the scores and calculate the total of squared scores (ΣX^2):

Sum of squared scores = ΣX^2

$= 16^2 + 12^2 + 17^2 + 18^2 + 16^2+ 25^2 + 22^2 + 24^2 + 32^2 + 11^2 + 9^2 + 12^2 + 13^2 + 8^2 + 11^2 + 12^2 + 14^2 + 12^2$

$= 256 + 144 + 289 + 324 + 256 + 625 + 484 + 576 + 1024 + 121 + 81 + 144 + 169 + 64 + 121 + 144 + 196 + 144$

$= 5162$

Step 3 Carry out the following essential intermediary calculations to be used in later steps. They are R, C, T and something called the correction factor.

$$C = \frac{C_1^2 + C_2^2 + C_3^2}{\text{Number of scores per sleep deprivation condition}}$$

$$= \frac{77^2 + 91^2 + 116^2}{6}$$

$$= \frac{5929 + 8281 + 13,456}{6}$$

$$= \frac{27,666}{6}$$

$$= 4611.000$$

$$R = \frac{R_1^2 + R_2^{\,2}}{\text{Number of scores per alcohol condition}}$$

$$= \frac{182^2 + 102^2}{9}$$

$$= \frac{33{,}124 + 10{,}404}{9}$$

$$= \frac{43{,}528}{9}$$

$$= 4836.444$$

$$T = \frac{T_1^2 + T_2^2 + T_3^2 + T_4^2 + T_5^2 + T_6^2}{\text{Number of scores per cell}}$$

$$= \frac{45^2 + 59^2 + 78^2 + 32^2 + 32^2 + 38^2}{3}$$

$$= \frac{2025 + 3482 + 6084 + 1024 + 1024 + 1444}{3}$$

$$= \frac{15{,}082}{3}$$

$$= 5027.333$$

$$\text{Correction factor} = \frac{\text{Grand total}^2}{\text{Number of scores}} = \frac{G^2}{N} = \frac{284^2}{18} = \frac{80{,}656}{18} = 4480.889$$

Thus
$$C = 4611.000$$
$$R = 4836.444$$
$$T = 5027.333$$

$$\frac{G^2}{N} = 4480.889 \text{ (i.e. correction factor)}$$

Also $\Sigma X^2 = 5162$ (from step 2).

Enter the following calculations into the analysis of variance summary table (Table 22.21).

Step 4 Calculate the sum of squares for the independent variable alcohol (i.e. $SS_{[alcohol]}$). (The elements of the calculation have already been calculated in step 3.)

$$SS_{[alcohol]} = R - \frac{G^2}{N}$$

$$= 4836.444 - 4480.889$$

$$= 355.555$$

The degrees of freedom for $SS_{[alcohol]}$ = the number of conditions (or levels) of the alcohol variable $- 1 = 2 - 1 = 1$.

Table 22.21 **Analysis of variance summary table**

Source of variation	Sums of squares	Degrees of freedom	Mean square	*F*-ratio
Main effects:				
Alcohol	355.555	1	355.555	31.67[a]
Sleep deprivation	130.111	2	65.555	5.84[a]
Interaction:				
Sleep deprivation with alcohol	60.778	2	30.389	2.71
'Error'	134.667	12	11.222	–
Total	681.111	17	–	–

[a] Significant at the 5% level.

Step 5 Calculate the sum of squares for the sleep deprivation variable. (The elements of this calculation have already been calculated in step 3.)

$$SS_{[sleep\ deprivation]} = C - \frac{G^2}{N}$$

$$= 4611.000 - 4480.889$$

$$= 130.111$$

The degrees of freedom = the number of conditions (or levels) of the sleep deprivation variable $- 1 = 3 - 1 = 2$.

Step 6 Calculate the interaction sum of squares (i.e. $SS_{[interaction]}$). (All of the elements of this calculation have already been calculated in step 3.) Insert these values.

$$SS_{[interaction]} = T - C - R + \frac{G^2}{N}$$

$$= 5027.333 - 4611.000 - 4836.444 + 4480.889$$

$$= 60.778$$

The degrees of freedom $SS_{[interaction]}$ are (the number of conditions (or levels) of the sleep deprivation variable $- 1) \times$ (the number of conditions (or levels) of the alcohol variable − 1) = (3 − 1) × (2 − 1) = 2 × 1 = 2 degrees of freedom.

Step 7 Calculate the error sum of squares. (This is based on the total sum of squares calculated in step 2 and T calculated in step 3.) Enter these values.

$$SS_{[error]} = \Sigma X^2 - T$$

$$= 5162 - 5027.333$$

$$= 134.667$$

The degrees of freedom for $SS_{[error]}$ are the number of scores − (number of rows) × (number of columns). Thus the degrees of freedom for error are 18 − (2 × 3) = 18 − 6 = 12. This value should be entered in the analysis of variance summary table.

Step 8 The main parts of the computation have now been completed and you should have entered the sums of squares and the degrees of freedom into the analysis of variance summary table. You also need to calculate the three F-ratios in Table 22.21 by dividing the main effect and interaction mean squares by the error mean squares.

Step 9 The statistical significance of each of these F-ratios is obtained by consulting Significance Table 22.1. If your value is larger than the listed value for the appropriate degrees of freedom then the F-ratio is statistically significant at the 5% level of significance. The column entry is the degrees of freedom for the particular main effect or interaction in question, the rows are always the degrees of freedom for error. As you can see, the two main effects in Table 22.21 are statistically significant whereas the interaction is not.

Interpretating the results Remember that the interpretation of any data should be based first of all on an examination of cell means and variances (or standard deviations) as in Table 22.22. The tests of significance merely confirm whether or not your interpretations can be generalised. It would appear from Table 22.22 that the cell means for the no-alcohol condition are relatively unaffected by the amount of sleep deprivation. However, in the alcohol conditions increasing levels of sleep deprivation produce a greater number of mistakes. There also appears to be a tendency for there to be more mistakes when the participants have taken alcohol than when they have not.

Reporting the results The results of this analysis may be written up as follows: 'A two-way ANOVA was carried out on variance on the data. The two main effects of sleep deprivation ($F = 31.67$, df = 2, 12, $p < 0.05$) and alcohol ($F = 5.84$, df = 1, 12, $p < 0.05$) were statistically significant. The number of errors related to the number of hours of sleep deprivation. Four hours of sleep deprivation resulted in an average of 12.83 errors, twelve hours of sleep deprivation resulted in an average of 15.17 errors, and twenty-four hours of sleep deprivation resulted in 19.33 errors on average. Consuming alcohol before the test resulted on average in 20.22 errors and the no-alcohol condition resulted in substantially fewer errors ($M = 15.78$). The interaction between sleep deprivation was not significant despite the tendency of the scores in the alcohol condition with 24 hours of sleep deprivation to be much higher than those in the other conditions ($F = 2.71$, df $= 2, 12$, ns). Inspection of the graph (Figure 22.1) suggests that there is an interaction since the alcohol and no-alcohol curves are not parallel. It would appear that the interaction is being hidden by the main effects in the ANOVA.'

The significant F-ratio for the main effect of sleep deprivation needs to be explored further by the use of multiple-comparisons tests (Chapter 23). Because there are only two alcohol conditions, this is unnecessary for independent variables having only two levels: there is no doubt where the differences lie in circumstances where there are only two values of an independent variable. Given the implications of the graph for the question of an interaction, it would be sensible to carry out multiple comparisons comparing all of the six cell means of the 2 × 3 ANOVA with each other (Chapter 23).

Table 22.22   **Table of means for the two-way ANOVA**

	Sleep deprivation			
	4 hours	**12 hours**	**24 hours**	
Alcohol	15.000	19.667	26.000	Row mean = 20.22
No alcohol	10.667	10.667	12.667	Row mean = 11.333
	Column mean = 12.833	Column mean = 15.167	Column mean = 19.333	Overall mean = 15.777

22.6 Three or more independent variables

The two-way ANOVA can be extended to include three or more independent variables although you are always restricted to analysing a single dependent variable. Despite this, it should be noted that the complexity of experimental research is constrained by a number of factors including the following:

1. Having a lot of different conditions in an experiment may involve a lot of research and planning time. Preparing complex sets of instructions for participants in the different experimental conditions, randomly assigning individuals to these groups and many other methodological considerations usually limit our level of ambition in research designs. In non-psychological disciplines, the logistics of experiments are different since the units may not

be people but, for example, seedlings in pots containing one of several different composts, with different amounts of fertiliser, and one of several different growing temperatures. These are far less time consuming.

2.   Interpreting ANOVA is more skilful than many researchers realise. Care is needed to interpret even a two-way analysis properly because main effects are prioritised in the calculation which results in main effects being credited with variation which is really due to interaction.

Since theoretically but not practically there is no limit to the number of independent variables possible in the analysis of variance the potential for complexity is enormous. However, caution is recommended when planning research. The problems of interpretation get somewhat more difficult the more independent variables there are. The complexity is largely the result of the number of possible *interactions*. Although there is just one interaction with a two-way analysis of variance, there are four with a three-way analysis of variance. The numbers accelerate rapidly with greater numbers of independent variables. As far as possible, we would recommend any psychologist to be wary of going far beyond a two-way analysis of variance without very careful planning and without some experience with these less complex designs.

It is possible to disregard the interactions and simply to analyse the different variables in the experiment as if they were several one-way experiments carried out at the same time. The interpretations would be simpler by doing this. However, this is rarely if ever done in psychological research and it is conventional always to consider interactions.

Imagine the following three-way or three-factor analysis of variance. The three independent variables are:

■ age – coded as either young or old
■ sex – coded as either male or female
■ noise – the research takes place in either a noisy or a quiet environment.

So this is a three-way ANOVA with a total of eight different conditions (2 ages × 2 sexes × 2 different noise levels). The dependent variable is the number of errors on a numerical memory test in the different conditions. The main features of this research are presented in Table 22.23.

Table 22.23 **A stylised three-way analysis of variance study**

| | Noisy conditions | | Quiet conditions | |
	Young	Old	Young	Old
Males				
Females				

The sheer number of comparisons possible between sections of the data causes problems. These comparisons are:

1. The main effect of sex – that is, comparing males and females irrespective of age or noise.

2. The main effect of age – that is, comparing young and old irrespective of sex or noise.

3. The main effect of noise – that is, comparing noisy and quiet conditions irrespective of age or sex.

4. The interaction of age and sex – that is, comparing age and sex groups ignoring the noise conditions. This would look like Table 22.24.

Table 22.24 **The interaction of age and sex**

	Young	**Old**
Males		
Females		

5. The interaction of age and noise – that is, comparing age and noise groups ignoring sex. This is shown in Table 22.25.

Table 22.25 **The interaction of age and noise**

Noisy conditions		**Quiet conditions**	
Young	**Old**	**Young**	**Old**

6. The interaction of noise and sex – that is, comparing the noise and sex groups ignoring age. This is shown in Table 22.26.

Table 22.26 **The interaction of noise and sex**

	Noisy conditions	**Quiet conditions**
Males		
Females		

7. There is a fourth interaction – the interaction of noise and sex and age which is represented by Table 22.27. Notice that the cell means of each of the conditions are involved in this.

Table 22.27 **The interaction of noise, sex and age**

	Noisy conditions		Quiet conditions	
	Young	Old	Young	Old
Males				
Females				

Although Table 22.27 looks like the format of the original data table (Table 22.23), the scores in the cells will be very different because all of the other sources of variation will have been removed.

The steps in calculating this three-way analysis of variance follow the pattern demonstrated earlier in this chapter but with extra layers of complexity:

1. The error term is calculated in the usual way by subtracting the cell mean from each score in a particular cell. The variance estimate of this table can then be calculated.

2. The main effect of sex is calculated by substituting the male mean for each of the male scores and the female mean for each of the female scores. The variance estimate of this table can then be calculated.

3. The age main effect is calculated by substituting the mean score of the young people for each of their scores and substituting the mean score of the old people for each of their scores. The variance estimate of this table can then be calculated.

4. The noise main effect is obtained by substituting the mean score in the noisy conditions for each score in the noisy conditions and substituting the mean score in the quiet conditions for each score in the quiet conditions. The variance estimate of this table can then be calculated.

5. The interaction of age and sex is arrived at by taking the table of scores with the error removed and then removing the age and sex difference simply by taking away the column mean and then the row mean. This is the same procedure as we applied to get the interaction in the two-way analysis of variance. The variance estimate of this table can then be calculated.

6. We arrive at the interaction of age and noise by drawing up a similar table and then taking away the appropriate age and noise means in turn. The variance estimate of this table can then be calculated.

7. We arrive at the interaction of noise and sex by drawing up a similar table and then taking away the appropriate noise and sex means in turn. The variance estimate of this table can then be calculated.

8. The three-way interaction (age × noise × sex) is obtained by first of all drawing up our table of the age × noise × sex conditions. We then take away the main effects by subtracting the appropriate age, noise and sex means from this table. But we also have to take away the two-way interactions of

age × noise, age × sex, and noise × sex by subtracting the appropriate means from the above table. Whatever is left is the three-way interaction. The variance estimate of this final table can then be calculated.

22.7 Notes and recommendations

■ Only when you have a 2 × 2 unrelated analysis of variance is the interpretation of the data relatively straightforward. For 2 × 3 or larger analyses of variance you need to read Chapter 23 as well.

■ Although at heart simple enough, the two-way analysis of variance is cumbersome to calculate by hand and is probably best done on a computer if you have anything other than small amounts of data.

■ Analysis of variance always requires a degree of careful interpretation of the findings and cannot always be interpreted in a hard-and-fast way. This is a little disconcerting given its apparent mathematical sophistication.

■ Before calculating the analysis of variance proper, spend a good deal of effort trying to make sense of the pattern of column, row and cell means in your data table. This should alert you to the major trends in your data. You can use your interpretation in combination with the analysis of variance summary table to obtain as refined an interpretation of your data as possible.

Chapter 23

Multiple comparisons in ANOVA

Just where do the differences lie?

Preparation

You will need a working knowledge of Chapters 19, 20 and 21 on the analysis of variance. Chapter 14 introduces the problem of multiple comparisons in the context of partitioning chi-square tables.

23.1 Introduction

When in research there are *more than two levels* of an *independent* variable it is not always obvious where the differences between conditions lie. There is no problem when you have only two groups of scores to compare in a one-way or a 2×2 ANOVA. However, if there are three or more different levels of any independent variable the interpretation problems multiply. Take, for example, Table 23.1 of means for a one-way analysis of variance.

Although the analysis of variance for the data which are summarised in this table may well be statistically significant, there remains a very obvious problem. Groups 1 and 2 have virtually identical means and it is Group 3 which has the exceptionally large scores. Quite simply we would be tempted to assume that Group 1 and Group 2 do not differ significantly and that any differences are due

Table 23.1 **Sample means in a one-way ANOVA**

	Group 1	Group 2	Group 3
Mean	5.6	5.7	12.9

Table 23.2 **Sample means in another one-way ANOVA**

	Group 1	Group 2	Group 3
Mean	5.6	7.3	12.9

to Group 3. Our eyes are telling us that only parts of the data are contributing to the significant ANOVA.

Although the above example is very clear, it becomes a little more fraught if the data are less clear-cut than this (Table 23.2). In this case, it may well be that all three groups differ from each other. Just by looking at the means we cannot know for certain since they may just reflect sampling differences.

Obviously it is essential to test the significance of the differences between the means for all *three* possible *pairs* of sample means from the three groups. These are:

Group 1 with Group 2
Group 1 with Group 3
Group 2 with Group 3

If there had been *four* groups then the pairs of comparisons would be:

Group 1 with Group 2
Group 1 with Group 3
Group 1 with Group 4
Group 2 with Group 3
Group 2 with Group 4
Group 3 with Group 4

This is getting to be a lot of comparisons.

23.2 Methods

There are a number of different procedures which you could employ to deal with this problem. One traditional approach involves comparing each of the pairs of groups using a *t*-test (or you could use one-way analysis of variance for two groups). So for the four-group experiment there would be six separate *t*-tests to calculate (Group 1 with Group 2, Group 1 with Group 3, etc.).

The problem with this procedure (which is not so bad really) is the number of separate comparisons being made. The more comparisons you make between pairs of variables the more likely is a significant difference merely due to chance (always the risk in inferential statistics). Similar procedures apply to the multifactorial (two-way, etc.) analysis of variance. You can compare different levels of any of the main effect pairs simply by comparing their means using a *t*-test or the equivalent. However, the multiple comparison difficulty remains unless you make an adjustment.

To cope with this problem a relatively simple procedure, the Bonferroni method is used. It assumes that the significance level should be shared between the *number* of comparisons made. So if you are making four comparisons (i.e. conducting four separate *t*-tests) then the appropriate significance level for the individual tests is as follows:

$$\text{Significance level for each test} = \frac{\text{Overall significance level}}{\text{Number of comparisons}}$$

$$= \frac{5\%}{4}$$

$$= 1.25\%$$

In other words, a comparison actually needs to be significant at the 1.25% level according to the significance tables before we accept that it is significant at the *equivalent* of the 5% level. This essentially compensates for our generosity in doing many comparisons and reduces the risk of inadvertently capitalising on chance differences. (We adopted this procedure for chi-square in Chapter 14.) Although this is the proper thing to do, we have often seen examples of analyses which fail to make this adjustment. Some researchers tend to stick with the regular 5% level per comparison no matter how many they are doing, although sometimes they point out the dangers of multiple comparisons without making an appropriate adjustment.

So long as you adjust your critical values to allow for the number of comparisons made, there is nothing much wrong with using multiple *t*-tests. Indeed, this procedure, properly applied, is a slightly 'conservative' one in that it errs in favour of the null hypotheses. However, there are better procedures for making multiple comparisons which are especially convenient when using a computer. These include such procedures as the Scheffé Test and the Duncan Multiple Range Test. The advantage of these is that they report directly significance levels which are adjusted for the numbers of comparisons being made.

Appendix K containes a table of *t*-values for use when there are a number of comparisons being made (i.e. multiple comparisons). Say you wished to test the statistical significance of the differences between pairs of groups in a three-group one-way analysis of variance. This gives three different comparisons between the pairs. The significant *t*-test values for this are found under the column for three comparisons.

23.3 Planned versus *a posteriori (post hoc)* comparisons

In the fantasy world of statisticians there is a belief that researchers are meticulous in planning the last detail of their statistical analysis in advance of doing research. As such an ideal researcher, one would have planned in advance precisely what pairs of cells or conditions in the research are to be compared. These choices are based on the hypotheses and other considerations. In other words, they are planned comparisons. More usual, in our experience, is that the details of the statistical analysis are decided upon *after* the data have been collected. Psychological theory is often not so strong that we can predict from it the precise pattern of outcomes we expect. Comparisons decided upon after the data have been collected and tabulated are called *a posteriori* or *post hoc* comparisons.

Since properly planned comparisons are not the norm in psychological research, for simplicity we will just consider the more casual situation in which comparisons are made as the data is inspected. (Basically, if your number of planned comparisons is smaller than your number of experimental conditions, then they can be tested by the multiple *t*-test *without* adjusting the critical values.)

There are a number of tests which deal with the situation in which multiple comparisons are being made. These include Dunnett's Test, Duncan's Test and others. The Scheffé Test will serve as a model of the sorts of things achieved by many of these tests and is probably as good as any other similar test for general application. Some other tests are not quite so stringent in ensuring that the appropriate level of significance is achieved.

23.4 The Scheffé Test for one-way ANOVA

Although this can be computed by hand without too much difficulty, the computer output of the Scheffé Test is particularly useful as it gives subsets of the groups (or conditions) in your experiment which do not differ significantly from each other. For example:

```
SUBSET  1
Group      Grp 3    Grp 1     Grp 2
mean       4.00     5.60      7.00
```

This means that Groups 1, 2 and 3 are not significantly different from each other. If you had significant differences between all three groups then you would have three subsets (Subset 1, Subset 2 and Subset 3) each of which contained just one group. If Groups 1 and 3 did not differ from each other but they both differed from Group 2 you would obtain something like

```
SUBSET  1
Group      Grp 3    Grp 1
mean       4.00     5.60

SUBSET  2
Group      Grp 2
mean       7.00
```

Calculation 23.1

Multiple comparisons: the Scheffé Test

The calculation of the Scheffé Test is straightforward once you have carried out an analysis of variance and have the summary table. The test tells you whether two group means in an ANOVA differ significantly from each other. Obviously the calculation has to be repeated for every pair of groups you wish to compare but no adjustments are necessary for the number of pairs of groups being compared. The following worked example is based on the data in Calculation 20.1. Table 23.3 reminds us about the data and Table 23.4 is the analysis of variance summary table for that calculation.

Table 23.3 **Data table for an unrelated analysis of variance**

Group 1 Hormone 1	Group 2 Hormone 2	Group 3 Placebo control
9	4	3
12	2	6
8	5	3
Mean = 9.667	Mean = 3.667	Mean = 4.000
$N_1 = 3$	$N_2 = 3$	$N_3 = 3$
		Overall mean = 5.778

Table 23.4 **Analysis of variance summary table**

Source of variation	Sum of squares	Degrees of freedom	Mean square (variance estimate)	F-ratio
Between groups	68.222	2	34.111	10.59[a]
Error (within-groups)	19.334	6	3.222	
Total	87.556	8	10.945	

[a] Significant at the 5% level

Step 1 The formula used is based on the F-distribution. It involves the two group means in question, the sample sizes in the relevant conditions and the error (within) mean square. All of these are to be found in Tables 23.3 and 23.4.

$$F = \frac{(\text{Mean of group}_1 - \text{Mean of group}_2)^2}{\text{Error mean square} \times \dfrac{N_1 + N_2}{N_1 \times N_2}}$$

$$= \frac{(9.667 - 3.667)^2}{3.222 \times \dfrac{3 + 3}{3 \times 3}}$$

$$= \frac{6.000^2}{3.222 \times \dfrac{6}{9}}$$

$$= \frac{36.000}{3.222 \times 0.667}$$

$$= \frac{36.000}{2.149}$$

$$= 16.75$$

Step 2 The significance of this F-ratio depends on the degrees of freedom. The degrees of freedom for the columns in Significance Table 22.1 are the number of groups being compared − 1 (i.e. 2 − 1 = 1 always). The degrees of freedom for the error term (i.e. number of scores − number of groups = 9 − 3 = 6) corresponds to the rows in Significance Table 22.1. This indicates that the difference between the mean of Group 1 and that of Group 2 is significant at the 5% level with the Scheffé Test.

Step 3 In essence, step 3 repeats steps 1 and 2 but compares Group 1 with Group 3 and Group 2 with Group 3. This gives us:

F when comparing Group 1 with Group 3 = 14.94 (significant at 5% level)

F when comparing Group 2 with Group 3 = 0.05 (not significant)

Interpreting the results The use of a multiple-comparisons test is necessary whenever there are more than two groups to compare in ANOVA. If there are only two groups then any further test is superfluous.

Reporting the results The results of this analysis may be written up as follows: 'The F-ratio for the overall analysis of variance was significant at the 5% level (F = 10.59, df = 2, 6, $p < 0.05$). Consequently, the Scheffé Test was used to compare pairs of group means in order to assess where the differences lie. It was found that at the 5% level of significance, Group 1 (M = 9.67) was significantly higher than Group 2 (M = 3.67) and Group 3 (M = 4.00) but that the means of Groups 2 and 3 did not differ from each other. Thus Hormone 1 was associated with higher levels of depression than either Hormone 2 or the placebo control which did not differ from each other.'

23.5 Multiple comparisons for multifactorial ANOVA

If your experimental design is multifactorial (that is, with two or more independent variables), multiple comparisons are tackled much as for the two-way ANOVA using exactly the same methods (including the adjusted multiple t-test procedure or the Scheffé Test). Of course, you would only need such a test if any of the independent variables (factors) has three or more different levels. Otherwise, the significance of the comparisons in the ANOVA is obvious from the ANOVA summary table since there are only two groups of scores to compare with each other (except for interactions).

If you have an independent variable with three or more different levels then multiple comparisons are important to tell you precisely where the significant differences lie. It would be possible to carry out multiple comparisons between every cell mean in the ANOVA but generally this would not be helpful. All one would do is to produce a table analogous to a one-way ANOVA by making the data in each cell of the multifactorial ANOVA into a column of the one-way ANOVA. The difficulty is that this multiplicity of comparisons would be practically uninterpretable since each cell consists of several sources of variation – the various main effects, for example.

It is much more useful and viable to employ multiple comparisons to compare the means of the several different levels of the independent variable(s). If there are four different levels of the independent variable, then one would essentially set out the table like a one-way ANOVA with four different levels of the independent variable. It is then possible to test the significance of the differences among the four means using, for example, the Scheffé Test.

23.6 Notes and recommendations

- If you have more than two sets of scores in the analysis of variance (or any other test for that matter), it is important to employ one of the procedures for multiple comparisons.

- Even simple procedures such as multiple t-tests are better than nothing, especially if the proper adjustment is made for the number of t-tests being carried out and you adjust the critical values accordingly.

- Modern computer packages, especially SPSS, have a range of multiple comparison tests. It is a fine art to know which is the most appropriate for your particular circumstances. Usually it is expedient to compare the results from several tests; often they will give much the same results, especially where the trends in the data are clear.

Recommended further reading

Howell, D. (1997). *Statistical Methods for Psychology* 4th Edition. Belmont, CA: Duxbury Press.

Chapter 24

More analysis of variance designs

Mixed-design ANOVA and analysis of covariance (ANCOVA)

24.1 Introduction

This chapter deals with two useful variants of the analysis of variance: the mixed design and the analysis of covariance. Although we are moving into quite advanced areas of statistics, the key to most statistical analysis lies more in the interpretation of simple statistics such as cell means. Avoid letting the complex calculations sometimes employed blind you to the major purpose of your analysis – understanding what your data say. The two new statistical procedures described in this chapter may appear to be very different but nevertheless they sometimes may be alternative ways of analysing much the same data.

The mixed design analysis of variance is similar to the two-way ANOVA described in Chapter 22. The big difference is that *one* of the independent variables is related and *one* is unrelated – hence the term mixed design. Thus it is used when participants take part in *all* of the conditions of one independent variable but in just *one* condition of the other variable. A good example of this type of design is when a pre-test has been given on the dependent variable before the different experimental treatments and a post-test given afterwards. So all participants are measured on both the pre-test and post-test making pre-test/post-test a related measure. Of course, the unrelated independent variable involves the important experimental manipulation.

The analysis of covariance (ANCOVA) described in this chapter is basically the unrelated analysis of variance (Chapter 21). The crucial difference is that an additional variable known as the covariate is measured in addition to the dependent variable. This covariate is a variable which correlates potentially with the *dependent* variable. The participants in the various conditions of the experiment may be different in terms of a covariate. Thus not all differences between the experimental conditions are due to the influence of the independent variable (experimental manipulation) on the dependent variable. In ANCOVA the scores on the dependent variable are adjusted so that they are equated on the covariate. Although the procedures do not actually give adjusted scores, the cell means for the adjusted scores are obtained. In experiments random assignment of participants to different conditions of the experiment is used so that any pre-existing differences between participants are randomly distributed. However, randomisation does not fully guarantee that participants are similar in all conditions for every study. Randomisation avoids systematic biases but it cannot ensure that there are no differences between participants in the different conditions prior to the experimental manipulation. Furthermore, non-experimental studies cannot employ randomisation properly. Pre-test measures can be thought of as covariates of the post-test measure and thus handled using the analysis of covariance as an alternative to the mixed design described above.

> **Design consideration** Before the introduction of computers, it was conventional in many of the variants of the analysis of variance to ensure that *all* conditions or cells had the same number of scores. The reason for this is that the calculations are simpler if this is the case. When carrying out laboratory studies, this is relatively easy to achieve even if it involves randomly discarding scores from some cells. However, it is possible to do any analysis of variance with unequal numbers of scores in each condition or cell. The calculations tend to be cumbersome and so it is best to use a computer package such as SPSS to reduce the computational load.
>
> The exception to this is the one-way analysis of variance described in Chapter 20 which can be calculated with no adjustments for unequal sample size. Of course, with the related one-way ANOVA it is not possible to have different numbers of participants in different conditions of the experiment since participants have to take part in all conditions.

24.2 Mixed designs and repeated measures

Repeated measures designs have the same subjects (or matched groups of subjects) measured in *all* conditions just as in the repeated measures one-way analysis of variance except that there are two or more independent variables. The repeated measures design is intended to increase the precision of research by measuring the error variance (residual variance) in a way which excludes the individual differences component. The individual difference component is obtained from the general tendency of individual participants to score relatively high or relatively low, say, irrespective of the experimental condition. The trend for each individual can simply be deducted from the error scores to leave (residual) error.

Fully repeated measures designs can be analysed but they are beyond the scope of this book (see Howell, 1997, for calculation methods). Some

Fixed versus random effects The issue of fixed versus random effects is a typical analysis of variance misnomer. It really means fixed or random choice of the different levels of an independent variable. The implication being that you can select the levels of a treatment (independent variable) either by a systematic decision or by choosing the levels by some random procedure.

Most psychological research assumes a *fixed effects* model and it is hard to find instances of the use of random effects. A fixed effect is where you as the researcher choose or decide or fix what the different values of the independent variable are going to be. In some cases you have no choice at all – a variable such as sex gives you no discretion since it has just two different values (male and female). Usually we just operate as if we have the choice of the different treatments for each independent variable. We simply decide that the experimental group is going to be deprived of sleep for five hours and the control group not deprived of sleep at all.

But there are many different possible amounts of sleep deprivation – no hours, one hour, two hours, three hours, four hours, and so forth. Instead of just selecting the number of hours of sleep deprivation on the basis of a particular whim, practicality or any other similar basis, it is possible to choose the amounts of sleep deprivation at random. We could draw the amount out of a hat containing the possible levels. In circumstances like these we would be using a *random effects* model. Because we have selected the hours of sleep deprivation at random, it could be said that our ability to generalise from our experiment to the effects of sleep deprivation in general is enhanced. We simply have chosen an unbiased way of selecting the amount of sleep deprivation after all.

Since the random effects model rarely corresponds to practice in psychological research it is not dealt with further in this book. Psychologists' research is more likely to be the result of agonising about time, money and other practical constraints on the choices available.

independent variables do not allow for repeated measures – sex, for example, is not a repeated measure since a person cannot change sex during the course of an experiment. Only where matching of groups on the basis of sex has been carried out is it possible to have sex as a repeated measure.

Much more common in psychology are *mixed designs* in which the repeated measure is on just some of the independent variables. Mixed designs are two- or more-way analyses of variance in which participants are measured in more than one experimental condition but not *every* experimental condition. (This means that for at least one of the independent variables in a mixed design, scores on different participants will be found in the different levels of this independent variable.) Usually you will have to check through the experimental design carefully in order to decide whether a researcher has used a mixed design, although many will stipulate the type of design.

One common mixed design is the pre-test/post-test design. Participants are measured on the dependent variable before and after the experimental treatment. This is clearly a related design since the same people are measured twice on the same dependent variable. However, since the experimental and control groups consist of different people, this comparison is unrelated. Hence this form of the pre-test/post-test design is a mixed design. This sort of design is illustrated in Table 24.1 (see Calculation 24.1). Imagine that the dependent variable is self-esteem measured in children before and after the experimental manipulation. The experimental manipulation involves praising half of the children (the experimental group) for good behaviour but telling the other half (the control group) nothing. Obviously this sort of design allows the researcher to test whether the two groups are similar prior to the experimental manipulation by comparing the experimental and control groups on the pre-test measure. The hypothesis that praise affects self-esteem suggests that the post-test measure should be different for the two groups. (Notice that the hypothesis predicts an interaction effect in which the related and unrelated independent variables interact to yield rather different scores for the experimental group and the control group on the post-test.)

In virtually all respects, the computation of the mixed design is like that for the two-way (unrelated) ANOVA described in Chapter 22. Both main effects and the interaction are calculated in identical fashion. The error is treated differently though. Although the *total* error is calculated by subtracting the cell mean from each of the data scores to leave the error score (as in Chapter 22), in the mixed design this error is then subdivided into two component parts: (a) the individual differences component and (b) the (residual) error component:

- the error due to individual differences is calculated and then used as the error term for the *unrelated* independent variable (this error term is often called 'subjects within groups')
- the (residual) error term is used as the error term when examining the effects of the related independent variable (this error term is often called 'B × subjects within groups').

Note the slight amendments made to the tables compared to those given in Chapter 22; columns headed 'subject' and 'subject mean' have been added. If there is variation in the subject mean column it shows that there is still an individual differences component in the scores in the main body of the table. Careful examination of (a) the column means and row means, (b) cell means, (c) subject means, and (d) the individual scores in the cells, will hint strongly whether there remains any variation due to (a) the main effects, (b) interaction, (c) individual differences, and (d) (residual) error.

If you feel confident with the two-way unrelated ANOVA described in Chapter 22, we suggest that you need to concentrate on step 2 and step 7 below as these tell you how to calculate the error terms. The other steps should be familiar.

Calculation 24.1

Mixed-design two-way unrelated analysis of variance: conceptual method

Table 24.1 **Example of a mixed ANOVA design**

	Subject	Pre-test measure	Post-test measure	Subject mean	
Control	S1	6	5	5.500	
	S2	4 Mean = 5.000	6 Mean = 6.000	5.000	Mean = 5.500
	S3	5	7	6.000	
Experimental	S4	7	10	8.500	
	S5	5 Mean = 5.667	11 Mean = 11.000	8.000	Mean = 8.333
	S6	5	12	8.500	
		Mean = 5.333	Mean = 8.500	Overall mean = 6.917	

The variance estimate for the data in Table 24.1 for $N - 1$ degrees of freedom is $76.89/11 = 11.67$. N is the number of scores.

Just to remind you, 11.67 is the variance estimate (or mean square) based on the twelve scores in Table 24.1. To avoid repetitious calculations with which you should now be familiar, we have given only the final stages of the calculation of the various variance estimates. This is to allow you to work through our example and check your calculations.

In the mixed-design ANOVA the following steps are then calculated.

Step 1 (between-subjects scores) Between-subjects scores are the data but with the pre-test/post-test difference eliminated. In other words, each subject's scores in the pre-test and post-test conditions are replaced by the corresponding subject mean. Thus the column means for the pre-test and post-test have the (residual) error removed since the remaining variation within the cells is due to individual differences. However, there still remains variation within the table due to individual differences as well as the main effects and interaction. (To be absolutely clear, the first entry of 5.500 for both the pre-test and post-test measure is obtained by averaging that first person's scores of 5 and 6 in Table 24.2.)

Table 24.2 **Table of between-subjects scores, i.e. with (residual) error removed**

	Subject	Pre-test	Post-test	Subject mean	
Control	S1	5.500	5.500	5.500	
	S2	5.000 Mean = 5.500	5.000 Mean = 5.500	5.000	Mean = 5.500
	S3	6.000	6.000	6.000	
Experimental	S4	8.500	8.500	8.500	
	S5	8.000 Mean = 8.333	8.000 Mean = 8.333	8.000	Mean = 8.333
	S6	8.500	8.500	8.500	
		Mean = 6.917	Mean = 6.917	Overall mean = 6.917	

The variance estimate for the between-subjects scores is $25.41 \div 5 = 5.08$ (df = number of subjects – 1, i.e. 6 – 1 = 5)

Step 2 (subjects within groups scores, i.e. individual difference component)   If we take away the cell mean from the scores in Table 24.2, we are left with the individual difference component for each subject for each score. Thus, S2's scores are on average –0.500 below the row mean. Table 24.3 gives the individual difference component of every score in the original data.

Table 24.3 **Subjects within groups scores, i.e. error due to individual differences removed**

	Subject	Pre-test	Post-test	Subject mean	
Control	S1	5.500 – 5.500 = 0.000	0.000	0.000	
	S2	5.000 – 5.500 = – 0.500	–0.500	–0.500	Mean = 0.000
	S3	6.000 – 5.500 = 0.500	0.500	0.500	
Experimental	S4	0.167	0.167	0.167	
	S5	–0.333	–0.333	–0.333	Mean = 0.000
	S6	0.167	0.167	0.167	
		Mean = 0.000	Mean = 0.000	Overall mean = 0.000	

The variance estimate for the subjects with groups scores is $1.32 \div 4 = 0.33$ (the df is the number of subjects – number of rows of data, i.e. 6 – 2 = 4).

You will see that these individual difference scores seem rather like error scores – they add to zero for each cell. Indeed they are error scores – the individual differences component of error. The variance estimate of the individual differences is used as the error variance estimate for calculating the significance of the control/experimental comparison (i.e. the *unrelated* independent variable).

Step 3 (experimental/control scores: main effect)   The best estimate of the effects of the experimental versus the control condition involves simply replacing each score for the control group with the control group mean

(5.500) and each score for the experimental group by the experimental group mean (8.333). This is shown in Table 24.4.

Table 24.4 **Main effect (experimental/control comparison)**

	Subject	Pre-test	Post-test	Subject mean	
Control	S1	5.500	5.500	5.500	
	S2	5.500	5.500	5.500	Mean = 5.500
	S3	5.500	5.500	5.500	
Experimental	S4	8.333	8.333	8.333	
	S5	8.333	8.333	8.333	Mean = 8.333
	S6	8.333	8.333	8.333	
		Mean = 6.917	Mean = 6.917	Overall mean = 6.917	

The variance estimate for the experimental/control main effect is 24.09 ÷ 1 = 24.09 (the df is the number of rows of data – 1, i.e. 2 – 1 = 1).

The statistical significance of the main effect of the experimental versus control manipulation independent variable involves the variance estimate for the main effects scores in Table 24.4 and the variance estimate for the individual differences error scores in Table 24.3. By dividing the former by the latter variance estimate, we obtain the F-ratio for testing the effects of the experimental versus control conditions. If this is significant then there is an overall difference between the control and experimental group scores.

Step 4 (within-subjects scores) Subtract the between-subjects scores (Table 24.2) from the data table (Table 24.1) and you are left the within-subjects scores. In other words, the scores in Table 24.5 are what is left when the effects of the experimental/control comparison and the individual difference component of the scores are removed. Notice that the subject means in Table 24.5 are all zero as are the row means. This indicates that there are no individual differences or differences due to the experimental/control comparison remaining in Table 24.5.

Table 24.5 **Within-subjects scores (i.e. the scores with individual differences and control/experimental differences eliminated)**

	Subject	Pre-test	Post-test	Subject mean	
Control	S1	0.5	–0.5	0.000	
	S2	–1.0	1.0	0.000	Mean = 0.000
	S3	–1.0	1.0	0.000	
Experimental	S4	–1.5	1.5	0.000	
	S5	–3.0	3.0	0.000	Mean = 0.000
	S6	–3.5	3.5	0.000	
		Mean = –0.909	Mean = 0.909	Overall mean = 0.000	

The variance estimate for this table is $51.48 \div 6 = 8.58$ (df is the number of scores minus the number of subjects $= 12 - 6 = 6$).

Step 5 (within-subjects independent variable main effect: pre-test/post-test scores) This is the main effect of the repeated measure. It is obtained simply by substituting the appropriate column average from the data table (Table 24.1) for each of the scores (Table 24.6).

Table 24.6 **The main effects of the pre-test/post-test comparison**

	Subject	Pre-test	Post-test	Subject mean	
Control	S1	5.333	8.500	6.917	
	S2	5.333	8.500	6.917	Mean = 6.917
	S3	5.333	8.500	6.917	
Experimental	S4	5.333	8.500	6.917	
	S5	5.333	8.500	6.917	Mean = 6.917
	S6	5.333	8.500	6.917	
		Mean = 5.333	Mean = 8.500		Overall mean = 6.917

The variance estimate for the pre-test/post-test main effect is $30.14 \div 1 = 30.14$ (the df is the number of columns of data -1, i.e. $2 - 1 = 1$).

Step 6 (the interaction of experimental/control with pre-test/post-test) The calculation of the interaction is much as for the two-way unrelated ANOVA (Chapter 22):

1. We can eliminate error by making every score in the data table the same as the cell mean (Table 24.7).

Table 24.7 **Removing (total) error from the data table**

	Subject	Pre-test	Post-test	Subject mean	
Control	S1	5.000	6.000	5.500	
	S2	5.000	6.000	5.500	Mean = 5.500
	S3	5.000	6.000	5.500	
Experimental	S4	5.667	11.000	8.300	
	S5	5.667	11.000	8.300	Mean = 8.333
	S6	5.667	11.000	8.300	
		Mean = 5.333	Mean = 8.5000		Overall mean = 6.917

2. We can eliminate the effect of the control versus experimental treatment by simply taking the corresponding row means away from all of the scores in Table 24.7 (Table 24.8).

Table 24.8   **Removing experimental/control main effect (total) error removed in previous step**

	Subject	Pre-test	Post-test	Subject mean	
Control	S1	5.000 – 5.500 = –0.500	0.500	0.000	
	S2	–0.500	0.500	0.000	Mean = 0.000
	S3	–0.500	0.500	0.000	
Experimental	S4	–2.666	2.667	0.000	
	S5	–2.666	2.667	0.000	Mean = 0.000
	S6	–2.666	2.667	0.000	
		Mean = –1.584	Mean = 1.584	Overall mean = 6.917	

3. Note that Table 24.8 still contains variation between its pre-test and post-test columns. We eliminate this by subtracting the corresponding column mean from each of the scores in the pre-test and post-test columns (Table 24.9).

Table 24.9   **Removing pre-test/post-test differences (error and experimental/control main effect already removed in previous two steps)**

	Subject	Pre-test	Post-test	Subject mean	
Control	S1	–0.500 – – 1.584 = 1.084	–1.084	0.000	
	S2	1.084	–1.084	0.000	Mean = 0.000
	S3	1.084	–1.084	0.000	
Experimental	S4	–1.082	1.083	0.000	
	S5	–1.082	1.083	0.000	Mean = 0.001
	S6	–1.082	1.083	0.000	
		Mean = 0.00	Mean = 0.00	Overall mean = 0.00	

Table 24.9 contains the scores for the interaction. The variance estimate for the interaction is 14.08 ÷ 1 = 14.08 (the df is the number of rows of data – 1 × the number of columns of data –1 (i.e. (2 – 1) x (2 – 1) = 1 × 1 = 1)).

Step 7 (pre-test/post-test × subjects within groups)

Earlier we explained that pre-test/post-test × subjects within groups is an error term which is in essence the (residual) error that we calculated in Chapter 21. It is actually quite easy to calculate the (residual) error simply by:

■ drawing up a total error table by subtracting the cell means from each score in the data table (Table 24.6) as we did for the two-way unrelated ANOVA in Chapter 22 and then

■ taking away from these (total) error scores the corresponding (residual) error in Table 24.8. In other words,

(Residual) error = (Total) error − Individual difference error

Most statistical textbooks present a rather more abstract computational approach to this which obscures what is really happening. However, to facilitate comparisons with other textbooks, if required, we will present the calculation using essentially the computational method.

The calculation of this error term involves taking the data (Table 24.1) and then (a) subtracting the interaction score (Table 24.9), (b) subtracting the individual differences score (Table 24.2), and (c) adding the between-subjects score (Table 24.6). Notice that the scores in Table 24.10 are just as we would expect of error scores – the cells all add up to zero. It is (residual) error since there is no variation left in the subject mean column.

Table 24.10 **The pre-test/post test × subjects within groups scores (i.e. (residual) error)**

	Subject	Pre-test	Post-test	Subject mean	
Control	S1	6−5.000−5.500+5.500 = 1.000	5−6.000−5.500+5.500 =−1.000	0.000	
	S2	4−5.000−5.000+5.500 =−0.500	6−6.000−5.000+5.500 = 0.500	0.000	Mean=
	S3	5−5.000−6.000+5.500 =−0.500	7−6.000−6.000+5.500 = 0.500	0.000	0.000
	S4	7−5.667−8.500+8.333 = 1.167	10−11.000−8.500+8.333 =−1.167	0.000	
	S5	5−5.667−8.00+8.333 =−0.334	12−11.000−8.500+8.333 = 0.833	0.000	Mean=
	S6	5−5.667−8.500+8.333 =−0.834	12−11.000−8.500+8.333 = 0.833	0.000	0.000
		Mean= 0.000	Mean= 0.000	Overall mean = 0.000	

The variance estimate for the pre-test/post-test × subjects within groups (or residual error) is 7.37 ÷ 4 = 1.84 (the df is (number of subjects − number of rows) × (number of columns − 1) = (6 − 2) × (2 − 1) = 4 × 1 = 1).

This (residual) error term is used in assessing the significance of the pre-test/post-test comparison as well as the interaction.

The various calculations in steps 1–7 can be made into an analysis of variance summary table. Table 24.11 is a summary table using the basic concepts we have included in this book; Table 24.12 is the same except that it uses the conventional way of presenting mixed designs in statistics textbooks.

Table 24.11 Analysis of variance summary table (using basic concepts)

Source of variation	Sums of squares	Degrees of freedom	Variance estimate	F-ratio
Unrelated				
Main effect (unrelated variable)	24.09	1	24.09	$\frac{24.09}{0.33} = 73.00^a$
Individual differences error	1.32	4	0.33	
Related				
Main effect (related variable)	30.14	1	30.14	$\frac{30.14}{1.84} = 16.38^a$
Interaction (related × unrelated variables)	14.08	1	14.08	$\frac{14.08}{1.84} = 7.65^a$
(Residual) error	7.37	4	1.84	

[a] Significant at the 5% level.

Table 24.12 Analysis of variance summary table (conventional textbook version)

Source of variation	Sums of squares	Degrees of freedom	Variance estimate	F-ratio
Between subjects				
A (Praise)	24.09	1	24.09	$\frac{24.09}{0.33} = 73.00^a$
Subjects within groups	1.32	4	0.33	
Within subjects				
B (Time)	30.14	1	30.14	$\frac{30.14}{1.84} = 16.38^a$
AB	14.08	1	14.08	$\frac{14.08}{1.84} = 7.65^a$
B × subjects within groups	7.37	4	1.84	

[a] Significant at the 5% level.

You might be wondering about the reasons for the two error terms. The (residual) error is merely that with no individual differences remaining, and in Chapter 21 we examined how removing individual differences helps to control error variation in related designs. Not surprisingly, it is used for the main effect and interaction which include related components. However, since the individual differences error contains only that source of variation, it makes a good error term for the unrelated scores comparison. After all, by getting rid of 'true' error variation the design allows a 'refined' error term for the unrelated comparison.

Perhaps we ought to explain why rather unusual names are used conventionally for the error terms in mixed ANOVAs. The reason is that the individual differences component of the scores cannot be estimated totally independently of the interaction between the main variables since they are both dependent on pre-test/post-test differences. Consequently the estimate of individual differences cannot be totally divorced from the interaction. It follows that both error terms ought to be labelled in ways which indicate this fact. On balance, then, you would be wise to keep to the conventional terminology.

Design consideration This sort of mixed design requires a significant interaction for the experimental hypothesis to be supported but does have the drawback that the main effect of the pre-test/post-test comparison may well be affected by this interaction. (Remember that ANOVA takes out main effects first and interactions can be confused for these.) Furthermore, the unrelated comparison can also be affected in the same way. A simpler, although not so thorough, analysis of these same data would be a *t*-test comparing the differences between the pre-test and post-test scores for the experimental and control groups.

The 'risks' in related subjects designs

The advantage of related designs is that the error component of the data can be reduced by the individual differences component. Similarly, in matched-subject designs the matching variables, if they are carefully selected because they correlate with the dependent variable, reduce the amount of error in the scores. However, there is a trade-off between reducing the error term and the reduction in degrees of freedom involved (Glantz and Slinker, 1990) since the degrees of freedom in an unrelated ANOVA error term are higher than for the related ANOVA error term. If one's matching variables are poorly related to the dependent variable or if the individual differences component of error is very small, there may be no advantage in using the related or matched ANOVA. Indeed, there can be a reduction in the power of the related ANOVA to reject your null hypothesis. This is a complex matter. The most practical advice is:

1. Do not employ matching unless you know that there is a strong relationship between the matching variables and the dependent variable (for example, it is only worthwhile matching subjects by their sex if you know that there is a sex difference in scores on the dependent variable).

2. Do whatever you can to reduce the error variance by standardising your methods and using highly reliable measures of the dependent variable.

Calculation 24.2

Mixed-design two-way analysis of variance: quick method

Calculation 24.1 gives a *conceptual* account of the two-way mixed-design analysis of variance calculation. That method illuminates the calculation of the two-way mixed-design analysis of variance but it is time consuming and rounding errors can affect it. The following calculation uses the computational formula for variance (p. 111) so it is quicker. Also remember that this calculation is only appropriate if you have equal numbers of scores in each cell. If not, you are far better using a computer program which can cope easily with unequal sample sizes which is the preferred solution. If you wish to do a hand calculation, then the simplest procedure is to delete scores *at random* from the larger cells until they are the same size as the smallest cell.

Step 1 We will analyse the data from Table 24.1. This involves a control group and an experimental group (the unrelated independent variable) together with a pre-test/post-test measure (the related independent variable). Table 24.13 reproduces these data but includes a number of totals instead of the means calculated in the previous method. These totals are:

■ the totals of each of the four cells (T_1, T_2, T_3, T_4)
■ the column totals (C_1, C_2)
■ the row totals (i.e. the control group total R_1, and the experimental group total R_2)
■ the subject totals (i.e. the totals for each participant P_1, P_2, etc.)
■ the grand total (G) or the total of all of the scores.

Table 24.13 **Data for the mixed-design ANOVA with some totals added**

Group	Subject	Pre-test	Post-test	Subject totals	Condition totals
Control	1	6	5	$P_1 = 11$	
	2	4	6	$P_2 = 10$	$R_1 = 33$
	3	5	7	$P_3 = 12$	
		$T_1 = 15$	$T_2 = 18$		
Experimental	4	7	10	$P_4 = 17$	
	5	5	11	$P_5 = 16$	$R_2 = 50$
	6	5	12	$P_6 = 17$	
		$T_3 = 17$	$T_4 = 33$		
		$C_1 = 32$	$C_2 = 51$		$G = 83$

Step 2 Square each of the scores and calculate the total of squared scores (ΣX^2):

$$\text{Sum of squared scores} = \Sigma X^2$$
$$= 6^2 + 4^2 + 5^2 + 7^2 + 5^2 + 5^2 + 5^2 + 6^2 + 7^2 + 10^2 + 11^2 + 12^2$$
$$= 36 + 16 + 25 + 49 + 25 + 25 + 25 + 36 + 49 + 100 + 121 + 144$$
$$= 651.000$$

Step 3 Carry out the following essential intermediary calculations to be used in later steps. They are R, C, T, P and the correction factor:

$$C = \frac{C_1^2 + C_2^2}{\text{Number of scores per related variable condition}}$$
$$= \frac{32^2 + 51^2}{6}$$
$$= \frac{1024 + 2601}{6}$$
$$= \frac{3625}{6}$$
$$= 604.167$$

$$R = \frac{R_1^2 + R_2^2}{\text{Number of scores per column}}$$
$$= \frac{33^2 + 50^2}{6}$$
$$= \frac{1089 + 2500}{6}$$

$$= \frac{3589}{6}$$

$$= 598.167$$

$$T = \frac{T_1^2 + T_2^2 + T_3^2 + T_4^2}{\text{Number of scores per cell}}$$

$$= \frac{15^2 + 18^2 + 17^2 + 33^2}{3}$$

$$= \frac{225 + 324 + 289 + 1089}{3}$$

$$= \frac{1927}{3}$$

$$= 642.333$$

$$P = \frac{P_1^2 + P_2^2 + P_3^2 + P_4^2 + P_5^2 + P_6^2}{\text{Number of scores per subject}}$$

$$= \frac{11^2 + 10^2 + 12^2 + 17^2 + 16^2 + 17^2}{2}$$

$$= \frac{121 + 100 + 144 + 289 + 256 + 289}{2}$$

$$= \frac{1199}{2}$$

$$= 599.500$$

$$\text{Correction factor} = \frac{\text{Grand total}^2}{\text{Number of scores}} = \frac{G^2}{N}$$

$$= \frac{83^2}{12}$$

$$= \frac{6889}{12}$$

$$= 574.083$$

Thus $C = 604.167$

$\quad\quad R = 598.167$

$\quad\quad T = 642.333$

$\quad\quad P = 599.500$

$$\frac{G^2}{N} = 574.083 \text{ (i.e. correction factor)}$$

Also $\Sigma X^2 = 651.000$ (from step 2).

Step 4 Calculate the sum of squares for the unrelated independent variable experimental/control group (i.e. $SS_{[experimental/control]}$). The elements of the calculation have already been calculated in step 3.) We can enter these values.

$$SS_{[experimental/control]} = R - \frac{G^2}{N}$$

$$= 598.167 - 574.083$$

$$= 24.084$$

The degrees of freedom for $SS_{[exp/con]}$ are the number of conditions (or levels) of the experimental/control variable minus one. Thus the degrees of freedom for the main effect of the independent variable experimental/control are $2 - 1 = 1$.

Table 24.14 **Analysis of variance summary table for calculation formula analysis**

Source of variation	Sums of squares	Degrees of freedom	Variance estimate (i.e. mean square)	F-ratio
Between subjects				
A (unrelated variable)	24.084	1	24.084	$\frac{24.084}{0.333} = 72.32^a$
Subjects within groups	1.333	4	0.333	
Within subjects				
B (time)	24.084	1	30.084	$\frac{30.084}{1.834} = 16.40^a$
AB	14.082	1	14.082	$\frac{14.082}{1.834} = 7.68^a$
B × subjects within groups	7.334	4	1.834	

[a] Significant at the 5% level.

Step 5 Calculate the sum of squares for subjects within groups ($SS_{[subjects\ within\ groups]}$):

$$SS_{[subjects\ within\ groups]} = P - R$$

$$= 599.500 - 598.167$$

$$= 1.333$$

The degrees of freedom for $SS_{[subjects\ within\ groups]}$ are the number of subjects minus the number of rows. There are six subjects and two rows of data, therefore the degrees of freedom $= 6 - 2 = 4$.

Step 5 Calculate the sum of squares for the related variable (i.e. the pre-test/post-test comparison.) This is $SS_{[time]}$.
$SS_{[time]}$:

$$SS_{[time]} = R - \frac{G^2}{N}$$

$$= 604.167 - 574.083$$

$$= 30.084$$

The degrees of freedom for $SS_{[time]}$ are the number of conditions (or levels) of the pre-test/post-test variable (i.e. independent variable) minus one. Thus the degrees of freedom for the main effect of the independent variable pre-test/post-test are $2 - 1 = 1$.

Step 6 Calculate the interaction between the related and unrelated variables (i.e. $SS_{[interaction]}$):

$$SS_{[interaction]} = P - R - C + \text{correction factor}$$

$$= 642.333 - 598.167 - 604.167 + 574.083$$

$$= 14.082$$

The degrees of freedom for $SS_{[interaction]}$ are (the number of conditions of the related independent variable $- 1$) $\times$ (the number of conditions of the unrelated independent variable $- 1$) $= (2 - 1) \times (2 - 1) = 1 \times 1 = 1$.

Step 7 Calculate (the sum of squares for the related variable) $\times$ (subjects within groups), that is $SS_{[related\ \times\ subjects\ within\ groups]}$:

$$SS_{[related\ x\ subjects\ within\ groups]} = \Sigma X^2 - T - P + R$$

$$= 651.000 - 642.333 - 599.500 + 598.167$$

$$= 7.334$$

The degrees of freedom for $SS_{[related\ x\ subjects\ within\ groups]} = $ (number of subjects $-$ number of rows) $\times$ (number of columns $- 1$) $= (6 - 2) \times (2 - 1) = 4 \times 1 = 4$.

Once you have entered the above calculations into an analysis of variance summary table (Table 24.14), the appropriate F-ratios need to be calculated as shown in that table and the significance of each F-ratio calculated. Significance Table 22.1 can be used for the 5% levels of significance (or Appendix J if other levels of significance are required). The degrees of freedom for the upper part of each F-ratio are to be found in the columns of this table; the degrees of freedom for the lower part of each F-ratio is the corresponding row of this table. As can be seen from Table 24.14, both the main effects and the interaction are significant.

Interpreting the results The interpretation of the mixed-design two-way ANOVA is virtually identical to the interpretation of any two-way ANOVA design such as the unrelated two-way analysis of variance in Chapter 23. It is the calculation of the error terms which is different and this does not alter the interpretation although obviously may affect the significance level.

Remember that the interpretation of any data should be based first of all on an examination of cell means and variances (or standard deviations) such as those to be found in Table 24.15. It is the pattern that you find in these which tells you just what the data say. The tests of significance merely confirm whether or not your interpretations may be generalised. An examination of Table 24.15 suggests that it is the experimental group at the post-test which has by far the highest mean score. There seems to be little difference between the other cells. This seems to suggest that there is an interaction between the two independent variables. The ANOVA summary table confirms this.

Reporting the results These results may be written up as follows: 'A mixed-design analysis of variance with praise as the unrelated independent variable and pre-test versus post-test as the related independent variable was carried out on the dependent variable self-esteem. The independent variable praise had a significant effect on self-esteem ($F = 72.32$, df $= 1, 4$; $p < 0.05$). The scores in the control group ($M = 5.50$) were significantly lower than those in the experimental group which was given praise ($M = 8.33$). Similarly, scores at the post-test were significantly higher in the post-test ($M = 8.50$) than in the pre-test ($M = 5.33$) ($F = 16.40$, df $= 1, 4$; $p < 0.05$). However, the hypothesis suggests that there is an interaction between the two independent variables such that the post-test measures of the experimental group given praise score more highly on the dependent variable than the other cells. There was a significant interaction ($F = 7.68$, df $= 1, 4$; $p < 0.05$). Furthermore, it would seem that it is the experimental groups following the praise manipulation which had the highest self-esteem scores. Table 24.15 shows the cell means for the four conditions of the experiment. It would appear that the variation between the cells is the result of the interaction effect and that the main effects are slight in comparison.'

Table 24.15 **Table of means for mixed ANOVA design**

	Pre-test measure	Post-test measure	
Control	Cell mean = 5.000	Cell mean = 6.000	Row mean = 5.500
Experimental	Cell mean = 5.667	Cell mean = 11.000	Row mean = 8.333
	Column mean = 5.333	Column mean = 8.500	Overall mean = 6.917

24.3 Analysis of covariance

The analysis of covariance (ANCOVA) is very much like the analysis of variance. The big difference is that it allows you to take account of any variable(s) which might correlate with the dependent variable (apart, of course, from any independent variables in your analysis of variance design). In other words, it is possible to adjust the analysis of variance for differences between your groups that might affect the outcome. For example, you might find that social class correlates with your dependent variable, and that social class differs for the groups in your ANOVA. Using ANCOVA you can adjust the scores on your dependent variable for these social class differences. This is in essence to equate all of the groups so that their mean social class is the same. Although it is possible to calculate ANCOVA by hand, we would recommend the use of a computer since you are likely to want to equate for several variables, not just one. Furthermore, you should check to see that your covariate does, in fact, correlate with the dependent variable otherwise your analysis becomes less sensitive, not more so.

Table 24.16 gives data that might be suitable for the analysis of covariance. The study is of the effects of different types of treatment on the dependent variable depression. For each participant, a pre-test measure of depression given prior to therapy is also given. Notice that the pre-test scores of Group 3, the no-treatment control group, tend to be larger on this pre-measure. Therefore, it could be that the apparent effects of therapy are to do with pre-existing differences between the three groups. Analysis of covariance could be used to allow for these pre-existing differences.

Table 24.16 **Example of analysis of covariance data**

Group 1 Psychotherapy		Group 2 Anti-depressant		Group 3 No-treatment control	
Independent variable Depression	Covariate Pre-test	Independent variable Depression	Covariate Pre-test	Independent variable Depression	Covariate Pre-test
27	38	30	40	40	60
15	32	27	34	29	52
22	35	24	32	35	57

Calculation 24.3

One-way analysis of covariance

The data are found in Table 24.16. The analysis of covariance involves a number of steps which remove the influence of the covariate on the dependent variable prior to calculating the analysis of variance on these adjusted scores. It is unnecessary to calculate the adjusted scores directly and adjusted sums of squares are used instead. The one-way analysis of covariance involves three major steps:

1. Calculating a one-way ANOVA on the dependent variable (depression) using exactly the same methods as found in Calculation 20.2.

2. Calculating a one-way ANOVA on the covariate (in this case the pre-test scores) again using exactly the same methods as found in Calculation 20.2.

3. Calculating a variation on the one-way ANOVA which involves the regression of the covariate on the dependent variable. In essence this is the covariation which is subtracted from the variation in the scores on the dependent variable to adjust them for the effect of the covariate.

The above steps are then used to calculate the analysis of covariance (ANCOVA).

Finally, in order to judge what the data say after the influence has been removed, we also need a table of the adjusted cell means for the dependent variable, i.e. what is left when the covariate is removed from the dependent variable.

Step 1 (one-way unrelated ANOVA on the dependent variable) For clarity we have given the data on the dependent variable in Table 24.17. Consult Calculation 20.2 for fuller details of calculating the one-way ANOVAs.

1. Calculate the sum of the squared scores by squaring each score on the dependent variable and adding to give the total:

$$\Sigma X^2 = 27^2 + 15^2 + 22^2 + 30^2 + 27^2 + 24^1 + 40^2 + 29^2 + 35^2 = 7309.000$$

2. Sum the scores to give:

$$G = 27 + 15 + 22 + 30 + 27 + 24 + 40 + 29 + 35 = 249.$$

3. Calculate the total number of scores on the dependent variable, $N = 9$.

4. Calculate the correction factor using the following formula:

$$\frac{G^2}{N} = \frac{249^2}{9} = 6889.000$$

5. Obtain the total sum of squares for the dependent variable by taking the sum of the squared scores minus the correction factor. This is $7309 - 6889.000 = 420.000$. This is entered into the ANOVA summary table for the dependent variable (Table 24.18).

6. Enter the degrees of freedom for the total sum of squares for the dependent variable. This is always $N - 1$ or the number of scores $- 1$ $= 9 - 1 = 8$.

7. The sum of squares between groups ($SS_{[between]}$) can be calculated as follows using the correction factor calculated above, the totals of each column and the number of scores in each column (e.g. N_1).

$$SS_{[between]} = \frac{T_1^2}{N_1} + \frac{T_2^2}{N_2} + \frac{T_3^2}{N_3} - \frac{G^2}{N}$$

$$= \frac{64^2}{3} + \frac{81^2}{3} + \frac{104^2}{3} - 6889.000$$

$$= 268.667$$

This value of the between-groups sum of squares for the dependent variable is entered into the ANOVA summary table (Table 24.18).

8. Enter the degrees of freedom for the between-groups sum of squares = columns − 1 = c − 1 = 3 − 1 = 2.

9. Calculate the error (i.e. error or within) sum of squares ($SS_{[error]}$) by subtracting the between-groups sum of squares from the total sum of squares:

$$SS_{[error]} = SS_{[total]} - SS_{[between]}$$

$$= 420.000 - 268.667$$

$$= 151.333$$

10. The degrees of freedom for error are the number of scores minus the number of columns = $N - c$ = 9 − 3 = 6.

Table 24.17 **Scores on the dependent variable**

Group 1	Group 2	Group 3
27	30	40
15	27	29
22	24	35

Table 24.18 ANOVA summary table for scores on the dependent variable

Source of variation	Sum of squares	Degrees of freedom	Mean square (variance estimate)	F-ratio
Between groups[dependent]	268.667	2	134.333	5.33[a]
Error[dependent]	151.333	6	25.222	
Total[dependent]	420.000	8		

[a] Significant at the 5% level.

Step 2 (unrelated ANOVA on the covariate) Again we can create a table of the covariate scores (Table 24.19) and carry out an unrelated ANOVA in exactly the same way as above for the dependent variable.

1. Calculate the sum of the squared scores by squaring each score on the covariate and adding to give the total:

$$\Sigma X^2 = 38^2 + 32^2 + 35^2 + 40^2 + 34^2 + 32^2 + 60^2 + 52^2 + 57^2$$
$$= 17026.$$

2. Sum the scores to give:

$$G = 38 + 32 + 35 + 40 + 34 + 32 + 60 + 52 + 57 = 380.$$

3. Calculate the total number of scores for the covariate, $N = 9$.

4. Calculate the correction factor using the following formula:

$$\frac{G^2}{N} = \frac{380^2}{9} = 16{,}044.444$$

5. Obtain the sum of squared scores for the covariate by taking the sum of the squared scores minus the correction factor. This is $17{,}026 - 16{,}044.444$ $= 981.556$. This is entered into the ANOVA summary table for the covariate (Table 24.20).

6. Enter the degrees of freedom for the total sum of squares for the dependent variable. This is always $N - 1$ or the number of scores $- 1$ $= 9 - 1 = 8$.

7. The sum of squares between groups ($SS_{[between]}$) can be calculated as follows using the correction factor which has already been calculated, the totals of each column and the number of scores in each column for the covariate (e.g. N_1)

$$SS_{[between]} = \frac{T_1^2}{N_1} + \frac{T_2^2}{N_2} + \frac{T_3^2}{N_3} - \frac{G^2}{N}$$

$$= \frac{105^2}{3} + \frac{106^2}{3} + \frac{169^2}{3} - 16{,}044.444$$

$$= 896.223$$

This value of the between-groups sum of squares for the covariate is entered into the ANOVA summary table (Table 24.20).

8. Also, enter the degrees of freedom for the between-groups sum of squares for the covariate $=$ columns $- 1 = c - 1 = 3 - 1 = 2$.

9. Calculate the error (i.e. error or within) sum of squares ($SS_{[error]}$) by subtracting the between-groups sum of squares from the total sum of squares:

$$SS_{[error]} = SS_{[total]} - SS_{[between]}$$

$$= 981.556 - 896.223$$

$$= 85.333$$

The degrees of freedom for error are the number of scores minus the number of columns = $N - c = 9 - 3 = 6$.

Table 24.19 **Scores on the covariate**

Group 1	Group 2	Group 3
38	40	60
32	34	52
35	32	57

Table 24.20 **ANOVA summary table for scores on the covariate**

Source of variation	Sum of squares	Degrees of freedom	Mean square (variance estimate)	F-ratio
Between groups[covariate]	896.223	2	448.112	31.51[a]
Error[covariate]	85.333	6	14.222	
Total[covariatet]	981.556	8		

[a] Significant at the 0.1% level.

Step 3 (calculating the covariation summary table) This is very similar to the calculation of the unrelated ANOVA but is based on the crossproducts of the dependent variable and covariate scores (Table 24.21). Basically it involves multiplying each dependent variable score by the equivalent covariate score. In this way it is similar to the calculation of the Pearson correlation coefficient which involves the calculation of the covariance. Table 24.21 can be used to calculate a summary table for the crossproducts (Table 24.22). The calculation is analogous to that for ANOVA in steps 1 and 2 above. The only substantial difference is that it involves calculation of the crossproducts of $X \times Y$ instead of X^2.

1. Calculate the overall (or grand) total of the X scores:

    $G_X = 27 + 15 + 22 + 30 + 27 + 24 + 40 + 29 + 35$
    $= 249$

2. Calculate the overall (or grand) total of the Y scores:

    $G_Y = 38 + 32 + 35 + 40 + 34 + 32 + 60 + 52 + 57$
    $= 380$

3. Calculate the number of scores for the dependent variable, $N = 9$.

4. Calculate the correction factor by substituting the already calculated values:

$$\text{Correction factor} = \frac{G_X \times G_Y}{N} = \frac{249 \times 380}{9} = \frac{94{,}620}{9} = 10{,}513.333$$

5. Calculate the number of scores for each group (N_1, N_2, N_3). In our example these are all 3 as the group sizes are equal but this does not have to be so.

6. Total degrees of freedom for the data table = the number of scores – 1
   = 9 – 1 = 8

7. Multiply each X score by the equivalent Y score to give the crossproducts and sum these crossproducts to give ΣXY which is the sum of crossproducts:

$$\begin{aligned}
\Sigma XY &= (27 \times 38) + (15 \times 32) + (22 \times 35) + (30 \times 40) + (27 \times 34) \\
&\quad + (24 \times 32) + (40 \times 60) + (29 \times 52) + (35 \times 57) \\
&= 1026 + 480 + 770 + 1200 + 918 + 768 + 2400 + 1508 + 1995 \\
&= 11{,}065
\end{aligned}$$

8. Obtain the total sum of covariation by subtracting the correction factor from the sum of crossproducts:

$$\text{Total sum of covariation} = \Sigma XY - \frac{G_X \times G_Y}{N}$$

$$= 11{,}065 - 10{,}513.333 = 551.667$$

9. These values of the total sum of covariation (551.667) and the degrees of freedom (8) can be entered into Table 24.22 (the summary table for covariation).

10. Sum the scores on the dependent variable and independent variables separately for each of the groups separately as in Table 24.21. This gives us $\Sigma X_1, \Sigma X_2, \Sigma X_3, \Sigma Y_1, \Sigma Y_2, \Sigma Y_3$, and since we have three groups in our instance.

11. The sum of the covariation between groups is calculated as follows:

Sum of covariation between groups =

$$\frac{\Sigma X_1 \Sigma Y_1}{N_1} + \frac{\Sigma X_2 \Sigma Y_2}{N_2} + \frac{\Sigma X_3 \Sigma Y_3}{N_3} - \frac{G_X G_Y}{N}$$

$$= \frac{64 \times 105}{3} + \frac{81 \times 106}{3} + \frac{104 \times 169}{3} = 551.667$$

$$= \frac{6720}{3} + \frac{8586}{3} + \frac{17576}{3} - 551.667$$

$$= 2240.000 + 2862.000 + 5858.667 - 10{,}513.333$$

$$= 447.334$$

12. The degrees of freedom for the covariation between groups is the number of groups $-1 = 3 - 1 = 2$.

13. These values of the sum of covariation between groups and degrees of freedom between groups can be entered in Table 24.22.

14. The sum of the covariation of error can be obtained now by subtracting the sum of the between-groups covariation from the total of covariation:

Sum of the covariation of error = Total of covariation
− Covariation between groups

= 551.667 − 447.334

= 104.333

15. This value of the covariation for error can now be entered into Table 24.22.

16. The degrees of freedom for error are calculated in a way which removes one degree of freedom for the covariation. This is simply the total number of scores – the number of groups $-1 = 9 - 3 - 1 = 5$. This can be entered in Table 24.22.

The above calculation steps for covariation are only superficially different from those for the analysis of variance in steps 1 and 2. They are actually different only so far as variance and covariance differ (pp. 65–6).

Table 24.21 **Data and crossproducts table**

Group 1			Group 2			Group 3		
X	Y	$X \times Y$	X	Y	$X \times Y$	X	Y	$X \times Y$
Dependent	Covariate		Dependent	Covariate		Dependent	Covariate	
27	38	1026	30	40	1200	40	60	2400
15	32	480	27	34	918	29	52	1508
22	35	770	24	32	768	35	57	1995
$\Sigma X =$	$\Sigma Y =$	$\Sigma XY=$	$\Sigma X=$	$\Sigma Y=$	$\Sigma XY=$	$\Sigma X=$	$\Sigma Y=$	$\Sigma XY=$
64	105	2276	81	106	886	104	169	5903
$\Sigma X \Sigma Y$			$\Sigma X \Sigma Y$			$\Sigma X \Sigma Y$		
$= 64 \times 105 = 6720$			$= 81 \times 106 = 8586$			$= 104 \times 169 = 17{,}576$		
$N_1 = 3$			$N_2 = 3$			$N_3 = 3$		

Grand total of all X scores $= \Sigma X = G_X = 64 + 81 + 104 + 249$
Grand total of all Y scores $= \Sigma Y = G_Y = 105 + 106 + 169 = 380$

Table 24.22 **Summary table for the covariation**

Source of variation	Sum of squares	Degrees of freedom	Mean square (variance estimate)	F-ratio
Between groups[covariation]	447.334	2		
Error[covariation]	104.333	6		
Total[covariation]	551.667	8		

Step 4 (calculating the ANCOVA summary table, i.e. the dependent table with the covariate partialled out) This is achieved by taking away the variation in the scores due to the covariate from the variation in the dependent variable. Once we have the three summary tables (dependent variable, covariate and crossproducts) then it is a fairly simply matter to calculate the adjusted dependent variable sums of squares and enter them into Table 24.23, the summary table for a one-way ANCOVA.

The formulae are:

$$SSError_{[adjusted]} = SSError_{[dependent]} - \frac{(Error_{[covariation]})^2}{SSError_{[covariate]}}$$

$$SSTotal_{[adjusted]} = SSTotal_{[dependent]} - \frac{(Total_{[covariation]})^2}{SSTotal_{[covariate]}}$$

Be very careful to distinguish between the covariation and the covariate.

These calculations are as follows:

$$SSError_{[adjusted]} = SSError_{[dependent]} - \frac{(Error_{[covariation]})^2}{SSError_{[covariate]}}$$

$$= 151.333 - \frac{104.333^2}{85.333}$$

$$= 151.333 - \frac{10885.375}{85.333}$$

$$= 151.333 - 127.563$$

$$= 23.77$$

$$SSTotal_{[adjusted]} = SSTotal_{[dependent]} - \frac{(Total_{[covariation]})^2}{SSTotal_{[covariate]}}$$

$$= 420.000 - \frac{(551.667)^2}{981.556}$$

$$= 420.000 - \frac{304336.479}{981.556}$$

$$= 420.000 - 310.055$$

$$= 109.945$$

Enter these values into the ANCOVA summary table (Table 24.23) and the sum of squares between obtained by subtracting the error sum of squares from the total sum of squares.

Note that the degrees of freedom for the error term in the ANCOVA summary table are listed as 5. This is because we have constrained the degrees of freedom by partialling out the covariate. The formula for the degrees of freedom for the adjusted error is number of scores − number of groups − 1 = 9 − 3 − 1 = 5.

Table 24.23 **ANCOVA summary table**

Source of variation	Sum of squares	Degrees of freedom	Mean square (variance estimate)	F-ratio
Between$_{[adjusted]}$	86.175	2	43.088	$\dfrac{43.088}{4.754} = 9.06^{a}$
Error$_{[adjusted]}$	23.770	5	4.754	
Total$_{[adjusted]}$	109.945	8		

^{a} Significant at the 5% level.

Step 5 The F-ratio in the ANCOVA summary table is calculated in the usual way. It is the between mean square divided by the error mean square. This is 9.06. The significance of this is obtained from Significance Table 22.1 for two and five degrees of freedom (or Appendix J if other levels of significance are required). We look under the column for two degrees of freedom and the row for five degrees of freedom. This indicates that our F-ratio is above the minimum value for statistical significance and is therefore statistically significant.

Step 6 (adjusting group means) No analysis of variance can be properly interpreted without reference to the means of the data table. This is not simple with ANCOVA as the means in the data are the means unadjusted for the covariate. Consequently it is necessary to adjust the means to indicate what the mean would be when the effect of the covariate is removed. The formula for this is as follows:

Adjusted group mean

$$= \text{Unadjusted group mean} - \left(\frac{\text{Error}_{[covariance]}}{\text{SSError}_{[covariate]}} \right.$$

$$\left. \times (\text{Group mean}_{[covariate]} - \text{Grand mean}_{[covariate]}) \right)$$

The unadjusted group means are merely the means of the scores on the dependent variable for each of the three groups in our example. These can be calculated from Table 24.17. The three groups means are: Group 1 = 27.000, Group 2 = 34.667 and Group 3 = 34.667.

The group means for the covariate can be calculated from Table 24.19. They are Group 1 = 35.333, Group 2 = 56.333 and Group 3 = 56.333.

The grand mean of the covariate is simply the mean of all of the scores on the covariate in Table 24.19 which equals 42.222 for our example.

The sums of squares for error have already been calculated. The sum of squares for error for the crossproducts is 104.333 and is found in Table 24.20. The sum of squares for error for the covariate is 85.333 and is found in Table 24.22.

We can now substitute all of these values into the formula and enter these values into Table 24.24.

Group 1: Adjusted mean = 30.27 obtained as follows:

$$21.333 - \left(\frac{104.333}{84.333} \times (35.000 - 42.222) \right)$$

$$= 21.333 - (1.237 \times - 7.222)$$

$$= 21.333 - - 8.934$$

$$= 30.267$$

Group 2: Adjusted mean = 35.52 obtained as follows

$$27.000 - \left(\frac{104.333}{84.333} \times (35.333 - 42.222) \right)$$

$$= 27.000 - (1.237 \times - 6.889)$$

$$= 27.000 - - 8.522$$

$$= 35.522$$

Group 3: Adjusted mean = 17.21 obtained as follows

$$34.667 - \left(\frac{104.333}{84.333} \times (56.333 - 42.222) \right)$$

$$= 34.667 - (1.237 \times - 14.111)$$

$$= 34.667 - 17.455$$

$$= 17.212$$

Table 24.24 **Unadjusted and adjusted means for depression**

Means	Group 1 Psychotherapy	Group 2 Antidepressants	Group 3 Control
Unadjusted	21.33	27.00	34.67
Adjusted	30.27	35.52	17.21

Notice how the adjusted means in Table 24.24 show a completely different pattern from the unadjusted means in this case.

Step 7 The simplest way of testing which of the adjusted means are different from the others is to use the Fisher Protected LSD (least significant difference) Test (Huitema, 1980). It is convenient since the component parts have largely been calculated by now. This test gives us an F-ratio with always one degree of freedom for the comparison and N – the number of groups – 1 = 9 – 3 – 1 = 5 in our example for the error. Because we have three groups, there are three possible comparisons between pairs of groups. We will show the calculation in full for the comparison between Groups 1 and 2:

$$F = \frac{(\text{Adjusted group}_1 \text{ mean} - \text{Adjusted group}_2 \text{ mean})^2}{\text{Mean square error adjusted} \times \left[\left(\dfrac{1}{N_1} + \dfrac{1}{N_2}\right) + \left(\dfrac{(\text{Covariate group}_1 \text{ mean} - \text{Covariate group}_2 \text{ mean})^2}{\text{Sum of squares of error for the covariate}}\right)\right]}$$

where:
adjusted Group$_1$ mean is found in Table 24.24
adjusted Group$_2$ mean is found in Table 24.24
mean square error adjusted is found in Table 24.23
Covariate Group$_1$ mean is found by consulting Table 24.19 and dividing the sum of covariate scores for the Group 1 by the number of scores for Group 1 = $\Sigma Y/N$ = 105/3 = 35.000
Covariate Group$_2$ mean is found in exactly the same way. Consult Table 24.19 and divide the sum of covariate scores for Group 2 by the number of scores = 106/3 = 35.333.
Sum of squares of error for the covariate is found in Table 24.20.

$$F = \frac{(30.27 - 35.52)^2}{4.754\left[\left(\dfrac{1}{3} + \dfrac{1}{3}\right) + \dfrac{(35.000 - 35.333)^2}{85.333}\right]}$$

$$= \frac{5.25^2}{4.754\left[(0.333 + 0.333) + \dfrac{(-0.333)^2}{85.333}\right]}$$

$$= \frac{27.563}{4.754\left(0.666 + \dfrac{0.111}{85.333}\right)}$$

$$= \frac{27.563}{4.754(0.666 + 0.001)}$$

$$= \frac{27.563}{4.754(0.667)}$$

$$= \frac{27.563}{3.171}$$

$$= 8.692$$

This value of the F-ratio with one and five degrees of freedom is statistically significant at the 5% level. So the adjusted means of Group 1 and Group 2 are significantly different from each other.

We also carried out the comparisons between Group 1 and Group 3 (the obtained F-ratio of 5.98 was not significant at the 5% level) and Group 2 and Group 3 (the obtained F-ratio 12.09 was statistically significant at the 5% level).

Interpreting the results The analysis of covariance makes it clear that the post-test measures of depression differ overall once the pre-test differences are controlled. However, by considering the means of the adjusted levels of depression it seems clear that the depression scores of the control groups were actually lower than those of either of the treatment groups. In other words, once pre-test levels of depression are adjusted for, then the obvious interpretation is that depression is actually being increased by the treatment rather than being reduced relative to the control group. The multiple-comparisons test indicates that the significant differences are between the antidepressant group and the control group and the psychotherapy group and the control group. The two treatment groups did not differ significantly from each other.

Reporting the result This analysis may be written up as follows: 'An analysis of covariance (ANCOVA) was applied to the three groups (psychotherapy, antidepressant, and no-treatment control) in order to see whether the different treatments had an effect on post-test levels of depression controlling for pre-test depression. There was found to be a significant effect of the type of treatment (ANCOVA, $F= 9.06$, df $= 2, 5$; significant at the 5% level). The unadjusted means indicated that depression was higher in the control group ($M = 34.67$), than with psychotherapy ($M = 21.33$) or with antidepressant treatment ($M = 35.52$). However, this seems to be the result of the influence of the covariate (pre-therapy levels of depression as measured at the pre-test) since the adjusted means for the groups indicate that the least depression is found in the untreated control group ($M = 17.21$), compared with the psychotherapy group ($M = 30.27$) and the antidepressant group ($M = 35.52$). Thus, the two treatment conditions increased depression relative to the control group. This was confirmed in a comparison of the adjusted means using the Fisher Protected LSD Test. The analysis indicated that Group 1 (psychotherapy) and Group 2 (antidepressant) differed significantly ($F= 8.69$, df $= 1, 5$; significant at the 5% level). Group 2 (antidepressant) and Group 3 (control condition) differed significantly ($F = 12.09$, df $= 1, 5$; significant at the 5% level). Group 1 (psychotherapy) and Group 3 (control) did not differ significantly ($F = 5.98$, df $= 1, 5$; not significant at the 5% level).'

24.4 Notes and recommendations

■ Research designs which require complex statistics such as the above ANOVAs are difficult and cumbersome to implement. Use them only after careful deliberation about what it is you really need from your research.

■ Avoid the temptation to include basic demographic variables such as age and sex routinely as independent variables in the analysis of variance. If they are key factors then they should be included, otherwise they can merely lead to complex interactions which may be hard to interpret and not profitable when you have done so.

Recommended further reading

Cramer, D. (1998). *Fundamental Statistics for Social Research: Step-by-step Calculations and Computer Techniques using SPSS for Windows.* London: Routledge, chapters 9 & 10.

Glantz, S.A. and Slinker, B.K. (1990). *Primer of Applied Regression and Analysis of Variance.* New York: McGraw-Hill.

Chapter 25

Statistics and the analysis of experiments

Preparation

Make sure that you understand hypotheses (Chapter 10), and nominal category data versus numerical score data (Chapter 1).

25.1 Introduction

Feeling jaded and listless? Don't know what stats to use to analyse your experiment? Make money from home. Try Professor Warburton's Patent Stats Pack. All the professional tricks revealed. Guaranteed not to fail. Gives hope where there is no hope. Professor Warburton's Stats Pack troubleshoots the troubleshooters.

Since the death of Professor Warburton in 1975, through thrombosis of the wallet, his Patent Stats Pack had been feared lost. Libraries on three continents were searched. Miraculously it was discovered after many years in Australia in a trunk under the bed of a dingo farmer. Auctioned recently at Sotheby's to an unknown buyer – reputedly a German antiquarian – it broke all records. Controversy broke out when scholars claimed that Professor Warburton was a fraud and never held an academic appointment in his life. To date, it has not been possible to refute this claim.

These are vile slurs against Professor Warburton who many regard as the founder of the post-modernist statistics movement and the first person to deconstruct statistics. Judge for yourself.

25.2 The Patent Stats Pack

Principle 1   Practically nothing needs to be known about statistical calculations and theory to choose appropriate procedures to analyse your data. The characteristics of your research are the main considerations – not knowledge of statistics books.

Principle 2   Ideally you should not undertake research without being able to sketch out the likely features of your tables and diagrams.

Principle 3 You *can* make a silk purse out of a sow's ear. First catch your silk pig . . . A common mistake is thinking that the data as they are collected are the data as they will be analysed. Sometimes, especially when the statistical analysis has not been planned prior to collecting data, you may have to make your data fit the available statistical techniques. Always remember that you may need to alter the format of your data in some way in order to make them suitable for statistical analysis. These changes include:

- adding scores from several variables to get a single overall or composite variable

- separating a variable into several different components (especially where you have collected data as frequencies in nominal categories and have allowed multiple answers).

25.3 Checklist

The following are the major considerations which will help you choose an appropriate statistical analysis for your data.

1. Write down your hypothesis. Probably the best way of doing this is to simply fill in the blanks in the following:

   'My hypothesis is that there is a relationship between
   Variable 1 _____ and Variable 2 _____ '

   Do not write in the names of more than two variables. There is nothing to stop you having several hypotheses. Write down as many hypotheses as seems appropriate – but only *two* variable names per hypothesis. Treat each hypothesis as a separate statistical analysis.

   If you cannot name the two variables you see as correlated then it is possible that you wish only to compare a single sample with a population. In this case check out the single-sample chi-square (Chapter 14) or the single-sample t-test (Chapter 12).

2. If you cannot meet the requirements of 1 above then you are possibly confused about the purpose of the research. *Go no further until you have sorted this out* – do not blame statistics for your conceptual muddle. Writing out your hypotheses until they are clear may sound like a chore but it is an important part of statistical analysis.

3. Classify each of the variables in your hypothesis into either of the following two categories:

   (a) numerical score variables

   (b) nominal (category) variables – and count the number of categories.

4. Based on 3, decide which of the following statements is true of your hypothesis:

(a) I have *two* numerical score variables: Yes/No
(if yes then go to 5)

(b) I have *two* nominal category variables: Yes/No
(if yes then go to 6)

(c) I have *one* nominal category variable and *one* numerical score variable: Yes/No
(if yes then go to 7)

5. If you answered yes to 4(a) above (i.e. you have two numerical score variables) then your statistical analysis involves the correlation coefficient. This might include Pearson correlation, Spearman correlation, or regression. Turn to Chapter 29 on the analysis of questionnaire research for ideas of what is possible.

6. If you answered yes to 4(b), implying that you have two nominal category variables, then your statistical analysis has to be based on contingency tables using chi-square or closely related tests. The range available to you is as follows:

(a) chi-square

(b) Fisher Exact Probability Test for 2×2 or 2×3 contingency tables, especially if the samples are small or expected frequencies low

(c) The McNemar Test if you are studying *change* in the same sample of people.

The only problem which you are likely to experience with such tests is if you have allowed the participants in your research to give more than one answer to a question. If you have, then the solution is to turn each category into a separate variable and code each individual according to whether or not they are in that category. So, for example, in a frequency table such as Table 25.1 it is pretty obvious that multiple responses have been allowed since the total of the frequencies is in excess of the sample size of 50. This table could be turned into four new tables:

- Table 1: The number of vegetarians (19) versus the number of non-vegetarians (31)
- Table 2: The number of fast food preferrers (28) versus the non-fast food preferrers (22)
- Table 3: Italian preferrers (9) versus Italian non-preferrers (41)
- Table 4: Curry preferrers (8) versus non-curry preferrers (42)

7. If you answered yes to 4(c) then the nominal (category) variable is called the *independent* variable and the numerical score variable is called the *dependent* variable. The number of categories for the independent variable partly determines the statistical tests you can apply:

Table 25.1   Food preferences of a sample of 50 teenagers

Food type	Frequency
Vegetarian	19
Fast food	28
Italian	9
Curry	8

(a) If you have two categories for the independent (nominal category) variable then:

   (i) the *t*-test is a suitable statistic (Chapters 12 and 13)

   (ii) the one-way analysis of variance is suitable (Chapters 20 and 21).

   The choice between the two is purely arbitrary as they give equivalent results. Remember to check whether your two sets of scores are independent or correlated/related. If your scores on the dependent variable are correlated then it is appropriate to use the related or correlated versions of the *t*-test (Chapter 12) and the analysis of variance (Chapter 21).

(b) If you have *three or more* categories for the independent (nominal category) variable then your choice is limited to the one-way analysis of variance. Again, if your dependent variable features correlated or related scores, then the related or correlated one-way analysis of variance can be used (Chapters 19 and 20).

> **Design consideration** If it becomes clear that the basic assumptions of parametric tests are violated by your data (which for all practical purposes means that the distribution of scores is *very* skewed), then you might wish to employ a nonparametric equivalent (Chapter 18 and Appendix B2).

Sometimes you may decide that you have *two or more independent* variables for each dependent variable. Here you are getting into the complexities of the analysis of variance and you need to consult Chapters 22 and 24 for advice.

25.4 Special cases

Multiple items to measure the same variable

Sometimes instead of measuring a variable with a single question or with a single technique, that variable is measured in several ways. Most likely is that a

Table 25.2 An aid to selecting appropriate statistical analyses for different experimental designs

Type of data	One sample compared with known population	Two independent samples	Two related samples	Two or more independent samples	Two or more related samples	Two or more independent variables
Nominal (category) data	One-sample chi-square	Chi-square	McNemar Test	Chi-square	Not in this book[a]	Chi-square
Numerical score data	One-sample t-test	Unrelated t-test, unrelated one-way ANOVA	Related t-test, related one-way ANOVA	Unrelated ANOVA	Related ANOVA	Two-way etc. ANOVA
Numerical score data which violates assumptions of parametric tests	Not in this book[a]	Mann–Whitney U-test	Wilcoxon Matched Pairs Test	Kruskal–Wallis (Appendix B2)	Friedman (Appendix B2)	Not in this book[a]

[a] These are fairly specific nonparametric tests which are rarely used.

questionnaire has been used which contains several questions pertaining to the same thing. In these circumstances you will probably want to combine these questions to give a single numerical score on that variable. The techniques used to do this include the use of standard scores and factor analysis (which are described in Chapters 5 and 26). Generally by combining these different indicators of a major variable together to give a single score you improve the reliability and validity of your research. The combined scores can be used as a single variable and analysed with t-tests or analyses of variance, for example.

Assessing change over time

The simplest way of studying change over time is to calculate the difference between the first testing and the second testing. This is precisely what a repeated measures t-test, for example, does. However, these difference scores can themselves be used in whatever way you wish. In particular, it would be possible to compare difference scores from two or more different samples in order to assess if the amount of change over time depended on sex or any other independent variable. In other words, it is unnecessary to have a complex analysis of variance design which includes time as one independent variable and sex as the other.

25.5 Notes and recommendations

- Nobody ever learned to play a musical instrument simply by reading a book and never practising. It takes a little time to become confident in choosing appropriate statistical analyses.
- Simple statistical analyses are not automatically inferior to complex ones.
- Table 25.2 should help you choose an appropriate statistical procedure for your experimental data. It is designed to deal only with studies in which you are comparing the *means* of two or more groups of scores. It is not intended to deal with correlations between variables.

Part 4

More advanced correlational statistics

Chapter 26

Partial correlation
Spurious correlation, third variables, suppressor variables

Preparation
Revise the Pearson correlation coefficient (Chapter 7) if necessary. What do we mean by a causal relationship?

26.1 Introduction

The partial correlation coefficient is particularly useful when trying to make causal statements from field research. It is not useful in experimental research where different methods are used to establish causal relationships. Look at the following research outlines taking as critical a viewpoint as possible:

Project 1 Researchers examine the published suicide rates in different geographical locations in the country. They find that there is a significant relationship between unemployment rates in these areas and suicide rates. They conclude that unemployment causes suicide.

Project 2: Researchers examine the relationship between shoe size and liking football matches. They find a relationship between the two but claim that it would be nonsense to suggest that liking football makes your feet grow bigger.

Although both of these pieces of research are superficially similar, the researchers draw rather different conclusions. In the first case it is suggested that unemployment *causes* suicide whereas in the second case the researchers are reluctant to claim that liking football makes your feet grow bigger. The researchers in both cases may be correct in their interpretation of the correlations but should we take their interpretations at face value? The short answer is no, since correlations do not prove causality in themselves.

In both cases, it is possible that the relationships obtained are spurious (or artificial) ones which occur because of the influence of other variables which the researcher has not considered. So, for example, the relationship between shoe size and liking football might be due to sex – men tend to have bigger feet than women and tend to like football more than women do. So the relationship between shoe size and liking football is merely a consequence of sex differences. The relationship between unemployment and suicide, similarly, could be due to the influence of a third variable. In this case the variable might be social class. If we found, for example, that being from a lower social class was associated with a greater likelihood of unemployment *and* with being more prone to suicide, this would suggest that the relationship between unemployment and suicide was due to social class differences, not because unemployment leads directly to suicide.

Partial correlation is a statistically precise way of calculating what the relationship between two variables would be if one could take away the influence of one (or more) additional variables. Sometimes this is referred to as *controlling for a third variable* or *partialling out a third variable*. In essence it revises the value of your correlation coefficient to take into account third variables.

> **Design consideration** Partial correlation can never prove that causal relationships exist between two variables. The reason is that partialling out a third, fourth or fifth variable does not rule out the possibility that there is an additional variable which has not been considered which is the cause of the correlation. However, partial correlation may be useful in examining the validity of claims about specified variables which might be causing the relationship. Considerations of causality are a minor aspect of partial correlation.

26.2 Theoretical considerations

Partial correlation can be applied to your own data if you have the necessary correlations available. However, partial correlation can also be applied to published research without necessarily obtaining the original data itself – so long as the appropriate correlation coefficients are available. All it requires is that the values of the correlations between your two main variables and the possible third variable are known. It is not uncommon to have the necessary tables of correlations published in books and journal articles although the raw data (original scores) are rarely included in published research.

A table of correlations between several variables is known as a correlation matrix. Table 26.1 is an example featuring the following three variables: numerical intelligence test score (which we have labelled X in the table), verbal intelligence test score (which we have labelled Y in the table), and age (which we have labelled C in the table) in a sample of 30 teenagers.

Notice that the diagonal from top left to bottom right consists of 1.00 repeated three times. This is because the correlation of numerical score with itself, verbal score with itself, and age with itself will always be a perfect relationship ($r = 1.00$) –

Table 26.1   **A correlation matrix involving three variables**

	Variable X Numerical score	Variable Y Verbal score	Variable C Age in years
Variable X Numerical score	1.00	0.97	0.80
Variable Y Verbal score	0.97	1.00	0.85
Variable C Age in years	0.80	0.85	1.00

it has to be since you are correlating exactly the same numbers together. Also notice that the matrix is symmetrical around the diagonal. This is fairly obvious since the correlation of the numerical score with the verbal score has to be exactly the same as the correlation of the verbal score with the numerical score. More often than not a researcher would report just half of Table 26.1, so the correlations would look like a triangle. It doesn't matter which way of doing things you choose.

Remember that we have used the letters X, Y and C for the different columns and rows of the matrix. The C column and C row are the column and row respectively for the *control* variable (age in this case).

Not only is partial correlation an important statistical tool in its own right, it also forms the basis of other techniques such as multiple regression (Chapter 28).

26.3 The calculation

The calculation of the partial correlation coefficient is fairly speedy so long as you have a correlation matrix ready made. Assuming this, the calculation should cause no problems. Computer programs for the partial correlation will normally be capable of calculating the correlation matrix for you, if necessary. Calculation 26.1 works out the relationship between verbal and numerical scores in the above table controlling for age ($r_{XY.C}$).

Calculation 26.1

Partial correlation coefficient

The calculation is based on the correlations found in Table 26.1

Formula:

$$r_{XY.C} = \frac{r_{XY} - (r_{XC} \times r_{YC})}{\sqrt{1 - r_{XC}^2} \ \sqrt{1 - r_{YC}^2}}$$

where:

$r_{XY.C}$ = correlation of verbal and numerical scores with age controlled as denoted by C

r_{XY} = correlation of numerical and verbal scores (= 0.97)

r_{XC} = correlation of numerical scores and age (the control variable) (= 0.80)

r_{YC} = correlation of verbal scores and age (the control variable) (= 0.85).

Using the values taken from the correlation matrix in Table 26.1 we find that:

$$r_{XY.C} = \frac{0.97 - (0.80 \times 0.85)}{\sqrt{1 - 0.80^2} \ \sqrt{1 - 0.85^2}}$$

$$= \frac{0.97 - (0.68)}{\sqrt{1 - 0.64} \ \sqrt{1 - 0.72}}$$

$$= \frac{0.29}{\sqrt{0.36} \ \sqrt{0.28}}$$

$$= \frac{0.29}{0.6 \times 0.53}$$

$$= \frac{0.29}{0.32}$$

$$= 0.91$$

Thus controlling for age has hardly changed the correlation coefficient – it decreases only very slightly from 0.97 to 0.91.

Interpreting the results   A section on interpretation follows. However, when interpreting a partial correlation you need to consider what the unpartialled correlation is. This is the baseline against which the partial correlation is understood. Although usually we would look to see if partialling reduces the size of the correlation it can increase it.

Reporting the results   The following is one way of reporting this analysis: 'Since age was a correlate of both verbal and numerical ability, it was decided to investigate the effect of controlling for age on the correlation. After partialling, the correlation of 0.97 declined slightly to 0.91. However, this change is very small and the correlation remains very significant so age was having little or no effect on the correlation between verbal and numerical abilities.'

26.4 Interpretation

What does this mean? The original correlation between numerical and verbal scores of 0.97 is reduced to 0.91 when we control for age. This is a very small amount of change and we can say that controlling for age has no real influence on the original correlation coefficient.

The following is the original pattern of relationships between the three variables:

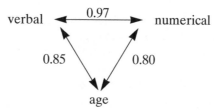

The partial correlation essentially removes all the variation between verbal scores and age and also between numerical scores and age. This is rather like making these correlations zero. But, in this case, when we make these correlations zero we still find that there is a very substantial correlation between verbal and numerical scores:

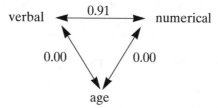

This is an important lesson since it suggests that controlling for a third variable does not always affect the correlation, despite the fact that in this case the control variable age had quite substantial relationships with both verbal and numerical ability scores. *This should be a warning that simply showing that two variables are both correlated with a third variable does not in itself establish that the third variable is responsible for the main correlation.*

Despite this, often the partial correlation coefficient substantially changes the size of the correlation coefficient. Of course, it is important to know that a third variable does not change the correlation value. In contrast, the example in Section 26.7 and Calculation 26.3 shows a major change following partialling.

Calculation 26.2

Statistical significance of the partial correlation

The calculation of statistical significance for the partial correlation can be carried out simply using tables of the significance of the Pearson correlation coefficient such as Significance Table 10.1 or the table in Appendix C. However, in order to do this you will need to adjust the sample size by subtracting three. Thus if the sample size is 10 for the Pearson correlation it is $10 - 3 = 7$ for the partial correlation coefficient with 1 variable controlled. So in our example in Table 26.1 which was based on a sample of 30 teenagers, we obtain the 5% significant level from the table in Appendix C by finding the 5% value for a sample size of $30 - 3 = 27$. The minimum value for statistical significance at the 5% level is 0.367 (two-tailed).

Interpreting the results   The statistical significance of the partial correlation coefficient is much the same as for the Pearson correlation coefficient on which it is based. A statistically significant finding means that the partial correlation coefficient is unlikely to have been drawn from a population in which the partial correlation is zero.

Reporting the results   The statistical significance of the partial correlation may be reported in exactly the same way as for any correlation coefficient. The degrees of freedom are different since they have to be adjusted for the number of control variables. If the sample size for the correlation is 10, then subtract 3 to give 7 degrees of freedom if just one variable is being controlled for. In other words, subtract the total number of variables including the two original variables plus all of the control variables. So if there were 4 control variables in this example, the degrees of freedom become $10 - 2 - 4 = 4$.

26.5 Multiple control variables

It may have struck you that there might be several variables that a researcher might wish to control for at one and the same time. For example, a researcher might wish to control for age and social class at the same time, or even age, social class and sex. This can be done relatively easily on a computer but is rather cumbersome to do by hand.

There are a number of terms that are used which are relatively simple if you know what they mean:

1. *Zero*-order correlation – the correlation between your main variables (e.g. r_{XY}).
2. *First*-order partial correlation – the correlation between your main variables controlling for just *one* variable (e.g. $r_{XY.C}$).
3. *Second*-order partial correlation – the correlation between your main variables controlling for *two* variables at the same time (the symbol for this might be $r_{XY.CD}$).

Not surprisingly, we can extend this quite considerably; for example, a *fifth*-order partial correlation involves *five* control variables at the same time (e.g. $r_{XY.CDEFG}$). The principles remain the same no matter what order of partial correlation you are examining.

26.6 Suppressor variables

Sometimes you might find that you actually obtain a low correlation between two variables which you had expected to correlate quite substantially. In some instances this is because a third variable actually has the effect of reducing or suppressing the correlation between the two main variables. Partial correlation is useful in removing the inhibitory effect of this third variable. In other words, it can sometimes happen that controlling the influence of a third variable results in a *larger* correlation. Indeed, it is possible to find that an initially negative correlation becomes a positive correlation when the influence of a third variable is controlled.

26.7 An example from the research literature

Baron and Straus (1989) took the officially reported crime rates for rapes from most US states and compared these with the circulation figures for soft-core pornography in these areas. The correlation between rape rates and the amounts of pornography over these states was 0.53. (If this confuses you, the correlations are calculated 'pretending' that each state is like a person in calculating the correlation coefficient.) The temptation is to interpret this correlation as suggesting that pornography leads to rape. Several authors have done so.

However, Howitt and Cumberbatch (1990) took issue with this. They pointed out that the proportions of divorced men in these areas also correlated substantially with both pornography circulation rates and rape rates. The data are listed in Table 26.2.

Table 26.2   **Correlation between rape, pornography and divorce**

	Variable X Rape rates	Variable Y Pornography circulation	Variable C Proportion of divorced men
Variable X Rape rates	1.00	0.53	0.67
Variable Y Pornography circulation		1.00	0.59
Variable C Proportion of divorced men			1.00

It might be the case that rather than pornography causing rape, the apparent relationship between these two variables is merely due to the fact that divorced men are more likely to engage in these 'alternative sexual activities'. It is a simple matter to control for this third variable, as set out in Calculation 26.3.

Calculation 26.3

Partial correlation coefficient for rape and pornography controlling for proportion of divorced men

Formula:

$$r_{XY.C} = \frac{r_{XY} - (r_{XC} \times r_{YC})}{\sqrt{1 - r_{XC}^2} \ \sqrt{1 - r_{YC}^2}}$$

where:

$r_{XY.C}$ = correlation of rape rates with pornography controlling for proportion of divorced men

r_{XY} = correlation of rape and pornography (= 0.53)

r_{XC} = correlation of rape and proportion of divorced men (= 0.67)

r_{YC} = correlation of pornography and proportion of divorced men (= 0.59).

Using the values taken from the correlation matrix in Table 26.2 we find that:

$$r_{XY.C} = \frac{0.53 - (0.67 \times 0.59)}{\sqrt{1 - 0.67^2} \ \sqrt{1 - 0.59^2}}$$

$$= 0.22$$

In this case, the correlation when the third variable is taken into account has changed substantially to become much nearer zero. It would be reasonable to suggest that the partial correlation coefficient indicates that there is *no* causal relationship between pornography and rape – quite a dramatic change in interpretation from the claim that pornography causes rape. The argument is not necessarily that the proportion of divorced men directly causes rape and the purchase of pornography. However, since it is an unlikely hypothesis that rape and pornography *cause* divorce then the fact that partialling out divorce reduces greatly the correlation between rape and pornography means that our faith in the original 'causal' link is reduced.

26.8 An example from a student's work

It is becoming increasingly common to teach children with special educational needs in classrooms along with other children rather than in special schools. Butler (1995a) measured the number of characteristics a sample of 14 teachers possessed which have been held to be of special importance in the effective teaching of special needs children. These qualities would include 'empathy towards special needs children', 'attitude towards integrating special needs children' and about ten others.

In order to assess the quality of the learning experience, the student researcher time-sampled children's task-centred behaviour. By this is meant the number of time periods during which the child was concentrating on the task in hand rather than, say, just wandering around the classroom causing a nuisance. The researcher rated one special needs child and one 'normal' child from each teacher's class. She found that there was a very high correlation of 0.96 between the number of qualities that a teacher possessed and the amount of time that the special needs children spent 'on task' (df = 12, $p < 0.01$). Interestingly the correlation of the measure of teacher qualities with the behaviour of normal children in the class was only 0.23. The student used partial correlation to remove the task-oriented behaviour of the 'normal' children in order to control for the extent to which teacher qualities had a beneficial effect on ordinary teaching. This made absolutely no difference to the correlation between the number of qualities the teacher possessed and the amount of time special needs children spent on educational tasks. In other words, the student could be confident that she had identified qualities of teachers which were especially beneficial to special needs children.

In terms of the research design there might be some worries, as the student was well aware. In particular, in an ideal research design there would be a second observer rating the behaviour of the children in order to check the consistency of the ratings between different observers.

26.9 Notes and recommendations

■ If you are doing a *field* rather than a laboratory project check your research hypotheses. If they appear to suggest that one variable *causes* another then do consider using partial correlation. It can potentially enhance one's confidence about making causal interpretations if a significant correlation remains after partialling. However, caution should still be applied since there always remains a risk that an additional variable suppresses the relationship between your two main variables.

■ Do not forget that even after partialling out third variables, any causal interpretation of the correlation coefficient remaining has to be tentative. No correlation coefficient (including partial correlation coefficients) can establish causality in itself. You establish causality largely through your research design, not the statistics you apply.

- ◼ Do not overlook the possibility that you may need to control more than one variable.

- ◼ Do not assume that partial correlation has no role except in seeking causal relationships. Sometimes, for example, the researcher might wish to control for male–female influences on a correlation without wishing to establish causality. Partial correlation will reveal the strength of a non-causal relationship having controlled for a third variable. Causality is something the researcher considers; it is not something built into a correlation coefficient as such.

- ◼ Do not forget to test the statistical significance of the partial correlation – as shown above, it is very easy.

Chapter 27

Factor analysis

Simplifying complex data

Preparation
Review variance (Chapter 5), correlation coefficient (Chapter 7), and correlation matrix (Chapter 26).

27.1 Introduction

Researchers frequently collect large amounts of data. Sometimes, speculatively, they add extra questions to a survey without any pressing reason. With data on so many variables, it becomes difficult to make sense of the complexity of the data. With questionnaires, one naturally seeks patterns in the correlations between questions. However, the sheer number of interrelationships makes this hard. Take the following brief questionnaire:

Item 1: It is possible to bend spoons by rubbing them
    Agree strongly   Agree   Neither   Disagree   Disagree strongly

Item 2: I have had 'out of body' experiences
    Agree strongly   Agree   Neither   Disagree   Disagree strongly

Item 3: Satanism is a true religion
    Agree strongly   Agree   Neither   Disagree   Disagree strongly

Item 4: Tarot cards reveal coming events
    Agree strongly   Agree   Neither   Disagree   Disagree strongly

Item 5: Speaking in tongues is a peak religious experience
    Agree strongly   Agree   Neither   Disagree   Disagree strongly

Item 6: The world was saved by visiting space beings
    Agree strongly   Agree   Neither   Disagree   Disagree strongly

Item 7: Most people are reincarnated
    Agree strongly   Agree   Neither   Disagree   Disagree strongly

Item 8: Astrology is a science, not an art
   Agree strongly   Agree   Neither   Disagree   Disagree strongly

Item 9: Animals have souls
   Agree strongly   Agree   Neither   Disagree   Disagree strongly

Item 10: Talking to plants helps them to grow
   Agree strongly   Agree   Neither   Disagree   Disagree strongly

Agree strongly could be scored as 1, agree scored as 2, neither as 3, disagree as 4, and disagree strongly as 5. This turns the words into numerical scores. Correlating the answers to each of these 10 questions with each of the others for 300 respondents, generates a large correlation matrix (a table of all possible correlations between all of the possible pairs of questions). Ten questions will produce 10^2 or 100 correlations. Although the correlation matrix is symmetrical about the diagonal from top left to bottom right, there remain 45 *different* correlations to examine. Such a matrix might be much like the one in Table 27.1.

It is not easy to make complete sense of this; the quantity of information makes overall interpretation difficult. Quite simply, large matrices are too much for our brains to comprehend. This is where factor analysis can be beneficial. It is a technique which helps you overcome the complexity of correlation matrices. In essence, it takes a matrix of correlations and generates a much smaller set of 'supervariables' which characterise the main trends in the correlation matrix.

Table 27.1 **Correlation matrix of 10 items**

	Item 1	Item 2	Item 3	Item 4	Item 5	Item 6	Item 7	Item 8	Item 9	Item 10
Item 1	1.00	0.50	0.72	0.30	0.32	0.20	0.70	0.30	0.30	0.10
Item 2	0.50	1.00	0.40	0.51	0.60	0.14	0.17	0.55	0.23	0.55
Item 3	0.72	0.40	1.00	0.55	0.64	0.23	0.12	0.17	0.22	0.67
Item 4	0.30	0.51	0.55	1.00	0.84	0.69	0.47	0.44	0.56	0.35
Item 5	0.32	0.60	0.64	0.84	1.00	0.14	0.77	0.65	0.48	0.34
Item 6	0.20	0.14	0.23	0.69	0.14	1.00	0.58	0.72	0.33	0.17
Item 7	0.70	0.17	0.12	0.47	0.77	0.58	1.00	0.64	0.43	0.76
Item 8	0.30	0.55	0.17	0.44	0.65	0.72	0.64	1.00	0.27	0.43
Item 9	0.30	0.23	0.22	0.56	0.48	0.33	0.43	0.27	1.00	0.12
Item 10	0.10	0.55	0.67	0.35	0.34	0.17	0.76	0.43	0.12	1.00

These 'supervariables' or factors are generally much easier to understand than the original matrix.

27.2 A bit of history

Factor analysis is not a new technique – it dates back to shortly after the First World War. It is an invention largely of psychologists, originally to serve a very specific purpose in the field of mental testing. As you are probably aware, there are numerous psychological tests of different sorts of intellectual ability. The purpose of factor analysis was to detect which sorts of mental skills tend to go together and which are distinct abilities. It has proven more generally useful and is used in the development of psychological tests and questionnaires. Personality, attitude, intelligence and aptitude tests are often based on it since it helps select which items from the tests and measures to retain. By using factors, it is possible to obtain 'purer' measures of psychological variables. Not surprisingly, then, some theorists have used it extensively. The personality theories of researchers Raymond Cattell and Hans Eysenck (Cramer, 1992) are heavily dependent on factor analysis. The development of high speed electronic computers has made the technique relatively routine since no longer does it require months of hand calculations.

27.3 Concepts in factor analysis

In order to understand factor analysis, it is useful to start with a simple and highly stylised correlation matrix such as the one in Table 27.2.

You can probably detect that there are *two* distinct clusters of variables. Variables A, C and E all tend to correlate with each other pretty well. Similarly, variables B, D and F all tend to correlate with each other. Notice that the

Table 27.2 **Stylised correlation matrix between variables A to F**

	Variable A	Variable B	Variable C	Variable D	Variable E	Variable F
Variable A	1.00	0.00	0.91	–0.05	0.96	0.10
Variable B	0.00	1.00	0.08	0.88	0.02	0.80
Variable C	0.91	0.08	1.00	–0.01	0.90	0.29
Variable D	–0.05	0.88	–0.01	1.00	–0.08	0.79
Variable E	0.96	0.02	0.90	–0.08	1.00	0.11
Variable F	0.10	0.80	0.29	0.79	0.11	1.00

Table 27.3 **Stylised correlation matrix with variable names added**

	Batting	Cross-words	Darts	Scrabble	Juggling	Spelling
Batting	1.00	0.00	0.91	−0.05	0.96	0.10
Crosswords	0.00	1.00	0.08	0.88	0.02	0.80
Darts	0.91	0.08	1.00	−0.01	0.90	0.29
Scrabble	−0.05	0.88	−0.01	1.00	−0.08	0.79
Juggling	0.96	0.02	0.90	−0.08	1.00	0.11
Spelling	0.10	0.80	0.29	0.79	0.11	1.00

members of the first cluster (A, C, E) do not correlate well with members of the second cluster (B, D, F) – they would not be very distinct clusters if they did. In order to make the clusters more meaningful, we need to decide what variables contributing to the first cluster (A, C, E) have in common; next we need to explore the similarities of the variables in the second cluster (B, D, F). Calling the variables by arbitrary letters does not help us very much. But what if we add a little detail by identifying the variables more clearly and relabelling the matrix of correlations as in Table 27.3?

Interpretation of the clusters is now possible. Drawing the clusters from the table we find:

1st Cluster
Variable A = skill at batting
Variable C = skill at throwing darts
Variable E = skill at juggling

2nd Cluster
Variable B = skill at doing crosswords
Variable D = skill at doing the word game 'Scrabble'
Variable F = skill at spelling

Once this 'fleshing out of the bones' has been done, the meaning of each cluster is somewhat more apparent. The first cluster seems to involve a general skill at hand–eye coordination; the second cluster seems to involve verbal skill.

This sort of interpretation is easy enough in clear-cut cases like this and with small correlation matrices. Life and statistics, however, are rarely that simple. Remember that in Chapter 26 on partial correlation we found that a zero correlation between two variables may become a large positive or negative correlation when we take away the influence of a third variable or a suppressor variable which is hiding the true relationship between two main variables. Similar sorts of

Table 27.4   **Factor loading matrix**

Variable	Factor 1	Factor 2
Skill at batting	0.98	−0.01
Skill at crosswords	0.01	0.93
Skill at darts	0.94	0.10
Skill at Scrabble	−0.07	0.94
Skill at juggling	0.97	−0.01
Skill at spelling	0.15	0.86

things can happen in factor analysis. Factor analysis enables us to handle such complexities which would be next to impossible by just inspecting a correlation matrix.

Factor analysis is a mathematical procedure which reduces a correlation matrix containing many variables into a much smaller number of factors or supervariables. A supervariable cannot be measured directly and its nature has to be inferred from the relationships of the original variables with the abstract supervariable. However, in identifying the clusters above we have begun to grasp the idea of supervariables. The abilities which made up Cluster 2 were made meaningful by suggesting that they had verbal skill in common.

The *output* from a factor analysis based on the correlation matrix presented above might look rather like the one in Table 27.4.

What does this table mean? There are two things to understand:

1. Factor 1 and Factor 2 are like the clusters of variables we have seen above. They are really variables but we are calling them supervariables because they take a large number of other variables into account. Ideally there should only be a small number of factors to consider.

2. The numbers under the columns for Factor 1 and Factor 2 are called *factor loadings*. Really they are nothing other than correlation coefficients recycled with a different name. So the variable 'skill at batting' correlates 0.98 with the supervariable which is Factor 1. 'Skill at batting' does not correlate at all well with the supervariable which is Factor 2 (the correlation is nearly zero at −0.01). Factor loadings follow all of the rules for correlation coefficients so they vary from −1.00 through 0.00 to +1.00.

We interpret the meaning of Factor 1 in much the same way as we interpreted the clusters above. We find the variables which correlate best with the super-variable or factor in question by looking at the factor loadings for each of the factors in turn. Usually you will hear phrases like 'batting, darts and juggling load highly on Factor 1'. All this means is that they correlate highly with the super-variable, Factor 1. Since we find that batting, darts and juggling all correlate well with Factor 1, they must define the factor. We try to see what batting, darts and juggling have in common – once again we would suggest that hand–eye coordination is the common element. We might call the factor hand–eye coordination. Obviously there is a subjective element in this since not everyone would interpret the factors identically.

27.4 Decisions, decisions, decisions

This entire section can be ignored by the faint-hearted who are not about to carry out a factor analysis.

Now that you have an idea of how to interpret a factor loading matrix derived from a factor analysis, it is time to add a few extra complexities. As already mentioned, factor analysis is more subjective and judgemental than most statistical techniques you have studied so far. This is not solely because of the subjectivity of interpreting the meaning of factors. There are many variants of factor analysis. By and large these are easily coped with as computers do most of the hard work. However, there are four issues that should be raised as they underlie the choices to be made.

Rotated or unrotated factors

The most basic sort of factor analysis is the principal components method. It is a mathematically based technique which has the following characteristics:

1. The factors are extracted in order of magnitude from the largest to smallest in terms of the amount of variance explained by the factor. Since factors are variables they will have a certain amount of variance associated with them.

2. Each of the factors explains the *maximum amount* of variance that it possibly can.

The amount of variance 'explained' by a factor is related to something called the *eigenvalue*. This is easy to calculate since it is merely the *sum* of the *squared* factor loadings of a particular factor. Thus the eigenvalue of a factor for which the factor loadings are 0.86, 0.00, 0.93, 0.00, 0.91 and 0.00 is $0.86^2 + 0.00^2 + 0.93^2 + 0.00^2 + 0.91^2 + 0.00^2$ which equals 2.4.

But maximising each successive eigenvalue or amount of variance is a purely mathematical choice which may not offer the best factors for the purposes of understanding the conceptual underlying structure of a correlation matrix. For this reason, a number of different criteria have been suggested to determine the 'best' factors. Usually these involve maximising the number of high factor loadings on a factor and minimising the number of low loadings (much as in our stylised example). This is not a simple process because a factor analysis generates several factors – adjustments to one factor can adversely affect the satis-factoriness of the other factors. This process is called *rotation* because in pre-computer days it involved rotating (or twisting) the axes on a series of scatter-grams until a satisfactory or 'simple' (i.e. easily interpreted) factor structure was obtained. Nowadays we do not use graphs to obtain this simple structure but procedures such as Varimax do this for us. Principal components are the unadjusted factors which explain the greatest amounts of variance but are not always particularly easy to interpret.

These are quite abstract ideas and you may still feel a little confused as to which to use. Experimentation by statisticians suggests that the rotated factors tend to reveal underlying structures a little better than unrotated ones. We would recommend that you use rotated factors until you find a good reason not to.

Orthogonal or oblique rotation

Routinely researchers will use *orthogonal rotations* rather than *oblique rotations*. The difference is not too difficult to grasp if you remember that factors are in essence variables, albeit supervariables:

1. Orthogonal rotation simply means that none of the factors or 'supervariables' are actually allowed to correlate with each other. This mathematical requirement is built into the computational procedures.
2. Oblique rotation means that the factors or 'supervariables' are allowed to correlate with each other (although they can end up uncorrelated) if this helps to simplify the interpretation of the factors. Computer procedures such as Promax produce correlated or oblique factors.

There is something known as *second-order factor analysis* which can be done if you have correlated factors. Since the oblique factors are supervariables which correlate with each other, it is possible to produce a correlation matrix of the correlations between factors. This matrix can then be factor-analysed to produce new factors. Since second-order factors are 'factors of factors' they are very general indeed. You cannot get second-order factors from uncorrelated factors since the correlation matrix would contain only zeros. Some of the controversy amongst factor analysts is related to the use of such second-order factors.

How many factors?

We may have misled you into thinking that factor analysis reduces the number of variables that you have to consider. It can, but not automatically so, because in fact without some intervention on your part you could have as many factors as variables you started off with. This would not be very useful as it means that your factor matrix is as complex as your correlation matrix. Furthermore, it is difficult to interpret all of the factors since the later ones tend to be 'junk' and consist of nothing other than error variance.

You need to limit the number of factors to those which are 'statistically significant'. There are no commonly available and universally accepted tests of the significance of a factor. However, one commonly accepted procedure is to ignore any factor for which the eigenvalue is less than 1.00. The reason for this is that a factor with an eigenvalue of less than 1.00 is not receiving its 'fair share' of variance by chance. What this means is that a factor with an eigenvalue under 1.00 cannot possibly be statistically significant – although this does not mean that those with an eigenvalue greater than 1.00 are actually statistically significant. For most purposes it is a good enough criterion although skilled statisticians might have other views.

Another procedure is the Scree test. This is simply a graph of the amount of variance explained by successive factors in the factor analysis. The point at which the curve flattens out indicates the start of the non-significant factors.

Getting the number of factors right matters most of all when one is going to rotate the factors to a simpler structure. If you have too many factors the variance tends to be shared very thinly.

Communality

Although up to this point we have said that the diagonal of a correlation matrix from top left to bottom right will consists of ones, an exception is usually made in factor analysis. The reason for this is quite simple if you compare the two correlation matrices in Tables 27.5 and 27.6.

Table 27.5 **Correlation matrix 1**

	Variable A	Variable B	Variable C
Variable A	1.00	0.50	0.40
Variable B	0.50	1.00	0.70
Variable C	0.40	0.70	1.00

Table 27.6 **Correlation matrix 2**

	Variable A	Variable B	Variable C
Variable A	1.00	0.12	0.20
Variable B	0.12	1.00	0.30
Variable C	0.20	0.30	1.00

You will notice that Matrix 1 contains substantially higher correlation coefficients than Matrix 2. Consequently the ones in the diagonal of Matrix 2 contribute a disproportionately large amount of variance to the matrix compared to the equivalent ones in Matrix 1 (where the rest of the correlations are quite large anyway). The factors obtained from Matrix 2 would largely be devoted to variance coming from the diagonal. In other words, the factors would have to correspond more-or-less to variables A, B and C. Hardly a satisfactory simplification of the correlation matrix. Since most psychological data tend to produce low correlations, we need to do something about the problem.

The solution usually adopted is to substitute different values in the diagonal of the correlation matrix in place of the ones seen above. These replacement values are called the *communalities*. Theoretically, a variable can be thought of as being made of three different types of variance:

1. Specific variance – variance which can only be measured by that variable and is specific to that variable.

2. Common variance – variance which a particular variable has in common with other variables.

3. Error variance – just completely random variance which is not systematically related to any other source of variance.

A correlation of any variable with itself is exceptional in that it consists of all of these types of variance (that is why the correlation of a variable with itself is 1.00), whereas a correlation between two different variables consists only of variance that is common to the two variables (common variance).

Communality is in essence the correlation that a variable would have with itself based solely on common variance. Of course, this is a curious abstract concept. Obviously it is not possible to know the value of this correlation directly since variables do not come ready broken down into the three different types of variance. All that we can do is estimate as best we can the communality. The highest correlation that a variable has with any other variable in a correlation matrix is used as the communality. This is shown in Table 27.7.

So if we want to know the communality of Variable A we look to see what its highest correlation with anything else is (in this case it is the 0.50 correlation with Variable B). Similarly we estimate the communality of Variable B as 0.70 since

Table 27.7   **Correlation matrix 1 (communality *italicised* in each column)**

	Variable A	Variable B	Variable C
Variable A	1.00	0.50	0.40
Variable B	*0.50*	1.00	*0.70*
Variable C	0.40	*0.70*	1.00

Table 27.8   **Correlation matrix 1 but using communality estimates in the diagonal**

	Variable A	Variable B	Variable C
Variable A	0.50	0.50	0.40
Variable B	0.50	0.70	0.70
Variable C	0.40	0.70	0.70

Table 27.9   **Part of a factor loading matrix**

	Factor 1	Factor 2
Variable A	0.50	0.70
Variable B	0.40	0.30

this is its highest correlation with any other variable in the matrix. Likewise the communality of Variable C is also 0.70 since this is its highest correlation in the matrix with another variable. We then substitute these communalities in the diagonal of the matrix as shown in Table 27.8.

These first estimates can be a little rough and ready. Normally in factor analysis, following an initial stab using methods like this, better approximations are made by using the 'significant' factor loading matrix in order to 'reconstruct' the correlation matrix. For any pair of variables, the computer multiplies their two loadings on each factor, then sums the total. Thus if part of the factor loading matrix was as shown in Table 27.9, the correlation between Variables A and B is $(0.50 \times 0.40) + (0.70 \times 0.30) = 0.20 + 0.21 = 0.41$. This is not normally the correlation between Variables A and B found in the original data but one based on the previously estimated communality and the significant factors. However, following such a procedure for the entire correlation matrix does provide a slightly different value for each communality compared with our original estimate. These new communality estimates can be used as part of the factor analysis. The whole process can be repeated over and over again until the best possible estimate is achieved. This is usually referred to as a process of *iteration* – successive approximations to give the best estimate.

Actually, as a beginner to factor analysis you should not worry too much about most of these things for the simple reason that you could adopt an 'off the peg' package for factor analysis which, while not satisfying every researcher, will do the job pretty well until you get a little experience and greater sophistication.

27.5 Exploratory and confirmatory factor analysis

So far, we have presented factor analysis as a means of simplifying complex data matrices. In other words, factor analysis is being used to explore the structure (and, as a consequence, the meaning) of the data. This is clearly a very useful analytical tool. Of course, the danger is that the structure obtained through these essentially mathematical procedures is assumed to be the basis for a definitive interpretation of the data. This is problematic because of the inherent variablity of most psychological measurement which suggests that the factors obtained in exploratory factor analysis may themselves be subject to variability.

As a consequence, it has become increasingly common to question the extent to which exploratory factor analysis can be relied upon. One development from this is the notion of confirmatory factor analysis. Put as simply as possible, confirmatory factor analysis is a means of confirming that the factor structure obtained in exploratory factor analysis is robust and not merely the consequence of the whims of random variability in one's data. Obviously it would be silly to take the data and re-do the factor analysis. That could only serve to check for computational errors. However, one could obtain a new set of data using more or less the same measures as in the original study. Then it is possible to factor-analyse these data to test the extent to which the characteristics of the original factor analysis are reproduced in the fresh factor analysis of fresh data. In this way, it may be possible to confirm the original analysis.

27.6 An example of factor analysis from the literature

Butler (1995b) points out that children at school spend a lot of time looking at the work of their classmates. Although the evidence for this is clear, the reasons for their doing so are not researched. She decided to explore children's motives for looking at the work of other children and proposed a four-component model of the reasons they gave. Some children could be concerned mainly about learning to do the task and developing their skills and mastery of a particular type of task; other children might be more concerned with the quality of the product of their work. Furthermore, a child's motivation might be to evaluate themselves (self-evaluation); on the other hand, their primary motivation might be in terms of evaluating the product of their work on the task. In other words, Butler proposed two dichotomies which might lead to a four-fold categorisation of motivations for looking at other children's work (Table 27.10).

Based on this sort of reasoning, the researcher developed a questionnaire consisting of 32 items, 'Why I Looked at Other Children's Work'. Raters allocated

Table 27.10   **Butler's model of reasons to look at the work of others**

	Product improvement	Self-improvement
Performance oriented	Doing better than others with little effort	Comparing task skills with those of others
Mastery oriented	Wanting to learn and improve	Checking whether own work needs improving

a number of items to each of the above categories and the best eight items in each category were chosen for this questionnaire. An example of a question from this questionnaire is:

I wanted to see . . . if my work is better or worse than others

The children's answers had been coded from 1 to 5 according to their extent of agreement with the statements.

Each child was given a page of empty circles on which they drew many pictures using these circles as far as possible. When this had been completed, they answered the 'Why I Looked at Other Children's Work' questionnaire. The researcher's task was then to establish whether her questionnaire actually consisted of the four independent 'reasons' for looking at the work of other children during the activity.

An obvious approach to this questionnaire is to correlate the scores of the sample of children on the various items on the questionnaire. This produced a 32×32 correlation matrix which could be factor-analysed to see whether the four categories of motives for looking at other children's work actually emerged:

> 'Principal-components analysis[1] with oblique rotation[2] yielded five factors with eigenvalues greater than 1.0[3] which accounted for 62% of the variance[4] . . . Three factors corresponded to the mastery-oriented product improvement (MPI), performance-oriented product improvement (PPI), and performance-oriented self-evaluation (PSE) categories, but some items loaded high on more than one factor[5]. Items expected a priori to load on a mastery-oriented self-evaluation (MSE) category formed two factors. One (MSE) conformed to the original conceptualization, and the other (checking procedure [CP]) reflected concern with clarifying task demands and instructions.' (Butler, 1995b, p. 350, superscripts added)

The meaning of the superscripted passages is as follows:

1. Principal components analysis was the type of factor analysis employed – it means that communalities were *not* used. Otherwise the term 'principal axes' is used where communalities have been estimated.

2. Oblique rotation means that the factors may well correlate with each other. That is, if one correlates the factor loadings on each factor with the factor loadings on each of the other factors, a correlation matrix would be produced in which the correlations may differ from zero. Orthogonal rotation would have produced a correlation matrix of the factors in which the correlation coefficients are all zero.

3. This means that there are five factors which are potentially statistically significant – the minimum value of a potentially significant eigenvalue is 1.0 although this is only a *minimum* value and no guarantee of statistical significance.

Table 27.11   Butler's factor loading matrix

Item: I wanted to see . . .	Performance-oriented self-evaluation	Mastery-oriented product improvement	Checking procedures	Performance-oriented product improvement	Mastery-oriented self-evaluation
Who had the most ideas	0.61			-0.37	
Whose work was best	0.74				
If others had better ideas than me	0.68				
Whether there were ideas I hadn't thought of		0.68			0.34
Ideas which would help me develop my own ideas		0.68			
If I'd understood what to do			0.85		
Whether my drawings were appropriate			0.86		
If I was working at the appropriate speed					0.63
How I was progressing on this new task					0.70
I didn't want to hand in poor work				0.67	
I didn't want my page to be emptier than others'				0.74	

Factor loadings with absolute values less than 0.30 are not reported. Table adapted from Butler (1995b).

4. These five factors explain 62% of the variance, apparently. That is, the sum of the squared factor loadings on these five factors is 62% of the squared correlation coefficients in the 32 × 32 correlation matrix.

5. In factor analysis, some items may load on more than one factor – this implies that they are measuring aspects of more than one factor.

Table 27.11 gives an adapted version of the factor analysis table in which some items have been omitted for simplicity's sake in the presentation.

You will notice from Table 27.11 that many factor loadings are missing. This is because the researcher has chosen not to report low factor loadings on each factor. This has the advantage of simplifying the factor loading matrix by emphasising the stronger relationships. The disadvantage is that the reporting of the analysis is incomplete and it is impossible for readers of the report to explore the data further. (If the original 32 × 32 correlation matrix had been included then it would be possible to reproduce the factor analysis and carry out variants on the original analysis.)

The researcher has inserted titles for the factors in the matrix. Do not forget that these titles are arbitrary and the researcher's interpretation. Consequently, you may wish to consider the extent to which her titles are adequate. The way to do this is to examine the set of questions which load highly on each of the factors to see whether a radically different interpretation is possible. Having done this you may feel that Butler's interpretations are reasonable. Butler's difficulty is that she has five factors when her model would predict only four. While this means that she is to a degree wrong, her model is substantially correct because the four factors she predicted appear to be present in the factor analysis. The problem is that some of the questionnaire items do not appear to measure what she suggested they should measure.

Some researchers might be tempted to re-do the factor analysis with just four factors. The reason for this is that the proper number of factors to extract in factor analysis is not clear-cut. Because Butler used a minimal cut-off point for significant factors (eigenvalues of 1.0 and above), she may have included more factors than she needed to. It would strengthen Butler's argument if such a reanalysis found that four factors reproduced Butler's model better. However, we should stress that factor analysis does not lead to hard-and-fast solutions and that Butler would be better confirming her claims by the analysis of a fresh study using the questionnaire.

27.7 Notes and recommendations

■ Do not be afraid to try out factor analysis on your data. It is not difficult to do if you are familiar with using simpler techniques on a computer

■ Do not panic when faced with output from a factor analysis. It can be very lengthy and confusing because it contains things that mere mortals simply do not want to know. Usually the crucial aspects of the factor analysis are to be found towards the end of the output. If in doubt, do not hesitate to contact your local expert – computer output is not always user friendly.

■ Take the factor analysis slowly – it takes a while to build your skills sufficiently to be totally confident.

■ Do not forget that interpreting the factors can be fairly subjective – you might not always see things as other people do and it might not be you who is wrong.

■ Factor analysis can be applied only to correlations calculated using the Pearson correlation formula.

Recommended further reading

Bryman, A. and Cramer, D. (1999). *Quantitive Data Analysis with SPSS Release 8 for Windows: A Guide for Social Scientists.* London, Routledge, chapter 11.
Child, D. (1970). *The Essentials of Factor Analysis.* London: Holt, Rinehart & Winston.
Kline, P. (1994). *An Easy Guide to Factor Analysis.* London, Routledge.
Tabachnick, B. G. and Fidell, L. S. (1996). *Using Multivariate Statistics* (3rd edition), New York: HarperCollins, chapter 13.

Chapter 28

Multiple regression and multiple correlation

Preparation

Revise Chapter 8 on simple regression and the standard error in relation to regression. You should also be aware of standard scores from Chapter 5 and the coefficient of determination for the correlation coefficient in Chapter 7. Optimal understanding of this chapter is aided if you understand the concepts of partial correlation and zero-order correlation described in Chapter 26.

28.1 Introduction

Traditionally, psychologists have assumed that the primary purpose of research is to isolate the influence of one variable on another. So researchers might examine whether paternal absence from the family during childhood leads to poor mathematical skills in children. The fundamental difficulty with this is that other variables which might influence a child's mathematical skills are ignored. In real life, away from the psychology laboratory, variables do not act independently of each other. An alternative approach is to explore the complex pattern of variables which may relate to mathematical skills. Numerous factors may be involved in mathematical ability including maternal educational level, the quality of mathematical teaching at school, the child's general level of intelligence or IQ, whether or not the child went to nursery school, the sex of the child and so forth. We rarely know all the factors which might be related to important variables such as mathematical skills before we begin research; so we will tend to include variables which turn out to be poor predictors of the criterion. Multiple regression quite simply helps us choose empirically the most effective set of predictors for any criterion.

Multiple regression can be carried out with scores or standardised scores (*z*-scores). Standardised multiple regression has the advantage of making the regression values directly analogous to correlation coefficients. The consequence of this is that it is easy to make direct comparisons between the influence of different variables. In unstandardised multiple regression the variables are left in their original form. Standardised and unstandardised multiple regression are usually done simultaneously by computer programs.

28.2 Theoretical considerations

> The techniques described in this chapter concern *linear* multiple regression which assumes that the relationships between variables fall approximately on a straight line.

Multiple regression is an extension of simple (or bivariate) regression (Chapter 8). In simple regression, a single dependent variable (or criterion variable) is related to a single independent variable (or predictor variable). For example, marital satisfaction may be regressed against the degree to which the partners have similar personalities. In other words, can marital satisfaction be predicted from the degree of personality similarity between partners? In multiple regression, on the other hand, the criterion is regressed against several potential predictors. For example, to what extent is marital satisfaction related to various factors such as socio-economic status of both partners, similarity in socio-economic status, religious affiliation, similarity in religious affiliation, duration of courtship, age of partners at marriage and so on? Of course, personality similarity might be included in the list of predictors studied.

Multiple regression serves two main functions:

1. To determine the minimum number of predictors needed to predict a criterion. Some of the predictors which are significantly related to the criterion may also be correlated with each other and so may not all be necessary to predict the criterion. Say, for example, that the two predictors of attraction to one's spouse and commitment to one's marriage both correlate highly with each other and that both these variables were positively related to the criterion of marital satisfaction (although marital commitment is more strongly related to marital satisfaction than is attraction to the spouse). If most of the variation between marital satisfaction and attraction to the spouse was also shared with marital commitment, then marital commitment alone may be sufficient to predict marital satisfaction. Another example of this would be the industrial psychologist who wished to use psychological tests to select the best applicants for a job. Obviously a lot of time and money could be saved if redundant or very overlapping tests could be weeded out, leaving just a minimum number of tests which predict worker quality.

2. To explore whether certain predictors remain significantly related to the criterion when other variables are controlled or held constant. For example, marital commitment might be partly a function of religious belief so that those who are more religious may be more satisfied with their marriage. We may be interested in determining whether marital commitment is

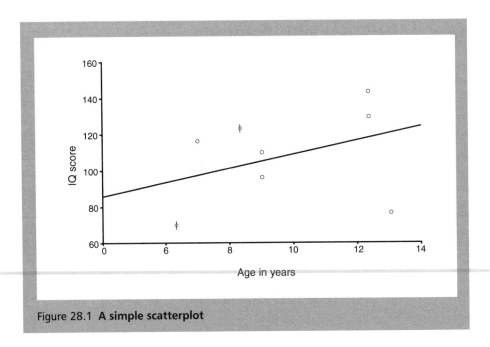

Figure 28.1 **A simple scatterplot**

still significantly related to marital satisfaction when strength of religious belief is controlled.

To explain multiple regression, it is useful to remember the main features of simple regression:

1. Simple regression can be represented by the scatterplot in Figure 28.1 in which values of the criterion are arranged along the vertical axis and values of the predictor are arranged along the horizontal axis. For example, marital satisfaction may be the criterion and personality similarity the predictor. Each point on the scatterplot indicates the position of the criterion and predictor scores for a particular individual in the sample. The relationship between the criterion and the predictor is shown by the slope of the straight line through the points on the scattergram. This 'best fitting' straight line is the one which minimises the (squared) distances between the points and their position on the line. This slope is known as the regression coefficient.

2. The intercept constant is the point at which the regression line intersects or cuts the vertical axis, in other words, the value on the vertical axis when the value on the horizontal axis is zero.

3. To determine the predicted score of the criterion from a particular score of the predictor, we draw a line parallel to the vertical axis from the score on the horizontal axis to the regression line. From here we draw a second line

parallel to the horizontal axis to the vertical axis, which gives us the predicted score of the criterion.

4. Unless there is a perfect relationship between the predictor and the criterion, the predicted score of the criterion will usually differ from the actual score for a particular case.

5. Unlike the correlation coefficient, regression is dependent on the variability of the variables involved. This makes regressions on different samples and different variables very difficult to compare. However, we can standardise the scores on the predictor and the criterion variables. By expressing them as standard scores (i.e. z-scores), each variable will have a mean of 0 and a standard deviation of 1. Furthermore, the intercept or intercept constant will always be 0 in these circumstances.

Regression equations

Simple regression is usually expressed in terms of the following regression equation:

Y	$=$	a	$+$	bX
predicted score on criterion variable		intercept constant		regression coefficient × predictor score

In other words, to predict a particular criterion score, we multiply the particular score of the predictor by the regression coefficient and add to it the intercept constant. Note that the values of the intercept constant and the regression coefficient remain the same for the equation, so the equation can be seen as describing the relationship between the criterion and the predictor.

When the scores of the criterion and the predictor are standardised to z-scores, the regression coefficient is the same as Pearson's correlation coefficient and ranges from +1.00 through 0.00 to –1.00.

In multiple regression, the regression equation is the same except that there are several predictors and each predictor has its own (partial) regression coefficient:

$$Y = a + b_1X_1 + b_2X_2 + b_3X_3 + \ldots$$

A partial regression coefficient expresses the relationship between a particular predictor and the criterion controlling for, or partialling out, the relationship between that predictor and all the other predictors in the equation. This ensures that each predictor variable provides an independent contribution to the prediction.

The relationship between the criterion and the predictors is often described in terms of the percentage of variance of the criterion that is *explained* or *accounted for* by the predictors. (This is much like the coefficient of determination for the correlation coefficient.) One way of illustrating what the partial regression coefficient means is through a Venn diagram (Figure 28.2) involving the criterion Y and the two predictors X_1 and X_2. Each of the circles signifies the amount of variance of one of the three variables. The area shaded in Diagram

28.2(a) is common only to X_1 and Y and represents the variance of Y that it shares with variable X_1. The shaded area in Figure 28.2(b) is shared only by X_2 and Y and signifies the amount of variance of Y that it shares with variable X_2. Often a phrase such as 'the amount of variance explained by variable X' is used instead of 'the amount of variance shared by variable X'. Both terms signify the amount of overlapping variance.

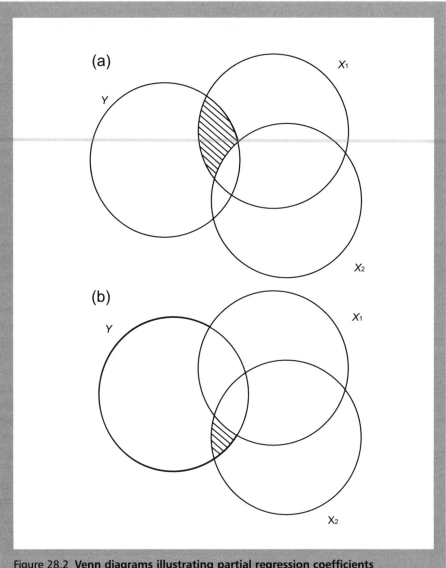

Figure 28.2 **Venn diagrams illustrating partial regression coefficients**

The number of regression equations that can be compared in a multiple regression increases exponentially with the number of predictors. With only *two* predictors, the maximum number of regression equations that can be examined is three – the two predictors on their own and the two combined:

1. $Y = a + b_1X_1$
2. $Y = a + b_2X_2$
3. $Y = a + b_1X_1 + b_2X_2$

With *three* predictors (X_1, X_2 and X_3) the number of regression equations that can be looked at is seven – three with only one predictor, three with two predictors and one with all three predictors:

1. $Y = a + b_1X_1$
2. $Y = a + b_2X_2$
3. $Y = a + b_3X_3$
4. $Y = a + b_1X_1 + b_2X_2$
5. $Y = a + b_1X_1 + b_3X_3$
6. $Y = a + b_2X_2 + b_3X_3$
7. $Y = a + b_1X_1 + b_2X_2 + b_3X_3$

To work out the number of regression equations that can be compared with any number of predictors, we raise 2 to the power of the number of predictors and subtract 1 from the result. In the case of three predictors this is 7 ($2^3 - 1 = 8 - 1 = 7$).

Design considerations Regression can involve the raw scores or standard scores. Computers will usually print out both sorts.

1. Regression involving 'standard scores' gives regression coefficients which can more readily be compared in terms of their size since they range between +1.0 and –1.0 like simple correlation coefficients (i.e. Pearson correlation). In other words, the predictor variables are comparable irrespective of the units of measurement on which they were originally based. This is just like any other standard scores (Chapter 5).

2. Regression involving 'non-standard scores' or raw scores is about the 'nuts and bolts' of prediction. Like our account of simple regression, it provides predicted numerical values for the criterion variable based on an individual's scores on the various predictor variables. However, the size of the regression coefficient is no indication of the importance of the unstandardised predictor since the size is dependent on the units of measurement involved.

Selection

Since multiple regression is particularly useful with a large number of predictors, such an analysis involves many regression equations. Obviously the complexity of the analysis could be awesome. In order not to have to look at every potential equation, a number of different approaches have been suggested for selecting and testing predictors. These approaches include *hierarchical* (or *blockwise*) *selection* and *stepwise selection*. Hierarchical selection enters predictors into the regression equation on some practical or theoretical consideration. Stepwise selection employs statistical criteria to choose the smallest set of predictors which best predict the variation in the criterion. In contrast to these methods, entering all predictors into the regression equation is known as *standard* multiple regression. Finally, comparing all possible sets of predictors is called *setwise* regression.

1. In *hierarchical selection* predictors are entered singly or in blocks according to some practical or theoretical rationale. For example, potentially confounding variables such as socio-demographic factors may be statistically controlled by entering them first into the regression equation. Alternatively, similar variables may be grouped (or 'blocked') together and entered as a block, such as a block of personality variables, a block of attitude variables and so on. The computer tells us the net influence of each block in turn.

2. In *stepwise selection* the predictor with the highest zero-order correlation is entered first into the regression equation if it explains a significant proportion of the variance of the criterion. The second predictor to be considered for entry is that which has the highest partial correlation with the criterion. If it explains a significant proportion of the variance of the criterion it is entered into the equation. At this point the predictor which was entered first is examined to see if it still explains a significant proportion of the variance of the criterion. If it no longer does so, it is dropped from the equation. The analysis continues with the predictor which has the next highest partial correlation with the criterion. The process stops when no more predictors are entered into or removed from the equation.

28.3 Stepwise multiple regression example

Since we will need to use hierarchical multiple regression to carry out path analysis in the next chapter, we will illustrate stepwise multiple regression in the present chapter. Our example asks whether a person's educational achievement (the criterion variable) can be predicted from their intellectual ability, their motivation to do well in school and their parents' interest in their education (the predictor variables). The minimum information we need to carry out a multiple regression is the number of people in the sample and the correlations between all the variables. It has been suggested that with stepwise regression it is desirable to

Table 28.1 **Correlation matrix for a criterion and three predictors**

	Educational achievement	Intellectual ability	School motivation
Intellectual ability	0.60		
School motivation	0.40	0.30	
Parental interest	0.20	0.20	0.30

Table 28.2 **The regression output**

Predictor variables	r	B	Beta	R^2 increments
Intellectual ability	0.60	0.84	0.53	0.36
School motivation	0.40	0.24	0.24	0.05

$$R^2 = .41$$
$$\text{Adjusted } R^2 = .40$$
$$R^0 = .64$$

Note B weights can only be calculated with data on means and standard deviations.

have 40 times more cases than predictors. Since we have three predictors, we will say that we have a sample of 120 cases. (However, much reported research fails to follow this rule of thumb.) In order to interpret the results of multiple regression it is usually necessary to have more information than this but for our purposes the fictitious correlation matrix presented in Table 28.1 should be sufficient.

The calculation of multiple regression with more than two predictors is complicated and so will not be shown. However, the basic results of a stepwise multiple regression analysis are given in Table 28.2. What this simple example shows is that only two of the three 'predictors' actually explain a significant percentage of variance in educational achievement.

These two variables are intellectual ability and school motivation. The first variable to be considered for entry into the regression equation is the one with the highest zero-order correlation with educational achievement. This variable is intellectual ability. The *proportion* of variance in educational achievement explained or predicted by intellectual ability is the square of its correlation with educational achievement which is 0.36 ($0.6^2 = 0.36$). The next predictor to be considered for entry into the regression equation is the variable which has the highest partial correlation with the criterion. These partial correlations have not been presented; however, school motivation is the predictor variable with the highest partial correlation with the criterion variable educational achievement.

School motivation explains a further significant increment of 0.05 in variance. The two predictors together explain 0.41 of the variance of educational achievement. The figure of the total proportion of variance explained is arrived at either by adding together the increments for R^2 (the multiple correlation squared) which are 0.36 and 0.05 or by squaring the overall R (the multiple correlation) which is 0.64^2 or 0.41. The multiple correlation is likely to be bigger the smaller the sample and for more predictors. Consequently, this figure is usually adjusted for the size of the sample and the number of predictors, which reduces it in size somewhat. Furthermore, as can be seen from Table 28.2, R^2 also can be expressed as increments. Finally, the partial regression or beta coefficients for the regression equation containing the two predictors are also shown in Table 28.2 and are 0.53 for intellectual ability and 0.24 for school motivation. We can write this regression equation as follows:

$$\text{Educational achievement} = a + 0.53 \times \text{intellectual ability} + 0.24 \times \text{school motivation}$$

According to our fictitious example, the weight of intellectual ability is greater than that of school motivation in predicting educational achievement.

Design consideration There is a concept, *multicollinearity*, which needs consideration when planning a multiple-regression analysis. This merely refers to a situation in which several of the predictor variables correlate with each other very highly. This results in difficulties because small sampling fluctuations may result in a particular variable appearing to be a powerful predictor while other variables may appear to be relatively weak predictors. So Variables A and B, both of which predict the criterion, may correlate with each other at, say, 0.9. However, because Variable A, say, has a *minutely* better correlation with the criterion it is selected first by the computer. Variable B then appears to be a far less good predictor. When the intercorrelations of your predictor variables are very high, perhaps above 0.8 or so, then the dangers of multicollinearity are also high. In terms of research design, it is a well known phenomenon that if you measure several different variables using the same type of method then there is a tendency for the variables to intercorrelate simply because of that fact. So, if all of your measures are based on self-completion questionnaires or on ratings by observers then you may find strong intercorrelations simply because of this. Quite clearly, care should be exercised to ensure that your predictor measures do not intercorrelate highly. If multicollinearity is apparent then be very careful about claiming that one of the predictors is far better than another.

The main points you need to consider in relation to the analysis are:

1. The R^2 increments tell you how much your prediction improved as the computer adds in more variables at a time. In the above example, we can see that intellectual ability is by far the most useful predictor.

2. Be careful not to be confused by the unstandardised regression coefficients (B) and the standardised regression coefficients (beta). We are using beta values in the above. Beta regression coefficients are rather like correlation coefficients since they are calculated by effectively transforming each score on a variable into a standard score (Chapter 5). However, because of other adjustments made, the beta regression coefficients are closer to partial correlation coefficients. Nonetheless, it is best to use the standardised regression coefficients (betas) as they are easy to interpret, each regression coefficient being comparable to the other. You would use the unstandardised (B) regression coefficients if you are trying to make predictions from the values of the predictor variable to the criterion variable.

28.4 An example from the published literature

Munford (1994) examined the predictors of depression in African-Americans. The research involved her administering the following measures:

1. The Beck Depression Inventory.

2. The Rosenberg Self-esteem Scale.

3. The Hollingshead Two-factor Index of Social Position. This is a measure of the occupational social class and educational standards (i.e. a measure of social class).

4. The gender (self-reported sex) of the individual.

5. The Racial Identity Attitude Scale which measures several different stages in the development of racial identity:

   (a) Pre-encounter: the stage before black people become exposed to racism. It is the stage at which they accept the definitions of themselves imposed by the white racist community

   (b) Encounter: the stage where identity is challenged by direct experiences of racism

   (c) Immersion: the individual is learning to value his or her own race and culture

   (d) Internalisation: the individual has achieved a mature and secure sense of his or her own race and identity.

As one might expect, Munford was interested in the relationship between depression as measured by the Beck Depression Inventory (the criterion variable)

Table 28.3 **Summary of stepwise multiple regression: self-esteem, gender, social class and racial identity attitudes as predictors of depression**

Predictor	R^2 increments	R^2 (adj) total	Beta F
Self-esteem	0.37	0.37	134.10
Pre-encounter	0.02	0.39	8.97
Encounter	0.01	0.41	4.71
Sex	0.01	0.42	4.77

Adapted from Munford, 1994

and the remaining variables (the predictor variables). She computed a correlation matrix between all of the variables, but as this involved 28 different correlation coefficients it is obvious that she needed a means of simplifying its complexity. She subjected her correlation matrix to a stepwise regression which yielded the outcome shown in Table 28.3.

As you can see, many of the predictors are not included in the table, indicating that they were not significant independent predictors of depression (thus social class and internalisation, for example, are excluded). Self-esteem is the best predictor of depression – those with the higher self-esteem tended to have lower depression scores. One cannot tell this directly from the table as it presents squared values which would have lost any negative signs. *We have to assess the direction of the relationship from the correlation matrix of all of the variables together.* The correlation matrix (not shown) reveals a negative correlation (–0.61) between self-esteem and depression.

Although pre-encounter, encounter and sex all contribute something to the prediction, the increment in the amount of variation explained is quite small for each of them. Thus R^2 for pre-encounter is only 0.02 which means (expressed as a percentage) that the increase in variation explained is only 2% (i.e. 0.02 × 100%).

Beta F in essence reports F-ratios (Chapter 19) for each of the predictor variables. All of those presented are statistically significant since otherwise the variable in question would not correlate significantly with the depression.

28.5 Notes and recommendations

■ Multiple regression is only practicable in most cases using a computer since the computations are numerous.

■ Normally one does not have to compute the correlation matrix independently between variables. The computer program usually does this on the raw scores. There may be a facility for entering correlation matrices which might be useful once in a while when you are reanalysing someone else's correlation matrix.

■ Choose hierarchical selection for your multiple regression if you are trying to test out theoretical predictions or if you have some other rationale. One advantage of this is that you can first of all control for any social or demographic variables (sex, social class, etc.) which might influence your results. Then you can choose your remaining predictors in any order which you think best meets your needs.

■ Choose stepwise selection methods in circumstances in which you simply wish to choose the best and smallest set of predictors. This would be ideal in circumstances in which you wish to dispense with time-consuming (and expensive) psychological tests, say in an industrial setting involving personnel selection. The main considerations here are entirely practical.

Recommended further reading

Cramer, D. (1998). *Fundamental Statistics for Social Research: Step-by-step Calculations and Computer Techniques using SPSS for Windows*, London: Routledge, chapter 7.

Glantz, S.A. and Slinker, B.K. (1990). *Primer of Applied Regression and Analysis of Variance.* New York: McGraw-Hill.

Pedhazur, E. J. (1982). *Multiple Regression in Behavioral Research: Explanation and Prediction* (2nd edition). New York: Holt, Rinehart & Winston, chapter 6.

Tabachnick, B. G. and Fidell, L. S. (1996). *Using Multivariate Statistics* (3rd edition). New York: HarperCollins, chapter 5.

Chapter 29

Path analysis

Preparation
Path analysis requires that you understand the basic principles of multiple regression (Chapter 27).

29.1 Introduction

As modern psychology has increasingly drawn from real problems and non-laboratory research methods, the problems of establishing what variables affect other variables have changed. Laboratory experiments in which causal linkages are determined by random assignment of individuals to an experimental and control group have been supplemented by a wish to understand people better in their natural environment. Causal modelling is merely a generic name for attempts to explore the patterns of interrelationships between variables in order to suggest how some variables might be causally influencing others. Of course, some suggestions might be rather better than others; some theoretical links might not fare well against actual data. In path analysis it is possible to estimate how well a particular suggested pattern of influences fits the known data. The better the model or causal pattern fits the actual data then the more likely we are to believe that the model is a useful theoretical development.

There is no suggestion intended that this will inevitably provide indisputable evidence that a particular causal model is the only possibility. Path analysis simply seeks to describe a particular path which explains the relationships among the variables well, and precisely; variables which we failed to include in our analysis might be rather better. Of course, we can exclude some causal pathways on logical grounds. For example, childhood experiences might possibly influence our adult behaviour. So it is reasonable to include childhood experiences as influences on adult behaviour. However, the reverse pattern is not viable. Our childhood experiences cannot possibly be caused by our adult behaviour; the temporal sequence is wrong. In other words, some causal models are not so viable as others for logical reasons.

Figure 29.1 **Possible path from marital love to remaining married**

29.2 Theoretical considerations

Path analysis involves specifying the assumed causal relationships among several variables. Take, for example, the variables (1) marital satisfaction, (2) remaining married, and (3) the love between a couple. A reasonable assumption is that couples who love one another are more likely to be satisfied with their marriage and consequently are more likely to stay together. This pattern of assumed relationships is described as a causal model. Such a pattern of influences (or causal model) can be presented as a *path diagram* as in Figure 29.1. In this, variables to the left (marital love) are thought to influence variables towards the right (marital satisfaction and remaining married). Right-facing arrows between variables indicate the causal direction. So marital love causes marital satisfaction which in turn is responsible for remaining married.

However, relationships between variables in themselves do not establish that marital love really causes marital satisfaction. There are four possible causal relationships between two variables:

1. As suggested by our model, marital love may increase marital satisfaction.
2. The opposite effect may occur with marital satisfaction heightening marital love.
3. Both variables may affect each other, marital love bringing about marital satisfaction and marital satisfaction enhancing marital love. This kind of relationship is variously known as a *two-way*, *bidirectional*, *bilateral*, *reciprocal* or *non-recursive* relationship.
4. The relationship may not really exist but may appear to exist because both variables are affected by some further confounding factor(s). For example, both marital love and marital satisfaction may be weaker in emotionally unstable people and stronger in emotionally stable people. This creates the impression that marital love and marital satisfaction are related when they are not, because emotionally unstable people are lower in both marital love and marital satisfaction while emotionally stable people are higher in both. This fourth sort of relationship is known as a *spurious* one.

In path analysis a distinction is often made between *exogenous* and *endogenous* variables:

Figure 29.2 **Influence of endogenous variables on relationship between marital love and remaining married**

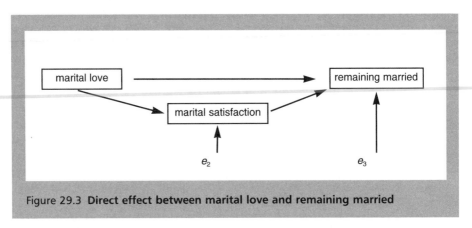

Figure 29.3 **Direct effect between marital love and remaining married**

1. An exogenous variable is one whose assumed causes have not been measured or tested.
2. An endogenous variable is one for which one or more possible causes have been measured and have been posited in the causal model.

So, in the above model, marital love is an exogenous variable while marital satisfaction and remaining married are endogenous variables.

There will be some variation in endogenous variables which is unaccounted for or unexplained by causal variables in the model. This unexplained variance in an endogenous variable is indicated by vertical arrows pointing towards that variable as shown in the path diagram in Figure 29.2. For example, the variance in marital satisfaction *not* explained by marital love is represented by the vertical arrow from e_2. Similarly, the variance in remaining married unaccounted for by marital satisfaction is depicted by the vertical arrow from e_3. The e stands for *error* – the term used to describe unexplained variance. The word *residual* is sometimes used instead to refer to the variance that remains to be explained.

In this model marital love is assumed to have an *indirect* effect on remaining married through its effect on marital satisfaction. However, marital love may also have a *direct* effect on remaining married as shown in the path diagram of Figure 29.3.

Figure 29.4 **Path coefficients**

Path coefficients

The values of the direct effects are known as *path coefficients*. They are usually the standardised beta coefficients taken from multiple regression analyses (see Chapter 28). In other words, they are essentially correlation coefficients. The values of the paths reflecting error (or residual) variance are known as error or residual path coefficients.

We will use the symbol p_1 for the path coefficient for the direct effect of marital love on marital satisfaction, p_2 for the direct effect of marital love on remaining married, and p_3 for the direct effect of marital satisfaction on remaining married. We will refer to the paths reflecting error variance for marital variance and remaining married respectively as p_4 and p_5. These are shown in Figure 29.4.

To calculate these path coefficients we need to calculate the following two regression equations:

Marital satisfaction = $a + p_1$ marital love

Remaining married = $b + p_2$ marital love + p_3 marital satisfaction

(In the above equations a and b are intercept coefficients for the regression equations. Intercept coefficients are the points at which the regression lines cut

Figure 29.5 **Actual values of path coefficients inserted**

the vertical axis. They are identified with different symbols simply because they will have different values. We can largely ignore them for the present purposes.)

Suppose that the correlation between marital love and marital satisfaction is 0.50, between marital love and remaining married 0.40 and between marital satisfaction and remaining married 0.70 for a sample of 100 couples. The path coefficients are the standardised beta coefficients for these two equations which are:

Marital satisfaction = a + 0.50 marital love

Remaining married = b + 0.07 marital love + 0.67 marital satisfaction

In other words the path coefficient for p_1 is 0.50, for p_2 0.07 and for p_3 0.67 as shown in Figure 29.5.

Since there is only one predictor variable in the first regression, the standardised beta coefficient of 0.50 is the same as the zero-order correlation of 0.50 between marital love (the predictor variable) and marital satisfaction (the criterion variable). (If there are several predictors then partial correlation coefficients would be involved.) Note that the path coefficient between marital love and remaining married is virtually zero (0.07) and statistically not significant. This means that marital love does not directly affect remaining married. The path coefficient (0.67) between marital satisfaction and remaining married differs little from the correlation (0.70) between them. This indicates that the relationship between marital satisfaction and remaining married is not due to the spurious effect of marital love.

To determine an indirect effect (such as that between marital love and remaining married which is mediated by marital satisfaction), the path coefficient between marital love and marital satisfaction (0.50) is multiplied by the path coefficient between marital satisfaction and remaining married (0.67). This gives an indirect effect of 0.335 (0.50 × 0.67 = 0.335). To calculate the total effect of marital love on remaining married, we add the direct effect of marital love on remaining married (0.07) to its indirect effect (0.335) which gives a sum of 0.405. The total effect of one variable on another should be, within rounding error, the same as the zero-order correlation between the two variables. As we can see, the total effect of marital love on remaining married is 0.405, which is very close to the value of the zero-order correlation of 0.40. In other words, path analysis breaks down or decomposes the correlations between the endogenous and exogenous variables into their component parts, making it easier to see what might be happening. So, for example, the correlation between marital love and remaining married is decomposed into (a) the indirect effect of marital love on remaining married, and (b) the direct effects of marital love on marital satisfaction and of marital satisfaction on remaining married. Doing this enables us to see that although the correlation between marital love and remaining married is moderately strong (0.40), this relationship is largely mediated indirectly through marital satisfaction.

The correlation between marital satisfaction and remaining married can also be decomposed into the direct effect we have already calculated (0.67) and a spurious component due to the effect of marital love on both marital satisfaction and remaining married. This spurious component is the product of the direct effect of marital love on marital satisfaction (0.50) and of marital love on remaining married (0.07) which gives 0.035 ($0.50 \times 0.07 = 0.035$). This is clearly a small value. We can reconstitute the correlation between marital satisfaction and remaining married by summing the direct effect (0.67) and the spurious component (0.035) which gives a total of $0.67 + 0.035 = 0.705$. This value is very similar to the original correlation of 0.70.

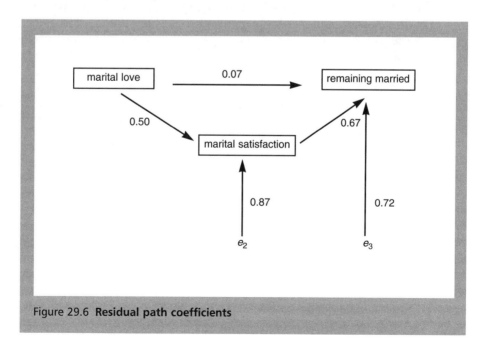

Figure 29.6 **Residual path coefficients**

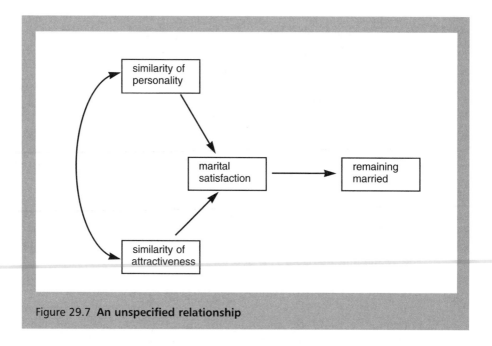

Figure 29.7 **An unspecified relationship**

To calculate the proportion of variance not explained in an endogenous variable we subtract the adjusted multiple R squared value for that variable from 1. The adjusted multiple R squared value is 0.24 for marital satisfaction and 0.48 for remaining married. So 0.76 (1 – 0.24 = 0.76) or 76% of the variance in marital satisfaction is not explained, and 0.52 (1 – 0.48) or 52% of the variance in remaining married is not explained. In path analysis it is assumed that the variables representing error are unrelated to any other variables in the model (otherwise it would not be error). Consequently, the error path coefficient is the correlation between the error and the endogenous variable which can be obtained by taking the square root of the proportion of unexplained variance in the endogenous variable. In other words, the residual path coefficient is 0.87 ($\sqrt{0.76} = 0.87$) for marital satisfaction and 0.72 ($\sqrt{0.52} = 0.72$) for remaining married (Figure 29.6).

Where there is a relationship between two variables whose nature is not known or specified, this relationship is depicted in a path diagram by a curved double-headed arrow. Suppose, for example, the two exogenous variables of similarity in personality and similarity in physical attractiveness, which were assumed to influence marital satisfaction, were known to be related but this relationship was thought not to be causal. This relationship would be shown in a path diagram as in Figure 29.7.

The correlation between these two exogenous variables is not used in calculating the effect of these two variables on marital satisfaction and remaining married.

Table 29.1 **Original and recomposed correlations**

Pairs of variables	Original correlations	Recomposed correlations
Marital love and marital satisfaction	0.50	0.500
Marital love and remaining married	0.40	0.405
Marital satisfaction and remaining married	0.70	0.705

Generalisation

To determine whether our path analysis is generalisable from the sample to the population, we calculate how well our model reflects the original correlation matrix between the variables in that model using the large sample chi-square test. This will not be described here other than to make these two points:

1. If this chi-square test is statistically significant, then this means that the model does not fit the data.

2. Other things being equal, the larger the sample, the more likely it is that the chi-square test is statistically significant and the model is to be rejected.

In terms of our model in Figure 29.6, we can see that the recomposed correlations for the model are very similar to the original correlations between the three variables as shown in Table 29.1.

Not all models will demonstrate this feature. It is always true when the model is just-identified. Identification is an important concept in path analysis. However, it is somewhat complex and so can only be presented in outline here. There are three types of identification:

1. *Just-identified*. This means that all the variables in the path analysis are connected by unidirectional paths (single-headed arrows). Actually even with the arrows entirely reversed in direction this would still be the case. Since the standardised beta coefficients are essentially correlation coefficients, this entirely reversed model would fit our data just as well as our preferred model. In other words, the recomposed correlations for this reversed just-identified model are just the same as for the forward model. *The reconstituted correlations for any just-identified model are similar to the original correlations. Consequently it is not possible to use the match between the model and the data as support for the validity of the model.*

2. *Under-identified*. In this there are assumed to be one or more bidirectional pathways (double-headed arrows between variables). For example, the relationship between marital love and marital satisfaction may be thought of as being reciprocal, both variables influencing each other. Since it is impossible

to provide an estimate of the influence of marital love on marital satisfaction which is entirely independent of the influence of marital satisfaction on marital love, it is not possible to say what the unique estimate for these pathways would be. Consequently we would need to modify our model to avoid this. That is, we need to respecify it as a just-identified or an over-identified model.

3. *Over-identified.* In an over-identified model it is assumed that some pairs of variables do not relate. Using our example, an over-identified model assumes that there is no relationship between two pairs of variables. For instance, take the following model which postulates that marital love does not lead directly to remaining married:

marital love → marital satisfaction → remaining married

This is over-identified since there are two ways in which the path coefficients could be estimated:

(a) the path coefficient between marital satisfaction and remaining married could simply reflect the correlation between these two variables (i.e. 0.70), or

(b) the correlation between marital satisfaction and remaining married could be estimated by dividing the correlation between marital love and remaining married (0.40) by that between marital love and marital satisfaction (0.50).

29.3 An example from published research

Path analysis can be as simple or as complex as the researchers' theories about the interrelationships between variables in their research. Increasing the numbers of variables under consideration accelerates the complexity in the path diagram. Not only does the analysis look more daunting if many variables are involved, but the path diagram becomes harder to draw. In this section we will discuss a path analysis by Wagner and Zick (1995) of the causes of blatant ethnic prejudice. It is fairly well known and established that there is a relationship between people's level of formal education and their expressions of prejudice: the more prejudiced tend to have the least formal education. This suggests that there is something about education which leads to less prejudice but what is the mechanism involved? Does education act directly to reduce prejudice or does it do so indirectly through some mediating variable (Figure 29.8)?

Thus there are two possible paths: (1) the *direct* path from formal education to blatant prejudice, and (2) the *indirect* path which involves a mediating variable(s).

Of course, the apparent complexity of this path diagram can be increased if several mediating variables are used rather than just one. Furthermore, if several direct variables are used instead of just formal education, the diagram will

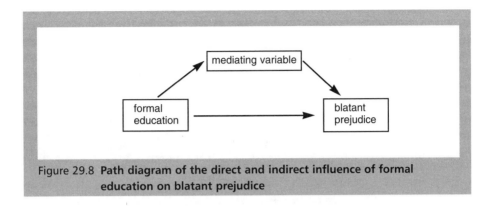

Figure 29.8 **Path diagram of the direct and indirect influence of formal education on blatant prejudice**

become increasingly complex. Wagner and Zick (1995) collected information in a number of European countries on several potential mediating variables linking formal education and blatant prejudice:

1. Individual (relative) deprivation: the feeling of an individual that he or she is economically deprived compared with other people.

2. Group (relative) deprivation: the feeling that one's social group (e.g. ethnic group) has fared badly economically compared with the rest of society.

3. Perceived incongruency: the incompatibility between an ethnic group's values and those dominant in society.

4. Political conservatism: the individual's position on the political left-wing to right-wing dimension.

5. National pride: pride in being a member of the national group (e.g. French or German).

6. Contact with foreign people: the numbers of foreign people living in one's neighbourhood.

Although this list of mediating variables far from exhausts the possibilities, it does provide measures of a number of variables which empirical studies have related to blatant ethnic prejudice.

In addition, the researchers had other measures which they could have included in the path diagram (e.g. sex and age) but omitted because the researchers did not consider them relevant to their immediate task. However, they were used by the researchers as control variables, as we shall see. There was another variable, *social strata*, which was a measure of social class. This was included in the path diagram by the researchers as social class was actually affected by a person's level of education.

There is no mystery about the path diagram; it is merely one of several path diagrams which the researchers could have studied. Most of the possibilities were ignored and the researchers concentrated on why those with the most

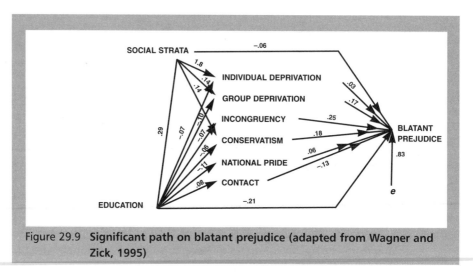

Figure 29.9   **Significant path on blatant prejudice (adapted from Wagner and Zick, 1995)**

formal education tend to express the least blatant prejudice. Drawing the diagram is a paper-and-pencil task based on elaborating the simple path diagram in Figure 29.8. Wagner and Zick's path diagram is shown in Figure 29.9. It includes both direct and indirect (mediated) relationships. Arrows pointing more or less towards the right are the only ones included as these indicate possible causal directions. Having drawn the elaborated diagram, the researchers inserted the values of the relationships between the variables (i.e. path coefficients which are in essence correlation coefficients) next to the appropriate arrows. The researchers omitted arrows (pathways) when the path coefficient did not reach statistical significance. However, because the sample was big (N = 3788), very small values were significant at the 5% level. The square of e = 0.83 in Figure 29.9 indicates how much variation in blatant prejudice is *unexplained* by the path diagram.

The path coefficients themselves were taken from Table 29.2. As you can see, this contains a lot of information. The following are the main considerations:

1. A zero-order correlation is merely the Pearson correlation coefficient as described in Chapter 7. First-order, second-order, etc., correlations are partial correlations as described in Chapter 26.

2. The upper triangle of the matrix in the table is merely a correlation matrix involving the range of measures in the path diagram with age and sex added.

3. Because the sample size was very large (N = 3788), many of the correlations account for very little variance although they are statistically significant; the correlation of 0.04 is statistically significant but its coefficient of determination or amount of variation shared by the two variables is 0.04^2 or 0.0016 or 0.16%.

4. Correlation coefficients are not used in the path analysis but are used in a multiple regression to obtain the beta weights.

Table 29.2   Zero-order correlations between variables (upper part) and results of a path analysis (lower part)

	Age	Sex	Educ.	Strata	Ind. dep.	Group dep.	Incongr.	Conser.	Pride	Contact	Prejud.
Age		-0.02	-0.28*	-0.01	0.07*	0.03†	0.06*	0.13*	0.18*	-0.24*	0.23*
Sex	-0.02		-0.07*	-0.02	0.04†	0.02	-0.02	0.02	-0.01	-0.14*	0.04*
Education	-0.28*b	-0.08*b		0.27*	-0.13*	-0.14*	-0.08*	-0.05*	-0.15*	0.17*	-0.34*
Social strata	0.07*b	0.01b	0.29*b		-0.20*	-0.17*	-0.02	0.13*	-0.02	0.34†	-0.14*
Individual deprivation	0.05*b	0.03b	-0.07†b	-0.18*b		0.30*	0.01	-0.09*	-0.07*	-0.08*	0.12*
Group deprivation	0.01b	0.01b	-0.10*b	-0.14*b	0.28*c		0.12*	0.01	0.03†	0.01	0.25*
Incongruency	0.04†b	-0.02b	-0.07*b	-0.00b	-0.02c	0.11*c		0.09*	0.04†	-0.01	0.32*
Conservatism	0.12*b	0.02b	-0.06†b	0.14*b	-0.07*c	-0.03c	0.08*c		0.23*	-0.10*	0.24*
National pride	0.15*b	-0.01b	-0.11*b	0.01b	-0.09*c	0.04c	0.01c	0.20*c		-0.09*	0.18*
Contact	-0.22*b	-0.13*b	0.09*b	0.01b	-0.08*c	0.06†c	0.01c	-0.07*c	-0.03c		-0.21
Blatant prejudice	0.08*b	0.00b	-0.21*b	-0.06*b	0.03†b	0.17*b	0.25*b	0.18*b	0.06*b	-0.13*b	

b: beta-coefficient from a simultaneous regression.
c: partial correlation with the effects of age, sex, education and social strata partialled out unless otherwise indicated: Pearson correlation coefficient.
*$p \leq 0.01$; †$p \leq 0.05$.
Table reproduced from Wagner and Zick (1995) © John Wiley and Sons Limited. Reproduced with permission.

5. Wagner and Zick (1995) carried out a simultaneous multiple regression on the correlation matrix in order to predict blatant prejudice from age, sex, formal education, social strata and the mediating variables (individual deprivation, group deprivation, etc.).

6. The beta weights from this multiple regression are indicated by a letter b in the lower half of the matrix in Table 29.2.

7. The coefficients marked c in the lower half of the matrix in Table 29.2 are partial correlations which take away the effects of age, sex, education and social strata from the relationships between the pairs of variables. That is, one needs to insert in the *indirect* pathways the correlations having removed the influence of age, sex, education and social strata. In other words, the coefficients marked c are the fourth-order correlation coefficients (partial correlations) controlling for age, sex, education and social strata simultaneously. Although this procedure is perfectly adequate, it is more conventional to use hierarchical multiple regression to achieve much the same end.

The authors describe the results of their path analysis as follows:

'The path analysis shows that the predictors of ethnic prejudice mentioned above are determined by formal education, even though some of the direct paths from education are relatively weak. However, for individual and group relative deprivation and for political conservatism, social strata mediates part of the determination by formal education. The influence of mediating variables means that the covariation of formal education and ethnic prejudice can be partially explained especially by variations in social strata, group deprivation, incongruency, conservatism, and acceptance of contact with foreigners. In addition to this, the path analysis indicates a strong direct path from education to blatant prejudice which cannot be explained by the mediation variables measured. A chi-square analysis shows that a restricted model without the assumption of a direct path from education to prejudice is significantly worse than the full model presented (chi-square = 84.02, df = 1). Thus, the path analysis demonstrates that part of the educational differences in ethnic outgroup rejection can be accounted for by the mediating psychological variables, even though a substantial proportion of the covariance of respondents' education and outgroup rejection remained unexplained.' (Wagner and Zick, 1995, pp. 53–54)

Major points which might clarify the above paragraph include:

1. Education influences variables which influence blatant prejudice. Often the influences are very weak. Most studies would use far smaller sample sizes so the tiny coefficients sometimes obtained in the study would be dismissed as not significant.

2. The chi-square tests whether the indirect paths model is significantly improved by adding in the direct path from formal education to blatant

prejudice. The results of the analysis suggest that the direct + indirect effects model is superior to the indirect effects alone model.

29.4 Notes and recommendations

- Path analysis requires a degree of mastery of statistical concepts which many students will not achieve during their degree course. Anyone who is convinced that it is appropriate for their research will need to consult supplementary sources and any local expert who might be available.

- The complexity of path analysis should not be allowed to interfere with one's critical faculties. A path analysis cannot be any better than the quality of the data which go into it.

- Path analysis involves exploring data in ways which seem alien to those who feel that statistics should be a hard-and-fast discipline in which there is only one right way of doing things. It is an example of a statistical technique which is an exploratory tool rather than a fixed solution to a fixed problem.

Recommended further reading

Bryman, A. and Cramer, D. (1999). *Quantitive Data Analysis with SPSS Release 8 for Windows: A Guide for Social Scientists*. London: Routledge, chapter 10.

Pedhazur, E.J. (1982). *Multiple Regression in Behavioral Research. Explanation and Prediction* (2nd edition). New York: Holt, Rinehart & Winston, chapter 15.

Chapter 30

The analysis of a questionnaire/survey project

Preparation
Review correlation (Chapter 8) and regression (Chapter 9).

30.1 Introduction

This chapter examines the analysis of questionnaire and/or survey projects. A lot of research planned by students adopts this style. The key feature is the number of variables involved; this type of research tempts researchers to write lengthy questionnaires with numerous items. It takes little effort to write a question, even less to write a poor question. Still less time is required to answer the questions if they are in a closed-ended format in which just one alternative is circled. An exploratory or pilot study will not always identify faulty questions and, more often than not, the pressures on students' time are such that pilot studies are rudimentary and based on very few individuals.

Some students, wanting to get closer to the experiences of the participants in their research, choose to ask the questions themselves rather than have a self-completion questionnaire. However, the basic problem remains very much the same – too much data. The difference is that with the open-ended interview approach the data have to be coded in a form suitable for statistical analysis. The coding process has its own problems – largely what coding categories to use and whether the categories used are easily used by the coders. Profound disagreements between the coders suggest either that the categories are inadequate or that they have been very poorly defined.

Of course, there are student projects which utilise ready-made questionnaires purchased from a supplier of psychological tests and measures. Although there are numerous questions involved, these are reduced to a single 'score' or measurement (or sometimes a small number of sub-scores). The groundwork of turning the questionnaire into a small number of 'scores' has already been done by its writers and will not be elaborated upon here.

30.2 The research project

Sarah Freeman is a bright young psychology student who has partied for most of her time at university. So when it is time to plan a research project she has little background knowledge of psychological research and theory. Stuck for a final-year project she designs a piece of research based on her main interest in life – thinking about sex. Her project explores the hypothesis that a religious upbringing leads to sexual inhibitions. Naturally, her supervisor is reluctant to let Sarah loose on the public at large and so insists that the research is carried out on a consenting sample of fellow students. Pressured by deadlines for coursework essays, she hastily prepares a questionnaire which she pushes under bedroom doors in the Elisha Briggs Hall of Residence. Participants in the research are to return the completed questionnaires to her via the student mail system.

Her questionnaire is a simple enough affair. Sarah's questions – with spelling corrected – are as follows.

(1) My gender is
     Male   Female

(2) My degree course is _____

(3) I am _____ years of age

(4) My religion is _____

(5) I would rate my religious faith as:
     Very strong   Strong   Neither   Weak   Very weak

(6) I attend a place of worship _____ per year

(7) My faith in God is important to me
     Strongly agree   Agree   Neither   Disagree   Strongly disagree

(8) I am a virgin
     Agree   Disagree

(9) I am sexually promiscuous
     Strongly agree   Agree   Neither   Disagree   Strongly disagree

(10) I fantasise about sex with several partners at the same time
      Strongly agree   Agree   Neither   Disagree   Strongly disagree

(11) I feel guilty after sex with more than three people at the same time
      Strongly agree   Agree   Neither   Disagree   Strongly disagree

(12) Oral sex is an abomination
      Strongly agree   Agree   Neither   Disagree   Strongly disagree

(13) Sadomasochism is appealing to me
      Strongly agree   Agree   Neither   Disagree   Strongly disagree

(14) I like sex
     *Once a week   Twice a week   Every day   Every morning   All the time
                                              and evening*

(15) Pornography
     Is disgusting   Is a stimulant   Is best home made

Suddenly Sarah sees the light of day – just a few months before she finishes at university and is launched onto the job market. Despite being due for submission, the project is in a diabolical mess. No more partying for her – she has become a serious-minded student (well, sort of) and she is determined to resurrect her flagging and ailing attempts at research. No longer does she burn the candle at one end – she now burns it at both ends trying to make sense of statistics and research methods books. Pretty dry stuff it all is. If only she had spent some time on statistics in her misspent youth she would not have been in this hole. Can she get out of the mess?

The short answer is no. The longer answer is that she could improve things considerably with a well-thought-out analysis of her data. Research has to be carefully planned to be at its most effective. She needed to consider her hypotheses, methods and statistical analysis in advance of even collecting the data. Sarah is paying for the error of her ways. One positive aspect of all this is that Sarah can at least show that she is aware of the major issues and problems with her sort of research.

30.3 The research hypothesis

Although statistics is not particularly concerned about the details of the hypotheses underlying research, a clear statement of the purposes of the research often transforms the analysis of haphazardly planned research. Of course, it is by far the best to plan meticulously before doing your research. However, this does not always happen in research – even in research by professionals.

Simply stated, Sarah's research aims to find out whether there is a relationship between religious upbringing and sexual inhibitions. The trouble with this is that it is unclear quite what is meant by a religious upbringing – does it matter which sort of religion or how intensely it is part of family life? Furthermore, it is unclear what she means by sexual inhibitions – for example, not carrying out certain activities might be the result of inhibitions but it may also be that the person does not find them arousing.

Given the limited range of questions which Sarah included in her questionnaire, we might suggest to her that she has several measures of religiousness:

1. The first is what religion they claim to be. The range is wide and includes fundamentalist, Roman Catholic, Protestant, Muslim and a variety of other religions. Is it possible for Sarah to make suggestions as to which religions are most likely to encourage sexual repression – perhaps she thinks that Roman Catholicism, Islam and fundamentalism are the religions most likely

to inculcate sexual inhibitions. If so, she could formulate a hypothesis which relates aspects of the religion to sexual inhibition.

2. There is a question about actual attendance at church. It could be that involvement in the religious community is a key variable in the influence of religion on sexual inhibitions. This might be specified as a hypothesis.

3. There are two questions which involve the importance of religious beliefs in the lives of the respondents. Again, a hypothesis might specify religious beliefs as the important element in the possible relationship.

In terms of her measures of sexual activity, there are some very obvious things to point out. The first is that it is very difficult to relate any of the sex questions to sexual inhibition as such. Some of the questions deal with frequency of sexual activities, some deal with sexual fantasy, and others deal with somewhat 'unusual' sexual practices. Probably Sarah is stuck with a fatal flaw in her research – that is, she failed to *operationalise* her concept properly; she may not have turned her *idea* of sexual inhibitions into a *measure* of that thing. It may or may not be that her measures do reflect sexual inhibitions. This is really a matter of the validity of her measures for her purposes. At the level of superficial validity of the questions we may have our doubts. Clearly Sarah might have done better to include some questions which ask about sexual inhibitions. In the circumstances it might be appropriate for Sarah to reformulate her hypothesis to suggest that religious upbringing influences sexual behaviours and sexual fantasy. At least this might make more sense in terms of her questionnaire. Unfortunately there is a downside to this – sexual inhibition seemed to be a psychologically interesting concept.

30.4 Initial variable classification

It is useful for the novice researcher to classify the variables that they have collected into category variables and numerical scores:

1. You should remember that psychologists frequently turn answers on a verbal scale into numerical scores. So questions 5, 7, 9, 10, 11, 12, 13 and 14 of Sarah's questionnaire all have fixed answer alternatives. Although they do not involve numbers, it is conventional in psychological research to impose a numerical scale of 1 to 5 onto these answer categories. The reason for this is that the categories have verbal labels which imply increasing quantities of something. Scaling from 1 to 5 is arbitrary but has been shown to work pretty well in practice.

2. Some variables which appear at first to be just nominal categories can be turned into numerical scores simply and easily. The classic example of this in research is the variable gender which consists of just two categories: male and female. Innumerable research reports code the gender variable numerically as 1 = male and 2 = female. The logic is obvious, the numerical codings implying different quantities of the variable femaleness (or maleness). However, such variables can legitimately be treated in either way.

Table 30.1 **Sarah's 15 questions classified as category or score variables**

Nominal or category variables	Numerical score variables	Other
Question 1: Gender[a]	Question 1: Gender[a]	
Question 2: Degree course		
	Question 3: Age	
Question 4: Religion		
	Question 5: Faith	
	Question 6: Attend	
	Question 7: God	
	Question 8: Virgin	
	Question 9: Promiscuous	
	Question 10: Fantasise	
	Question 11: Guilty	
	Question 12: Oral	
	Question 13: Sadomasochism	
	Question 14: Like sex	
Question 15: Pornography		

[a] Means that the variable may be placed in more than one column.

So, with these points in mind, we can classify each of our variables as 'category' or 'numerical score' or 'other' – meaning anything we are uncertain about (as in Table 30.1).

This is quite promising in terms of statistical analysis as 12 out of the 15 variables can be classified as numerical scores. This allows some of the more powerful correlational statistical techniques to be used if required. This still leaves three variables classified as categories. These are the degree course the student is taking, their religion and their views on pornography. These are probably quite varied in terms of their answers anyway. So, Sarah may find that there may be 20 or more different degree courses included in the list of replies with only a few students in each of these 20 or more categories. Similarly, the religion question could generate a multiplicity of different replies. *As they stand, these three variables are of little use in statistical analysis – they need to be recoded in some way.*

30.5 Further coding of data

It is difficult to know why Sarah included the degree course question – it does not seem to have much to do with the issues at hand – so one approach is to discreetly ignore it. Probably a better approach is to recode the answers in a simple but appropriate way. One thing which could be done is to recode them as science or arts degree courses. In other words, the degree course could be coded as 1 if it is science and 2 if it is arts. If this is done then the variable could be classified as a numerical score much as the gender variable could be.

The religion question is more of a problem. Given that the answers will include Catholics, Mormons, Baptists, and many more, the temptation might be to classify the variable simply as *religion given* versus *no religion given*. However, this may not serve Sarah's purposes too well since it may be that the key thing is whether the religion is sexually controlling or not. One approach that Sarah could take is to obtain the services of people who are knowledgeable about various religions. They could be asked to rate the religions in terms of their degree of sexual control over their members. This could be done on a short scale such as:

| *Very sexually controlling* | *Sexually controlling* | *Not sexually controlling* |

This would transform the religion variable into a numerical scale if ratings were applied from 0 to 2, for example. Those not mentioning a religion might be deemed to be in the 'not sexually controlling' category. Obviously Sarah should report the degree of agreement between the raters of the religion (i.e. the interrater reliability).

Of course, Sarah might decide to categorise the religions in a category form:

1. None
2. Fundamentalist
3. Catholic
4. Protestant
5. Muslim
6. Other

Unfortunately, this classification retains the nominal category characteristics of the original data although reducing the numbers of categories quite substantially.

The question about pornography seems to be a natural nominal category variable given the response alternatives. Perhaps it is best to treat it as such although it could be recoded in such a way that the 'is a stimulant' and 'is best home made' answers are classified together as being pro-pornography while the 'is disgusting' answer is given a different score. There are no hard-and-fast rules about these decisions and at some stage you have to come to terms with the fact that some choices seem almost arbitrary. That does not mean that you should not try to base your decisions on rational arguments as far as possible.

30.6 Data cleaning

There is little point in retaining variables in your research which contain little or no variance. It is particularly important with analyses of questionnaire-type materials to systematically exclude useless variables since they can create misleading impressions at a later stage.

The important steps are as follows:

1. Draw up or print out frequency counts of the values of each variable you have. This can be done as frequency tables or histograms/bar charts. It should become obvious to you if virtually every participant in the research gives much the same answer to a question. Consider deleting such non-discriminating questions.

2. In the case of variables which have a multiplicity of different values, you might consider recoding these variables into a small number of ranges. This might apply in the case of the age question in Sarah's research.

3. Where you find empty or virtually empty response categories then consider combining categories. Some categories may contain just a few cases. These are probably useless for your overall analysis.

30.7 Data analysis

A relatively simple approach

If Sarah follows our advice, all or virtually all of the variables will be coded as numerical scores. Any variables not coded in this way will have to be analysed by statistics suitable for category data – this might be the chi-square but more likely they will be treated as different values of the independent variable for the analysis of variance or a similar test. We would recommend, as far as possible within the requirements of your hypotheses, that all variables are transformed into numerical scores.

Accepting this, it would be a relatively simple matter to calculate the correlations between all of the variables in Sarah's list and each other. The trouble with this is that this results in a rather large correlation matrix of 15 × 15 correlation coefficients – in other words a table of 225 coefficients. Although the table will be symmetrical around the diagonal of the matrix, this still leaves over 100 different correlations. It is not the purpose of statistical analysis to pour complexity on your research; statistics are there to simplify as far as is possible.

In Sarah's research, the sex questions are quite numerous. She has eight different questions about sexual matters. Obviously it would be satisfactory if there were some way of combining these different answers in order that a single measure of 'sexual inhibition' could be developed. One simple thing that might be done is simply to add the scores on the questions together. This would require the following:

1. That the different questions are scored in the same direction. Looking at Sarah's questionnaire we see that, for example, the question 'I like sex' if

scored numerically from left to right would give a bigger score to those who liked sex most often. However, the answers to the question on sadomasochism if scored numerically from left to right would give a lower score to those who liked sadomasochistic sex. It is necessary to recode her answers in such a way that they are consistent. In this case all the answers which are more sexual could be rescored as necessary to make the high scores pro-sex.

2. That the standard deviations of scores on questions to be added together are similar, otherwise the questions with the biggest standard deviations will swamp the others. If they differ radically, then it is best to convert each score on a variable to a standard score and then add up answers to several questions (Chapter 5).

A similar sort of thing could be done with the three religious questions although it might be equally appropriate, given their relatively small number, to treat them as three separate variables.

In order to test her hypotheses, Sarah could correlate the sex and religion variables together. A significant relationship in the predicted direction would support Sarah's hypotheses. (It would be equally appropriate to apply t-tests or analyses of variance with religion as the independent variable and sex questions as the dependent variables.)

The advantage of using correlations is that it is then possible to control for (or partial out) obvious background variables which might influence the relationships found. In this study gender and age are of particular interest since both of them might relate to our main variables of interest. Partial correlation could be used to remove the influence of gender and age from the correlation between religion and sexual inhibition.

A more complex approach

Given the number of questions Sarah has included on her questionnaire, it is arguable that she ought to consider using factor analysis on the sex questions to explore the pattern of interrelations between the variables. She may well find that the answers to the sex questions tend to cluster together to form small groups of questions which tend to measure separate aspects of sex. For example, questions which deal with unusual sexual practices might group together.

Factor analysis would identify the important clusters or factors. In addition, factor analysis will usually give factor scores which are weighted scores for each individual on each factor separately. These are expressed on the same scale and so are comparable. In other words, they have already been expressed in terms of standard scores.

It is then possible to relate scores on the religion variable(s) with scores on each of the factors just as before. Partialling out gender and age might also be appropriate.

An alternative complex approach

One could also employ multiple regression (Chapter 28). Probably the best approach is to use religion as the dependent (criterion) variable(s) and the separate sex variables as the independent (predictor) variables. In this way it is possible to find out which of the sex variables contribute to the prediction of the religious experiences of the participants in childhood. Sarah may find that only certain of the questions are particularly and independently related to religion. Actually, Sarah could control for age and gender by forcing them into the regression early in the analysis.

30.8 Notes and recommendations

- Although statistics can help structure poor data, it is impossible to remedy all faults though statistics. Research design and planning is always vital.
- Statistics is useful in simplifying complex data into a small number of variables. Unfortunately, for most practical purposes it is impossible to do this without resorting to computer analysis. This is because of the sheer number of variables to be analysed.
- Do not let your partying outstrip your studying.

Part 5

Assorted advanced techniques

Chapter 31

Statistical power analysis
Do my findings matter?

Preparation

Significance testing and the correlation coefficient are the basic ideas. Since this chapter contrasts with much of current practice in the use of statistics by academic psychologists, a degree course at the University of Real Life might help.

One of the most neglected questions in statistical analysis is that of whether or not the researcher's findings are of any real substance. Obviously part of the answer depends very much on the particular research question being asked. One needs to address issues such as (a): Is this a theoretically important issue? (b) Is this an issue of social relevance? and (c) Will this research actually help people? None of these are statistical matters. Statistics can help quantify the strength of the relationships established in the research. Very few research publications seriously discuss this issue with respect to the research they describe.

31.1 Statistical significance

Students sometimes get confused as to the meaning of significance in statistics. Perhaps it is a pity that the word significance was ever used in this context since all that it actually means is that it is reasonable to generalise from your sample data to the population. That is to say, significance merely tells you the extent to which you can be confident that your findings are not simply artifacts of your particular sample or samples. It has absolutely nothing to do with whether or not there are really substantial trends in your data. Researchers tend to keep a little quiet about the substance of their findings, preferring merely to report the statistical significance. It is common – but bad – practice to dwell on statistical significance, but this is encouraged by the fact that publication of one's research in psychology depends very much on obtaining statistical significance.

The size of the samples being used has a profound effect on the statistical significance of one's research. A correlation of 0.81 is needed to be statistically significant at the 5% level with a sample size of 6. However, with a much larger sample size (say, 100), one only requires a correlation of 0.20 to be statistically significant at the 5% level. In other words, with a large enough sample size quite small relationships can be statistically significant.

We have already seen that the *squared* correlation coefficient basically gives us the proportion of the total variance shared by two variables. Sometimes r^2 is referred to as the *coefficient of determination*. With a correlation of $r = 1.00$ the value of r^2 is still 1.00 (i.e. the total amount of variance). That means that all of the variation in one of the variables is predictable from the other variable. In other words, 100% of the variation on one variable is determinable from the variation in the other variable. Expressed graphically it would mean that all of the points on a scattergram would fit perfectly on a straight line. If, however, the correlation between two variables is 0.2 then this means that r^2 equals 0.04. That is to say that the two variables have only 4% of their variance in common. This is not very much at all despite the fact that such a small correlation may well be statistically significant if the sample size is large enough. The scatterplot of such a small correlation has points which tend to scatter quite a lot from the best-fitting straight line between the points – in other words there is a lot of error variance compared to the strength of the relationship between the two variables.

31.2 Method and statistical power

Before going any further, we should emphasise that the quality of your research methods is an important factor determining the strength of the relationships found in your research. Sloppy research methods or poor measurements are to be avoided at all costs. Anything which introduces measurement error into your research design will reduce the apparent trends in the research. So, for example, a laboratory experimenter must take scrupulous care in standardising her or his procedures as far as possible.

This is clearly demonstrated if we consider a researcher trying to assess the relationship between children's ages and their heights in a sample of pre-school children. An excellent method for doing this would be to obtain each child's birth certificate to obtain his or her age and to take the child down to the local clinic to have the child's height precisely measured by the clinic nurse who is experienced at doing so. In these circumstances there is probably very little we can do further to maximise our chances of assessing the true relationship between age and height in children.

A much sloppier way of doing this research on the relation between children's ages and heights might be as follows. The researcher asks the child's nursery teacher to estimate the child's height and tells them to guess if they complain that they do not know. The children's ages are measured by asking the children themselves. It is pretty obvious that these measures of age and height are a little rough and ready. Using these approximate measures we would expect rather poor correlations between age and height – especially compared with the previous, very precise method. In other words, the precision of our measurement procedures has an important influence on the relationships we obtain.

The difference between the two studies is that the second researcher is using very unreliable measures of height and age compared with the very reliable measures of the first researcher. There are a number of ways of measuring reliability in psychology including interrater reliability which is essentially the correlation between a set of measurements taken by person A with those taken by person B. So, for example, we would expect that the birth certificate method of measuring age would produce high correlations between the calculations of two different people, and that asking the children themselves would not produce very reliable measures compared with the answer we would get from the same children even the next day.

If you can calculate the reliability of your measurements, it is possible to adjust the correlation between two measures. This essentially inflates the reliability coefficients to equal 1.00. In other words, you get the correlation between age and height assuming that the measures were totally reliable. The formula for doing this is:

$$r_{x \infty y \infty} = \frac{r_{xy}}{\sqrt{r_{xx} \, r_{yy}}}$$

The symbol $r_{x \infty y \infty}$ is the coefficient of attenuation. It is merely the correlation between variables x and y if these variables were perfectly reliable. The symbols r_{xx} and r_{yy} are the reliability coefficients of the variables x and y.

Often in research we do not have estimates of the reliability of our measures so the procedure is not universally applicable.

31.3 Size of the effect in studies

Although it is relatively easy to see the size of the relationships in correlation research, it is not quite so obvious in relation to experiments which have been analysed using t-tests, chi-square, or a nonparametric test such as the Wilcoxon Matched Pairs. One of the approaches to this is to find ways of turning each of these statistics into a correlation coefficient. Generally this is computationally easy. The resulting correlation coefficient makes it very easy to assess the size of your relationships as it can be interpreted like any other correlation coefficient.

Chi-square

It is easy to turn a 2 × 2 chi-square into a sort of correlation coefficient by substituting the appropriate values in the following formula:

$$r_{phi} = \sqrt{\frac{\text{chi-square}}{N}}$$

r_{phi} is simply a Pearson correlation coefficient for frequency scores. In fact, it is merely a special name for the Pearson correlation coefficient formula used in these circumstances. Interpret it more or less like any other correlation coefficient. It is always positive because chi-square itself can only have positive values. Remember that N in the above formula refers to the number of subjects and *not* to the degrees of freedom.

If your chi-square is bigger than a 2 × 2 table, you can calculate the *contingency coefficient* instead. The formula for this is:

$$\text{Contingency coefficient} = \sqrt{\frac{\text{chi-square}}{\text{chi-square} + N}}$$

As above, N in this case is the sample size, *not* the number of degrees of freedom.

It is possible to interpret the contingency coefficient *very approximately* as if it were a Pearson correlation coefficient. But avoid making precise parallels between the two.

The *t*-test

Essentially what is done here is to turn the *independent variable* into numerical values. That is to say, if the research design has, say, an experimental and a control group we code one group with the value 1 and the other group with the value 2. Take the research design in Table 31.1, for example, which compares men and women in terms of level of job ambition (the dependent variable).

Of course, normally we would analyse the difference between the means in terms of the *t*-test or something similar. However, we can correlate the scores on the dependent variable (job ambition) if we code the independent variable as 1 for a man and 2 for a woman (Table 31.2). The two sets of scores can then be correlated using a Pearson correlation. This should be a simple calculation for

Table 31.1   **Scores of men and women on a dependent variable**

Men	Women
5	2
4	1
9	3
6	2
4	1
7	6
5	2
1	2
4	

Table 31.2 Arranging the data in Table 31.1 so that the sex can be correlated with the dependent variable

Score on dependent variable (job ambition)	Score on independent variable sex (men coded as 1, women coded as 2)
5	1
4	1
9	1
6	1
4	1
7	1
5	1
1	1
4	1
2	2
1	2
3	2
2	2
1	2
6	2
2	2
2	2

you. However, if you have already worked out your *t*-values for the *t*-test you can use the following formula to enable you to calculate the correlation quicker:

$$r_{bis} = \sqrt{\frac{t^2}{t^2 + df}}$$

where *t* is the value of the *t*-statistic and df equals the degrees of freedom for the *t*-test.

Do not worry too much about r_{bis} since it is merely the Pearson correlation coefficient when one variable (e.g. sex) has just one of two values.

31.4 An approximation for nonparametric tests

We have to approximate to obtain a correlation coefficient for nonparametric tests such as the Mann–Whitney U-test. One possible procedure is to work out the statistic (e.g. Mann–Whitney U-test), check its probability value (significance level), and then look up what the value of the *t*-test would be for that same significance level and sample size. For example, if we get a value of the Mann–Whitney U of 211 which we find to be significant at the 5% level (two-tailed test) on a sample of 16 subjects, we could look up in the *t*-table the value of *t* which would be significant at the 5% level (two-tailed test) on a sample of 16 subjects (i.e. the degrees of freedom $= 14$). This value of t is 2.15 which could be substituted in the formula:

$$r_{bis} = \sqrt{\frac{t^2}{t^2 + df}}$$

31.5 Analysis of variance (ANOVA)

It is possible to compute from analysis of variance data a correlation measure called *eta*. This is analogous to a correlation coefficient but describes a curvilinear rather than the linear relationship which the Pearson correlation coefficient does. It is of particular use in the analysis of variance since it is sometimes difficult to know which of the independent variables explains the most variance. The probability value of an *F*-ratio in itself does not enable us to judge which of the independent variables accounts for the largest amount of the variance of the dependent variable. Table 31.3 is a summary table from an analysis of variance considering the influence of intelligence and social class on a dependent variable. It is difficult to know from the table whether intelligence or social class explains more of the variance.

In order to calculate the value of eta for any of the variables all we need to do is substitute in the following formula:

$$eta = \sqrt{\frac{\text{treatment df} \times F\text{-ratio}}{(\text{treatment df} \times F\text{-ratio}) + \text{within df}}}$$

So, for example, if we take intelligence then we substitute the values from Table 31.3 in the formula:

$$eta = \sqrt{\frac{2 \times 8.9}{(2 \times 8.9) + 108}}$$

$$= \sqrt{\frac{17.8}{17.8 + 108}}$$

Table 31.3 **Analysis of variance summary table**

Source of variance	Sums of squares	Degrees of freedom	Mean square	*F*-ratio	Signifi-cance
Intelligence	1600	2	800	8.9	1%
Social class	2400	3	800	8.9	1%
Interaction	720	6	120	1.3	ns
Within (error)	9720	108	90		

31.4 Analysis of variance summary table with values of eta added

Source of variance	Sums of squares	Degrees of freedom	Mean square	*F*-ratio	Signifi-cance	Eta η
Intelligence	1600	2	800	8.9	1%	0.38
Social class	2400	3	800	8.9	1%	0.44
Interaction	720	6	120	1.3	ns	0.26
Within (error)	9720	108	90			

$$= \sqrt{\frac{17.8}{125.8}}$$

$$= \sqrt{0.1415}$$

$$= 0.38$$

If we do a similar calculation for the two other sources of variation we can extend our summary table to include eta (Table 31.4). What this extra information tells us is that social class accounts for more variation in the dependent variable than does either intelligence or the interaction.

31.6 Notes and recommendations

■ *Do not* expect the things in this chapter to feature regularly in other researchers' reports. They tend to get ignored despite their importance.

■ *Do* be aware of the need to assess the degree of explanatory power obtained in your research as part of your interpretation of the value of your findings. All too frequently psychologists seek statistical significance and forget that their findings may be trivial in terms of the amount of variance explained.

■ *Do* try to design your research in such a way that the error and unreliability are minimised as far as possible.

Chapter 32

Meta-analysis

Combining and exploring statistical findings from previous research

Preparation

Review statistical power (Chapter 31). In particular, make sure that you understand the difference between statistical significance and statistical power.

32.1 Introduction

Meta-analysis is a general term to describe statistical techniques which allow a researcher to analyse the pattern of findings from a variety of published and unpublished studies into a particular research question. Most statistical analyses investigate the data from a single research study. However, when we review the research literature we frequently find a number of studies researching similar hypotheses and similar variables. Such studies can vary enormously in terms of the method they employ (for example, field studies versus laboratory studies) or the populations they sample (for example, students versus the general population). Sometimes a number of studies may find positive evidence in favour of the hypothesis whereas others support the reverse trend. The main objectives of meta-analysis are as follows:

1. To assess the strength of relationships over a range of studies and, if possible, to combine these into a single overall indicator of the relationship.

2. To assess the influence of various characteristics of pertinent studies (the type of sample, the type of method, etc.) on the strength of the relationships found in the studies.

Meta-analysis involves some new concepts. Although relatively rare in student work, a meta-analysis is a feasible proposition where time and resources are available for a thorough literature search.

A crucial feature of any research study is the process of reviewing the available empirical literature on a particular topic. To date, meta-analysis has not routinely been applied to these reviews. Usually a meta-analysis is carried out as an independent exercise because of a number of difficulties in its use:

1. Because meta-analysis is a study of studies, it is necessary to obtain copies of relevant reports and publications dealing with the statistical analysis of the relationship in question. Sometimes these may have to be obtained, say, from other libraries (or from the researchers themselves if the study has been recently published). Sometimes publications will be untraceable. The process of obtaining research reports costs time and there may be financial charges involved. Since there may be a bias towards the publishing of significant research findings, ideally a meta-analysis should also include unpublished research findings. These can be even more difficult to identify and obtain.

2. The meta-analyst needs to be familiar with computerised database searches. Unless a variety of databases are searched using a variety of keywords, significant research studies may be overlooked. Published articles and books may be sources of additional studies which have not been found using the databases.

3. There is inconsistency in the reporting of research findings. Sometimes important pieces of information are missing. A meta-analysis can be done with very minimal information – sample size and significance level. If statistical power or effect size were routinely reported for every research study there would be no problem. Increasingly, journals are requiring this information. Nevertheless, meta-analysts may have to use a range of formulae to transpose published findings into measures of power or effect size.

4. There is a good deal of non-computer work involved in meta-analysis. Meta-analysis is not available on any of the standard statistical packages. However, much of the work is computationally easy with just a hand calculator. Computers can be useful in later stages of the analysis but they are far from essential.

5. Meta-analysis involves defining the variables and types of study of interest with some precision. This requires some understanding of the field of study which is difficult to achieve within the timescale of student projects.

It is to be hoped that readers will not be too deterred by the above comments. After all, they imply diligence, planning, hard work and understanding of the chosen field of research. These are reasonable targets for any researcher whether or not using meta-analysis.

Criticisms of meta-analysis usually apply equally to conventional reviews of the empirical studies. So, for example, problems of retrieval of studies, biases in selection of statistically significant findings in research publications, glossing over details in particular studies and similar issues are common to both meta-analytic and other attempts to synthesise the literature.

This chapter provides a practical introduction to meta-analysis which should be sufficient to guide students through the major stages involved. It does not pretend to be an exhaustive coverage.

32.2 The Pearson correlation coefficient as the effect size

Effect size is the central concept in meta-analysis. It means exactly what it says – the size of the effect of one variable on a second. In other words, the effect size indicates the amount of relationship between one variable and another variable in a standardised way. This should not be confused with a causal effect, though in controlled experiments it may actually mean causal effect. Ultimately, and largely for practical reasons, the most convenient measure of effect size is the Pearson correlation coefficient between the two variables (say the independent variable and the dependent variable). In Chapter 31 the correlation coefficient was used as a measure of statistical power (i.e. the strength of the relationship between the two variables). Statistical power is not the same as statistical significance, which is about generalising from a sample to a population. The larger the correlation coefficient between two variables, the larger the effect of one variable on the other. Thus statistical power and effect size are pretty much the same thing.

Chapter 31 also showed just how easy it is to convert a number of different statistical tests such as the t-test and chi-square into a Pearson correlation coefficient. It is the ease of such conversions that ensures the Pearson correlation coefficient's practical utility as a measure of effect size. Irrespective of the nature of the statistical analysis reported by the researcher in the primary report, it is highly likely that a correlation coefficient can be obtained from this information. The minimum information required is significance level and sample size.

Do not assume that effect size is useful only when comparing independent variables and dependent variables in experimental studies. Meta-analysis can be used in virtually any type of study. Also, remember that the techniques can be useful when combining the results of just two studies.

32.3 Other measures of effect size

Cohen's d is the other common measure of effect size. Its major disadvantage is that it can be more difficult to calculate from the statistical analyses usually presented in reports of psychological research. Cohen's d is the difference between the mean of one group of participants and the mean of the other group adjusted by dividing by the standard deviation of the scores. In other words, it is the difference between the two groups standardised by dividing by the standard deviation. Just as we can turn any score into a z-score by dividing the score by the standard deviation, we can generate a standardised effect score by dividing the unstandardised effect size (for example, the difference between the experimental and control group) by the size of the standard deviation of the scores. Expressed as a formula, Cohen's d is:

$$\text{Cohen's } d = \frac{\text{Mean of Group A} - \text{Mean of Group B}}{\text{Standard deviations of both groups of scores pooled together}}$$

The standard deviation is obtained by subtracting the experimental group scores from the experimental group's mean and subtracting the control group scores from the control group's mean. These difference scores are then pooled (combined) as a first step in computing their standard deviation. This can be a complex matter especially when the sample sizes are different as you may remember from our discussion of the unrelated t-test (Chapter 13). Although there is a similarity, it is not true to say that Cohen's d is the same as the t-test despite overlaps in their calculation. In the t-test the division is by the standard error of the difference between the sample means; in Cohen's d, the division is by the standard deviation of the pooled groups of scores. (In essence the two standard deviations are combined arithmetically.)

Although Cohen's d is commonly used in meta-analysis, it is not quite as flexible in use as the Pearson correlation coefficient. Most important is the fact that it is much easier to estimate the Pearson correlation coefficient from the minimal information that researchers sometimes supply. We saw in Chapter 31 how we can calculate a correlation coefficient from a range of tests of significance. This is not so easy with Cohen's d.

32.4 Effects of different characteristics of studies

Modern meta-analyses are not simply about determining the effect size over a range of studies. They also try to estimate what characteristics of studies may be responsible for large effect sizes and what characteristics of studies may be responsible for smaller effect sizes. It is usual to select a range of possible study variables which may be related to effect size. These may include:

- the gender of the participants
- the size of the study
- the quality of the study as rated by a panel of psychologists or from the prestige of the journal in which the study was published
- whether the study involved behavioural rather than attitudinal measures
- the sex of the researcher
- whether the study was a laboratory experiment or field study
- any other variable that the meta-analyst judges to be pertinent and which can

be assessed from the primary published reports of studies or by other means such as ratings by experts.

This list is not the ideal or complete list. The study variables you choose may be very different from the above list which should not simply be routinely applied without further consideration.

The selection of study variables is a subjective matter in the sense that it depends on knowledge, skill and a degree of insight. These are much the same characteristics that are required by any researcher. Note that the information the meta-analyst wants may not be given in the available research reports – for example, the researcher may not have analysed data for males and females separately.

The basic procedures for investigating the influence of study variables on effect size are very simple. So if a meta-analyst wished to study effect size in studies involving female participants compared with those involving male participants, the following effect sizes could be calculated:

1. The overall (combined) effect size for relevant studies irrespective of the sex of the participants.

2. The overall (combined) effect size for female participant studies.

3. The overall (combined) effect size for male participant studies.

It may well be that the overall effect size is more-or-less the same for both males and females. However, the male and female effect sizes could be very different. Such a simple analysis may be insufficient for the analyst's particular purposes. For example, the analysis would be a little more complicated if the analyst wished to compare the effect sizes for young males, young females, older males and older females. This would involve the calculation of effect sizes for the four different age/sex combinations (see Table 32.1).

Not all meta-analyses investigate the influence of study characteristics. Carry out such an analysis only if it is relevant to your purposes.

Table 32.1 **Meta-analysis table for different age and sex combinations**

	Young	**Older**
Males	$r = 0.32$	$r = 0.13$
	$r = 0.45$	$r = -0.03$
	$r = 0.35$	
Females		
	$r = 0.22$	$r = -0.04$
	$r = 0.12$	$r = 0.05$
	$r = 0.15$	$r = 0.15$
		$r = 0.11$

32.5 First steps in meta-analysis

Step 1: Define the variables of interest to you

Decide precisely which two variables you are investigating in your meta-analysis. (Other pairs of variables can also be considered and treated in the same way in parallel.) This is in essence deciding the nature of the research hypothesis to be tested.

Step 2: Plan your database search

Plan your search for relevant studies involving your chosen variables. This search should involve a computer search of the relevant databases. Perusing studies referred to in relevant research publications may generate additions to your list of relevant studies. Of course, you may wish to omit certain types of study because they are not relevant or do not meet other criteria. It is important to do this using stipulated criteria rather than on whims. If possible, seek out unpublished studies.

Table 32.2   Equivalent effect sizes expressed as Cohen's *d* and Pearson correlation coefficients

Pearson *r*	Cohen's *d*	Pearson *r*	Cohen's *d*	Pearson *r*	Cohen's *d*	Pearson *r*	Cohen's *d*	Pearson *r*	Cohen's *d*
0.00	0.00	0.20	0.41	0.40	0.87	0.60	1.50	0.80	2.67
0.01	0.02	0.21	0.43	0.41	0.90	0.61	1.54	0.81	2.76
0.02	0.04	0.22	0.45	0.42	0.93	0.62	1.58	0.82	2.87
0.03	0.06	0.23	0.47	0.43	0.95	0.63	1.62	0.83	2.98
0.04	0.08	0.24	0.49	0.44	0.98	0.64	1.67	0.84	3.10
0.05	0.10	0.25	0.52	0.45	1.01	0.65	1.71	0.85	3.23
0.06	0.12	0.26	0.54	0.46	1.04	0.66	1.76	0.86	3.37
0.07	0.14	0.27	0.56	0.47	1.06	0.67	1.81	0.87	3.53
0.08	0.16	0.28	0.58	0.48	1.09	0.68	1.85	0.88	3.71
0.09	0.18	0.29	0.61	0.49	1.12	0.69	1.91	0.89	3.90
0.10	0.20	0.30	0.63	0.50	1.15	0.70	1.96	0.90	4.13
0.11	0.22	0.31	0.65	0.51	1.19	0.71	2.02	0.91	4.39
0.12	0.24	0.32	0.68	0.52	1.22	0.72	2.08	0.92	4.69
0.13	0.26	0.33	0.70	0.53	1.25	0.73	2.14	0.93	5.06
0.14	0.28	0.34	0.72	0.54	1.28	0.74	2.20	0.94	5.51
0.15	0.30	0.35	0.75	0.55	1.32	0.75	2.27	0.95	6.08
0.16	0.32	0.36	0.77	0.56	1.35	0.76	2.34	0.96	6.86
0.17	0.35	0.37	0.80	0.57	1.39	0.77	2.31	0.97	7.98
0.18	0.37	0.38	0.82	0.58	1.42	0.78	2.49	0.98	9.85
0.19	0.39	0.39	0.85	0.59	1.46	0.79	2.58	0.99	14.04

Step 3: Obtain research reports

Obtain copies of research reports containing the statistical analyses of the relevant studies. These may be available in your local university or college library, but sometimes they have to be ordered from other libraries. The authors of recently published studies may be contacted by mail or e-mail to obtain copies of reports. Databases usually contain an adequate address for the senior author. Remember that at the very minimum, you need a significance level and sample size to calculate an effect size.

Sometimes a previous meta-analytic study may supply you with details of otherwise unobtainable studies. It may be possible to use the effect sizes reported in this earlier meta-analysis. Cohen's d is easily converted to r (and vice versa) by using Table 32.2. This table also serves as a ready reference to compare effect sizes expressed as r with those given as Cohen's d.

Table 32.3   **Converting various tests of significance to a correlation coefficient**

Statistic	Formula for converting to Pearson correlation	Notes
t-test	$r_{BIS} = \sqrt{\dfrac{t^2}{t^2 + df}}$	Can be used for a related or unrelated t-test
Chi-square	$r = \sqrt{\dfrac{\text{Chi-square}}{N}}$	Only use this formula for a 2 × 2 chi-square
Cohen's d	Convert to r using Table 32.2	Useful if no source of data from a study is available other than another meta-analysis
Nonparametric test	$r = \dfrac{z}{\sqrt{N}}$	Alternatively convert to parametric equivalent and substitute this value in formula (see pp. 375–6)
Pearson correlation coefficient and variants	No conversion necessary	These are already the value of the effect size
Most common tests of significance and when only significance level and sample size given	$r = \dfrac{z}{\sqrt{N}}$	Convert the significance level to z using Table 32.4. Then divide by the square root of the sample size involved

Step 4: Calculating effect sizes for each study

A standard measure of effect size should be calculated for each of the relationships between the variables for each study reviewed. Our chosen measure of effect size is the Pearson correlation coefficient or r. Some studies may report this value or some other measure of effect size but usually they do not. Where effect sizes are not reported they need to be calculated by the meta-analyst.

It is usually possible to use the test of significance reported in the original analysis to calculate the effect size r. Table 32.3 gives this conversion for common tests of significance. We have already seen some of these in Chapter 31.

However, sometimes this information is missing from the primary source. If you know the sample size and the significance level, then the following formula can be used to approximate to the effect size irrespective of the particular test of significance involved. The significance levels should be converted to their one-tailed equivalents if they are given as two-tailed probabilities.

$$r = \frac{z}{\sqrt{N}}$$

The value of z for the significance level is obtained by consulting Table 32.4. So, if the significance level for a particular study is 0.7% (i.e. the probability is 0.007), then the value of z obtained from Table 32.4 is 2.44. Assuming that the one-tailed significance level is based on 40 participants, the effect size is:

$$r = \frac{2.44}{\sqrt{40}}$$

$$r = \frac{2.44}{6.325}$$

$$= 0.39$$

This is a good approximation given the limited information required. The formula has obvious advantages for use with uncommon tests of significance or those for which a conversion formula to r is not available. It can also be used to convert *non*parametric significance levels to effect sizes. Of course, significance levels are not always reported very precisely which may cause problems especially when the findings are *not* significant at the 5% level. Just what is the effect size for this? Some authors report it as an effect size of zero though clearly this is not likely to be the case. Others take it as the 50% or 0.5 level of significance. In these circumstances it would be better to estimate the effect size from the formulae in Table 32.3 if at all possible.

At the end of this step you should have values or estimated values of the effect size for each of the studies you are using in your meta-analysis. If you are unable to give an effect size because of incomplete information in the original report of a study or because the report was unobtainable, it will have to be omitted. This omission should be reported in your report of your meta-analysis.

Table 32.4 *z*-distribution for converting one-tailed probability levels to *z*-scores

Find the appropriate significance or probability level (*p*) value from the table below, the required *z*-score is adjacent to the *right*.

Reverse this process if you wish to convert your *z*-score back to a significance or probability level.

Remember that a probability needs to be multiplied by 100% to get the percentage probability.

p	*z*	*p*	*z*	*p*	*z*	*p*	*z*	*p*	*z*
0.00001	4.265	0.19	0.878	0.40	0.253	0.61	0.279	0.82	−0.915
0.0001	3.719	0.20	0.842	0.41	0.228	0.62	−0.306	0.83	−0.954
0.001	3.090	0.21	0.806	0.42	0.202	0.63	−0.332	0.84	−0.995
0.01	2.326	0.22	0.772	0.43	0.176	0.64	−0.359	0.85	−1.036
0.02	2.054	0.23	0.739	0.44	0.151	0.65	−0.385	0.86	−1.080
0.03	1.881	0.24	0.706	0.45	0.126	0.66	−0.413	0.87	−1.126
0.04	1.751	0.25	0.675	0.46	0.100	0.67	−0.440	0.88	−1.175
0.05	1.645	0.26	0.643	0.47	0.075	0.68	−0.468	0.89	−1.227
0.06	1.555	0.27	0.613	0.48	0.050	0.69	−0.496	0.90	−1.282
0.07	1.476	0.28	0.583	0.49	0.025	0.70	−0.524	0.91	−1.341
0.08	1.405	0.29	0.553	0.50	0.000	0.71	−0.553	0.92	−1.405
0.09	1.341	0.30	0.524	0.51	−0.025	0.72	−0.583	0.93	−1.476
0.10	1.282	0.31	0.496	0.52	−0.050	0.73	−0.613	0.94	−1.555
0.11	1.227	0.32	0.468	0.53	−0.075	0.74	−0.643	0.95	−1.645
0.12	1.175	0.33	0.440	0.54	−0.100	0.75	−0.675	0.96	−1.751
0.13	1.126	0.34	0.413	0.55	−0.126	0.76	−0.706	0.97	−1.881
0.14	1.080	0.35	0.385	0.56	−0.151	0.77	−0.739	0.98	−2.054
0.15	1.036	0.36	0.359	0.57	−0.176	0.78	−0.772	0.99	−2.326
0.16	0.995	0.37	0.332	0.58	−0.202	0.79	−0.806		
0.17	0.954	0.38	0.306	0.59	−0.228	0.80	−0.842		
0.18	0.915	0.39	0.279	0.60	−0.253	0.81	−0.878		

Step 5: Combining effect sizes over a number of studies

One aim of meta-analysis is to combine the findings of several studies (or a selected subset of studies such as those involving female participants) into a single composite effect size. The obvious way of doing this is to average the effect sizes. However, the simple numerical average of the effect sizes can give a distorted value particularly when some of the values of the correlation coefficients are large. Instead we average the effect sizes by converting each *r* into a *z*-score (z_r) for the correlation coefficient using Table 32.5. This table is of

Table 32.5   **Extended table of Fisher's z_r transformation of the correlation coefficient**

r	z_r	r	z_r	r	z_r	r	z_r	r	z_r	r	z_r	r	z_r
0.01	0.10	0.41	0.436	0.801	1.101	0.841	1.225	0.881	1.380	0.921	1.596	0.961	1.959
0.02	0.020	0.42	0.448	0.802	1.104	0.842	1.228	0.882	1.385	0.922	1.602	0.962	1.972
0.03	0.030	0.43	0.460	0.803	1.107	0.843	1.231	0.883	1.389	0.923	1.609	0.963	1.986
0.04	0.040	0.44	0.472	0.804	1.110	0.844	1.235	0.884	1.394	0.924	1.616	0.964	2.000
0.05	0.050	0.45	0.485	0.805	1.113	0.845	1.238	0.885	1.398	0.925	1.623	0.965	2.014
0.06	0.060	0.46	0.497	0.806	1.116	0.846	1.242	0.886	1.403	0.926	1.630	0.966	2.029
0.07	0.070	0.47	0.510	0.807	1.118	0.847	1.245	0.887	1.408	0.927	1.637	0.967	2.044
0.08	0.080	0.48	0.523	0.808	1.121	0.848	1.249	0.888	1.412	0.928	1.644	0.968	2.060
0.09	0.090	0.49	0.536	0.809	1.124	0.849	1.253	0.889	1.417	0.929	1.651	0.969	2.076
0.10	0.100	0.50	0.549	0.810	1.127	0.850	1.256	0.890	1.422	0.930	1.658	0.970	2.092
0.11	0.110	0.51	0.563	0.811	1.130	0.851	1.260	0.891	1.427	0.931	1.666	0.971	2.110
0.12	0.121	0.52	0.576	0.812	1.133	0.852	1.263	0.892	1.432	0.932	1.673	0.972	2.127
0.13	0.131	0.53	0.590	0.813	1.136	0.853	1.267	0.893	1.437	0.933	1.681	0.973	2.146
0.14	0.141	0.54	0.604	0.814	1.139	0.854	1.271	0.894	1.442	0.934	1.689	0.974	2.165
0.15	0.151	0.55	0.618	0.815	1.142	0.855	1.274	0.895	1.447	0.935	1.697	0.975	2.185
0.16	0.161	0.56	0.633	0.816	1.145	0.856	1.278	0.896	1.452	0.936	1.705	0.976	2.205
0.17	0.172	0.57	0.648	0.817	1.148	0.857	1.282	0.897	1.457	0.937	1.713	0.977	2.227
0.18	0.182	0.58	0.663	0.818	1.151	0.858	1.286	0.898	1.462	0.938	1.721	0.978	2.249
0.19	0.192	0.59	0.678	0.819	1.154	0.859	1.290	0.899	1.467	0.939	1.730	0.979	2.273
0.20	0.203	0.60	0.693	0.820	1.157	0.860	1.293	0.900	1.472	0.940	1.738	0.980	2.298
0.21	0.213	0.61	0.709	0.821	1.160	0.861	1.297	0.901	1.478	0.941	1.747	0.981	2.323
0.22	0.224	0.62	0.725	0.822	1.163	0.862	1.301	0.902	1.483	0.942	1.756	0.982	2.351
0.23	0.234	0.63	0.741	0.823	1.166	0.863	1.305	0.903	1.488	0.943	1.764	0.983	2.380
0.24	0.245	0.64	0.758	0.824	1.169	0.864	1.309	0.904	1.494	0.944	1.774	0.984	2.410
0.25	0.255	0.65	0.775	0.825	1.172	0.865	1.313	0.905	1.499	0.945	1.783	0.985	2.443
0.26	0.266	0.66	0.793	0.826	1.175	0.866	1.317	0.906	1.505	0.946	1.792	0.986	2.477
0.27	0.277	0.67	0.811	0.827	1.179	0.867	1.321	0.907	1.510	0.947	1.802	0.987	2.515
0.28	0.288	0.68	0.829	0.828	1.182	0.868	1.325	0.908	1.516	0.948	1.812	0.988	2.555
0.29	0.299	0.69	0.848	0.829	1.185	0.869	1.329	0.909	1.522	0.949	1.822	0.989	2.599
0.30	0.310	0.70	0.867	0.830	1.188	0.870	1.333	0.910	1.528	0.950	1.832	0.990	2.647
0.31	0.321	0.71	0.887	0.831	1.191	0.871	1.337	0.911	1.533	0.951	1.842	0.991	2.700
0.32	0.332	0.72	0.908	0.832	1.195	0.872	1.341	0.912	1.539	0.952	1.853	0.992	2.759
0.33	0.343	0.73	0.929	0.833	1.198	0.873	1.346	0.913	1.545	0.953	1.863	0.993	2.826
0.34	0.354	0.74	0.951	0.834	1.201	0.874	1.350	0.914	1.551	0.954	1.875	0.994	2.903
0.35	0.365	0.75	0.973	0.835	1.204	0.875	1.354	0.915	1.557	0.955	1.886	0.995	2.995
0.36	0.377	0.76	0.996	0.836	1.208	0.876	1.358	0.916	1.564	0.956	1.897	0.996	3.106
0.37	0.388	0.77	1.020	0.837	1.211	0.877	1.363	0.917	1.570	0.957	1.909	0.997	3.250
0.38	0.400	0.78	1.045	0.838	1.214	0.878	1.367	0.918	1.576	0.958	1.921	0.998	3.453
0.39	0.412	0.79	1.071	0.839	1.218	0.879	1.371	0.919	1.583	0.959	1.933	0.999	3.800
0.40	0.424	0.80	1.098	0.840	1.221	0.880	1.376	0.920	1.589	0.960	1.946		

the correlation coefficient expressed as a normal distribution. It is different from the z-distribution so take care. The several values of z_r are then summed and averaged by dividing by the number of values. This average can then be turned back into the combined effect size by using Table 32.5 in the reverse mode. (That is, you look for your value of the combined z_r in the right-hand side of the pairs of columns and find the value of r to the left of this.)

Thus if we wish to calculate the average effect size from three studies with the following effect sizes

Study A: $r = 0.3$
Study B: $r = 0.7$
Study C: $r = 0.5$

we convert each to their z_r by using Table 32.5. These values are 0.310, 0.867 and 0.549 respectively. The numerical average of these is $(0.310 + 0.867 + 0.549)/3 = 0.575$. We can then reconvert this value to an overall effect size by using Table 32.5 in reverse. The effect size r for the three studies combined is therefore 0.52.

It is possible that a particular study has findings in the reverse direction from those of the majority. In this case its effect size is given a negative value. Thus the overall effect size will be reduced.

Step 6: The significance of the combined studies

The significance level of the combined studies can also be assessed. Once again the simple numerical average of the probability levels is misleading. Intuitively we may appreciate that this simple average makes no allowance for the greatly increased sample size obtained by combining studies. There are numerous different ways of combining significance levels from a range of studies to give an overall significance level, each having different advantages or disadvantages. The simplest and one of the most satisfactory methods is to convert each significance level into a z-score using Table 32.4. Rather than divide by the number of z-scores to obtain the average, the sum of the z-scores is divided by the square root of the number of z-scores:

$$z = \frac{\Sigma z}{\sqrt{N}}$$

Thus if the significance levels from a set of studies are 0.08, 0.15, and 0.02, each of these is converted to a z-score using Table 32.4. This gives us z-scores of 1.405, 1.036 and 2.054 respectively. These z-scores are summed and divided by the square root of the number of z-scores using the above formula:

$$z = \frac{1.405 + 1.036 + 1.054}{\sqrt{3}}$$

$$= \frac{3.495}{1.732}$$

$$= 2.018$$

This average z is converted back into a significance level using Table 32.4. In this case, this gives a combined significance level of 0.022 (or 2.2%).

Note that if the findings of a study are in the *reverse* direction from those of the majority, the corresponding z-score is given a negative sign. Once again, this tends to reduce the overall significance level.

Step 7: Comparing effect sizes from studies with different characteristics

Finally, what if one wished to compare effect sizes between studies with different characteristics? For example, what if one wanted to know whether studies involving female participants differed from those involving male participants in terms of their effect size? The easiest way of doing this is to turn your data into a table like Table 32.6. In this table the effect sizes for the male and female studies are listed in separate columns. It is then a relatively simple matter to compare these two sets of effect size 'scores' using the Mann–Whitney U-test (Calculation 18.3) or the t-test (Calculation 13.1). This is an approximate procedure in the eyes of some experts since all studies are considered equal although they may differ in terms of the sample size. Despite criticisms of such an approach, it uses familiar statistics and may well be sufficiently powerful for most purposes.

Table 32.6 **Illustrating the comparison of effect sizes for different study characteristics**

Effect sizes of studies of males	Effect sizes of studies of females
0.27	0.41
0.15	0.52
0.22	0.43
0.29	0.47
Mean = 0.23	Mean = 0.45

There is a significant difference between these two groups as assessed by either the Mann-Whitney U-test or the unrelated t-test. Thus the effect sizes are greater in studies which involved female participants than in studies involving male participants. If you choose the t-test, it might be advantageous to convert your effect sizes to z_r values since this will reduce the undue influence of extreme values a little.

32.6 Illustrative example

There is evidence that men's physiological responses to sexually explicit pictures may differentiate sex offenders from non-offenders and non-sex offenders. Physiological response in these studies by plethysmographs which either measure changes in the volume of the penis or changes in the circumference of the penis. The latter measure is generally not well regarded. The data reported are fictitious but help to illustrate the processes involved in meta-analysis.

Step 1: Define the variables of interest to you

In this case the researchers wished to review the available studies which might indicate whether physiological responses to sexual images could be used to differentiate sex offenders from other men. Consequently the independent variable was sex offender versus non-offender or non-sex offender and the dependent variable was measured by scores on a plethysmograph assessment of the men's response to erotic pictures.

Step 2: Plan your database search

The researchers searched the psychological abstract database (PsychLit) and also the medical science database using the keywords plethysmograph, sex offender, rapist, paedophile and molester. Furthermore, as the field is relatively small, the researchers were able to write to one hundred researchers in the field requesting relevant research reports either published or unpublished.

Step 3: Obtain research reports

The researchers found nine studies from their database search to be obtained from their own or other university libraries. These are listed in column 1 of Table 32.7 but they also received two additional unpublished studies from their request to key researchers. Table 32.7 also includes information relevant to calculating the effect size gleaned from these reports and information about possible study variables.

Step 4: Calculating an effect size for each study

Table 32.7 lists the information obtained from each study relevant to calculating the effect size. The formula (or table) used is mentioned and the final column provides effect sizes expressed as r for each of the studies. Edwards's study, however, is so lacking in the statistical detail provided that it has been deleted by the meta-analysts.

Table 32.7 Illustrative summary of studies and the conversion of statistics to effect sizes

Study (fictitious)	Effect size information	Sig.	Plethysmograph measure	Control group	Effect size formula	Effect size r
Brown (1976)	Chi-square value given as 4.06 with 1 degree of freedom based on N of 73 cases	0.05	Circumference	Prisoners	$r = \sqrt{\dfrac{\text{Chi-square}}{N}}$	0.24
Grey (1998)	Gives effect size as r = 0.54	?	Volume	Prisoners	None needed	0.54
Black (1983)	F given as significant at 0.01 with 20 cases	0.01	Circumference	Prisoners	$r = \dfrac{z}{\sqrt{N}}$	0.52
White (1995)	t-value given as 2.31 with 34 cases (i.e. df = 32)	0.025	Volume	Non-prisoners	$r_{BIS} = \sqrt{\dfrac{t^2}{t^2 + df}}$	0.37
Jones (1966)	t-test reported as 1.45, df=54	0.10	Circumference	Non-prisoners	$r_{BIS} = \sqrt{\dfrac{t^2}{t^2 + df}}$	0.19
Williams (1987)	Mann-Whitney U significant at 1% level based on 47 cases	0.01	Circumference	Non-prisoners	$r = \dfrac{z}{\sqrt{N}}$	0.34
Parton (unpublished)	Related t = 2.53, df = 10, this was a matched design in which prisoners served as own control	0.025	Volume	Prisoners	$r_{BIS} = \sqrt{\dfrac{t^2}{t^2 + df}}$ (This formula works with related t-tests)	0.49
Carter (unpublished)	t = 1.67 with total N = 23	0.075	Circumference	Prisoners	$r_{BIS} = \sqrt{\dfrac{t^2}{t^2 + df}}$	0.34
Elliot (1999)	Cohen's d given as 0.45	0.001	Circumference	Prisoners	Convert to r with Table 32.2	0.22
Smith (1989)	F reported as significant at 0.03 with df = 1, 54 (i.e. N = 56)	0.03	Volume	Non-prisoners	$r = \dfrac{z}{\sqrt{N}}$	0.50
Edwards (1953)	t-value not reported. Findings not significant at 5% level with sample size 14	> 0.05 or set at p = 0.50	Circumference	Prisoners	Use of formula too crude because of uncertainty about exact significance and no other statistics (alternatively r could be set at 0.00)	Study ignored

Step 5: Combining effect sizes over a number of studies

The meta-analyst combined the effect sizes for all of the studies by converting each effect r into a z_r, averaging these, and finally converting back to an effect size. This involves turning each effect size correlation into a Fisher z_r using Table 32.5. The effect sizes in order are 0.24, 0.54, 0.52, 0.37, 0.19, 0.34, 0.49, 0.34, 0.22, 0.50 according to Table 32.7. Remember that the final study has been discarded from the analysis. The average of the corresponding z_rs is:

average z_r

$$= \frac{0.245 + 0.604 + 0.576 + 0.388 + 0.192 + 0.354 + 0.536 + 0.354 + 0.224 + 0.549}{10}$$

$$= \frac{4.022}{10}$$

$$= 0.4022$$

This value of z_r according to Table 32.5 corresponds to an average of the effect sizes of 0.40 (this is obtained by looking for the average z_r of 0.4022 in the body of Table 32.5 and reading off the value of r which corresponds to this value of the averaged z_r).

This process could be repeated to obtain, say, the overall effect size of the volume measure and the circumference measure separately.

Step 6: The significance of the combined studies

The overall significance of the combined studies is obtained by turning each significance level into the corresponding z-score using Table 32.4. The various z-scores are then summed and divided by the square root of the number (N) of significance levels employed. Note that for two studies the significance level is not reported or is not precise enough. Thus the calculation is based on just nine studies. The formula for z is:

$$z = \frac{\Sigma z}{\sqrt{N}}$$

This gives:

$$z = \frac{1.645 + 2.326 + 1.960 + 1.281 + 2.326 + 1.960 + 1.440 + 3.090 + 1.880}{\sqrt{9}}$$

$$= \frac{18.842}{3}$$

$$= 6.29$$

Remember that this is the value of z which has to be converted back to a significance level using Table 32.4. Thus the combined significance level is 0.001 or 0.1%.

Step 7: Comparing effect sizes from studies with different characteristics

Because there is some question whether the circumference measure is as good as the volume measure, the overall effect sizes were calculated for the circumference measure studies and the volume measure studies separately. This yielded the data in Table 32.8.

Table 32.8 **Effect size data for volume measures and circumference penile measures compared**

Effect sizes of studies involving volume measure	Effect sizes of studies involving circumference measure
0.54	0.24
0.37	0.52
0.49	0.19
0.50	0.34
	0.34
	0.22
Mean = 0.48	Mean = 0.37

Comparing these overall effect sizes, it would seem that there are some grounds for thinking that circumference studies produce the smallest effect size implying that they are inferior at identifying sex offenders from other men. This comparison is significant at only the 0.067 level with a Mann–Whitney test but significant at 0.04 with the unrelated t-test. Using z_r instead of the effect size made no substantial difference to the outcome. This seems reasonably strong evidence that the volume measure tends to produce greater effects than the circumference measures.

A similar analysis comparing the effect of having a prisoner versus a non-prisoner control group showed no significant difference in terms of effect size using the same tests of significance.

32.7 Comparing a study with a previous study

Meta-analysis is useful when you are replicating another researcher's study as it provides a method of combining the results of the two studies. Furthermore, you can test to see if your effect size is significantly different from that found in the previous research. The formula involves converting each effect size to z_r using Table 32.5 and then subtracting one from the other and making other calculations involving N (the sample sizes) as in the following formula:

$$z = \frac{r_1 - r_2}{\sqrt{\dfrac{1}{N_1 - 3} + \dfrac{1}{N_2 - 3}}}$$

Thus if the effect sizes under consideration are 0.43 (with $N = 25$) and 0.62 (with $N = 47$) then these are first converted to z_r using Table 32.5. This gives us values of 0.460 and 0.725. The calculation is then:

$$z = \frac{0.460 - 0.725}{\sqrt{\dfrac{1}{25 - 3} + \dfrac{1}{47 - 3}}}$$

$$= \frac{-0.265}{\sqrt{\dfrac{1}{22} + \dfrac{1}{44}}}$$

$$= \frac{-0.265}{\sqrt{0.0455 + 0.0227}}$$

$$= \frac{-0.265}{\sqrt{0.0682}}$$

$$= \frac{-0.265}{0.261}$$

$$= 1.015$$

This value of z (*not* z_r) is turned into a significance level by using Table 32.4. This gives a probability value of 0.15 (or 15%) which is not statistically significant. Our conclusion in this case would be that the effect sizes of the two studies are similar and certainly not significantly different from each other. We could go on to report the effect size of the combined studies and the combined significance levels using the methods described above.

32.8 Notes and recommendations

■ This account of meta-analysis should convince you of the importance of reporting effect sizes for all studies you carry out. The most useful effect size formula is simply the Pearson's correlation coefficient between two variables.
■ When carrying out a literature review, it is a positive advantage to report the effect sizes for all of the important studies. This is more important than reporting statistical significance alone.

■ Experience will show that the difference between significant and non-significant findings can be very small indeed when their effect sizes are compared. Consequently you need to consider near-significant results carefully when evaluating the research literature.

Recommendation for further reading

Rosenthal, R. (1991). *Meta-analytic Procedures for Social Research*. Newbury Park, CA: Sage, especially chapters 1–4.

Chapter 33

Reliability in scales and measurement

Consistency and agreement

Preparation

The concept of correlation (Chapter 7) is an essential prerequisite to understanding the assessment of reliability. Chapter 21 on the correlated scores analysis of variance and Chapter 27 on factor analysis may also help with particular sections of this chapter.

33.1 Internal consistency of scales and measurements

An important role for statistics is in assessing the adequacy of psychological scales and measures. Usually in psychology, but not always, measures consist of several different components added together to give a total score on that measure. Thus many attitude and personality tests consist of a large number of questionnaire items which are combined to give a total score on some dimension of attitude or personality. Although the analysis of such scales using factor analysis (Chapter 27) is an important and necessary part of modern psychological test and measure construction, factor analysis is not the only approach to understanding the structure of a test or measure. In many circumstances a researcher may be concerned simply to obtain a fairly general measure of a particular psychological variable. In these circumstances, relatively simple checks on the structure of the measure may suffice. So, for example, a questionnaire designed to measure 'love' for one's partner might consist of several different questions. The researcher might wish to know the extent to which the items measure much the same thing. Generally speaking, if the items measure aspects of love then we would expect that they would intercorrelate with each other to a modest level at least. However, since it is the overall or total score on the measure of love which matters then we would expect:

1. That scores on each item correlate with the total score (this is item–total or item–whole correlation).

2. That a score based on half of the items of the scale would correlate with

scores based on the remainder of the scale (this is called split-half reliability which can be elaborated into Cronbach's coefficient alpha).

The procedures described in this chapter are about the *internal consistency* of psychological measures. Internal consistency is the extent to which all of the items constituting a measure are measuring much the same thing. If they are measuring similar things each item should correlate with the other items in the measure. Although this is referred to as reliability, it is a very different matter from reliability between two different points in time, for example.

Table 33.1 Data from ten cases from a four-item questionnaire

Person	Item 1	Item 2	Item 3	Item 4	Total score
1	1	3	5	6	15
2	2	1	1	2	6
3	1	1	1	1	4
4	5	2	4	2	13
5	6	4	3	2	15
6	5	4	5	6	20
7	4	5	3	2	14
8	2	1	2	1	6
9	1	2	1	1	5
10	1	1	2	2	6

33.2 Item-analysis using item–total correlation

Look at Table 33.1 It contains scores on four different items for ten different participants. There is also a total score given in the 'total' column consisting of the scores on each of Item 1, Item 2, Item 3 and Item 4. So the second participant has a total score of $2 + 1 + 1 + 2 = 6$. The correlations between the scores of the ten participants for Item 1 and the total score can be calculated with the Pearson correlation formula (Calculation 7.1). The value of the correlation is 0.74 which suggests that Item 1, for example, is a fairly good measure of what the total score on the measure is measuring.

Generally speaking, we would be happy with this scale given the relatively high item–total or item–whole correlation.

Table 33.2 Correlations of items with the total score on the scale

	Correlation with total score	Correlation with total score excluding item in question
Item 1	0.74	0.49
Item 2	0.84	0.71
Item 3	0.91	0.84
Item 4	0.76	0.55

Notice that when an item is excluded from the total score, its correlation with this adjusted total score is reduced. Thus, in Table 33.2 the correlation of Item 1 with the total score (based on summing Items 2, 3 and 4) is 0.49 as opposed to a correlation of 0.74 when all items are included. This more refined analysis does nothing to revise our opinion of the scale. Generally speaking, the items which seem to be the poorest are Items 1 and 4 which have the lowest item–total correlations.

Of course, four-item scales are unusual in psychological research. Normally we have many items. If we had a lot more items, we might be inclined to try to shorten the scale a little. The technique for doing this is simple. Delete the low-correlating items and re-do the analysis based on the shortened scale. Although our example is a short scale, if we wanted to reduce its length then we would probably wish to delete Item 1 since it has the worst correlation with the total score.

Table 33.3 gives the outcome of shortening the scale in this way. You will see that compared to the correlations in Table 33.2, the shortened scale has increased item–total correlations. In this sense, a better scale has been achieved by shortening it. The difficulty is that we can carry on deleting items and improving the internal consistency of the items but this may result in a shorter scale than we want. Usually it is best to exclude only the poorest of items. By doing so we leave a scale which covers a wide range of the aspects of the thing being measured. The appropriate scale length involves a degree of judgement.

A standard statistical package such as SPSS reduces the work in calculating item–total (item–whole) correlations of various sorts and makes shortening the number of items in the scale easy.

Table 33.3 **Correlations of shortened-scale items with the total score on that scale**

	Correlation with total score	Correlation with total score excluding item in question
Item 2	0.77	0.56
Item 3	0.94	0.87
Item 4	0.90	0.73

The results of this analysis can be written up as follows: 'An item–whole analysis was carried out on the items on the scale. As can be seen from Table 33.2, each item had a satisfactory correlation with the total score on all of the items combined. After the item–whole correlations had been recalculated with the item removed from the total score, there was a decline in the item–whole correlations. However, the relationships remained substantial and it was decided not to shorten the scale given that it consists of just four items.'

33.3 Split-half reliability

A computationally less demanding way of assessing the internal structure of a questionnaire is split-half reliability. Remember that internal reliability refers to the extent to which all of the items in a questionnaire (or similar measure) are assessing much the same thing. Split-half reliability simply involves computing scores based on half of the items and scores based on the other half of the items. The correlation between the scores for these two halves is the split-half reliability (more-or-less, but read on).

There are no rules for deciding which of the items should be in which half. There are common practices, however. Odd–even reliability is based on taking the odd-numbered items (1, 3, 5, etc.) as one set and the even-numbered items (2, 4, 6, etc.) as the other set. Alternatively, the first half of the items could be correlated with the second half. But there would be nothing against selecting the halves at random.

Calculation 33.1

Split-half reliability

Taking the data in Table 33.1, we could sum Items 1 and 2 for the total of the first half and sum Items 3 and 4 for the total of the second half. The correlation between the two halves is 0.477.

There is a further step. The difficulty is that we are correlating a scale half the length of our original scale with another scale half the length of our scale. Because of this, the reliability will be lower than for the full-length scale. Fortunately, it is quite easy to compute the reliability of a full scale from the reliability of half of the scale using the following formula:

$$\text{Full scale reliability} = \frac{2r_{hh}}{1 + r_{hh}}$$

Since we know the reliability of the half scale (r_{hh}) is 0.477, then the full scale reliability is:

$$\text{Full scale reliability} = \frac{2 \times 0.4771}{1 + 0.477}$$

$$= \frac{0.954}{1.477}$$

$$= 0.65$$

Thus the value of the split-half reliability is 0.65 when corrected to the full scale length. Standard computer statistics packages such as SPSS do most of the hard work for you.

> **Reporting the results** The results of this analysis may be written up as follows: 'The split-half reliability of the scale was found to be 0.65. This is a somewhat low value but given the exploratory nature of this research, the scale was nevertheless employed.' (As a rule of thumb, a value of about 0.8 or above would generally be seen as adequate evidence of reliability for general use.)

33.4 Alpha reliability

There is a problem with split-half reliability – its value will depend on which items are selected for each half. The odd–even reliability will not be the same as that found by comparing the first half of the items with the second half, for example. There is an obvious solution: calculate every possible split-half reliability having every possible combination of items in each half and then simply take the average of these. The average of all possible split-half reliabilities from a scale is known as *coefficient alpha*. We will calculate this from first principles and an alternative approach based on the analysis of variance.

Table 33.4 contains all of the possible ways of splitting four items into two halves. There are only three different ways of doing this with our short scale:

1. The total of Items 1 and 2 compared with the total of Items 3 and 4.
2. The total of Items 1 and 3 compared with the total of Items 2 and 4.
3. The total of Items 1 and 4 compared with the total of Items 2 and 3.

The reliability coefficients for these three different possibilities are to be found in Table 33.5. The average of the split-half coefficients corrected (adjusted) for length is coefficient alpha. So the average of 0.642 + 0.844 + 0.946 (or

Table 33.4 **Scores for all possible split-halves from four items**

Person	Split-half version 1		Split-half version 2		Split-half version 3	
	Items 1+2	Items 3+4	Items 1+3	Items 2+4	Items 1+4	Items 2+3
1	4	11	6	9	7	8
2	3	3	3	3	4	2
3	2	2	2	2	2	2
4	7	6	9	4	7	6
5	10	5	9	6	8	7
6	9	11	10	10	11	9
7	9	5	7	7	6	8
8	3	3	4	2	3	3
9	3	2	2	3	2	3
10	2	4	3	3	3	3

coefficient alpha) is 0.81. It is generally accepted that a coefficient alpha of 0.8 or above is satisfactory for psychological research.

This calculation may be feasible with a short scale of four items and a sample of ten individuals, but what, say, if the scale consisted of 100 items? The number of ways of sorting these 100 items into two separate sets of 50 is huge. Obviously the conceptually correct approach given so far would take too much computation time. The alternative hand-computation method is not quite so cumbersome but still time consuming. Basically it involves carrying out one-way analysis of variance for correlated scores on the data on each of the items. Thus the data would look like Table 33.6. Following through the procedure described under Calculation 21.1 would lead to the ANOVA summary table presented in Table 33.7. Values from this table are then substituted in the following computational formula for coefficient alpha:

$$\text{Coefficient alpha} = \frac{\text{Between-people variance} - \text{Error variance}}{\text{Between-people variance}}$$

$$= \frac{7.84 - 1.44}{7.84}$$

$$= \frac{6.40}{7.84}$$

$$= 0.82 \text{ (there is slight rounding error)}$$

This would be generally accepted as evidence of a satisfactory level of internal consistency since coefficients alpha above 0.8 are regarded as sufficient. The results of this analysis may be written up as follows: 'coefficient alpha was calculated for the scale and found to be 0.82 which is generally accepted to be satisfactory.'

It should be fairly obvious that hand-calculation of coefficient alpha even with this ANOVA method has little to recommend it. It might be useful to anyone who has access to a computer program for the correlated ANOVA but not to one which computes coefficient alpha directly. It need hardly be said that the use of a computer package such as SPSS which includes coefficient alpha is highly recommended.

Table 33.5   Correlations between split-halves and with corrections for shortened length

	Pearson correlation	Corrected for scale length
Items 1 + 2 with Items 3 + 4	0.477	0.642
Items 1 + 3 with Items 2 + 4	0.730	0.844
Items 1 + 4 with Items 2 + 3	0.898	0.946

Table 33.6 **Data on four-item questionnaire for ten cases arranged as for correlated one-way ANOVA**

Person	Item 1	Item 2	Item 3	Item 4
1	1	3	5	6
2	2	1	1	2
3	1	1	1	1
4	5	2	4	2
5	6	4	3	2
6	5	4	5	6
7	4	5	3	2
8	2	1	2	1
9	1	2	1	1
10	1	1	2	2
Cell mean	2.8	2.0	2.7	2.5

Table 33.7 **ANOVA summary table on four-item questionnaire data**

Source of variation	Sum of squares	Degrees of freedom	Mean square (or variance estimate)	F-ratio	Probability (significance)
Between treatments (i.e. between items)	1.00	3	Not needed	Not needed	Not needed
Between people (i.e. individual differences)	70.60	9	7.84		
Error (i.e. residual)	40.00	27	1.48		

33.5 Agreement between raters

Not all research involves psychological scales. Some research involves ratings by a pair of judges or even a panel of judges or assessors. Sometimes rating is used because it is felt that self-completion questionnaires might be inappropriate. Let us take the concept of dangerousness, i.e. the risk posed to members of the public by the release of sex offenders or mental hospital patients. One might be very unhappy about using self-completion questionnaires in these circumstances. It might be considered preferable to have expert clinical psychologists, forensic psychologists and psychiatrists interview the sex offenders or patients to assess the dangerousness of these people on release into the community. Let us assume that we have one clinical psychologist, one forensic psychologist and one psychiatrist who are used in a study of twelve sex offenders. Having interviewed each offender, read all case notes and obtained any further information they required, each of the three professionals rates each offender on a three-point dangerousness index:

■   a rating of 1 means that there is no risk to the public
■   a rating of 2 means that there is a moderate risk to the public
■   a rating of 3 means that there is a high risk to the public.

Their ratings of the twelve offenders are shown in Table 33.8.

Table 33.8 **The data from the three professionals for each of the twelve sex offenders**

	Clinical psychologist	**Forensic psychologist**	**Psychiatrist**
Offender 1	2	3	3
Offender 2	3	3	3
Offender 3	3	3	3
Offender 4	1	1	1
Offender 5	2	1	2
Offender 6	3	3	3
Offender 7	1	2	3
Offender 8	1	3	3
Offender 9	2	2	3
Offender 10	3	3	3
Offender 11	3	3	3
Offender 12	2	3	3

Table 33.9 **Correlations between the ratings of various professions**

	Forensic psychologist	**Psychiatrist**
Clinical psychologist	0.55	0.44
Forensic psychologist		0.83

Table 33.9 shows the Pearson correlations between the ratings of the three professionals. The figures seem to suggest a very high level of relationship between the forensic psychologist's and the psychiatrist's ratings. A correlation of 0.83 is, after all, a very strong relationship. The difficulty with this only becomes apparent when we examine Table 33.10 which gives agreements between the forensic psychologist and the psychiatrist. This is constructed by tabulating the forensic psychologist's ratings against those of the psychiatrist. The frequencies in the diagonal represent agreements, all other frequencies represent a degree of disagreement.

Table 33.10 **Agreements and disagreements between the forensic psychologist and the psychiatrist on ratings of sex offenders**

Forensic psychologist's ratings	Psychiatrist's ratings		
	1	2	3
1	1	1	0
2	0	0	2
3	0	0	8

At first sight it still might appear that there is strong agreement between the two sets of ratings. A total of nine out of the twelve ratings suggest perfect agreement. So what is the problem? A closer examination of Table 33.10 suggests that virtually all of the agreement occurs when the two experts rate the sex offender as a high risk to the public (rating 3). For the other two ratings they agree only one time out of four. This is a much lower level of agreement. Of course, if the experts rated all of the offenders as a high risk to the public then the agreement would be perfect – although they would not appear to be discriminating among levels of risk. If it were decided to release only sex offenders rated as a low risk to the public, only one sex offender would be released on the basis of the combined ratings of the psychiatrist and forensic psychologist. In other words, correlation coefficients are not very helpful when the exact agreement of raters is required.

The index of agreement between raters   needs to have the following characteristics:

1. It provides an index of the extent of overlap of ratings.
2. It should be sensitive to the problem that agreement is rather meaningless if both raters are using only one rating and do not vary their ratings.

Kappa is a useful index of agreement between a pair of raters since it is responsive to both of these things.

The kappa coefficient is calculated from the following formula:

$$\text{Kappa} = \frac{\text{Total frequency of agreement} - \text{Expected total frequency of agreement by chance}}{\text{Number of things rated} - \text{Expected total frequency of agreement by chance}}$$

Kappa can take negative values if the raters agree at less than chance level. It is zero if there is no agreement greater or lesser than chance. Coefficients approaching +1.00 indicate very good agreement between the raters.

Calculation 33.2

Kappa coefficient

The above data on the ratings of the forensic psychologist and the psychiatrist will be used to calculate kappa for their ratings.

Step 1 Draw-up a crosstabulation table of the data for the two raters and insert the marginal totals (i.e. the sum of frequencies for each row, the sum of frequencies for each column and the overall sum.) This is shown in Table 33.11.

Table 33.11 **Agreements and disagreements between the forensic psychologist and the psychiatrist on ratings of sex offenders with marginal totals added**

Forensic psychologist's ratings	Psychiatrist's ratings			Marginal totals
	1	2	3	
1	**1**	1	0	2
2	0	**0**	2	2
3	0	0	**8**	8
Marginal totals	1	1	10	Total = 12

Step 2 Calculate the frequencies of agreement. These are the frequencies in the diagonal of Table 33.11. They have been given in **bold**. So the frequency of agreements is $1 + 0 + 8 = 9$.

Step 3 Calculate the expected frequency of agreement by firstly calculating the following for each of the diagonals:

$$\text{Expected frequency} = \frac{\text{Column total} \times \text{Row total}}{\text{Total}}$$

Thus the expected frequency of agreement for ratings of 3 is the product of the column total of 10 and the row total of 8 divided by the overall total of 12. This is 80/12 or 6.667. Table 33.12 contains the results of these calculations.

Table 33.12 **Expected frequencies for agreement**

Forensic psychologist's ratings	Psychiatrist's ratings			Marginal totals
	1	2	3	
1	**0.167**			2
2	0	**0.167**	2	2
3	0	0	**6.667**	8
Marginal totals	1	1	10	Total = 12

Step 4 The expected total frequency of agreement by chance is therefore $0.167 + 0.167 + 6.667 = 7.001$.

Step 5 We can then substitute the values in the formula:

$$\text{Kappa} = \frac{\text{Total frequency of agreement} - \text{Expected total frequency of agreement by chance}}{\text{Number of things rated} - \text{Expected total frequency of agreement by chance}}$$

$$= \frac{9 - 7.001}{12 - 7.001}$$

$$= \frac{1.999}{4.999}$$

$$= 0.40$$

Interpreting the results Notice that although the actual agreement seems high at nine of the twelve ratings, coefficient kappa implies fairly low agreement. This reflects the relative lack of variability in the expert's ratings and the tendency for both to rate the offenders as 3 rather than any other value. Consequently, we can appreciate that coefficient kappa is superior to the simple proportion of agreement in assessing the reliability of ratings.

Reporting the results The results of this analysis can be written up as follows: 'Coefficient kappa was calculated on the relationship between the forensic psychologist's and the psychiatrist's ratings of dangerous. Despite there being a high level of agreement overall, it was found that kappa was only 0.4 suggesting that much of the apparent agreement was in fact due to both professionals using the highest dangerousness rating much of the time.'

33.6 Notes and recommendations

■ Although the methods employed in calculating internal reliability are straightforward, great care is needed to differentiate between internal reliability as assessed by the methods described in this chapter and measures of external reliability which are very different. External reliability includes the correlation between scores on a measure at two different points in time (i.e. test–retest reliability).

■ The difference between a correlation between scores and agreement between scores is very important. Remember that there can be a strong correlation between two variables with absolutely no match in the scores.

Recommended further reading

Tinsley, H.E.A. and Weiss D.J. (1975). Interrater reliability and agreement of subjective judgments. *Journal of Counselling Psychology*, **22**, 358–376.

Chapter 34

Confidence intervals

Preparation

Read the previous discussions of confidence intervals in Chapters 8 and 9. Revise the concepts of standard error and sampling distributions from Chapters 11 and 13.

34.1 Introduction

The concept of confidence intervals was described briefly in earlier chapters. Although confidence intervals have been used in psychological statistics for many years, recently their greater use has been advocated. More radically, it has been proposed that confidence intervals should replace statistical significance testing. However, both are informative approaches to statistical analysis and likely to coexist for a good many years. This chapter provides some information on the computation of confidence intervals for a variety of statistics already discussed. Despite the fact that any measure based on a sample has a confidence interval in theory, methods of calculating confidence intervals are not easily available for many statistical procedures.

Confidence intervals concern the estimates of population characteristics (parameters) based on a sample or samples taken from that population. The characteristics of samples tend to vary somewhat from the characteristics of the population from which they came – and from each other (Chapter 13). Consequently, estimates of the characteristics of a population based on a sample drawn from that population are unlikely to be exact. Nevertheless, they remain the best estimates we can have when ignorant of the exact details of the population. In previous chapters, we have used *point-estimates* of population parameters based on sample statistics. A point-estimate is merely a single figure estimate as opposed to a range. Thus if the mean of a sample is 5.3 then the point-estimate of the mean of the population is 5.3. Since this point-estimate is only our best guess from the characteristics of the sample, usually it only approximates the true population mean.

The alternative to point-estimates, the *confidence interval* approach, acknowledges the approximate nature of the point-estimate more directly. Confidence intervals give the range of values likely to include the population value. This range of likely values is called the confidence interval since it reflects the range of values likely to include the true population mean (if we only knew this). Thus, instead of saying that our estimate of the population mean is 5.3, we say that the population mean is likely to be in the range 4.0–6.6. By expressing our inference or estimate in this way, we reinforce the notion of uncertainty as to the precise value. So a confidence interval is simply the range of values of a statistic such as the mean or correlation which is likely to contain the true population mean. The size of the confidence interval will depend on the variability of scores. The more variable the scores in a sample, the larger the confidence interval has to be for any level of confidence.

There is an obvious problem with confidence intervals. We can never be absolutely certain how different a sample mean is from the mean of the population from which it was drawn (if we are basing our estimate on a sample). Consequently the following strategy is adopted. We state the range of sample means that includes (usually) the most likely 95% of sample means drawn at random from the population. In other words, the 95% confidence interval is the range of values we are 95% certain includes the 'true' population mean.

Chapter 13 explained how we take the characteristics of a sample to infer the most likely characteristics of the population from which that sample was taken. Furthermore, we can even calculate the distributions of samples taken from that inferred population. Remember that the *standard error* is the usual index of the amount of variability in sample means drawn at random from a population. Standard error is simply the standard deviation of sample means. The calculation

Table 34.1 **Table of t-values for 95% and 99% confidence intervals**

Degrees of freedom	t for 95% confidence	t for 99% confidence	Degrees of freedom	t for 95% confidence	t for 99% confidence
1	12.71	63.66	17	2.11	2.90
2	4.30	9.93	18	2.10	2.88
3	3.18	5.84	19	2.09	2.86
4	2.78	4.60	20	2.09	2.85
5	2.57	4.03	25	2.06	2.79
6	2.45	3.71	30	2.04	2.75
7	2.37	3.50	35	2.03	2.72
8	2.31	3.36	40	2.02	2.70
9	2.26	3.25	45	2.01	2.69
10	2.23	3.17	50	2.01	2.68
11	2.20	3.11	60	2.00	2.66
12	2.18	3.06	70	1.99	2.65
13	2.16	3.01	80	1.99	2.64
14	2.15	2.98	90	1.99	2.63
15	2.13	2.95	100	1.98	2.63
16	2.12	2.92	∞	1.96	2.58

Note: If the required number of degrees of freedom is missing, take the nearest lower number.

of standard error is a crucial phase in estimating confidence intervals for all parametric tests.

Normal distribution theory (Chapter 11) tells us that for *large* samples, 95% of sample means lie within plus or minus 1.96 standard deviations from the population mean. Thus if the standard error for samples has been calculated as 2.6, then 95% of sample means lie between –5.096 and +5.096 ($1.96 \times 2.6 = 5.096$) of the mean of our sample (i.e. the estimate of the population mean). If the sample mean is 10.00 then the confidence interval lies between 10.00 ± 5.096. That is, the confidence interval is between 4.934 and 15.096. Since this covers 95% of the most likely sample means, it is known as the 95% confidence interval. In other words, the 95% confidence interval is 4.93 to 15.10.

Confidence intervals can be set at other levels such as 99%. The more stringent 99% confidence interval involves multiplying the standard error by $2.576 = 2.576 \times 2.6 = 6.698$. The resulting 99% confidence interval would be 10.00 (the sample mean) plus and minus 6.698, or 3.30 to 16.70. So the more confident we want to be, the larger the confidence interval is. We can use tables of the z-distribution to work out other confidence intervals but the 95% and 99% are fairly conventional.

However, with small samples the z-distribution does not work perfectly. It is more usual to use the distribution of t (which is identical to that of z for large samples). With small samples, the value of t corresponding to our chosen confidence interval would be obtained from Table 34.1. This is distributed by the degrees of freedom. Thus if the degrees of freedom for a particular sample were 20, then the value of t for 95% confidence is 2.06 (from Table 34.1). So the confidence interval would be 2.06×2.6 on either side of the estimated population mean. That is, the 95% confidence interval would be to 4.64 to 15.36. The degrees of freedom will vary according to the statistical estimate in question.

Sometimes the concept *confidence limits* is used. Confidence limits are merely the extreme values of the *confidence interval*. In the above example, the 95% confidence limits are 4.64 and 15.36.

While this introduction explains confidence intervals in principle, their calculation varies from this pattern for some statistics.

34.2 The relationship between significance and confidence intervals

At first sight, statistical significance and confidence intervals appear dissimilar concepts. This is incorrect since they are both based on much the same inferential process. Remember that in significance testing we usually test the null hypothesis of no relationship between two variables. This usually boils down to a zero (or near-zero) correlation or to a difference of zero (or near-zero) between sample means. If the confidence interval does not contain this zero value then the obtained sample mean is statistically significant at 100% minus the confidence level. So if the 95% confidence interval is 2.30 to 8.16 but the null hypothesis would predict the population value of the statistic to be 0.00, then the null hypothesis is rejected at the 5% level of significance. In other words, confidence intervals contain enough information to judge statistical significance. However, statistical significance alone does not contain enough information to calculate confidence intervals.

Calculation 34.1

Confidence intervals for a population mean based on a single sample

Step 1   Calculate the standard error of the scores in the sample. The stages in doing this are given in Calculation 11.1. You will also need to calculate the mean of the sample and the degrees of freedom (i.e. sample size – 1).

Step 2   For the data in Table 11.1, the standard error is 0.58, the estimated population mean (the sample mean) is 5.00, and the degrees of freedom are 6 – 1 = 5 degrees of freedom.

Step 3   Decide what confidence level you require. We will use the 95% level. This is the minimum value of confidence in general use. If it was especially important that your confidence interval included the true population mean than you could use the 99% level or even the 99.9% level.

Step 4   Use Table 34.1 to find the value of t corresponding to the 95% confidence level. You need the row for the appropriate number of degrees of freedom (i.e. $N - 1 = 5$). This value of t is 2.57. Table 34.1 is merely a version of the table of the t-distribution that appears elsewhere in the book. It is included as some will find it initially less confusing to be able to look up the values directly.

Step 5   Calculate the confidence interval. It is the sample mean $\pm$ t × the standard error:

Step 6   Therefore, the 95% confidence interval for the population mean is 5.00 $\pm$ 2.57 × 0.58. This gives us a 95% confidence interval of 3.51 to 6.49.

Reporting the results   The results of this analysis may be written up as follows: 'The 95% confidence interval for the population mean was 3.51 to 6.49. As this interval does not include 0.00 then the null hypothesis that the sample comes from a population with a mean of 0.00 can be rejected at the 5% level of significance.'

Calculation 34.2

Confidence intervals for the unrelated t-test

Step 1 As most of the major steps in calculating the confidence interval involve steps in the calculation of the unrelated t-test, use Calculation 13.1 to calculate the necessary values.

Step 2 Make a note of the difference between the two sample means, the degrees of freedom $(N + N - 2)$, and the standard error of the difference between two sample means. For the example in Calculation 13.1 (Table 13.9), the difference between the sample means = 3.917, the degrees of freedom = 20 and the standard error = 1.392.

Step 3 Decide what level of confidence you require. This time we will use the 99% level of confidence.

Step 4 From Table 34.1, the t-value for 99% confidence with 20 degrees of freedom = 2.09.

Step 5 The confidence interval is obtained by taking the difference between the two sample means $\pm t \times$ the standard error.

Step 6 Thus the 99% confidence interval for the population of differences between sample means = 3.917 $\pm$ 2.09 $\times$ 1.392. Therefore the 99% confidence interval is 3.917 plus and minus 2.91 which gives a 99% confidence interval of 1.01 to 6.83.

Reporting the results The results of this analysis can be written up as follows: 'The 99% confidence interval for the difference in emotionality scores in two-parent and lone-parent families is 1.01 to 6.83. Since the null hypothesis holds that this difference is 0.00 then we can reject the null hypothesis at the 1% level of significance since the confidence interval does not include the value 0.00. The hypothesis that emotionality is different in two-parent and lone-parent families is supported at the 1% level of significance.'

Calculation 34.3

Related t-test

Step 1 Follow the calculation of the related t-test as described in Calculation 12.1. We will use that data to obtain the 95% confidence interval for the difference between the means.

Step 2 Make a note of the difference between the sample means, the degrees of freedom, and the standard error for your data. Calculation 12.1 yields a value of the difference between the sample means of –1.50, a standard error of the difference of 0.756 with 7 degrees of freedom.

Step 3 Decide what level of confidence you require. This time we are using the 95% level of confidence.

Step 4 From Table 34.1, the *t*-value for 95% confidence with 7 degrees of freedom = 2.37.

Step 5 The confidence interval is obtained by taking the difference between the two sample means ± the *t*-value × the standard error, i.e.

$$-0.15 \pm 2.37 \times 0.756$$
$$= -0.15 \pm 1.79$$
$$= -1.94 \text{ to } 1.54$$

Step 6 Thus the 95% confidence interval for the population of differences between sample means is –1.94 to 1.54.

Reporting the results   The results of this analysis can be written up as follows: 'The 95% confidence interval for the difference in eye contact at six months and nine months was –1.94 to 1.54. According to the null hypothesis this difference should be 0.00. Consequently, as this value is included in the 95% confidence interval then the null hypothesis is supported and the alternative hypothesis that eye contact is related to age is rejected.'

Calculation 34.4

Pearson correlation coefficient

Step 1 The calculation of the Pearson correlation coefficient is described in Calculation 7.1. Work through these steps for your data or compute the value of *r* using a computer.

Step 2 Make a note of the value of the correlation coefficient and the sample size. For the data in Table 7.1 the value of the correlation coefficient is –0.90 and the sample size is   10. We do *not* require the degrees of freedom for calculating the confidence interval for a Pearson correlation coefficient.

Step 3 To calculate the confidence interval, it is necessary to convert the correlation coefficient to its z_r using Table 32.5. Note that z_r is the Fisher normalised correlation coefficient. This table gives a value of z_r for a correlation of –0.90 as –1.472. The negative sign is added because the correlation is negative.

Step 4 The standard deviation of z_r is obtained using the formula:

$$\text{Standard deviation of } z_r = \frac{1}{\sqrt{N-3}}$$

Given that in our example the sample size N is 10, the standard deviation according to this formula is:

$$\text{Standard deviation of } z_r = \frac{1}{10-3}$$

$$= \frac{1}{\sqrt{7}}$$

$$= \frac{1}{2.646}$$

$$= 0.378$$

This standard deviation is distributed as for z so that the 95% confidence interval is 1.96 × the standard deviation. Thus the 95% confidence interval of z_r is the value of z_r for the correlation coefficient ± 1.96 × 0.378. That is, in our example, −1.472 ± 0.741. Therefore the 95% confidence interval for z_r is −0.731 to −2.213.

Step 5 The above is the confidence interval for z_r rather than for the original correlation coefficient. We can use Table 32.5 to convert this z_r back to the range of correlation coefficients. Thus the 95% confidence interval for the correlation coefficient is −0.62 to −0.97.

Interpreting the results You will notice that this confidence interval is *not* symmetrical around the sample correlation of −0.90. The correlation coefficient is not a linear variable so it cannot be added and divided as if it were. Hence the transformation to z_r which has linear characteristics.

Reporting the results The results of this analyis can be written up as follows. 'The 95% confidence interval for the Pearson correlation between musical and mathematical ability was −0.62 to −0.97. The null hypothesis suggests that this relationship will be 0.00. Since the value under the null-hypothesis was not included in the confidence interval, the null hypothesis of no relationship between musical and mathematical ability was rejected in favour of the alternative hypothesis that there is a negative correlation between mathematical and musical ability.'

34.3 Regression

There are several confidence intervals for even a simple regression analysis since regression involves several estimates of population parameters – the slope of the regression line, the cut point for the vertical axis and the predicted score from scores on the X variable.

Calculation 34.5

Confidence intervals for a predicted score

Step 1 Carry out the simple regression analysis according to Calculation 8.1. This will give the slope and the intercept (cut point) of the regression line. These can be used to calculate the most likely value of variable Y from a particular value of variable X. For a value of $X = 8$, the best prediction of Y is 3.37 for the data in Table 8.2.

Step 2 Calculate the Pearson correlation between variable X and variable Y in Table 8.2 using Calculation 7.1. This gives r as 0.616.

Step 3 Calculate the standard deviation of the Y variable scores using Calculation 5.1. The standard deviation of the Y scores is 1.72.

Step 4 Using the information calculated in the previous three steps, the standard error of the estimate of Y from a particular value of X is given by the following formula:

$$\text{Standard error of estimate of } Y = \text{sd of } Y \times \sqrt{\frac{1 - r^2}{N - 2}}$$

$$= 1.72 \times \sqrt{\frac{1 - 0.6115^2}{5 - 2}}$$

$$= 1.72 \times \sqrt{\frac{1 - 0.3788}{3}}$$

$$= 1.72 \times \sqrt{\frac{0.6212}{3}}$$

$$= 1.72 \times \sqrt{0.2071}$$

$$= 1.72 \times 0.4550$$

$$= 0.78$$

Step 5 This standard error can be converted to the confidence interval by multiplying the value of the standard error by the appropriate value of t. The degrees of freedom for this are $N - 2$. Table 34.1 indicates that the t-value for $N - 2$ or 3 degrees of freedom is 3.18 for the 95% confidence interval. This gives us a value of the confidence interval around the predicted Y score of 3.37 of $\pm 0.78 \times 3.18 = \pm 2.48$. Thus we can be 95% sure that the population value of Y predicted from X is within the range of 0.89 to 5.85.

Interpreting the results Of course, the confidence interval will vary numerically according to which X score is being used to predict Y. The size of the interval between the upper and lower confidence limits though does not vary. This is because the standard error is an average for all estimated Y scores.

Reporting the results The results of this analysis can be written up as follows: 'The 95% confidence interval for predicting musical ability from maths score was 0.89 to 5.85 for a point-prediction of 3.37.'

34.4 Other confidence intervals

In theory, any statistic (i.e. characteristic of a sample) will have a sampling distribution and, hence, a confidence interval. In practice, however, these can be obscure or unavailable.

34.5 Notes and recommendations

■ Confidence intervals for many statistical estimates are not easily obtained. Do not expect to find unusual confidence intervals explained in other than relatively difficult sources.

■ Standard statistical packages routinely calculate standard errors from which confidence intervals are relatively easy to derive.

Chapter 35

The analysis of complex contingency tables

Log-linear methods

Preparation

If you are hazy about contingency tables then look back to the discussion in Chapter 6. Also revise chi-square (Chapter 14) since it is involved in log-linear analyses. Log-linear shares concepts such as main effect and interaction with ANOVA which ought to be reviewed as general preparation (especially Chapter 22).

35.1 Introduction

In essence, log-linear methods are used for the analysis of complex contingency (or crosstabulation) tables. Data in Chapter 14 which were analysed using chi-square could be subjected to log-linear procedures although with no particular benefits. Log-linear goes further than this and comes into its own when dealing with three or more independent variables. Log-linear analysis identifies how the independent variables acting alone or in combination influence the frequencies in the cells of the contingency table. The frequencies can be regarded as if they are the dependent variable.

Some basic concepts need to be introduced:

■ *Interactions.* Like analysis of variance (ANOVA), log-linear analysis uses the concept of interactions between two or more independent variables. The concept is a little difficult to understand at first. It refers to the effects of the independent variables that cannot be explained by the effects of these independent variables acting separately. Much of this chapter is devoted to explaining the concept in more detail.

■ *Models.* A model in log-linear analysis is a statement (which can be expressed as a formula) which explains how the independent variables such as sex, age and social class result in the cell frequencies found in the contingency table. For example, one model might suggest that the pattern of frequencies in the

Table 35.1 **Possible model components for different sizes of contingency table**

Component of model	1	2	3	4	5
Overall mean (equal frequencies)	Yes	Yes	Yes	Yes	Yes
Main effects	A	A+B	A+B+C	A+B+C+D	A+B+C+D+E
Two-way interactions	–	A*B	A*B A*C B*C	A*B A*C A*D B*C B*D C*D	A*B A*C A*D A*E B*C B*D B*E C*D C*E
Three-way interactions			A*B*C	A*B*C A*B*D A*C*D B*C*D	A*B*C A*B*D A*B*E A*C*D A*C*E A*D*E B*C*D B*C*E B*D*E C*D*E
Four-way interactions				A*B*C*D	A*B*C*D A*B*C*E A*B*D*E B*C*D*E
Error	Yes	Yes	Yes	Yes	Yes

contingency table is the result of the independent influences of the variable sex and the variable age. There are probably other contending models for all but the simplest cases. An alternative model for this example is that the data are the result of the influence of variable social class plus the influence of variable sex *plus* the combined influence of variable sex interacting with the variable age. Table 35.1 gives the components of models for different numbers of independent variables in the contingency table. We will return to this later, but notice how the components include a constant (or the average frequency) *plus* the main effects of the independent variables *plus* interactive effects of the independent variables. Log-linear analysis helps a researcher to decide which of the possible models (i.e. which selection of the components in Table 35.1) is the best for the actual data. These different components will become clearer as we progress through this chapter. Model building can serve different purposes. Unless you have theoretical reasons for being interested in a particular model, then log-linear methods allow you to build up the model purely empirically.

■ *Goodness-of-fit.* This is simply the degree of match between the actual data and those values predicted on the basis of the model. Chi-square is a common measure of goodness-of-fit. Chi-square is zero if the observed data are exactly the same as the expected (or predicted) data. The bigger the value of chi-square, the greater the *misfit* between obtained and expected values. In Chapter 14, a significant value of chi-square caused us to reject the 'model' specified by the null hypothesis. A good fitting model would have a chi-square value approximating zero whereas a badly fitting model would have a large chi-square value.

■ *Pearson chi-square.* This is the version of chi-square used in Chapter 14 although common practice is simply to call it chi-square. The formula for the Pearson chi-square is:

$$\text{Pearson chi-square} \quad = \Sigma \, \frac{(\text{Observed} - \text{Expected})^2}{\text{Expected}}$$

The Pearson chi-square is used in log-linear analysis but it is not essential.

■ *Likelihood ratio chi-square.* This is the more common formula when doing log-linear analysis:

Likelihood ratio chi-square

$$= \Sigma \, \text{Observed frequency} \times \ln \text{ of } \frac{\text{Observed frequency}}{\text{Expected frequency}}$$

The term ln is a symbol for *natural logarithm*. Don't worry if you know nothing about natural logarithms. Although tables of natural logarithms are available, it is easier to obtain them from a scientific calculator (or the calculator built into Windows computer packages for instance). Observed frequency refers to the obtained data and expected frequency refers to the values expected according to the particular model being tested.

■ *Differences between Pearson and likelihood ratio chi-square.* The formula give slightly different values of chi-square for small sample sizes but converge as the sample sizes get large. Both formulae are often computed as measures of goodness of fit by computer programs for log-linear analysis. Nevertheless, it is best to concentrate on likelihood ratio chi-square in log-linear analysis because of its *additive* properties. This means that different components of chi-square can be added together to give the combined effects of different components of the chosen model. The Pearson chi-square does not act additively so cannot be used in this way. Hence its comparative unimportance in log-linear analysis.

Table 35.2 **Data to be modelled using log-linear analysis**

	Soap opera	**Crime drama**	**Neither**
Males	Observed = 27	Observed = 14	Observed = 19
Females	Observed = 17	Observed = 33	Observed = 9

35.2 A two-variable example

The distinctive approach of log-linear analysis can take a little time to absorb. Its characteristic logic is probably best explained by re-analysing an example from Chapter 14. The study of favourite types of television programme of males and females (Calculation 14.1) will be presented using the log-linear perspective. The data are given in Table 35.2 but they are exactly the same as the data in Table 14.8 in Chapter 14. The two independent variables were sex and favourite type of programme. In the (Pearson) chi-square analysis (Calculation 14.1) there is a sex difference in favourite type of television programme. Another way of putting this is that there is an interaction between a person's sex and their favourite type of television programme. (In Chapter 14, it was found that sex and favourite type of programme acting separately were insufficient to account for the data. The expected frequencies in that chapter are the frequencies expected on the basis of sex and programme effects having separate and unrelated effects. In Chapter 14, a significant value of chi-square meant that the distribution of cell frequencies could not be explained on the basis of this independent influence of sex and favourite programme type. The different sexes had different preferences. This would be an interaction in terms of log-linear analysis.)

A log-linear analysis of the data in Table 35.2 would examine possible underlying models (combinations of the independent variables) which might predict the obtained data. Theoretically, there are a number of possibilities according to log-linear analysis:

■ *Equal frequencies model.* This suggests that the observed cell frequencies are merely the total of cell frequencies divided equally between the cells. Since there are 119 observations in Table 35.2 and six cells then we would *expect* a frequency of 119/6 = 19.833 in each cell. Obviously this model, even if it fits the data best, is virtually a non-model.

■ *Main effects model.* This suggests that the observed cell frequencies are the consequence of the separate effects of the independent variables. While this might seem an important possibility if you recall main effects for ANOVA, in log-linear analysis, main effects are often trivial. The object of log-linear analysis is to account for the pattern of observed frequencies in the data. In

Table 35.2 note that there are slightly unequal numbers of males and females (60 males and 59 females) but, more importantly, the choices of the different programme types are unequal. That is, the different values of sex (male and female) and favourite television programme (soap opera, crime drama and neither) are not equally represented. For the main effect of sex, the inequality is small (60 males versus 59 females) but it is somewhat larger for the main effect of favourite television programme (44 choosing soap operas, 47 choosing crime dramas, and 28 choosing neither). The main effects merely refer to these inequalities which may be uninteresting in terms of the primary purpose of the analysis. In our example, a researcher is unlikely to be particularly interested in these main effects but much more interested if the interaction between sex and favourite programme type explains the data. In order for there to be *no* main effects, each of the categories of each of the independent variables would have to have the same frequency. This is rare in research.

■ *The interaction(s)*. An interaction is the effect of the interrelationship between the independent variables. In the present example, because we have only two independent variables, there is just one interaction which could be termed sex*favourite tv programme interaction. You will see from Table 35.1 that had there been more independent variables there would be more interactions to investigate. The number of interactions escalates with increasing numbers of independent variables (much as it does for ANOVA). Interactions interest researchers because they indicate the associations or correlations between independent variables.

The interactions and main effects are combined in log-linear analysis in order to see what main effects and what interactions are necessary to best account for (fit with) the observed data.

Log-linear analysis for this simple example involves the consideration of several different models.

Step 1: The equal frequencies model

In a manner of speaking this is the no-model model. It tests the idea that the cell frequencies require no explanation since they are equally distributed. This is *not* the same as the null hypothesis predictions made in Chapter 14 since these predicted not equal frequencies but *proportionate* frequencies according to the marginal totals. The equal frequencies model simply assumes that all of the cells of the contingency table have equal frequencies. Since we have a total frequency of 119 in the 6 cells of our analysis, the equal frequencies model predicts (expects) that there should be 119/6 or 19.833 in each cell as shown in Table 35.3. The likelihood ratio chi-square applied to this table is calculated in Table 35.4. Remember that the natural logarithms are obtained from a scientific calculator or one you find as a program on your computer. The use of natural logarithms is only important for understanding the basic calculation of log-linear.

Table 35.3 Contingency table for testing the equal frequencies model, i.e. the expected frequencies

	Soap opera	Crime drama	Neither	Total
Males	Observed = 27 Expected = 19.833	Observed = 14 Expected = 19.833	Observed = 19 Expected = 19.833	
Females	Observed = 17 Expected = 19.833	Observed = 33 Expected = 19.833	Observed = 9 Expected = 19.833	
Total				119

Table 35.4 Calculation of the fit of the equal frequencies model

Observed frequency	Expected frequency according to equal frequencies model	Observed ÷ expected	Natural logarithm of observed ÷ expected	Observed frequency × natural logarithm of observed ÷ expected
27	19.833	1.361	0.308	8.329
14	19.833	0.857	−0.154	−2.620
19	19.833	0.706	−0.348	−4.876
17	19.833	1.664	0.509	16.802
33	19.833	0.958	−0.043	−0.815
9	19.933	0.454	0.857	−7.111
				Total = 9.709

Likelihood ratio chi-square = 2 × total = 2 × 9.709 = 19.418

The fit of the equal frequencies model to the data is poor. The likelihood ratio chi-square is 19.418. This is the amount of misfit of that particular model to the data. (It is also the amount by which the main effects and the interactions can increase the fit of the best model to the data.)

The differences between the values expected according to the model and what is actually found in the data are known as the *residuals*. The residuals can be used to assess the fit of the model to the data in addition to the likelihood ratio chi-squares. Often, residuals are standardised so that comparisons can be made easily between the different cells, in which case they are known as standardised or adjusted residuals. The smaller the residuals the better the fit of the model to the data.

Step 2: The saturated model

The log-linear analysis of this data could be carried out in a number of ways since there are a variety of different models that could be tested. In general we will concentrate on the procedures which would commonly be employed when using computer programs such as SPSS. Often these compute the *saturated model* for you. A saturated model is one which includes all of the possible components as shown in Table 35.1 which, consequently, accounts perfectly for the data. That is, the values predicted by the saturated model are exactly the same as the data. Any model based on all of the components by definition accounts for the data perfectly. Since there is always a perfect correspondence or fit between the observed data and the predictions based on the likelihood ratio chi-square for the saturated model, this chi-square is always zero for the saturated model.

Table 35.5   **Contingency table for testing the saturated model**

	Soap opera	**Crime drama**	**Neither**	**Total**
Males	Observed = 27 Expected = 27.000	Observed = 14 Expected = 14.000	Observed = 19 Expected = 19.000	
Females	Observed = 17 Expected = 17.000	Observed = 33 Expected = 33.000	Observed = 9 Expected = 9.000	
Total				119

Table 35.5 gives the data and the expected frequencies for the saturated model. Notice, as we have already indicated, that the observed and expected frequencies for any cell of the contingency table are identical for this model. We will not bother to do this calculation. It is worth noting that computer programs often routinely increase the observed values by 0.5. This is done to avoid undesirable divisions by zero in the calculation while making very little difference to the calculation otherwise.

Step 3: Preparing to test for the main effects components of the model

The perfectly fitting model of the data (the saturated model) involves all possible components. It is not quite as impressive as the perfect fit suggests. We do not know what it is about our model which caused such a good fit. It could be the effects of sex, the effects of the type of programme, or the effects of the interaction of sex with type of programme, or any combination of these three possibilities. It could even mean that the equal frequencies model is correct if we had not already rejected that possibility. Further exploration is necessary to assess which of these components are contributing to the goodness-of-fit of the data to that predicted by the model. Any component of the model which does not increase the goodness-of-fit of the model to the data is superfluous since it does nothing to explain the data. (To anticipate a common practice in log-linear analysis, the corollary of this is also true: components are only retained if they *decrease* the fit of the model when they are *removed*.)

(Usually in the initial stages of log-linear analyses using a computer, similar components of the model are dealt with collectively. That is, the main effects of sex and favourite programme type are dealt with as if they were a unit of analysis. Had there been more than one interaction, these would also be dealt with collectively. At a later stage, it is usual to extend the analysis to deal with the combined components individually. That is, the data are explored in more detail in order to assess what main effects are actually influencing the data.)

To reiterate what we already have achieved we can say that we have examined two extremes of the model-building process: the saturated model and the equal frequencies model. We have established that the equal frequencies model is a poor fit to the data on this occasion (the saturated model is always a perfect fit). The misfit of the equal frequencies model to the data (likelihood ratio chi-square = 19.418) is the amount of improvement in fit achieved by the saturated model.

Step 4: TV programme type main effect

Main effects are one level of components in the saturated model. Understanding their calculation is fairly simple. Let us take the main effect of programme type. In order to predict the frequencies in the data based solely on the effects of the different programme type we simply replace each cell by the average of the frequencies in cells referring to that programme type. This in effect means that for our example we combine the data frequencies for the males and females who prefer soap operas and average this total by the number of cells involved (i.e. 2 cells). Twenty-seven males and 17 females claim to prefer soap operas so the total is 44 which is divided between the two cells involved in this case. This gives us a predicted frequency on the basis of the main effects model for programme type of 22.00 in each of the Soap Opera cells. This is shown in Table 35.6. The predicted value for Crime Drama is 14 + 13 divided by 2 which equals 13.50. The predicted value for the Neither category is 19 + 9 divided by 2 = 14.00. Again these can be seen in Table 35.6.

Now one can calculate the goodness of fit of this model simply by calculating the likelihood ratio chi-square for the data in Table 35.6. Just follow the model of the calculation in Table 35.4. The value of the likelihood ratio chi-square is

Table 35.6 **Table of data and expected frequencies based solely on the main effect of programme type**

	Soap opera	Crime drama	Neither	Total
Males	Observed = 27 Expected = 22.000	Observed = 14 Expected = 23.500	Observed = 19 Expected = 14.000	
Females	Observed = 17 Expected = 22.000	Observed = 33 Expected = 23.500	Observed = 9 Expected = 14,000	
Total	44	47	28	119

13.849. Compare this with the misfit based on the equal frequencies model (likelihood ratio chi-square = 19.418). It seems that there has been an improvement of 19.418 – 13.849 = 5.569 in the fit due to the programme main effect. (Remember that the bigger the likelihood ratio chi-square then the poorer the fit of the model to the data). Because the likelihood ratio chi-square has additive properties, this difference of 5.569 is the contribution of the main effect of programme type.

Step 5: Sex main effect

Because the frequencies of males and females in the data are nearly equal, there clearly is minimal main effect due to the independent variable sex in this case. Nevertheless this minimal value needs to be calculated. A similar procedure is adopted to calculate the main effects of sex. This time we need to sum the frequencies over the three different programme types for each sex separately and average this total frequency by the three programme types. Thus the observed frequencies for males in each of the three different programme type conditions is (27 + 14 + 19)/3 = 60/3 = 20. This gives a predicted value per male cell of 20. This is entered in Table 35.7. Similarly, the calculation for females is to sum the three observed frequencies and divide by the number of female cells. This is (17 + 33 + 9)/3 = 59/3 = 19.667. Again these values are entered in Table 35.7.

Table 35.7 **Table of data and expected frequencies based on the main effect of sex type**

	Soap opera	**Crime drama**	**Neither**	**Total**
Males	Observed = 27 Expected = 20.000	Observed = 14 Expected = 20.000	Observed = 19 Expected = 20.000	60
Females	Observed = 17 Expected = 19.667	Observed = 33 Expected = 19.667	Observed = 9 Expected = 19.667	59
Total				119

The likelihood ratio chi-square for the main effect of sex in Table 35.7 is 19.405. Compared with the value of 19.418 for the equal frequencies model, there is virtually no change, indicating the smallness of the sex difference in row frequencies. The improvement in fit due to sex alone is only 0.013.

Step 6: The main effects of programme type plus sex

This can now be obtained. It involves taking each cell in turn and working out the effect on the frequencies of the programme type and the sex concerned. This is done relative to the frequencies from the equal frequencies model (that is,

119/6 = 19.833 in every case). So, looking at Table 35.8, the expected frequency for Soap Operas is 22.000. This means that being a Soap Opera cell increases the frequency by 22.000 – 19.833 = 2.167. It may sound banal but in order to add in the effect of being a Soap Opera cell we have to add 2.167 to the expected frequencies under the equal frequencies model. Similarly, being a Crime Drama cell increases the frequency to 23.500 from our baseline equal frequencies expectation of 19.833. Being a Crime Drama cell increases the frequency by 23.500 – 19.833 = 3.667.

Table 35.8 Table of expected (predicted) frequencies based on adding the main effects of programme type and sex to the equal frequencies expectation

	Soap opera	Crime drama	Neither	Total
Males	Observed = 27 Expected = 19.833 + 2.167 + 0.167 = 22.167[a]	Observed = 14 Expected = 19.833 + 3.667 + 0.167 = 23.667[a]	Observed = 19 Expected = 19.833 + –5.833 + 0.167 = 14.167[a]	60
Females	Observed = 17 Expected = 19.833 + 2.167 + –0.166 = 21.834[a]	Observed = 33 Expected = 19.883 + 3.667 + –0.166 = 23.334[a]	Observed = 9 Expected = 19.883 + –5.833 + –0.166 = 13.834[a]	59
Total				119

[a] These hand-calculated values are very approximate and do not correspond to the best values for reasons discussed in the text.

In contrast, being in the Neither category tends to decrease the frequencies in the cell compared with the equal frequencies expectation of 19.833. From Table 35.7 we can see that the expected frequencies in the Neither column due to programme type are 14.000, which is below the equal frequencies expectation of 19.833. Thus, being a Neither cell changes frequencies by 14.000 – 19.833 = –5.833. That is, being Neither decreases frequencies by –5.833. In order to adjust the equal frequencies expectations for the programme type main effect we have to add 2.167 to the Soap Opera cells, add 3.667 to the Crime Drama cells and subtract 5.833 from (that is add –5.833 to) the Neither cells. This can be seen in Table 35.8.

We also need to make similar adjustments for the main effect of sex although these are much smaller. Compared with the equal frequencies value of 19.833, the male cells have an expected frequency of 20.000 which is an increase of 0.167. In order to adjust the equal frequencies baseline of 19.833 for a cell being Male we therefore have to add 0.167. This can be seen in Table 35.8. For Female cells, the expected frequency is 19.667, a reduction of 0.166. In short, we add –0.166 for a cell being Female. This is also shown in Table 35.8. (Of course, the additions and subtractions for the males and females should be identical, which they are within the limits of calculation rounding.)

At this point there is a big problem. That is, the values of the expected frequencies based on the main effects model gives the wrong answers according to computer output. For that matter, it does not give the same expected frequencies as given in the equivalent Pearson chi-square calculation we did in Chapter 14. Actually, the computer prints our expected frequencies which are the same as those calculated in Chapter 14. The problem is that we are not actually doing what the computer is doing. Think back to the two-way analysis of variance. These calculations worked as long as you have equal numbers of scores in each of the cells. Once you have unequal numbers, then the calculations have to be done a different way (and best of all by computer). This is because you are not adding effects proportionately once you have different cell frequencies. In log-linear analysis the problem arises because the marginal totals are usually unequal for each independent variable. This inequality means that simple linear additions and subtractions of main effects such as we have just done do not give the best estimates. That is in essence why a computer program is vital in log-linear analysis. Better estimates of expected frequencies are made using an iterative process. This means that an approximation is calculated but then refined by re-entering the approximation in recalculations. This is done repeatedly until a minimum criterion of change is found between calculations (i.e. between iterations). Computer programs allow you to decide on the size of this change and even the maximum number of iterations.

Now that we have some idea of how the adjustments are made for the main effects, even though we must rely on the computer for a bit of finesse, we will use the computer-generated values to finish off our explanation. Table 35.9 contains the observed and expected values due to the influence of the main effects as calculated by the computer's iterative process.

The value of the likelihood ratio chi-square for the data in Table 35.9 is, according to the computer, 13.841 (which is significant at 0.001 with df = 2). At this point, we can obtain the value of the sex*programme type interaction. We now know the following:

Table 35.9 Table of expected (predicted) frequencies based on adding the main effects of programme type and sex to the equal frequencies expectation as obtained by the iterative computer process

	Soap opera	Crime drama	Neither	Total
Males	Observed = 27	Observed = 14	Observed = 19	
	Expected = 22.18	Expected = 23.70	Expected = 14.72	
Females	Observed = 17	Observed = 33	Observed = 9	
	Expected = 21.82	Expected = 23.30	Expected = 13.88	
Total				

1. The fit of the saturated model which includes main effects plus the interaction is 0.000.
2. The fit of the model based on the two main effects is 13.841.
3. The fit of the model based on the equal frequencies model is 19.418.

It becomes a simple matter of subtraction to work out the improvement in fit due to the different components. Thus:

1. The increase in fit due to the two main effects = 19.418 – 13.841 = 5.577.
2. The increase in fit due to the interaction = 13.841 – 0.000 = 13.841.

These numerical values are likelihood ratio chi-squares. Only the interaction is statistically significant out of these major components. The main effect of programme type taken on its own would be statistically significant as it includes fewer degrees of freedom and has nearly the same likelihood ratio chi-square value. This is of no real interest as it merely shows that different proportions of people were choosing the different programme types as their favourites. In short, the interesting part of the model is the interaction which is statistically significant. Formally, this model is expressed simply as:

> Constant (i.e. equal frequency cell mean)
> + Programme main effect + A*B interaction

As the interaction is fairly simple, it is readily interpreted with the help of Table 35.8. So we can conclude that in order to model the data effectively we need the two-variable interaction. This we did in essence in Chapter 14 when interpreting the Pearson chi-square analysis of those data. Remember that the interaction is based on the residuals in that table (i.e. the differences between the observed and expected frequencies). As can be clearly seen, males are less inclined to choose crime dramas than women but are more inclined to choose soap operas.

35.3 A three-variable example

Interactions when the data have three or more independent variables become a little more difficult to understand. In any case, only when there are three or more independent variables does log-linear analysis achieve much more than the Pearson chi-square described in Chapter 14. Consequently it is important to study one of these more complex examples. Even though log-linear analysis usually requires the use of a computer using the iterative procedures, quite a lot can be achieved by trying to understand approximately what the computer is doing when it is calculating several second-order and higher-order interactions.

Table 35.1 gives the possible model components of any log-linear analysis for one to five independent variables. It is very unlikely that anyone would wish to use log-linear analysis when they have just one independent variable but it is useful to start from there just so that the patterns build up more clearly in the table. Computer programs can handle more independent variables than five but we are constrained by space and, moreover, log-linear analyses of ten independent variables are both atypical of psychological research designs and call for a great deal of statistical sophistication – especially experience with simpler log-linear analyses.

Basically, the more independent variables you have the more components there will be to the model. All models consist of main effects plus interactions plus the mean frequency per cell plus error. The last two can be largely ignored. The mean frequency per cell is the result of the influences of (possibly) numerous variables which the researcher has no control over and probably no knowledge of. The independent variables involved in model-building are those which might possibly cause differences between the frequencies in the different cells. These independent variables have to be measurable by the researcher too for them to be in the analysis. Error is present in any model but basically is assumed to be unrelated in any systematic way to the cell frequencies and can, if you wish, be ignored as a component of the model. Also note that the more independent variables in a model, the more complex the interactions.

Our example involves three independent variables. If you look in the column for three independent variables in Table 35.1 you will find listed all of the possible components of the model for that data. In this column there are three main effects (one for each of the independent variables), three two-way interactions between all possible distinct pairs taken from the three independent variables, and one three-way interaction. The analysis is much the same as for our earlier two-variable example but there are more components to add in. In particular, the meaning of the interactions needs to be clarified as there are now four of them rather than just one. Remember that it is usual to take similar levels of the model together for the initial model-fitting. Thus all the main effects are combined; all of the second-order interactions (two-variable interactions) together; all of the third-order (three-variable interactions) together and so forth. Only when this analysis is done is it usual to see precisely which combinations at which levels of the model are having an effect.

Table 35.10 A three-way contingency showing the relationship between sex, sexual abuse and physical abuse in a sample of psychiatric hospital patients

Variable B Sexual abuse	Variable C Physical abuse	Variable A Sex		Margin totals
		Female	Male	
Sexually abused	Physical abuse	45	55	100
	No physical	40	60	100
Not sexually abused	Physical abuse	55	45	100
	No physical	80	20	100
Margin totals		220	180	400

Our example involves the relationship between sex, sexual abuse and physical abuse in a sample of psychiatric patients. The data are to be found in Table 35.10 which gives the three-way crosstabulation or contingency table for our example. The numbers in the cells are *frequencies*. Each of the variables has been coded as a dichotomy: (a) female or male, (b) sexually abused or not, and (c) physically abused or not. (Variables could have more than two categories but this is not the case for these particular data.) The researchers are interested in explaining the frequencies in the table on the basis of the three *independent variables* – sex, sexual abuse and physical abuse – acting individually (main effects) or in combination (interactions). This would be described as a three-way contingency table because it involves *three independent variables*. It is worthwhile remembering that the more variables and the more categories of each variable the greater the sample size needs to be in order to have sufficient frequencies in each cell.

Two of the possible models are easily tested. They are the equal frequencies and the saturated models which are the extreme possibilities in log-linear analyses. The equal frequencies model simply involves the first row of Table 35.10 and no other influences. The saturated model includes all sources of influence in the table for the column for three independent variables.

Step 1: The equal frequencies model

The equal frequencies model is, in a sense the worst-fit scenario, for a model. It is what the data would look like if none of the independent variables in isolation or combination were needed to explain the data. The equal frequencies model

Table 35.11   The calculation of the likelihood ratio chi-square for the equal frequencies model

Observed frequency	Expected frequency according to the equal frequencies model	Observed ÷ expected	Natural logarithm of observed ÷ expected	Observed frequency × natural logarithm of observed ÷ expected
45	50.0	0.90	−0.1054	−4.741
40	50.0	0.80	−0.2231	−8.926
55	50.0	1.10	0.0953	5.242
80	50.0	1.60	0.4700	37.600
55	50.0	1.10	0.0953	5.242
60	50.0	1.20	0.1823	10.939
45	50.0	0.90	−0.1054	−4.741
20	50.0	0.40	−0.9163	−18.326

Total = 22.90

Likelihood ratio chi-square = 2 × sum of final column
= 2 × 22.290 = 44.580

merely describes what the data would look like if the frequencies were equally distributed through the cells of the table. As there are eight cells and a total of 400 observations, under the equal frequencies model it would be expected that each cell contains 400/8 = 50 cases. This model and the calculation of its fit with the observed data for which we are developing a model are shown in Table 35.11.

Just a reminder – the likelihood ratio chi-square is zero if the model fits the data exactly and increasingly bigger with greater amounts of misfit between the data and the data as predicted by the model. The chi-square value for the equal frequencies model is an indication of how much the independent variables and their interaction have to explain. The value of 44.58 obtained for the likelihood ratio chi-square on the equal frequencies model indicates that the data are poorly explained by that model. That is, there is a lot of variation in the frequencies which remains to be explained by other models than the equal frequencies model. Notice that the equal frequencies model only contains the mean frequency which is one of the potential components of all models. The equal frequencies value is sometimes called the constant. If it is zero or nearly zero then the equal frequencies model fits the model well. Do not get too excited if the equal frequencies model fits badly since the variation in frequencies between the cells might be explained by the main effects. To reiterate, main effects in the log-linear analysis are often of very little interest to psychologists. Only rarely will real-life data have no main effects in log-linear analysis since main effects occur when the categories of an independent variable are unequally distributed. In our data in Table 35.10, the marginal totals for physical abuse and sexual abuse are the same since equal numbers had been abused as had not been abused. Nevertheless, there is a possible main effect for sex since there are more females in the study than males. Whether or not this sex difference is significant has yet to be tested. So whatever the final model we select, it has already been clearly established that there is plenty of variation in the cell means to be explained by the main effects acting independently and the two-way interactions of pairs of these variables plus the three-way interaction of all of the variables.

Step 2: The saturated model

This model involves all of the possible independent variables acting separately and in combination. It includes all components given in Table 35.1 for a given number of independent variables. For a three-way contingency table the saturated model includes the mean frequency per cell (i.e.constant) plus the main effects plus the three two-variable interactions plus the three-variable interaction. Predictions based on the saturated model are exactly the same as the data themselves – they have to be since the saturated model includes every possible component of the model and so there is no other possible source of variation.

It is hardly worth computing the saturated model as it has to be a perfect fit to the data thus giving a likelihood ratio chi-square of 0.000. A zero value like this indicates a perfect fit between the observed data and the expectations (predictions) based on the model. Remember that for the saturated model, most computer programs will automatically add 0.5 to the observed frequencies to avoid divisions by zero which are unhelpful mathematically. This addition of 0.5 to each of the frequencies is not always necessary so some computer programs will give you the choice of not using it. Its influence is so negligible that the analysis is hardly affected.

Step 3: Building up the main effects model

The process of building up a model in log-linear analysis is fairly straightforward once the basic principles are understood, as we have seen. The stumbling block is the calculation of expected frequencies when marginal frequencies are unequal. They are unequal most of the time in real data. In these circumstances, only an approximate explanation can be given of what the computer is doing. Fortunately, as we have already seen, we can go a long way using simple maths.

Table 35.12 **The expected (or predicted) frequencies based on separate components of the model**

Data	Details of cell			Equal frequencies model	Main effects				Two-way interactions			
	Sex	Sexual abuse	Physical abuse		Sex	Sexual	Physical	All	Sex Sexual	Sex Physical	Sexual* Physical	All
45	Female	Yes	Yes	50.00	55.00	50.00	50.00	55.00	42.50	50.00	50.00	37.23
40	Female	Yes	No	50.00	55.00	50.00	50.00	55.00	42.50	60.00	50.00	47.77
55	Female	No	Yes	50.00	55.00	50.00	50.00	55.00	67.50	50.00	50.00	62.77
80	Female	No	No	50.00	55.00	50.00	50.00	55.00	67.50	60.00	50.00	72.33
55	Male	Yes	Yes	50.00	45.00	50.00	50.00	45.00	57.50	50.00	50.00	62.77
60	Male	Yes	No	50.00	45.00	50.00	50.00	45.00	57.50	40.00	50.00	52.23
45	Male	No	Yes	50.00	45.00	50.00	50.00	45.00	32.50	50.00	50.00	37.23
20	Male	No	No	50.00	45.00	50.00	50.00	45.00	32.50	40.00	50.00	27.77

Table 35.12 contains the expected frequencies based on different components of the model. Remember that the expected frequencies are those based on a particular model or component of the model. The first column contains the data (which are exactly the same as the predictions based on the saturated model already discussed). The fourth column gives the expected frequencies based on the equal frequencies model. This has already been discussed – the frequencies are merely the total frequencies averaged over the number of cells.

The next three cells have the major heading Main effects and there are separate columns for the main effect of sex, the main effect of sexual abuse, and the main effect of physical abuse. The fourth column headed All is for the added effect of these three main effects. How are these expected (predicted) values calculated? They are simply the averages of the appropriate cells. Thus for females, the four cells in Table 35.12 are 45, 40, 55 and 80 which totals 220. Thus if the cells in the Female column reflect only the effects of being female then we would expect all four Female cells to contain 220/4 = 55.00 cases. In Table 35.12, the expected frequencies under sex for the four Female cells are all 55.00. Similarly for the four remaining cells in that column which all involve males, the total male frequency is 180 so we would expect 180/4 or 45.00 in each of the Male cells.

Exactly the same process is applied to the Sexual abuse column. Two hundred of the cases were sexually abused in childhood whereas 200 were not. Thus we average the 200 sexually abused cases over the four cells in Table 35.12 which involve sexually abused individuals (i.e. 200/4 = 50.00). Then we average the 200 non-sexually abused individuals over the four cells containing non-sexually abused individuals (i.e. 200/4=50.00). Because there are equal numbers of sexually and non-sexually abused individuals no main effect of sexual abuse is present and all of the values in the Sexual abuse column are 50.00.

Given that there are also 200 physically abused and 200 non-physically abused cases, it is not surprising to find that all of the expected frequencies are 50.00 in the Physical abuse column too. The reasoning is exactly the same as for sexual abuse in the previous paragraph.

The combined main effects column labelled All is easily computed for our example. It is simply the combined individual effects of the three separate main effects. So it is the effect of sex plus sexual abuse plus physical abuse. Thus being female adds a frequency of five compared with the equal frequencies model figure of 50.00, being sexually abused adds zero and being physically abused adds zero. For example, for the first row which consists of 45 females who had been sexually abused and physically abused, we take the equal frequencies frequency of 50.00 and add 5 for being female + 0 for being sexually abused and + 0 for being physically abused. This gives the expected figure of 55.00 under the All main effects column.

To give another example, take the fifth row down where the data give a frequency of 55. This row refers to males who had been sexually abused and physically abused. Being male subtracts 5.00 from the equal frequency value, being sexually abused adds nothing and being physically abused also adds nothing. So our expected value is 50 − 5 + 0 + 0 = 45, the expected value for all of the main effects added together.

Step 4: The two-variable interactions

The two-way interactions are not difficult to estimate either. The two-way interaction for sex*sexual abuse is obtained by combining together the physical abuse categories. In our example, there are some who have been physically abused and some who have not among the females who had been sexually abused. Of these sexually abused females, 45 had been physically abused and 40 had not been physically abused. Combining these two frequencies and averaging them across the two relevant cells gives us:

$$\frac{45 + 40}{2}$$

$$= \frac{85}{2}$$

$$= 42.5$$

This is the value that you see under the sex*sexual abuse interaction for the first two rows.

If you need another example, take the last two rows which have values in the data column of 45 and 20. These rows consist of the males who had not been sexually abused. One row is those who had been physically abused and the other those who had not been physically abused. The two-way interaction of sex*sexual abuse is obtained by adding together the two different physical abuse categories and entering the average of these into the last two rows. So the frequencies are 45 and 20 which equals 65, which divided between the two relevant cells gives us 32.5. This is the value that you see for the sex*sexual abuse interaction for the final two rows.

What about the next interaction – sex*physical abuse? The calculation is basically the same. The only difficulty is that the rows corresponding to the cells we are interested in are physically further apart in the table. The sex*physical abuse interaction is obtained by combining the sexual abuse categories (i.e. the sexually abused and non-sexually abused). Let us take the females who had not been physically abused. These are the second and fourth rows. If we look at the observed values in the data these are frequencies of 40 and 80. The average of these is 60, and this is the value you find in the second and fourth rows of the sex*physical abuse interaction.

The sexual abuse*physical abuse interaction is calculated in a similar way – this time we combine the male and female groups for each of the four sexual abuse*physical abuse combinations. Take the sexually *and* physically abused individuals. These are to be found in rows 1 and 5. The data (observed) values for these rows are 45 and 55. This averages at 50.00 – the value of the entry for this two-way interaction in the first and fifth rows. (Actually all of the rows for this particular column have the same value indicating a lack of a sexual abuse*physical abuse interaction.)

The combined effects of the three two-way interactions cannot be seen directly from the table. This is because the values are based on an iterative process which involves several computational stages which are best done by the computer. The values in the last column of Table 35.12 are taken from SPSS computer output. Although we will not be showing this calculation here because of its complexity, we can show the essential logic although, as you will see, it gives slightly the wrong answers. All effects in log-linear analysis are additive so we should be able to combine the three two-way interactions in order to obtain the sum of the three two-way interactions.

This is quite simple. Compared with the equal frequencies mean frequency of 50.00 for each cell, what is the effect of each interaction? Taking the first row, we can see that the sex*sexual abuse interaction changes the score by –7.50 (i.e. 42.5 – 50.00), the sex*physical abuse interaction changes the score by 0.00 (i.e. 50.00 – 50.00) and the sexual abuse*physical abuse interaction changes the score by 0.00 (50.00 – 50.00). Adding these separate effects to the equal frequencies mean frequency of 50.00 we get:

$$50.00 + -7.50 + 0.00 + 0.00 = 42.50$$

This at first sight is the wrong answer since it is nowhere near the 37.23 obtained from the computer.

What we have not allowed for is the fact that these interactions also include the effect of the main effects. The main effects for this row combined to give a prediction of 55.00 compared with the equal frequencies mean of 50.00. That is to say, the main effects are increasing the prediction for this row by 5.00. This would have to be taken away from the prediction based on the interaction to leave the pure effects of the two-way interactions. So our value 42.50 contains 5.00 due to the main effects; getting rid of the main effects gives us the prediction of 37.50 based on the two-way interactions. This is pretty close to the 37.23 predicted by the model but not sufficiently so. The unequal marginal totals necessitate the adjustments made automatically by the iterative computer program. Had our marginal totals been a lot more unequal then our fit to the computer's value would have been much poorer. Simple methods are only suitable as ways of understanding the basics of the process.

If you would like another example of how the entries are computed, look at the final row of Table 35.12. The predicted values based on all the two-way interactions is 27.77. How is that value achieved? Notice that the two-way sex*sexual abuse interaction prediction is 32.50 which is 17.50 less than that according to the equal frequencies model prediction of 50.00; the sex*physical abuse prediction is 40.00, which is   10.00 less, and the sexual abuse*physical abuse prediction is 50.00, exactly the same. So to get the prediction based on the three two-way interactions together the calculation is the equal frequencies mean (50.00) + –17.50 + –10.00 + 0.00 = 22.50, but then we need to take away the influence of all the main effects which involves adding 5.00 this time. Thus we end up with a prediction of 27.50. Again this is not precisely the computer predicted value but it is close enough for purposes of explanation. Remember, it is only close because the main effects are small or zero.

What is the normal output of a computer program such as SPSS? The important point to remember is that it is usual to explore the model first of all as combined effects – the sum of the interactions, the sum of the main effects – rather than the individual components in the first analysis. For the data in Table 35.10 we obtained the information in Tables 35.13 and 35.14 from the computer by stipulating a saturated model.

What do Tables 35.13 and 35.14 tell us? Remember that when we assessed the fit of the data based on the equal frequencies model we obtained a likelihood ratio chi-square value of 44.580. This large value indicates a large misfit of the model to the data. (The smaller the size of chi-square the better the fit.) Notice that this value of chi-square is exactly the same (within the errors of rounding) as the chi-square value in Table 35.13 for the contribution of the main effects, two-way interactions and the three-way interactions. Thus 44.580 is the improvement in the fit of the model created by including the three different levels of effect *together*.

Table 35.13   **Tests of the increase in fit for the main effects and higher-order effects**

Level of effects	Types of effect involved	Degrees of freedom	Likelihood ratio chi-square	Probability
3	Three-way interaction	1	10.713	0.0011
2 (and above)	All the two-way interactions + the three-way interaction	4	40.573	0.0000
1 (and above)	All the main effects + the two-way interaction + the three-way interaction only	7	44.579	0.0000

Table 35.14   **Tests that the levels of effect are zero**

Level of effects	Types of effect involved	Degrees of freedom	Likelihood ratio chi-square	Probability
1	All the main effects only	3	4.007	0.2607
2	All the two-way interactions only	3	29.860	0.0000
3	Three-way interaction only	1	10.713	0.0011

If we take just the two-way and three-way interactions (omitting the main effects from the model), the improvement is a little less at 40.573 according to Table 35.13. Thus, remembering that likelihood ratio chi-square is linear – you can add and subtract values this means that the improvement in fit due to the main effects is 44.579 – 40.573 = 4.006 which within the limits of rounding error gives you exactly the same value as for all of the main effects only in Table 35.14 (the value in that table is 4.007).

If we take only the three-way interaction in Table 35.13 (i.e. omitting the two-way interaction and main effects from the model), we get a value of 10.713 for the amount of misfit. This is the value given in Table 35.14.

Where does the value for the two-way interactions come from? We have just found that the value for the main effect is 4.006 and the value for the three-way interaction is 10.713. If we take these away from the chi-square of 44.580 we get 44.580 – 4.006 – 10.713 = 29.861 for the contribution of the two-way interactions to the fit (exactly as can be found in Table 35.14 within the limits of rounding error).

It looks as if a good model for the data can exclude the main effects which are failing to contribute significantly to the goodness of fit even though the value of the likelihood ratio chi-square is 4.007. Thus a model based on the two-way and three-way interactions accounts for the data well.

Step 5: Which components account for the data?

This analysis has demonstrated the substantial contributions of the two-way and three-way interactions to the model's fit to the data. Since there is only one three-way interaction in this case, then there is no question what interaction is causing this three-way effect. There are three different two-way interactions for this model, not all of which may be contributing to the fit to the data. The way of checking for the relative influence of the different two-way interactions is to repeat the analysis but omitting one of the two-way interactions. This is easy to do on most computer programs. Doing this for the data in Table 35.10, we obtain the following:

- Based solely on sex*sexual abuse: chi-square = 15.036, df = 4, $p = 0.005$.
- Based solely on sex*physical abuse: chi-square = 36.525, df = 4, $p = 0.000$.
- Based solely on sexual abuse*physical abuse: chi-square= 44.579, df = 4, $p = 0.000$.

Working backwards, compared with the value of 44.580 for the misfit between the data and the equal frequencies model, there is no improvement in the fit by adding in the sexual abuse*physical abuse interaction since the value of likelihood ratio chi-square does not change (significantly) from that value 44.580. This means that the sexual abuse*physical abuse interaction contributes nothing to the model fit and can be dropped from the model.

Considering solely the sex*physical abuse interaction, there is a moderate improvement in fit. The maximum misfit of 44.580 as assessed by the likelihood ratio chi-square reduces to 36.526 when the sex*physical abuse interaction is included. This suggests that this interaction is quite important in the model and should be retained.

Finally, using solely the sex*sexual abuse interaction, the likelihood ratio chi-square value declines to 15.036 from the maximum of 44.579 suggesting that the sex*sexual abuse interaction has a substantial influence and improves the fit of the model substantially.

It should be remembered that there is a main effect for sex in all of the above two-way interactions except for the sexual abuse*physical abuse interaction where it is not present. (Check the marginal totals for the expected frequencies to see this.) In order to understand just how much change in fit is due to the two-way interaction we need to adjust for the main effect of sex which we have already calculated as a likelihood ratio chi-square of 4.007. So to calculate the likelihood ratio chi-square of the sex*physical abuse interaction we have to take 36.525 from 44.580 which gives a value for the improvement in fit

Table 35.15 **The amounts of fit caused by different components of the model**

Model	Likelihood ratio chi-square	Degrees of freedom	Prob.	Chi-square change
Saturated	0.000			–
All two-way interactions + all main effects (i.e. minus three-way interaction)	10.713	1	0.001	10.713[a]
Previous row less sex*sexual abuse	36.525	2	0.000	25.812[a]
Previous row less sexual abuse *physical abuse	36.525	3	0.000	0.000
Previous row less sex*physical abuse	40.573	4	0.000	4.048
Previous row less sexual abuse	40.573	5	0.000	0.000
Previous row less sex	44.579	6	0.000	4.006
Previous row less physical abuse	44.579	7	0.000	0.000

[a] Change significant at the 5% level.

of 8.054. This value is the improvement in fit due to the sex main effect and the sex*physical abuse interaction. So for the improvement in fit due to the sex*physical abuse interaction only we take 8.055 and subtract 4.007 to give a value of 4.048. This value is only roughly correct because of the unequal marginals involved which means that a better approximation will be achieved through an iterative process.

Table 35.15 gives the results of an analysis starting with the saturated model and gradually removing components. If a removed component is having an effect on the fit that there will be a non-zero value for the chi-square change for that row which needs to be tested for significance. The saturated model is a perfect fit (i.e. chi-square = 0.000) but taking away the three-way interaction increases the misfit to 10.713. This change (10.713 – 0.000) is the influence of the three-way interaction on the degree of fit. Taking away the interaction of sex*sexual abuse gives a chi-square change of 25.812 which indicates that the sex*sexual abuse interaction is having a big effect on the fit of the model.

When we take away sexual abuse*physical abuse there is a 0.000 chi-square change. This indicates that this interaction is doing nothing to improve the fit of the model. Thus the sexual abuse*physical abuse interaction may be dropped from the model.

Similarly the row of Table 35.15 where the main effect of sexual abuse is dropped has a zero likelihood ratio chi-square indicating the main effect of sexual abuse can be dropped from the model. Also the final row where the main effect of physical abuse is dropped also shows no change implying that this main effect can be dropped from the model. Actually only two of the components are statistically significant at the 5% level so that the model could be built on these solely. Our model then becomes:

mean frequency (i.e. equal frequencies mean) + sex*sexual abuse interaction + sex*sexual abuse* physical abuse interaction.

Step 6: More on the interpretation of log-linear analysis

By this stage it should be possible to attempt fitting a log-linear model. Of course, a little practice will be necessary with your chosen computer in order to familiarise yourself with its procedures. This is not too technical in practice with careful organisation and the creation of systematic tables to record the computer output. If these things are not done, the sheer quantity of frequently redundant computer output will cause confusion.

Specifying the best-fitting model using likelihood ratio chi-squares is *not* a complete interpretation of the model. This is much as the value of Pearson chi-square in Chapter 14 is insufficient without careful examination of the data. An important concept in this respect is that of residuals. A residual is merely the difference between the data and the data predicted on the basis of the model. These can be expressed merely as the data value minus the modelled value. So residuals may take positive or negative values and there is one residual per cell. Not only this, since in a log-linear analysis you may be comparing one or more components of the model with the data then several sets of residuals will have to be computed, and so you may be calculating different residuals for different components of the model or different models. Residuals can be standardised so that values are more easily compared one with another.

The good news is twofold. There is no difficulty in calculating simple residuals and computers generally do it for you anyway as part of calculating the model fit. If you look back to Table 35.12, you can easily calculate the residuals by subtracting any of the predicted model values from the actual data. The residuals for the saturated model are all zero of course, indicating a perfect fit. The residuals for the equal frequencies model are –5.00, –10.00, 5.00, 30.00, 5.00, 10.00, –5.00 and –30.00; that is the value of the frequency for that cell in the data – 50.000 in each case.

The other helpful thing when interpreting log-linear models is the estimated cell frequencies based on different components of the model. Remember that not only can you calculate these fairly directly but they are usually generated for you by the computer. The important thing about these estimated cell frequencies is that they tell you the trends in the data caused by, say, the interactions. For example, look at Table 35.12 and the column for the sex*sexual abuse interaction. You can see there that there are relatively few females who had been sexually abused and relatively more males who had been sexually abused in these data. It is best to compare these frequencies with the ones for the effects of the three main effects since the interaction figures actually include the effects of the main effects. Thus this comparison removes the main effects from the interaction.

Reporting the results

With something as complex as a log-linear analysis you might expect that writing up the results of the analysis will be complex. Indeed it can be and expect to write much more about your analysis than you would, for example, writing up the results of a correlation coefficient or a t-test. The purposes of log-linear analysis can be very varied, stretching from a fairly empirical examination of the data of the sort described earlier to testing the fit of a theoretical model to the actual data. Obviously there is no single sentence that can be usefully employed for describing the outcome of a log-linear analysis. Nevertheless certain things are very important. They are:

1. A table giving the data and the residuals for each of the models that you examine. Without this, the reader cannot assess precisely the form of the fit of the models to the data. Table 35.12 would be a useful format for doing this.

2. A table giving indications of the improvement in fit due to each component of the model. This will almost invariably be the likelihood ratio chi-square. Table 35.15 could be adapted to your particular data.

The text should discuss the final model which you have selected on the basis of your log-linear analysis. These could be expressed in terms of the components of the model which contribute significantly to the fit or, alternatively, as the lambda values mentioned in the Box below. Earlier in this chapter we have indicated the models for our two examples in a simple form.

Degrees of freedom   Using the computer means that you never need to actually calculate the degrees of freedom. However, if you understand their calculation from chi-square in Chapter 14, then you should have few problems with their calculation for log-linear. When reading degrees of freedom in tables, often they will include extra degrees of freedom for lower-level interactions or main effects. Adjustments may have to be made. Here are a few examples:

1. Total degrees of freedom are always the number of cells − 1.
2. Degrees of freedom for the equal frequencies model = 1.
3. Degrees of freedom for a main effect = total degrees of freedom divided by the number of different categories of the main effect.
4. Degrees of freedom for the saturated model = 0.

Remember that the degrees of freedom for *all* of the main effects, for example, is not the same as the degrees of freedom for any of the main effects taken separately.

Lambda   Often in log-linear analysis, the models are specified in terms of lambda (λ). This is simply the natural log of the influence of each of the different sorts of component of the cell frequencies. Thus a model may be built up from a succession of lambdas. These are given superscripts to denote what type of effect is involved: λ^A is the main effect of variable A and λ^{A*B} is the effect of the interaction of variables A and B. So an equation involving these and other components might be:

$$\text{Model} = \lambda + \lambda^A + \lambda^B + \lambda^{A*B}$$

This simply means that we add to the natural logarithm of the equal-cell mean or constant (λ), the natural logarithm of the main effects of the independent variable A (remember that this has positive and negative values), the natural logarithm of the main effects of the independent variable B, and the natural logarithm of the interaction of the independent variables A*B.

Hierarchical models Hierarchical models imply lower-order components and do not specify what these lower-order components are. Thus a hierarchical model may specify a four-variable interaction A*B*C*D. Any component involving A, B, C and D is assumed to be a component of that model. So the main effects A, B, C and D, the two-way interactions A*B, A*C, A*D, B*C, B*D and C*D, and the three-way interactions A*B*C, A*B*D, A*C*D and B*C*D are automatically specified as possible components in a hierarchical model. Notice that our examples employ a hierarchical approach.

35.4 Notes and recommendations

■ It is recommended that before analysing your own data with log-linear, that you reproduce our analyses in order to become familiar with the characteristics of your chosen computer program.

■ Confine yourself to small numbers of independent variables when first using log-linear analysis. Although computers may handle, say, ten independent variables, you may find it difficult without a lot of experience.

■ Log-linear analysis can include score variables.

■ Log-linear analysis is not as commonly used in psychological research as it is in other disciplines. The reason is the preference of psychologists for using score variables.

Recommended further reading

Agresti, A. (1996). *An Introduction to Categorical Data Analysis*. New York: Wiley, chapters 1–4.

Anderson, E.B. (1997). *Introduction to the Statistical Analysis of Categorical Data*. Berlin: Springer, chapters 2–4.

Appendix A

Testing for excessively skewed distributions

The use of nonparametric tests (Mann–Whitney U-test, Wilcoxon Matched Pairs Test) rather than parametric tests (unrelated *t*-test, related *t*-test) is conventionally recommended by some textbooks when the distribution of scores on a variable is significantly skewed (Chapter 18). There are a number of difficulties with this advice, particularly just how one knows that there is too much skew. It is possible to test for significant skewness. One simply computes a formula for the skewness and then divides this by the standard error of the skewness. If the resulting value equals or exceeds 1.96 then your skewness is significant at the 5% level (two-tailed test) and the null hypothesis that your sample comes from a symmetrical population should be rejected.

A.1 Skewness

The formula for skewness is:

$$\text{Skewness} = \frac{(\Sigma d^3) \times N}{\text{sd}^3 \times (N-1) \times (N-2)}$$

Notice that much of the formula is familiar: N is the number of scores, d is the deviation of each score from the mean of the sample, and sd is the estimated standard deviation of the scores (i.e. you use $N-1$ in the formula for standard deviation as described in Chapter 11).

What is different is the use of cubing. To cube a number you multiply it by itself twice. Thus the cube of 3 is $3 \times 3 \times 3 = 27$. A negative number cubed gives a negative number. Thus the cube of –4 is $(-4) \times (-4) \times (-4) = -64$.

We will take the data from Table 5.1 in Chapter 5 to illustrate the calculation of skewness. For simplicity's sake we will be using a definitional formula which involves the calculation of the sample mean. Table A1 gives the data in column 1 as well as the calculation steps to be followed. The number of scores, N, equals 9.

Table A.1   **Steps in the calculation of skewness**

Column 1 Age (years)	Column 2 Scores – sample mean	Column 3 Square values in column 2	Column 4 Cube values in column 2
20	20 – 23 = –3	9	–27
25	25 – 23 = 2	4	8
19	19 – 23 = –4	16	–64
35	35 – 23 = 12	144	1728
19	19 – 23 = –4	16	–64
17	17 – 23 = –6	36	–216
15	15 – 23 = –8	64	–512
30	30 – 23 = 7	49	343
27	27 – 23 = 4	16	64

ΣX = sum of scores = 207 $\Sigma d^2 = 354$ $\Sigma d^3 = 1260$

$\overline{X}$ = mean score = 23

For Table A1,

$$\text{Estimated standard deviation (sd)} \quad = \quad \sqrt{\frac{\Sigma d^2}{N-1}}$$

$$= \quad 6.652$$

Substituting this value and the values from the table in the formula for skewness we get:

$$\text{Skewness} \quad = \quad \frac{1260 \times 9}{6.652^3 \times (9-1) \times (9-2)}$$

$$= \quad \frac{11{,}340}{16{,}483.322}$$

$$= \quad 0.688$$

(Skewness could have a negative value.)

A.2   Standard error of skewness

The standard error of skewness involves calculating the value of the following formula for our particular sample size ($N = 9$):

$$\text{Standard error of skewness} = \sqrt{\frac{6 \times N \times (N-1)}{(N-2) \times (N+1) \times (N+3)}}$$

$$= \sqrt{\frac{432}{840}}$$

$$= \sqrt{0.514}$$

$$= 0.717$$

The significance of skewness involves a z-score:

$$z = \frac{\text{Skewness}}{\text{Standard error of skewness}}$$

$$= \frac{0.688}{0.717}$$

$$= 0.96$$

This value of z is lower than the minimum value of z (1.96) required to be statistically significant at the 5% level with a two-tailed test. Thus the scores are *not* extremely skewed. This implies that you may use parametric tests rather than nonparametric tests for comparisons involving this variable. Obviously you need to do the skewness test for the other variables involved.

For the related t-test, it is the skewness of the *differences* between the two sets of scores which needs to be examined, not the skewnesses of the two different sets of scores.

Appendix B1

Large sample formulae for the nonparametric tests

Sometimes you may wish to do a nonparametric test when the sample sizes exceed the tabulated values of the significance tables in Chapter 18. In these circumstances we would recommend using a computer. The reason is that ranking large numbers of scores is extremely time consuming and you risk making errors. However, if a computer is not available to do the analyses, you can make use of the following large sample formulae for nonparametric tests.

B1.1 Mann–Whitney U-test

$$z = \frac{U - \dfrac{n_1 \, n_2}{2}}{\sqrt{\left(\dfrac{n_1 \, n_2}{N(N-1)}\right)\left(\dfrac{N^3 - N}{12} - \Sigma \dfrac{t^3 - t}{12}\right)}}$$

U is as calculated in Chapter 18, n_1 and n_2 are the sizes of the two samples, and N is the sum of n_1 and n_2. t is a new symbol in this context: the number of scores tied at a particular value. Thus if you have three scores of 6 in your data, $t = 3$ for the score 6.

Notice that Σ precedes the part of the formula involving t. This indicates that for every score which has ties you need to do the calculation for the number of ties involved *and* sum all of these separate calculations. Where there are no ties, this part of the formula reduces to zero.

The calculated value of z must equal or exceed 1.96 to be statistically significant with a two-tailed test.

B1.2 Wilcoxon Matched Pairs Test

$$z = \frac{T - \dfrac{N(N+1)}{4}}{\sqrt{\dfrac{N(N+1)(2N+1)}{24}}}$$

T is the value of the Wilcoxon Matched Pairs statistic as calculated in Chapter 18. N is the number of pairs of scores in that calculation.

As before, z must equal or exceed 1.96 to be statistically significant with a two-tailed test.

Appendix B2

Nonparametric tests for three or more groups

Several nonparametric tests were described in Chapter 18. However, these dealt with circumstances in which only two sets of scores were compared. If you have three or more sets of scores there are other tests of significance which can be used. These are nowhere near so flexible and powerful as the Analyses of Variance described in Chapters 20 to 24.

B2.1 The Kruskal–Wallis three or more unrelated conditions test

The Kruskal–Wallis test is used in circumstances where there are *more than two* groups of independent or unrelated scores. All of the scores are *ranked* from lowest to highest irrespective of which group they belong to. The average rank in each group is examined. If the null hypothesis is true, then all groups should have more or less the same average rank.

Table B2.1 **Reading scores under three different levels of motivation**

High motivation	Medium motivation	Low motivation
17	10	3
14	11	9
19	8	2
16	12	5
18	9	1
20	11	7
23	8	6
21	12	
18	9	
	10	

Table B2.2 **Scores in Table B2.1 ranked from smallest to largest**

Row	High motivation	Medium motivation	Low motivation
	20	12.5	3
	18	14.5	10
	23	7.5	2
	19	16.5	4
	21.5	10	1
	24	14.5	6
	26	7.5	5
	25	16.5	
	21.5	10	
		12.5	
A	$\text{Mean rank} = \frac{198}{9} = 22.00$	$\text{Mean rank} = \frac{122}{10} = 12.20$	$\text{Mean rank} = \frac{31}{7} = 4.43$
B	$\text{Sum of ranks}^2 = 198^2 = 39204$	$\text{Sum of ranks}^2 = 122^2 = 14884$	$\text{Sum of ranks}^2 = 31^2 = 961$
C	$\text{Mean rank}^2 = \frac{39204}{9} = 4356.00$	$\text{Mean rank}^2 = \frac{14884}{10} = 1488.40$	$\text{Mean rank}^2 = \frac{961}{7} = 137.29$
D	R = sum of calculations in Row C = 4356.00 + 1488.40 + 137.29 = 5981.69		

Imagine that the reading abilities of children are compared under three conditions: (1) high motivation, (2) medium motivation, and (3) low motivation. The data might be as in Table B2.1. Different children are used in each condition so the data are unrelated. The scores on the dependent variable are on a standard reading test.

The scores are ranked from lowest to highest, ignoring the particular group they are in. Tied scores are given the average of the ranks they would have been given if they were different (Chapter 18). The results of this would look like Table B2.2, which also includes:

■ Row A: the mean rank in each condition

■ Row B: the square of the sum of the ranks in each condition

■ Row C: the square of the sum of ranks from Row B divided by the number of scores in each condition

■ Row D: R which equals the sum of the squares of the sums of ranks divided by the sample size, i.e. the sum of the figures in Row C.

The statistic, H, is calculated next using the following formula:

$$H = \frac{12R}{N(N+1)} - 3(N+1)$$

where R is the sum of the mean rank[2] in Row D in Table B2.2, and N is the number of scores ranked. Substituting,

$$H = \frac{12 \times 5981.69}{26 \, (26 + 1)} - 3 \, (26 + 1)$$

$$= \frac{71780.28}{702} - 81$$

$$= 102.251 - 81$$

$$= 21.25$$

The distribution of H approximates that of chi-square. The degrees of freedom is the number of different groups of scores minus 1. Thus the significance of H can be assessed against Significance Table 14.1 which tells us that our value of H needs to equal or exceed 6.0 to be significant at the 5% level (two-tailed test). Thus we reject our null hypothesis that reading was unaffected by levels of motivation.

B2.2 The Friedman three or more related samples test

This test is used in circumstances in which you have three or more *related* samples of scores. The scores for each participant in the research are ranked from smallest to largest separately. In other words the scores for Joe Bloggs are ranked from 1 to 3 (or however many conditions there are), the scores for Jenny Bloggs are also ranged from 1 to 3, and so forth for the rest. The test essentially examines whether the average ranks in the several conditions of the experiment are more or less equal as they should be if the null hypothesis is true.

Table B2.3 gives the scores in an experiment to test the recall of pairs of nonsense syllables under three conditions – high, medium and low distraction. The same participants were used in all conditions of the experiment.

Table B2.4 shows the scores ranked from smallest to largest for each participant in the research separately. Ties are given the average of the ranks that they would have otherwise been given.

Table B2.3 **Scores on memory ability under three different levels of distraction**

	Low distraction	Medium distraction	High distraction
John	9	6	7
Mary	15	7	2
Shaun	12	9	5
Edmund	16	8	2
Sanjit	22	15	6
Ann	8	3	4

Table B2.4 **Scores ranked separately for each participant**

	Low distraction	**Medium distraction**	**High distraction**
John	3	1	2
Mary	3	2	1
Shaun	3	1	1
Edmund	3	2	1
Sanjit	3	2	1
Ann	3	1	2
Row A	Sum of ranks = 18	Sum of ranks = 9	Sum of ranks = 8
Row B	Square = 18^2 = 324	Square = 9^2 = 81	Square = 8^2 = 64
Row C		R = sum of above squares = 324 + 81 + 64 = 469	

◼ Row A gives the sums of the ranks for each condition or level of distraction

◼ Row B gives the square of each sum of ranks for each conditon

◼ Row C gives the total, R, of the squared sums of ranks from Row B.

The value of R is entered in the following formula:

$$\chi_r^2 = \frac{12\,R}{nK\,(K+1)} - 3n\,(K+1)$$

where n is the number of participants (i.e. of rows of scores) = 6, and K is the number of columns of data (i.e. of different conditions) = 3. Therefore

$$\chi_r^2 = \frac{12 \times 469}{6 \times 3 \times (3+1)} - 3 \times 6 \times (3+1)$$

$$= \frac{5628}{72} - 72$$

$$= 6.17$$

The statistical significance of χ_r^2 is assessed using the chi-square table (Significance Table 14.1). The degrees of freedom are the number of conditions $- 1 = 3 - 1 = 2$. This table tells us that a value of 6.0 or more is needed to be statistically significant at the 5% level (two-tailed test). Thus, it appears that the null hypothesis that the conditions have no effect should be rejected in favour of the hypothesis that levels of distraction influence memory.

Appendix C

Extended table of significance for the Pearson correlation coefficient

The following table gives both two-tailed and one-tailed values for the significance of the Pearson correlation coefficient. Ignoring the sign of the correlation coefficient obtained, your value has to equal to or be larger than the value in the table in order to be statistically significant at the level of significance stipulated at the top of the column.

Sample size	Two-tailed: 10% One-tailed: 5%	Two-tailed: 5% One-tailed: 2.5%	Two-tailed: 2% One-tailed: 1%	Two-tailed: 1% One-tailed: 0.5%
3	0.988	0.997	1.000	1.000
4	0.900	0.950	0.980	0.990
5	0.805	0.878	0.934	0.959
6	0.729	0.811	0.882	0.917
7	0.669	0.754	0.833	0.875
8	0.621	0.707	0.808	0.834
9	0.582	0.666	0.750	0.798
10	0.549	0.632	0.715	0.765
11	0.521	0.602	0.685	0.735
12	0.497	0.576	0.658	0.708
13	0.476	0.553	0.634	0.684
14	0.458	0.532	0.612	0.661
15	0.441	0.514	0.592	0.641
16	0.426	0.497	0.574	0.623
17	0.412	0.482	0.558	0.606
18	0.400	0.468	0.543	0.590
19	0.389	0.456	0.529	0.575
20	0.378	0.444	0.516	0.561
21	0.369	0.433	0.503	0.549
22	0.360	0.423	0.492	0.537
23	0.352	0.413	0.482	0.526
24	0.344	0.404	0.472	0.515
25	0.337	0.396	0.462	0.505

Sample size	Two-tailed: 10% One-tailed: 5%	Two-tailed: 5% One-tailed: 2.5%	Two-tailed: 2% One-tailed: 1%	Two-tailed: 1% One-tailed: 0.5%
26	0.330	0.388	0.453	0.496
27	0.323	0.382	0.445	0.487
28	0.317	0.374	0.437	0.479
29	0.311	0.367	0.430	0.471
30	0.306	0.361	0.423	0.463
31	0.301	0.355	0.416	0.456
32	0.296	0.349	0.409	0.449
33	0.291	0.344	0.403	0.442
34	0.287	0.339	0.397	0.436
35	0.283	0.334	0.392	0.430
36	0.279	0.329	0.386	0.424
37	0.275	0.325	0.381	0.418
38	0.271	0.320	0.376	0.413
39	0.267	0.316	0.371	0.408
40	0.264	0.312	0.367	0.403
41	0.260	0.308	0.362	0.398
42	0.257	0.304	0.358	0.393
43	0.254	0.301	0.354	0.389
44	0.251	0.297	0.350	0.384
45	0.248	0.294	0.346	0.380
46	0.246	0.291	0.342	0.376
47	0.243	0.288	0.338	0.372
48	0.240	0.285	0.335	0.368
49	0.238	0.282	0.331	0.365
50	0.235	0.279	0.328	0.361
51	0.233	0.276	0.325	0.358
52	0.231	0.273	0.322	0.354
53	0.228	0.271	0.319	0.351
54	0.226	0.268	0.316	0.348
55	0.224	0.266	0.313	0.345
56	0.222	0.263	0.310	0.341
57	0.220	0.261	0.307	0.339
58	0.218	0.259	0.305	0.336
59	0.216	0.256	0.302	0.333
60	0.214	0.254	0.300	0.330
61	0.213	0.252	0.297	0.327
62	0.211	0.250	0.295	0.325
63	0.209	0.248	0.293	0.322
64	0.207	0.246	0.290	0.320
65	0.206	0.244	0.288	0.317
66	0.204	0.242	0.286	0.315
67	0.203	0.240	0.284	0.313
68	0.201	0.239	0.282	0.310

Sample size	Two-tailed: 10% One-tailed: 5%	Two-tailed: 5% One-tailed: 2.5%	Two-tailed: 2% One-tailed: 1%	Two-tailed: 1% One-tailed: 0.5%
69	0.200	0.237	0.280	0.308
70	0.198	0.235	0.278	0.306
71	0.197	0.234	0.276	0.304
72	0.195	0.232	0.274	0.302
73	0.194	0.230	0.272	0.300
74	0.193	0.229	0.270	0.298
75	0.191	0.227	0.268	0.296
76	0.190	0.226	0.266	0.294
77	0.189	0.224	0.265	0.292
78	0.188	0.223	0.263	0.290
79	0.186	0.221	0.261	0.288
80	0.185	0.220	0.260	0.286
81	0.184	0.219	0.258	0.285
82	0.183	0.217	0.257	0.283
83	0.182	0.216	0.255	0.281
84	0.181	0.215	0.253	0.280
85	0.180	0.213	0.252	0.278
86	0.179	0.212	0.251	0.276
87	0.178	0.211	0.249	0.275
88	0.176	0.210	0.248	0.273
89	0.175	0.208	0.246	0.272
90	0.174	0.207	0.245	0.270
91	0.174	0.206	0.244	0.269
92	0.173	0.205	0.242	0.267
93	0.172	0.204	0.241	0.266
94	0.171	0.203	0.240	0.264
95	0.170	0.202	0.238	0.263
96	0.169	0.201	0.237	0.262
97	0.168	0.200	0.236	0.260
98	0.167	0.199	0.235	0.259
99	0.166	0.198	0.234	0.258
100	0.165	0.197	0.232	0.256
200	0.117	0.139	0.164	0.182
300	0.095	0.113	0.134	0.149
400	0.082	0.098	0.116	0.129
500	0.074	0.088	0.104	0.115
1000	0.052	0.062	0.074	0.081

Appendix D

Table of significance for the Spearman correlation coefficient

The following table gives both two-tailed and one-tailed values for the significance of the Spearman correlation coefficient. Ignoring the sign of the correlation coefficient obtained, your value has to equal or be larger than the value in the table in order to be statistically significant at the level of significance stipulated at the top of the column. Do not use the following table if you used the Pearson correlation coefficient approach described in Calculation 7.2. It is in most applications an approximation. The following table should only be used when the calculation has used the formula described in Calculation 7.3 and there are ties.

Sample size	Two-tailed: 10% One-tailed: 5%	Two-tailed: 5% One-tailed: 2.5%	Two-tailed: 2% One-tailed: 1%	Two-tailed: 1% One-tailed: 0.5%
5	0.900	–	–	–
6	0.829	0.886	0.943	–
7	0.714	0.786	0.893	–
8	0.643	0.738	0.833	0.881
9	0.600	0.683	0.783	0.833
10	0.564	0.648	0.745	0.858
11	0.520	0.620	0.737	0.814
12	0.496	0.591	0.703	0.776
13	0.475	0.566	0.673	0.743
14	0.456	0.544	0.646	0.714
15	0.440	0.524	0.623	0.688
16	0.425	0.506	0.602	0.665
17	0.411	0.490	0.583	0.644
18	0.399	0.475	0.565	0.625
19	0.388	0.462	0.549	0.607
20	0.377	0.450	0.535	0.591

Sample size	Two-tailed: 10% One-tailed: 5%	Two-tailed: 5% One-tailed: 2.5%	Two-tailed: 2% One-tailed: 1%	Two-tailed: 1% One-tailed: 0.5%
21	0.368	0.438	0.521	0.576
22	0.359	0.428	0.508	0.562
23	0.351	0.418	0.497	0.549
24	0.343	0.409	0.486	0.537
25	0.336	0.400	0.476	0.526
26	0.329	0.392	0.466	0.515
27	0.323	0.384	0.457	0.505
28	0.317	0.377	0.448	0.496
29	0.311	0.370	0.440	0.487
30	0.305	0.364	0.433	0.478
31	0.300	0.358	0.425	0.470
32	0.295	0.352	0.418	0.462
33	0.291	0.346	0.412	0.455
34	0.286	0.341	0.406	0.448
35	0.282	0.336	0.400	0.442
36	0.278	0.331	0.394	0.435
37	0.274	0.327	0.388	0.429
38	0.270	0.322	0.383	0.423
39	0.267	0.318	0.378	0.418
40	0.263	0.314	0.373	0.412
41	0.260	0.310	0.368	0.407
42	0.257	0.306	0.364	0.402
43	0.254	0.302	0.360	0.397
44	0.251	0.299	0.355	0.393
45	0.248	0.295	0.351	0.388
46	0.245	0.292	0.347	0.384
47	0.243	0.289	0.344	0.380
48	0.240	0.286	0.340	0.376
49	0.237	0.283	0.336	0.372
50	0.235	0.280	0.333	0.368
51	0.233	0.277	0.330	0.364
52	0.230	0.274	0.326	0.361
53	0.228	0.272	0.323	0.357
54	0.226	0.269	0.320	0.354
55	0.224	0.267	0.317	0.350
56	0.222	0.264	0.314	0.347
57	0.220	0.262	0.311	0.344
58	0.218	0.260	0.309	0.341
59	0.216	0.257	0.306	0.338
60	0.214	0.255	0.303	0.335
61	0.212	0.253	0.301	0.332
62	0.211	0.251	0.298	0.330
63	0.209	0.249	0.296	0.327

Sample size	Two-tailed: 10% One-tailed: 5%	Two-tailed: 5% One-tailed: 2.5%	Two-tailed: 2% One-tailed: 1%	Two-tailed: 1% One-tailed: 0.5%
64	0.207	0.247	0.294	0.324
65	0.206	0.245	0.291	0.322
66	0.204	0.243	0.289	0.319
67	0.202	0.241	0.287	0.317
68	0.201	0.239	0.285	0.315
69	0.199	0.238	0.283	0.312
70	0.198	0.236	0.280	0.310
71	0.197	0.234	0.278	0.308
72	0.195	0.233	0.277	0.306
73	0.194	0.231	0.275	0.303
74	0.193	0.229	0.273	0.301
75	0.191	0.228	0.271	0.299
76	0.190	0.226	0.269	0.297
77	0.189	0.225	0.267	0.295
78	0.187	0.223	0.266	0.293
79	0.186	0.222	0.264	0.292
80	0.185	0.221	0.262	0.290
81	0.184	0.219	0.261	0.288
82	0.183	0.218	0.259	0.286
83	0.182	0.216	0.257	0.284
84	0.181	0.215	0.256	0.283
85	0.179	0.214	0.254	0.281
86	0.178	0.213	0.253	0.279
87	0.177	0.211	0.251	0.278
88	0.176	0.210	0.250	0.276
89	0.175	0.209	0.248	0.274
90	0.174	0.208	0.247	0.273
91	0.173	0.207	0.246	0.271
92	0.172	0.205	0.244	0.270
93	0.172	0.204	0.243	0.268
94	0.171	0.203	0.242	0.267
95	0.170	0.202	0.240	0.266
96	0.169	0.201	0.239	0.264
97	0.168	0.200	0.238	0.263
98	0.167	0.199	0.237	0.261
99	0.166	0.198	0.235	0.260
100	0.165	0.197	0.234	0.259
200	0.117	0.139	0.165	0.183
300	0.095	0.113	0.135	0.149
400	0.082	0.098	0.117	0.129
500	0.074	0.088	0.104	0.115
1000	0.052	0.062	0.074	0.081

Appendix E

Extended table of significance for the t-test

The following table gives two-tailed and one-tailed significance values for the *t*-test. The value of *t* which you obtain (ignoring sign) in your calculation has to equal or be larger than the listed value in order to be statistically significant at the level of significance given at the top of each column.

For the related *t*-test the degrees of freedom are the *number of pairs* of scores – 1.

For the unrelated *t*-test the degrees of freedom are the number of scores – 2.

Degrees of freedom	Two-tailed: 10% One-tailed: 5%	Two-tailed: 5% One-tailed: 2.5%	Two-tailed: 2% One-tailed: 1%	Two-tailed: 1% One-tailed: 0.5%
1	6.314	12.706	31.820	63.657
2	2.920	4.303	6.965	9.925
3	2.353	3.182	4.541	5.841
4	2.132	2.776	3.747	4.604
5	2.015	2.571	3.365	4.032
6	1.943	2.447	3.365	3.708
7	1.895	2.365	2.998	3.500
8	1.860	2.306	2.897	3.355
9	1.833	2.262	2.821	3.250
10	1.813	2.228	2.764	3.169
11	1.796	2.201	2.718	3.106
12	1.782	2.179	2.681	3.055
13	1.771	2.160	2.650	3.012
14	1.761	2.145	2.625	2.977
15	1.753	2.132	2.603	2.947
16	1.746	2.120	2.583	2.921
17	1.740	2.110	2.567	2.898
18	1.734	2.101	2.552	2.878
19	1.729	2.093	2.539	2.861
20	1.725	2.086	2.528	2.845

Degrees of freedom	Two-tailed: 10% One-tailed: 5%	Two-tailed: 5% One-tailed: 2.5%	Two-tailed: 2% One-tailed: 1%	Two-tailed: 1% One-tailed: 0.5%
21	1.721	2.080	2.518	2.831
22	1.717	2.074	2.508	2.819
23	1.714	2.069	2.500	2.807
24	1.711	2.064	2.492	2.797
25	1.708	2.064	2.485	2.787
26	1.706	2.055	2.479	2.779
27	1.703	2.052	2.473	2.771
28	1.701	2.048	2.467	2.763
29	1.699	2.045	2.462	2.756
30	1.697	2.042	2.457	2.750
31	1.696	2.039	2.453	2.744
32	1.694	2.037	2.449	2.739
33	1.692	2.035	2.445	2.733
34	1.691	2.032	2.441	2.728
35	1.690	2.030	2.438	2.724
36	1.688	2.028	2.434	2.720
37	1.687	2.026	2.431	2.715
38	1.686	2.024	2.429	2.712
39	1.685	2.023	2.426	2.708
40	1.684	2.021	2.423	2.704
41	1.683	2.020	2.421	2.701
42	1.682	2.018	2.418	2.698
43	1.681	2.017	2.416	2.695
44	1.680	2.017	2.414	2.692
45	1.679	2.014	2.412	2.690
46	1.679	2.013	2.410	2.687
47	1.678	2.012	2.408	2.685
48	1.677	2.011	2.408	2.682
49	1.677	2.010	2.405	2.680
50	1.676	2.009	2.403	2.678
51	1.675	2.008	2.402	2.676
52	1.675	2.007	2.400	2.674
53	1.674	2.006	2.399	2.672
54	1.674	2.005	2.397	2.670
55	1.673	2.004	2.396	2.668
56	1.672	2.003	2.395	2.667
57	1.672	2.002	2.394	2.665
58	1.672	2.002	2.392	2.663
59	1.671	2.001	2.391	2.662
60	1.671	2.000	2.390	2.660
61	1.670	2.000	2.389	2.659
62	1.670	1.999	2.388	2.658
63	1.669	1.998	2.387	2.656

Degrees of freedom	Two-tailed: 10% One-tailed: 5%	Two-tailed: 5% One-tailed: 2.5%	Two-tailed: 2% One-tailed: 1%	Two-tailed: 1% One-tailed: 0.5%
64	1.669	1.998	2.386	2.655
65	1.669	1.997	2.385	2.654
66	1.668	1.997	2.384	2.652
67	1.668	1.996	2.383	2.651
68	1.668	1.995	2.383	2.650
69	1.667	1.995	2.382	2.649
70	1.667	1.994	2.381	2.648
71	1.667	1.994	2.380	2.647
72	1.666	1.994	2.379	2.646
73	1.666	1.993	2.379	2.645
74	1.666	1.993	2.378	2.644
75	1.665	1.992	2.377	2.643
76	1.665	1.992	2.376	2.642
77	1.665	1.991	2.376	2.641
78	1.665	1.991	2.375	2.640
79	1.664	1.990	2.375	2.640
80	1.664	1.990	2.374	2.639
81	1.664	1.990	2.373	2.638
82	1.664	1.989	2.373	2.637
83	1.663	1.989	2.372	2.636
84	1.663	1.989	2.372	2.636
85	1.663	1.988	2.371	2.635
86	1.663	1.988	2.370	2.634
87	1.663	1.988	2.370	2.634
88	1.662	1.987	2.369	2.633
89	1.662	1.987	2.369	2.632
90	1.662	1.987	2.369	2.632
91	1.662	1.986	2.368	2.631
92	1.662	1.986	2.368	2.630
93	1.661	1.986	2.367	2.630
94	1.661	1.986	2.367	2.629
95	1.661	1.985	2.366	2.629
96	1.661	1.985	2.366	2.628
97	1.661	1.985	2.365	2.627
98	1.661	1.984	2.365	2.627
99	1.660	1.984	2.365	2.626
100	1.660	1.984	2.364	2.626
200	1.653	1.972	2.345	2.601
300	1.650	1.968	2.339	2.592
400	1.649	1.966	2.336	2.588
500	1.648	1.965	2.334	2.586
1000	1.646	1.962	2.330	2.581
∞	1.645	1.960	2.326	2.576

Appendix F

Table of significance for Chi-square

The following table gives one-tailed and two-tailed significance values for chi-square. The obtained value of chi-square has to equal or exceed the listed value to be statistically significant at the level at the top of the column.

Degrees of freedom	5%	1%
1 (One-tailed)[a]	2.705	5.412
1 (2-tailed)	3.841	6.635
2 (2-tailed)	5.992	9.210
3 (2-tailed)	7.815	11.345
4 (2-tailed)	9.488	13.277
5 (2-tailed)	11.070	15.086
6 (2-tailed)	12.592	16.812
7 (2-tailed)	14.067	18.475
8 (2-tailed)	15.507	20.090
9 (2-tailed)	16.919	21.666
10 (2-tailed)	18.307	23.209
11 (2-tailed)	19.675	24.725
12 (2-tailed)	21.026	26.217

[a] It is correct to carry out a one-tailed chi-square only when there is just 1 degree of freedom.

Appendix G

Extended table of significance for the sign test

Your value must be smaller than or equal to the listed value to be significant at the level stipulated at the top of the column.

N	Two-tailed: 5% One-tailed: 2.5%	Two-tailed: 2% One-tailed: 1%	Two-tailed: 1% One-tailed: 0.5%
5	0		
6	0	0	
7	0	0	
8	1	0	0
9	1	1	0
10	1	1	0
11	2	1	0
12	2	2	1
13	3	2	1
14	3	2	1
15	3	3	2
16	4	3	2
17	4	4	2
18	5	4	3
19	5	4	3
20	5	5	3
21	6	5	4
22	6	5	4
23	7	6	5
24	7	6	5
25	7	7	5
26	8	8	6
27	9	8	6
28	9	8	7
29	10	9	7

N	Two-tailed: 5% One-tailed: 2.5%	Two-tailed: 2% One-tailed: 1%	Two-tailed: 1% One-tailed: 0.5%
30	10	9	7
31	10	10	8
32	11	10	8
33	11	10	9
34	12	11	9
35	12	11	9
36	13	12	10
37	13	12	10
38	13	12	11
39	14	13	11
40	14	13	11
41	15	14	12
42	15	14	12
43	16	15	13
44	16	15	13
45	16	15	13
46	17	16	14
47	17	16	14
48	18	17	15
49	18	17	15
50	19	18	15
51	19	18	16
52	20	18	16
53	20	19	17
54	20	19	17
55	21	20	17
56	21	20	18
57	22	21	18
58	22	21	19
59	23	21	19
60	23	22	19
61	24	22	20
62	24	23	20
63	24	23	21
64	25	24	21
65	25	24	22
66	26	25	22
67	26	25	22
68	27	25	23
69	27	26	23
70	28	26	24
71	28	27	24
72	28	27	24

Degrees of freedom	Two-tailed: 5% One-tailed: 2.5%	Two-tailed: 2% One-tailed: 1%	Two-tailed: 1% One-tailed: 0.5%
73	29	28	25
74	29	28	25
75	30	29	26
76	30	29	26
77	31	29	27
78	31	30	27
79	32	30	27
80	32	31	28
81	33	31	28
82	33	32	29
83	33	32	29
84	34	32	30
85	34	33	30
86	35	33	30
87	35	34	31
88	36	34	31
89	36	35	32
90	37	35	32
91	37	36	33
92	38	36	33
93	38	36	34
94	38	37	34
95	39	37	34
96	39	38	35
97	40	38	35
98	40	39	36
99	41	39	36
100	41	40	37
200	88	86	81
300	135	132	127
400	183	180	174
500	231	228	221
1000	473	468	459

Appendix H

Table of significance for the Wilcoxon Matched Pairs Test

Your value must be smaller than or equal to the listed value to be significant at the level stipulated at the top of the column.

Number of pairs of scores	Two-tailed: 5% One-tailed: 2.5%	Two-tailed: 2% One-tailed: 1%	Two-tailed: 1% One-tailed: 0.5%
6	2	1	–
7	4	2	–
8	6	4	0
9	8	6	2
10	11	8	3
11	14	11	5
12	17	14	7
13	21	17	10
14	26	21	13
15	31	25	16
16	36	30	20
17	42	35	24
18	47	40	28
19	54	46	33
20	60	52	37
21	68	59	42
22	76	66	47
23	84	74	54
24	92	81	60
25	101	90	67
26	111	98	74
27	121	107	82
28	131	117	90
29	141	127	99

Number of pairs of scores	Two-tailed: 5% One-tailed: 2.5%	Two-tailed: 2% One-tailed: 1%	Two-tailed: 1% One-tailed: 0.5%
30	153	137	108
31	164	148	117
32	176	159	127
33	188	171	137
34	201	183	147
35	215	195	158
36	228	208	169
37	242	222	181
38	257	235	193
39	272	250	206
40	288	264	219
41	304	279	232
42	320	295	246
43	337	311	260
44	354	327	275
45	372	344	290
46	390	361	305
47	409	379	321
48	428	397	337
49	447	415	354
50	467	434	371
51	488	454	389
52	508	474	407
53	530	494	425
54	551	515	444
55	574	536	463
56	596	558	483
57	619	580	503
58	643	602	524
59	667	625	545
60	692	649	566
61	716	673	588
62	742	697	610
63	768	722	633
64	794	747	656
65	821	773	679
66	848	799	703
67	876	825	728
68	904	852	752
69	932	880	778
70	961	908	803

Number of pairs of scores	Two-tailed: 5% One-tailed: 2.5%	Two-tailed: 2% One-tailed: 1%	Two-tailed: 1% One-tailed: 0.5%
71	991	936	29
72	1021	965	856
73	1051	994	883
74	1082	1024	910
75	1113	1054	938
76	1145	1084	967
77	1178	1115	995
78	1210	1147	1025
79	1243	1179	1054
80	1277	1211	1084
81	1311	1244	1115
82	1346	1278	1146
83	1381	1311	1177
84	1416	1346	1209
85	1452	1380	1241
86	1488	1415	1274
87	1525	1451	1307
88	1563	1487	1340
89	1600	1523	1374
90	1639	1560	1409
91	1677	1598	1444
92	1717	1636	1479
93	1756	1674	1515
94	1796	1713	1551
95	1837	1752	1588
96	1878	1792	1625
97	1919	1832	1662
98	1961	1872	1700
99	2004	1913	1739
100	2047	1955	1778
200	8702	8444	7944
300	20,101	19,628	18,710
400	36,294	35,565	34,154
500	57,308	56,290	54,318
1000	235,222	232,344	226,772

Appendix I

Table of significance for the Mann-Whitney U-test

5% significant values level for the Mann-Whitney U statistic (one-tailed test)

Your value must be in the listed ranges for your sample sizes to be significant at the 5% level, i.e. to accept the hypothesis. In addition, you should have predicted which group would have the smaller sum of ranks.

				Sample size for larger group							
5	6	7	8	9	10	11	12	13	14	15	20
0–4	0–5	0–6	0–8	0–9	0–11	0–12	0–13	0–15	0–16	0–18	0–25
21–25	25–30	29–35	32–40	36–45	39–50	43–55	47–60	50–65	54–70	57–75	75–100
0–5	0–7	0–8	0–10	0–12	0–14	0–16	0–17	0–19	0–21	0–23	0–32
25–30	29–36	34–42	38–48	42–54	46–60	50–66	55–72	59–78	61–82	67–90	88–120
0–6	0–8	0–11	0–13	0–15	0–17	0–19	0–21	0–24	0–26	0–28	0–39
29–35	34–42	38–49	43–56	48–63	53–70	58–77	63–84	67–91	72–98	77–105	101–140
0–8	0–10	0–13	0–15	0–18	0–20	0–23	0–26	0–28	0–31	0–33	0–47
32–40	38–48	43–56	49–64	54–72	60–80	65–88	70–96	76–104	81–112	87–120	113–160
0–9	0–12	0–15	0–18	0–21	0–24	0–27	0–30	0–33	0–36	0–39	0–54
36–45	42–54	48–63	54–72	60–81	66–90	72–99	78–108	84–117	90–126	96–135	126–180
0–11	0–14	0–17	0–20	0–24	0–27	0–31	0–34	0–37	0–41	0–44	0–62
39–50	46–60	53–70	60–80	66–90	73–100	79–110	86–120	93–130	99–140	106–150	138–200
0–12	0–16	0–19	0–23	0–27	0–31	0–34	0–38	0–42	0–46	0–50	0–69
43–55	50–66	58–77	65–88	72–99	79–110	87–121	94–132	101–143	108–154	115–165	151–220
0–13	0–17	0–21	0–26	0–30	0–34	0–38	0–42	0–47	0–51	0–55	0–77
47–60	55–72	63–84	70–96	78–108	86–120	94–132	102–144	109–156	117–168	125–180	163–240
0–15	0–19	0–24	0–28	0–33	0–37	0–42	0–47	0–51	0–56	0–61	0–84
50–65	59–78	67–91	76–104	84–117	93–130	101–143	109–156	118–169	126–182	134–195	176–260
0–16	0–21	0–26	0–31	0–36	0–41	0–46	0–59	0–56	0–61	0–66	0–92
54–70	61–82	72–98	81–112	90–126	99–140	108–154	109–168	126–182	135–196	144–210	188–280
0–18	0–23	0–28	0–33	0–39	0–44	0–50	0–55	0–61	0–66	0–72	0–100
57–75	67–90	77–105	87–120	96–135	106–150	115–165	125–180	153–195	144–210	153–225	200–300
0–25	0–32	0–39	0–47	0–54	0–62	0–69	0–77	0–84	0–92	0–100	0–138
75–100	88–120	101–140	113–160	126–180	138–200	151–220	163–240	200–260	188–280	200–300	262–400

The above table has been adapted and extended from Table I of R.P. Runyon and A. Haber (1989). *Fundamentals of Behavioral Statistics*. New York: McGraw-Hill. With the kind permission of the publisher.

1% significant values level for the Mann-Whitney *U* statistic (two-tailed test)

Your value must be in the listed ranges for your sample sizes to be significant at the 1% level, i.e. to accept the hypothesis at the 1% level.

Sample size for larger group											
5	6	7	8	9	10	11	12	13	14	15	20
0 / 25	0–1 / 29–30	0–1 / 34–35	0–2 / 38–40	0–3 / 42–45	0–4 / 46–50	0–5 / 50–55	0–6 / 54–60	0–7 / 58–65	0–7 / 67–70	0–8 / 67–75	0–13 / 87–100
0–1 / 29–30	0–2 / 34–36	0–3 / 39–42	0–4 / 44–48	0–5 / 49–54	0–6 / 54–60	0–7 / 59–66	0–9 / 63–72	0–10 / 68–78	0–11 / 71–82	0–12 / 78–90	0–18 / 102–120
0–1 / 34–35	0–3 / 39–42	0–4 / 45–49	0–6 / 50–56	0–7 / 56–63	0–9 / 61–70	0–10 / 67–77	0–12 / 72–84	0–13 / 78–91	0–15 / 83–98	0–16 / 89–105	0–24 / 116–140
0–2 / 38–40	0–4 / 44–48	0–6 / 50–56	0–7 / 57–64	0–9 / 63–72	0–11 / 69–80	0–13 / 75–88	0–15 / 81–96	0–17 / 87–104	0–18 / 94–112	0–20 / 100–120	0–30 / 130–160
0–3 / 42–45	0–5 / 49–54	0–7 / 56–63	0–9 / 63–72	0–11 / 70–81	0–13 / 77–90	0–16 / 81–99	0–18 / 90–108	0–20 / 89–117	0–22 / 104–126	0–24 / 101–135	0–36 / 144–180
0–4 / 46–50	0–6 / 54–60	0–9 / 61–70	0–11 / 69–80	0–13 / 77–90	0–16 / 84–100	0–18 / 92–110	0–21 / 99–120	0–24 / 97–130	0–26 / 114–140	0–29 / 111–150	0–42 / 158–200
0–5 / 50–55	0–7 / 59–66	0–10 / 67–77	0–13 / 75–88	0–16 / 83–99	0–18 / 92–110	0–21 / 90–111	0–24 / 108–132	0–27 / 106–143	0–30 / 124–154	0–33 / 132–165	0–48 / 172–220
0–6 / 54–60	0–9 / 63–72	0–12 / 72–84	0–15 / 81–96	0–18 / 90–108	0–21 / 99–120	0–24 / 108–132	0–27 / 117–144	0–31 / 115–156	0–34 / 134–168	0–37 / 143–180	0–54 / 186–240
0–7 / 58–65	0–10 / 68–78	0–13 / 78–91	0–17 / 87–104	0- 20 / 97–117	0–24 / 106–130	0–27 / 116–143	0–31 / 125–156	0–34 / 135–169	0–38 / 144–182	0–42 / 153–195	0–60 / 200–260
0–7 / 63–70	0–11 / 71–82	0–15 / 83–98	0–18 / 94–112	0–22 / 104–126	0–26 / 114–140	0–30 / 124–154	0–34 / 134–168	0–38 / 144–182	0–42 / 154–196	0–46 / 164–210	0–67 / 213–280
0–8 / 67–75	0–12 / 78–90	0–16 / 89–105	0–20 / 100–120	0–24 / 111–135	0–29 / 121–150	0–33 / 132–165	0–37 / 143–180	0–42 / 153–195	0–46 / 164–210	0–51 / 174–225	0–73 / 227–300
0–13 / 87–100	0–18 / 102–120	0–24 / 116–140	0–30 / 130–160	0–36 / 144–180	0–42 / 158–200	0–48 / 172–220	0–54 / 186–240	0–60 / 200–260	0–67 / 213–280	0–73 / 227–300	0–105 / 295–400

The above table has been adapted and extended from Table I of R.P. Runyon and A. Haber (1989). *Fundamentals of Behavioral Statistics*. New York: McGraw-Hill. With the kind permission of the publisher.

Table of significance values for the *F*-distribution

5% significance levels for *F*-distribution for testing differences in variance estimates between two samples (one-tailed test)

Your value has to equal or be larger than the tabled value to be significant at the 5% level, i.e. to accept the hypothesis. In addition, you should have predicted which of the variance estimates is the larger.

Degrees of freedom smaller variance estimate (Denominator)	Degrees of freedom larger variance estimate (Numerator)					
	5	7	10	20	50	∞
5	3.453	3.368	3.297	3.207	3.147	3.105
6	3.107	3.015	2.937	2.836	2.770	2.722
7	2.883	2.785	2.703	2.595	2.523	2.471
8	2.727	2.624	2.538	2.425	2.348	2.293
10	2.522	2.414	2.323	2.201	2.117	2.055
12	2.394	2.283	2.188	2.060	1.970	1.904
15	2.273	2.158	2.059	1.924	1.828	1.755
20	2.158	2.040	1.937	1.794	1.690	1.607
30	2.049	1.927	1.820	1.667	1.552	1.456
50	1.966	1.841	1.729	1.568	1.441	1.327
100	1.906	1.778	1.663	1.494	1.355	1.214
∞	1.847	1.774	1.599	1.421	1.263	1.000

5% significant values of the *F*-ratio for ANOVA (one-tailed test)

Your value has to equal or be larger than the tabled value to be significant at the 5% level, i.e. to accept the hypothesis. You should also have predicted which group of scores has the highest mean. Only the *column* for 1 degree of freedom should be used for one-tailed testing.

Degrees of freedom for error or within-cells mean square (or variance estimate)	Degrees of freedom for between-treatments mean square (or variance estimate)					
	1	2	3	4	5	8
1	39.862	49.500	53.593	55.833	57.240	63.325
2	8.526	9.000	9.162	9.243	9.293	9.491
3	5.538	5.463	5.391	5.343	5.309	5.134
4	4.545	4.325	4.191	4.107	4.051	3.761
5	4.060	3.780	3.619	3.520	3.453	3.105
6	3.776	3.463	3.289	3.181	3.107	2.722
7	3.590	3.257	3.074	2.961	2.883	2.471
8	3.458	3.113	2.924	2.806	2.727	2.293
9	3.360	3.007	2.813	2.693	2.611	2.160
10	3.285	2.925	2.728	2.605	2.522	2.056
13	3.136	2.763	2.560	2.434	2.347	1.847
15	3.073	2.695	2.490	2.361	2.273	1.755
20	2.975	2.589	2.380	2.249	2.158	1.608
30	2.881	2.489	2.276	2.142	2.049	1.457
60	2.791	2.393	2.177	2.041	1.946	1.292
∞	2.711	2.303	2.084	1.945	1.848	1.000

1% significance levels for *F*-distribution for testing differences in variance estimates between two samples (two-tailed test)

Your value has to equal or be larger than the tabled value to be significant at the 1% level for a two-tailed test, i.e. to accept the hypothesis.

Degrees of freedom smaller variance estimate (Denominator)	Degrees of freedom larger variance estimate (Numerator)					
	5	7	10	20	50	∞
5	10.967	10.456	10.051	9.553	9.238	9.020
6	8.746	8.260	7.874	7.396	7.091	6.880
7	7.460	6.993	6.620	6.155	5.858	5.649
8	6.632	6.178	5.814	5.359	5.065	4.859
10	5.636	5.200	4.849	4.405	4.115	3.909
12	5.064	4.640	4.296	3.858	3.569	3.361
15	4.556	4.142	3.805	3.372	3.081	2.868
20	4.103	3.699	3.368	2.938	2.643	2.421
25	3.855	3.457	3.129	2.699	2.400	2.169
30	3.699	3.305	2.979	2.549	2.245	2.006
50	3.408	3.020	2.698	2.265	3.081	1.683
100	3.206	2.823	2.503	2.067	1.735	1.427
∞	3.017	2.639	2.321	1.878	1.523	1.000

5% significant values of the F-ratio for ANOVA (two-tailed test)

Your value has to equal or be larger than the tabled value to be significant at the 1% level for a two-tailed test, i.e. to accept the hypothesis.

Degrees of freedom for error or within-cells mean square (or variance estimate)	Degrees of freedom for between-treatments mean square (or variance estimate)					
	1	2	3	4	5	∞
1	4050.000	5000.000	5400.000	5620.000	5760.000	6370.000
2	98.502	99.000	99.166	99.249	99.299	99.499
3	34.116	30.817	29.458	28.710	28.237	26.125
4	21.198	18.000	16.694	15.977	15.522	13.463
5	16.258	13.274	12.060	11.392	10.967	9.020
6	13.745	10.925	9.780	9.148	8.746	6.880
7	12.246	9.547	8.451	7.847	7.460	5.649
8	11.259	8.649	7.591	7.006	6.632	4.859
9	10.562	8.021	6.992	6.422	6.057	4.311
10	10.044	7.559	6.552	5.994	5.636	3.909
13	9.074	6.701	5.739	5.205	4.862	3.165
15	8.683	6.359	5.417	4.893	4.556	2.868
20	8.096	5.849	4.938	4.431	4.103	2.421
30	7.563	5.390	4.510	4.018	3.699	2.006
60	7.077	4.977	4.126	3.649	3.339	1.601
∞	6.637	4.605	3.782	3.319	3.017	1.000

Appendix K

Table of significant values of *t* when making multiple *t*-tests

The following table gives the 5% significance values for two-tailed *t*-tests when you are making up to ten unplanned comparisons. The number of comparisons you decide to make is up to you and does not have to be the maximum possible. This table can be used in any circumstances where you have multiple *t*-tests.

Degrees of freedom	Number of comparisons being made									
	1	2	3	4	5	6	7	8	9	10
1	12.706	25.452	38.188	50.923	63.657	76.390	89.124	101.856	114.589	127.321
2	4.303	6.205	7.649	8.860	9.925	10.886	11.769	12.590	13.360	14.089
3	3.182	4.177	4.857	5.392	5.841	6.231	6.580	6.895	7.185	7.453
4	2.776	3.495	3.961	4.315	4.604	4.851	5.067	5.261	5.437	5.598
5	2.571	3.163	3.534	3.810	4.032	4.219	4.382	4.526	4.655	4.773
6	2.447	2.969	3.288	3.521	3.708	3.863	3.997	4.115	4.221	4.317
7	2.365	2.841	3.128	3.335	3.500	3.636	3.753	3.855	3.947	4.029
8	2.306	2.752	3.016	3.206	3.355	3.479	3.584	3.677	3.759	3.833
9	2.262	2.685	2.933	3.111	3.250	3.364	3.462	3.547	3.622	3.690
10	2.228	2.634	2.870	3.038	3.169	3.277	3.368	3.448	3.518	3.581
11	2.201	2.593	2.820	2.981	3.106	3.208	3.295	3.370	3.437	3.497
12	2.179	2.560	2.780	2.934	3.055	3.153	3.236	3.308	3.371	3.428
13	2.160	2.533	2.746	2.896	3.012	3.107	3.187	3.257	3.318	3.373
14	2.145	2.510	2.718	2.864	2.977	3.069	3.146	3.213	3.273	3.326
15	2.132	2.490	2.694	2.837	2.947	3.036	3.112	3.177	3.235	3.286
16	2.120	2.473	2.673	2.813	2.921	3.008	3.082	3.146	3.202	3.252
17	2.110	2.458	2.655	2.793	2.898	2.984	3.056	3.119	3.174	3.222
18	2.101	2.445	2.639	2.774	2.878	2.963	3.034	3.095	3.149	3.197
19	2.093	2.433	2.625	2.759	2.861	2.944	3.014	3.074	3.127	3.174
20	2.086	2.423	2.613	2.744	2.845	2.927	2.996	3.055	3.107	3.153

Degrees of freedom	Number of comparisons being made									
	1	2	3	4	5	6	7	8	9	10
21	2.080	2.414	2.601	2.732	2.831	2.912	2.980	3.038	3.090	3.135
22	2.074	2.406	2.591	2.720	2.819	2.898	2.966	3.023	3.074	3.119
23	2.069	2.398	2.582	2.710	2.807	2.886	2.953	3.010	3.059	3.104
24	2.064	2.391	2.574	2.700	2.797	2.875	2.941	2.997	3.047	3.091
25	2.064	2.385	2.566	2.692	2.787	2.865	2.930	2.986	3.035	3.078
26	2.055	2.379	2.559	2.684	2.779	2.856	2.920	2.975	3.024	3.067
27	2.052	2.373	2.553	2.676	2.771	2.847	2.911	2.966	3.014	3.057
28	2.048	2.369	2.547	2.670	2.763	2.839	2.902	2.957	3.005	3.047
29	2.045	2.364	2.541	2.663	2.756	2.832	2.894	2.949	2.996	3.038
30	2.042	2.360	2.536	2.657	2.750	2.825	2.887	2.941	2.988	3.030
31	2.039	2.356	2.531	2.652	2.744	2.818	2.880	2.934	2.981	3.022
32	2.037	2.352	2.526	2.647	2.739	2.812	2.874	2.927	2.974	3.015
33	2.035	2.348	2.522	2.642	2.733	2.807	2.868	2.921	2.967	3.008
34	2.032	2.345	2.518	2.638	2.728	2.801	2.863	2.915	2.961	3.002
35	2.030	2.342	2.515	2.633	2.724	2.797	2.857	2.910	2.955	2.996
36	2.028	2.339	2.511	2.630	2.720	2.792	2.853	2.905	2.950	2.990
37	2.026	2.336	2.508	2.626	2.715	2.788	2.848	2.900	2.945	2.985
38	2.024	2.334	2.505	2.622	2.712	2.784	2.844	2.895	2.940	2.980
39	2.023	2.331	2.502	2.619	2.708	2.780	2.839	2.891	2.936	2.976
40	2.021	2.329	2.499	2.616	2.704	2.776	2.836	2.887	2.931	2.971
41	2.020	2.327	2.496	2.613	2.701	2.772	2.832	2.883	2.927	2.967
42	2.018	2.325	2.494	2.610	2.698	2.769	2.828	2.879	2.923	2.963
43	2.017	2.323	2.491	2.607	2.695	2.766	2.825	2.875	2.920	2.959
44	2.017	2.321	2.489	2.605	2.692	2.763	2.822	2.872	2.916	2.955
45	2.014	2.319	2.487	2.602	2.690	2.760	2.819	2.869	2.913	2.952
46	2.013	2.317	2.485	2.600	2.687	2.757	2.816	2.866	2.910	2.949
47	2.012	2.316	2.483	2.598	2.685	2.755	2.813	2.863	2.907	2.946
48	2.011	2.314	2.481	2.595	2.682	2.752	2.810	2.860	2.904	2.943
49	2.010	2.312	2.479	2.593	2.680	2.750	2.808	2.857	2.901	2.940
50	2.009	2.311	2.477	2.591	2.678	2.747	2.805	2.855	2.898	2.937
51	2.008	2.309	2.476	2.589	2.676	2.745	2.803	2.853	2.896	2.934
52	2.007	2.308	2.474	2.588	2.674	2.743	2.801	2.850	2.893	2.932
53	2.006	2.307	2.472	2.586	2.672	2.741	2.798	2.848	2.891	2.929
54	2.005	2.306	2.471	2.584	2.670	2.739	2.797	2.846	2.889	2.927
55	2.004	2.304	2.469	2.583	2.668	2.737	2.795	2.844	2.887	2.925
56	2.003	2.303	2.468	2.581	2.667	2.735	2.793	2.842	2.885	2.922
57	2.002	2.302	2.467	2.579	2.665	2.734	2.791	2.840	2.882	2.920
58	2.002	2.301	2.465	2.578	2.663	2.732	2.789	2.838	2.881	2.918
59	2.001	2.300	2.464	2.577	2.662	2.730	2.787	2.836	2.879	2.916
60	2.000	2.299	2.463	2.575	2.660	2.729	2.786	2.834	2.877	2.915
61	2.000	2.298	2.462	2.574	2.659	2.727	2.784	2.833	2.875	2.913

Degrees of freedom	Number of comparisons being made									
	1	2	3	4	5	6	7	8	9	10
62	1.999	2.297	2.461	2.573	2.658	2.726	2.782	2.831	2.873	2.911
63	1.998	2.296	2.460	2.571	2.656	2.724	2.781	2.829	2.872	2.909
64	1.998	2.295	2.459	2.570	2.655	2.723	2.779	2.828	2.870	2.908
65	1.997	2.295	2.458	2.569	2.654	2.721	2.778	2.826	2.869	2.906
66	1.997	2.294	2.457	2.568	2.652	2.720	2.777	2.825	2.867	2.905
67	1.996	2.293	2.456	2.567	2.651	2.719	2.775	2.824	2.866	2.903
68	1.995	2.292	2.455	2.566	2.650	2.718	2.774	2.822	2.864	2.902
69	1.995	2.291	2.454	2.565	2.649	2.716	2.773	2.821	2.863	2.900
70	1.994	2.291	2.453	2.564	2.648	2.715	2.772	2.820	2.862	2.899
71	1.994	2.290	2.452	2.563	2.647	2.714	2.770	2.818	2.860	2.898
72	1.994	2.289	2.451	2.562	2.646	2.713	2.769	2.817	2.859	2.896
73	1.993	2.289	2.450	2.561	2.645	2.712	2.768	2.816	2.858	2.895
74	1.993	2.288	2.450	2.560	2.644	2.711	2.767	2.815	2.857	2.894
75	1.992	2.287	2.449	2.559	2.643	2.710	2.766	2.814	2.856	2.893
76	1.992	2.287	2.448	2.559	2.642	2.709	2.765	2.813	2.854	2.891
77	1.991	2.286	2.447	2.558	2.641	2.708	2.764	2.812	2.853	2.890
78	1.991	2.285	2.447	2.557	2.640	2.707	2.763	2.811	2.852	2.889
79	1.990	2.285	2.446	2.556	2.640	2.706	2.762	2.810	2.851	2.888
80	1.990	2.284	2.445	2.555	2.639	2.705	2.761	2.809	2.850	2.887
81	1.990	2.284	2.445	2.555	2.638	2.705	2.760	2.808	2.849	2.886
82	1.989	2.283	2.444	2.554	2.637	2.704	2.759	2.807	2.848	2.885
83	1.989	2.283	2.444	2.553	2.636	2.703	2.759	2.806	2.847	2.884
84	1.989	2.282	2.443	2.553	2.636	2.702	2.758	2.805	2.846	2.883
85	1.988	2.282	2.442	2.552	2.635	2.701	2.757	2.804	2.845	2.882
86	1.988	2.281	2.442	2.551	2.634	2.701	2.756	2.803	2.845	2.881
87	1.988	2.281	2.441	2.551	2.634	2.700	2.755	2.803	2.844	2.880
88	1.987	2.280	2.441	2.550	2.633	2.699	2.755	2.802	2.843	2.880
89	1.987	2.280	2.440	2.550	2.632	2.699	2.754	2.801	2.842	2.879
90	1.987	2.280	2.440	2.549	2.632	2.698	2.753	2.800	2.841	2.878
91	1.986	2.279	2.439	2.548	2.631	2.697	2.752	2.800	2.841	2.877
92	1.986	2.279	2.439	2.548	2.630	2.696	2.752	2.799	2.840	2.876
93	1.986	2.278	2.438	2.547	2.630	2.696	2.751	2.798	2.839	2.876
94	1.986	2.278	2.438	2.547	2.629	2.695	2.750	2.797	2.838	2.875
95	1.985	2.277	2.437	2.546	2.629	2.695	2.750	2.797	2.838	2.874
96	1.985	2.277	2.437	2.546	2.628	2.694	2.749	2.796	2.837	2.873
97	1.985	2.277	2.436	2.545	2.627	2.694	2.748	2.795	2.836	2.873
98	1.984	2.276	2.436	2.545	2.627	2.693	2.748	2.795	2.836	2.872
99	1.984	2.276	2.435	2.544	2.626	2.692	2.747	2.794	2.835	2.871
100	1.984	2.276	2.435	2.544	2.626	2.692	2.747	2.793	2.834	2.871
∞	1.960	2.241	2.394	2.498	2.576	2.638	2.690	2.734	2.773	2.807

References

Baron, L. and Straus, M. (1989). *Four Theories of Rape: A State-Level Analysis*. New Haven, CT: Yale University Press.

Blalock, H.M. (1972). *Social Statistics*. New York: McGraw-Hill.

Bryman, A. and Cramer, D. (1999). *Quantitive Data Analysis with SPSS Release 8 for Windows: A Guide for Social Scientists*. London: Routledge.

Butler, C. (1995a). Teachers' qualities, resources and involvement of special needs children in mainstream classrooms. Unpublished thesis, Department of Social Sciences, Loughborough University.

Butler, R. (1995b). Motivational and informational functions and consequences of children's attention to peers' work. *Journal of Educational Psychology*, **87**(3), 347–360.

Cramer, D. (1992). *Personality and Psychotherapy*. Milton Keynes: Open University Press.

Cramer, D. (1998). *Fundamental Statistics for Social Research: Step-by-step Calculations and Computer Techniques using SPSS for Windows*, London: Routledge.

Crighton, D. and Towl, G. (1994). The selection and recruitment of prison officers. *Forensic Update: A Newsletter for Forensic Psychologists*, **39**, 4–7.

Donnerstein, E. (1980). Aggressive erotica and violence against women. *Journal of Personality and Social Psychology*, **39**(2), 269–277.

Gillis, J.S. (1980). *Child Anxiety Scale Manual*. Champaign, Il: Institute of Personality and Ability Testing.

Glantz, S.A. and Slinker, B.K. (1990). *Primer of Applied Regression and Analysis of Violence*. New York: McGraw-Hill.

Howell D. (1997). *Statistical Methods for Psychology* 4th edition. Belmont, CA: Duxbury Press.

Howitt, D. and Cumberbatch, G. (1990). *Pornography: Impacts and Influences*. London: Home Office Research and Planning Unit.

Huitema, B.E. (1980). *The Analysis of Covariance and its Alternatives*. New York: Wiley.

Johnston, F.A. and Johnston, S.A. (1986). Differences between human figure drawings of child molesters and control groups. *Journal of Clinical Psychology*, **42**(4), 638–647.

Kerlinger, F.N. (1986). *Foundations of Behavioural Research*. New York: Holt, Rinehart & Winston.

Kline, P. (1994). *An Easy Guide to Factor Analysis*. London: Routledge.

Munford, M.B. (1994). Relationship of gender, self-esteem, social class and racial identity to depression in blacks. *Journal of Black Psychology*, **20**, 157–174.

Pedhazur, E. J. (1982). *Multiple Regression in Behavioral Research: Explanation and Prediction* (2nd edition). New York: Holt, Rinehart & Winston.

Rosenthal, J.A. (1988). Patterns of reported child abuse and neglect. *Child Abuse and Neglect*, **12**, 263–271.

Szostak, H. (1995). Competitive performance, anxiety and perceptions of parental pressure in young tennis players. Unpublished thesis, Department of Social Sciences, Loughborough University.

Tabachnick, B. G. and Fidell, L. S. (1996). *Using Multivariate Statistics* (3rd edition), New York: HarperCollins.

Tinsley, H.E.A. and Weiss D.J. (1975). Interrater reliability and agreement of subjective judgments. *Journal of Counselling Psychology*, **22**, 358–376.

Wagner, U. and Zick, A. (1995). The relation of formal education to ethnic prejudice: its reliability, validity and explanation. *European Journal of Social Psychology*, **25**, 41–56.

Index

addition rule 162
  calculation 164
Agresti, A. 441
alpha reliability 400–2
alternative hypothesis 102–3, 203
analysis of covariance 269–99
  calculation 287–98
  comparing adjusted means 297–8
  covariate 287
  example 287
  means after adjustment 295–6
analysis of variance
  fixed vs. random effects 271
  three factors 257–61
analysis of variance correlated scores
  214–229
  calculation 219–25
  matching 224
  significance table 230
  summary table 219, 225
  types of research appropriate 222–3
analysis of variance mixed designs
  269–99
  between subjects scores 273–4
  fixed vs. random effect 271
  interaction 276–8
  main effects 275–6
  problems 280
  residual error 272
  subjects within groups 274
  within subjects variance 275–6

analysis of variance multiple
  comparisons 262–3
analysis of variance one-way unrelated
  195–213
  calculation 204–12
  degrees of freedom 201–4
  quick formulae degrees of freedom
    204
  significance table for 200
  summary table 208–9
analysis of variance two-way 231–61
  2 x 3 244
  calculation 252–7
  degrees of freedom error 246
  degrees of freedom main effects
    247
  dependent variable 243–4
  error 245–6
  error variance estimate 246
  F-ratios 250–2
  independent variable 244
  interaction 245–6, 248–50, 250–2
  levels of treatment 244
  main effect 245–7
  main effects vs. interactions 249–50
  multivariate 231
  significance table 249
  summary table 251, 248
  ways 231
Anderson, E. B. 441
asymmetry 25

bands of scores   17, 56
bar chart   14–15
Baron, L.   315, 475
between groups variance   209
bimodal distributions   23, 37
Blalock, H.M.   141, 475
Bryman, A.   333, 359, 475
Butler, C.   317, 475
Butler, R.   329, 322, 475

Castellan, N.J.   186
Cattell, Raymond   321
cells   143
Child, D.   333
chi-square   142–5, 181
    alternatives to   152
    calculation   147–50, 156–8
    chi-square degrees of freedom   146
    chi-square single sample   156–8
    combining categories/samples   152
    formula   147
    one sample   156–8
    partitioning   150
    related designs   158–60
    significance 5% and 1% table   147
    small expected frequencies   151, 160
    with known populations   156–8
choosing a statistical test   300–5
    table for   304
coefficient of determination   72
Cohen's d 380–1, 384
    table   383
combined categories   11
comparing mean, median and mode
    25
compound bar chart   58–9
    bad example   58
compound histogram   59–60
confidence intervals   89, 97–8, 407–15
    limits   409
    mean   410
    Pearson correlation   412–13
    regression   413–15
    related t-   411–12
    unrelated t-   411

contingency tables   143
correlated measures designs   115
correlated scores   126–7
correlation coefficients   62–79
counterbalancing   117
covariance   65–6
    formula   67
Cramer, D.   299, 321, 333, 345, 359, 475
Crighton, D.   155, 475
critical values   104
crosstabulation or contingency tables
    57–60, 143
Cumberbatch, G.   316, 475
cumulative frequencies   37–9
curvilinear correlation   70–1

data exploration   2
degrees of freedom   108, 112, 119,
    201–4
dependent variable in t-test   118
descriptive statistics   1–2
determination, coefficient of   72
diagrams   9–19
    nominal data   10–15
    numerical scores   15–18
    relationships   53–61
directional hypotheses   103
directional predictions   172
directionless or nondirectional tests
    167
distorted curves   34–6
Donnerstein, E.   170, 475

error scores   201
    estimating   202
estimated standard deviation   111
estimated standard error   112, 119
estimated variance   29, 111
Eysenck, Hans   321
expected frequencies   144
    calculating   144–6

F-ratio test   189–94
    calculation   191–4
    formula   191

significance table   190
factor analysis   63, 319–33
  communality   326
  confirmatory   328–9
  correlation matrix   320
  example   329–32
  exploratory   328–9
  factor loadings   323–4
  history   321
  number of factors   325–6
  orthogonal vs. oblique   325
  rotation   324
  second-order factors   325
factorials, table of   153
Fidell, L. S.   333, 345, 476
Fisher exact probability test   152
  2 x 3 formula   155
  calculation   153–5
five point scale   16
fixed vs. random effects, analysis of
    variance   271
frequencies   6, 8
  calculation   11–12
  cumulative   37–9
  percentage   11–12
  simple   11
frequency curves   31–2
  bimodal, multimodal   23, 37
Friedman Test   186, 448–9

Gillis, J.S.   78, 475
Glantz, S. A.   299, 345, 475

histogram   16, 31
Howell, D.   268, 475
Howitt, D.   315, 475
Huitema, B. E.   297, 475

independent variable in t-test   118
individual differences   225–7
inferential statistics   2
interactions
  analysis of variance   232–4, 250–2
  log-linear analysis   416–17, 420,
    424–9, 432–9

intercept   83
internal consistency   396–406
  alpha reliability   400–2
  inter-rater agreement   402–6
  item-total   397–8
  Kappa coefficient   402–6
  split-half reliability   399–400
interquartile range   25

Johnston, F.A.   169, 476
Johnston, S.A.   169, 476

Kappa coefficient   402–6
Kerlinger, F. N.   476
Kline, P.   333, 476
Kruskal–Wallis Test   186, 446–8
kurtosis   35–6

large sample formulae   445
least squares solution   81
leptokurtic   35–6
Likert-scale/questionnaire   16
log-linear   416–41
  degrees of freedom   440
  goodness-of fit   418
  hierarchical models   441
  lambda   440
  likelihood ratio chi-square   418
  models   416–18

Mann–Whitney U-test   182–5, 445
  calculation   182–5
  large sample   445
  significance table   185
Marascuilo, L.A.   186
matching   117, 216, 224
Maxwell, A.W.   160
McNemar Test   158–60
McSweeney, M.   186
mean, arithmetic   21–2
  calculation   22
  formula   21
mean deviation   26
measurement
  category   5

measurement (*continued*)
  equal-interval 7
  formal 6
  interval 7
  nominal 5, 7
  numerical 5
  ordinal 7
  rank 7
  ratio 7
  scales 6
  scores 5
  types of 5
median 23–4
mesokurtic 35–6
meta-analysis 378–95
  calculation 383–9
  combining effect sizes 386–9
  conversion table for different effect
      size measures 383
  effect size 380–1
  formulae for conversions 384
  study characteristics 381–2, 389
mode 22
multicollinearity 342
multimodal distributions 23, 37
multiple comparisons 262–6
  multifactorial comparisons
      267–8
  multiple *t*-tests 242–3
  numbers of comparisons 242
  planned vs. a posteriori 264–5
  Scheffé test 265–7
multiple regression 334–45
  blockwise 340
  example 343–4
  functions 335–6
  hierarchical 340
  multicollinearity 342
  regression equations 337–9
  selection of predictors 340
  standardised 334
  stepwise 340–1
multiplication rule 162–3
  calculation 165–6
Munford, M.B. 343–4, 476

negative correlation 63–4
non-directional predictions 172–3
nonparametric statistics 176–86
  parametric equivalents 176
  problems of 177
normal curve 31–3, 110–11
null hypothesis 102–3, 203
numerical scores 5

observed frequencies 144
obtained score 201
one-tail predictions 173–4
one-tailed testing 172–5
  requirements of 174–5
outliers 70–1
  reasons to delete 70

partial correlation 62, 309–18
  calculation 311–12, 316
  causality 308
  multiple controls 314–15
  orders of 315–16
  significance table 314
  statistical significance 314
partitioning chi-square 150–2
path analysis 346–59
  direct effect 348
  endogenous variables 347–8
  example 354–9
  exogenous variables 347–8
  just-identified 353
  over identified 354
  path coefficients 349–53
  two-way relationships 347
  under-identified 353
Pearson Correlation Coefficient 62
  calculation 67–70
  example of use 78
  formula 67
  quick formula 67
  significance table 105
  significance testing 99–108
Pearson Product Moment Correlation
      Coefficient 62
Pedhazur, E. J. 345, 359, 476

percentage probabilities   162
percentiles   39
perfect correlation   64
pictogram   15
pie diagrams   12–14
   calculating slices   13
   poor example   13
platykurtic   35–6
planned or *a priori* comparisons   264
point estimates   407
population   93
positive correlation   63
post hoc or *a posteriori* comparisons
      264–68
pre-test/post-test   269–99
probability   161–6
proportions   52
public opinion polls   53

questionnaires, analysis of   360–8
   data cleaning   365–6

random samples, characteristics of
      95–7
random sampling   94–7
range   25
ranking tests   176–85
regression, simple   80–90
   calculation   85–7
   confidence intervals   88–9
   correlation vs. regression   84
   formula for intercept   86
   formula for prediction   86–7
   formula for slope   85
   least squares solution   83
   number of regression lines   84
   problems with regression   87
   scattergrams   81
   slope   83–4, 86–7
   standard errors   87–9
   theory   82–5
   X-axis   81
   Y-axis   81
regression line   54
regression to the mean   161

related measures designs   116
relationships   53–61
   diagrams for numerical scores   54–7
repeated measures designs   116
Rosenthal, J. A.   170, 476
Rosenthal, R.   395

sample   93
sampling distribution   109
scattergram   54–7
scatterplot   54–7
Scheffé test   265–7
selecting a statistical test   300–5
   table for   304
Siegel, S.   186
sigma sign   21
Sign test calculation   178–80
   significance table   179
significance levels, reporting   167–71
   examples from publications   169–71
   significance over different studies
         164
significance tables
   chi-square   459
   F-distribution   468–71
   Mann-Whitney U 466–7
   Pearson correlation   450–2
   sign test   460–2
   Spearman correlation   453–5
   t-test   456–8
   Wilcoxon Matched Pairs   463–5
significance testing   72, 93–8, 100–1
   repeated   163–4
skewness   25, 34–5, 442–4
   formula   442
   negative   34–5
   positive   34–5
   standard error of   443–4
Slinker, B. K.   299, 345, 475
slope   83–4
Spearman's rho   73–8, 181
   calculation with and without tied
         ranks   74–5
   calculation with no tied ranks   74–7
   formula   74

Spearman's rho (*continued*)
  formula without ties   76
  significance of   106–8
  significance table   107
standard deviation   41–52
  calculation   43–5
  formula, defining   43
  formula, quick   44
  use of   47–8, 52
standard deviation estimate   111
standard error calculation   112–13
standard error of difference between
    sample means   133–5
standard error of means   109–14
standard normal distribution   48–51
  significance table   50
statistical power analysis   372–7
  ANOVA   376–7
  chi-square   374–5
  eta   376–7
  nonparametric tests   376
  size of effects   374–7
  t-test   375–6
statistical significance   372–3
Straus, M.   315, 475
sunflowers   56–7
suppressor variables   315
surveys, analysis of   360–8
  data cleaning   365–6
Szostak, H.   47, 476

t-distribution   118–19
t-score   120
t-test related   115–26
  calculation   121–3
  examples of designs   115–16
  formula   120
  significance table   140
  significance test   126
t-test unrelated   127–41
  dissimilar variances   140–1
  examples of designs   127–8
  null hypothesis   129, 131, 133

standard error   134–7
Tabachnick, B. G.   333, 345, 476
tables   9–19
  nominal data   10–15
  numerical scores   15–18
  relationships   53–61
Tinsley, H. E. A.   406, 476
treatment levels   232
true scores   197–201
  estimating   202
Towl, G.   155, 475
two-tailed testing   172–5
type 1 error   106
type 2 error   106

variability   25–9
variables   4–5
variance   26–9
  formula, computing   28
  formula, defining   27
variance estimate   29, 111
variance ratio test   189–94
  calculation   191–4
  formula   191
  significance table of *F*   190
Venn diagram   337–8

Wagner, U.   354–8, 476
Weiss, D. J.   406, 476
Wilcoxon Matched Pairs Test
    180–2
  Large sample   445
  significance table   181
within groups variance   209

Yates's correction   159

z-score   46–52
  calculation   46–7
  formula   47
zero correlation   64–5
zero point   7
Zick, A.   354–8, 476